IONIAN VISION

By the same author

The Great Island: A Study of Crete

Ionian Vision

Greece in Asia Minor 1919-1922

Michael Llewellyn Smith

ST. MARTIN'S PRESS
NEW YORK

AFFILIATED PUBLISHERS: Macmillan Limited, London
also at Bombay, Calcutta, Madras and Melbourne

To Colette

Contents

List of Illustrations

Maps

Illustration Acknowledgements

The author and publishers are grateful to the following for permission to reproduce photographs: Historical and Ethnological Museum, Athens for Nos. 1, 11; Markezinis Collection for Nos. 2, 3, 4, 5, 6, 7, 8, 16; Benaki Museum, Athens for No. 9; Admiral G. Lambrinopoulos for No. 10; Radio Times Hulton Picture Library for Nos. 13, 14, 15.

This story carried us back to classic times. It is true Greek tragedy, with Chance as the ever-ready handmaid of Fate. However the Greek race might have altered in blood and quality, their characteristics were found unchanged since the days of Alcibiades. As of old, they preferred faction above all other interests, and as of old in their crisis they had at their head one of the greatest of men. The interplay between the Greek love of party politics and the influence exercised over them by Venizelos constitutes the action of the piece. The scene and the lighting are the Great War; and the theme, 'How Greece gained the Empire of her dreams in spite of herself, and threw it away when she awoke.'

Winston Churchill,
The World Crisis: the Aftermath, p. 379

Some Place Name Variants

The same place often has a different name in Turkish and Greek. The following table may help those readers who are used to one version and find another in the text or the maps. The first column gives the Turkish version (slightly Anglicized so as to avoid the use of cedillas and diacritical marks). The second column gives the Greek version (again sometimes Anglicized) where this differs substantially from the Turkish. The third column gives further variant spellings such as are found in British sources.

Turkish	Greek	Other variants
Afyon Karahisar		Afium Karahissar, etc.
Ak Hisar	Axarios	
Alashehir	Philadelphia	
Ankara		Angora
Antakya		Antioch
Antalya	Attaleia	Adalia
Aydin		Aidin
Ayvali	Kydonies	Aivali
Bandirma	Panormos	Panderma
Bergama	Pergamos	
Bodrum	Halicarnassus	
Chanakalle		Chanak
Edirne	Adrianople	
Edremit	Adramytteion	
Eregli	Heraclea	
Gemlik	Kios	
Iskenderun		Alexandretta
Istanbul	Constantinople	
Izmir	Smyrna	
Izmit	Nicomedia	Ismid, Ismidt, etc.
Iznik	Nicaea	
R. Kizil	R. Halys	
Manisa	Magnesia	
R. Menderes	R. Meander	
Trabzon	Trebizond	

Preface

This book has its origins in a doctoral thesis submitted at the University of Oxford, entitled *The Greek Occupation of Asia Minor, 1919–22, and the National Schism.* This thesis, which may be consulted in the Bodleian Library, contains more reference material and a longer bibliography than the present work. I have made substantial changes in the main text also, and added much new narrative.

All Greek titles are given in translated form only in the references; but the bibliography provides the original Greek titles (transliterated) as well as their English translations. Transliteration from Greek and Turkish is a problem. Consistency is possible, but those who achieve it (e.g. Arnold Toynbee in his book *The Western Question in Greece and Turkey*) pay a price in infelicities (such as the name Ghúnaris) which are logical but look odd to readers familiar with other forms (e.g. Gounaris). My versions are inconsistent, but comprehensible.

I should like to acknowledge the help and advice of the Directors and staffs of the Benaki Museum, the National Archives and the Library of Parliament, Athens; Mr A. J. P. Taylor and the staff of the Beaverbrook Library, London; Madame Marie Argyropoulou, who allowed me to see her late husband's unpublished papers; Dr J. K. Campbell; Professor D. Dakin; Miss Lesley Duffield, who typed the manuscript; Mr P. Gounarakis; Mrs Isobel Lawes, who prepared the index; Mr V. J. G. Stavridi, who lent me the papers of his father, Sir John Stavridi; Miss Joanna Stavridi; Dr Theodore Stephanides; Admiral Sir Bertram Thesiger and Lady Thesiger, who allowed me to use Admiral Thesiger's unpublished 'Naval Memories'; and my wife.

I owe a special debt to two Greek historians and men of affairs: Mr Spyros B. Markezinis, for his generous advice on historical questions and practical help over illustrations; and Mr A. A. Pallis for his encouragement, advice and personal reminiscences.

I am most grateful too to Mrs Markezinis for allowing me to use photographs from her rich collection.

Many others helped with letters: among them, Mr Desmond Allhusen, Mr G. Apostolopoulos, Colonel W. A. Asher, Mrs Ellen Buckingham, Mr Hugh Bulley, Mrs H. Rosamund Craies, Mrs Teresa Crosfield, Mr Edward Doylemesh, Dr T. Doxiades, Mrs K. H. Johnston, Lieutenant-Commander P. K. Kemp, Lord Kinross, Major Kemâl Kutluoğlu, Mr G. M. Lee, Mr H. N. Lyster, Mr Ian Lyster, Captain F. P. Morris, Mrs Ethel O'Carroll, Mr C. F. R. Routh, Mr Geoffrey Rowell, Mr W. Rusby, Mr T. A. Sanson, Commander R. H. Stokes-Rees, Lieutenant-Colonel F. H. Thompson, Mr David Tudor-Pole, Mr Denys J. Voaden, and Mr R. Wilkinson.

1 | The Great Idea

The Kingdom of Greece is not Greece; it is merely
a part, the smallest, poorest part of Greece.

John Kolettis in 1844

On 2 August 1868 a son was born to Olga, wife of the young King
George of Greece. The kingdom which the prince was to rule
over was a poor, cramped piece of Balkan territory, carved out of
the sprawling Ottoman Empire by an invincible Greek nationalist spirit and a reluctant European diplomacy. The Peloponnese, a few hundred square miles of mainland stretching only as
far north as a line from Arta in the west to Volos and mount
Pelion in the east, and a handful of the Greek islands, were all
that the turbulent Greek warlords and politicians of the recent
struggle for independence could extract from the Great Powers
of Europe. For the Greeks this was not enough. These were the
feverish outward-looking years of the new kingdom, the years of
the 'Great Idea' of a revived Greek empire, a Byzantium rising
in new splendour across the dolphin-torn Aegean sea. For the
dreamers in their studies lined with the ancient Greek classics,
the politicians on the rostrum developing a nationalist rhetoric
to encompass the new horizons which opened up before the
nation, the chatterers in pavement cafés, there were few limits to
what in an ideal world would be Greek. Crete, Thessaly, Epirus,
Macedonia, Thrace, the Aegean islands, these were patently
areas of Hellenism. Farther off were Cyprus, the Dodecanese, the
Ionian coastlands of Asia Minor, even Pontus on the Black
Sea.

These were the dreams into which the heir to the Glucksberg
dynasty was born. They called him Constantine, a name rich in
nationalist associations. It was a Constantine who had founded
Constantinople, the great city which symbolized the illusory
golden age and summoned up the inextinguishable nostalgia of
the Greek race. It was another Constantine, surnamed Palaeologus, who died defending the Byzantine city against the invading
Ottoman Turks in 1453 – a heroic and unavailing defence of
Christendom against what the Greeks believed to be the

encroaching tide of barbarism. The name of the young Crown Prince revived such submerged racial memories – even if it was plausibly suggested that he was named not after Palaeologus but after his uncle, the Grand Duke Constantine Constantinovich, Queen Olga's favourite brother.

Constantine was appointed Duke of Sparta when only one month old. There was something symbolic here too. The new and liberal Greek constitution introduced in the early years of King George's reign forbade the award of titles of nobility or distinction to Greek citizens. A lively debate in the Greek parliament greeted the announcement of the title. It was entirely characteristic that the first controversy to arise over the Crown Prince concerned a constitutional issue.

The Greek royal family was European and cosmopolitan, shallowly rooted in the hard Greek soil. It was only five years since George had arrived in Greece, after the brusque ejection of his predecessor the Bavarian prince Otho, the first king of independent Greece. George's father, King Christian IX of Denmark, held a central position in the network of dynastic alliances of nineteenth-century Europe. Of his sons, one succeeded him, one assumed the throne of Norway as King Haakon, and one ascended the throne of Greece. Of his daughters the elder became the Tsaritsa Maria, wife of Alexander III of Russia; the younger, Alexandra, married Edward Prince of Wales and became Queen of England. Thus George and through him Greece were intimately connected with the ruling houses of Europe. His marriage in 1867 to Olga, daughter of Tsar Alexander II's younger brother, the Grand Duke Constantine, brought new and stronger ties with Russia.

The Greece of the mid-nineteenth century was stirred by an awakening conviction of the historic inevitability of the expansion of the kingdom to embrace the unredeemed portion of the Greek nation. The politician John Kolettis who, with King Otho, represented the Great Idea in its wilder political aspect, voiced this conviction in the National Assembly in January 1844:

The Kingdom of Greece is not Greece; it is merely a part, the smallest, poorest part of Greece. The Greek is not only he who inhabits the Kingdom, but also he who inhabits Ioannina or Salonika or Serres or Adrianoupolis or Constantinople or Trebizond or Crete or Samos or any other region belonging to Greek history or the Greek race.... There are two great centres of Hellenism. Athens is the capital of the Kingdom. Constantinople is the great capital, the City, the dream and hope of all Greeks.[1]

The idea that Greece (the ideal Greece, not yet realized in fact) comprised not just the kingdom but the whole area inhabited by the Greek nation, was symbolized in the title given to the new King George I in the constitution of 1864 – 'King of the Hellenes', not King of Greece.

The Idea was not merely the sentimental product of nineteenth-century medievalists; it was, in one of its aspects, centuries old and deeply rooted in the Greeks' national and religious consciousness. This aspect was the recovery of Constantinople for Christendom, the reestablishment of the universal Christian Byzantine Empire which had fallen in 1453. Ever since this time the recovery of St Sophia and the city had been handed down from generation to generation as the destiny and aspiration of the Greek Orthodox. The idea of the reestablishment of the universal Christian Empire took root in the mind of the Greeks as a yearning for the return of Constantinople, less and less related, as time passed, to the specific aim of the reestablishment of a Byzantine Empire in anything like its previous form.

The ferment of new ideas which preceded the Greek war of independence and followed the foundation of the Greek kingdom revived and transformed this yearning, giving it a new political content. Around the turn of the century, the ambition of some of the Phanariots, the class of educated Greeks from Constantinople who had gradually acquired great political and economic power within the administrative structure of the Ottoman Empire, was to complete their infiltration of the Empire from within and revive Byzantium in this way. But the Greek war of independence and the creation of the Greek state put an end to such ambitions at least for many years to come, both by provoking Turkish hostility to the Greek element within the Empire and because the new state acted as focus of Greek energy and a magnet to Greek administrative talent.

The new kingdom was a state formed on the western model, under the influence of western European political theory; it was the antithesis of the multinational Byzantine (or indeed Ottoman) theocracy. To the old yearning for Constantinople, rooted in the religious instincts of the Greek people, were now added new feelings – a consciousness of *territory* as being Greek, a feeling for frontiers, a conviction that the nation, or race, should be coincident with the new state, and therefore that the millions of Greeks within the Ottoman Empire must be 'redeemed' – all feelings associated with modern nationalism.

The Great Idea therefore in the mid-nineteenth century came to contain at least three different strands. Strictly interpreted, it was the romantic dream of a revival of the Byzantine–Greek Empire centred on Constantinople. Less strictly it was the aspiration for Greek cultural and economic dominance within the Ottoman Empire, leading to its gradual subversion from within by a natural process which need not entail a violent clash between the rival Greek and Turkish nations. Thirdly, the Idea could be interpreted in terms of the modern nation state, as the progressive redemption of the Greek *irridenta* by their incorporation in the Greek kingdom, which entailed a head-on clash with the Ottoman Empire. Though all these conceptions survived into the twentieth century, it was the third which prevailed. The ideal world was one thing, the real another. It took more than thirty years for the independent kingdom to take the first step in the realization of these grandiose ambitions.

When Prince George, aged only seventeen and without experience of politics or Balkan manners, came from Denmark in 1863 to take up the throne for which the Great Powers (especially Britain) had pronounced him suitable, the British Government handed over the Ionian Islands to Greece as the new king's dowry. Corfu, the richest jewel in this string of islands, still shows traces of the British way of life in the cricket games played between its two clubs (Byron and Corfu Athletic) and visiting British teams, and in the ginger beer which the spectators drink while watching the game.

In 1881 the frontier of Greece was pushed north to include the rich plains of Thessaly – a further success but still for the Greeks no more than a provisional settlement. The next territories on the nationalist agenda were Crete and Macedonia.

King George was an easy-going, shrewd operator who soon learned to cope with the wily Greek politicians by whom he was surrounded, dividing them and ruling by the exercise of patronage, and operating nearly enough within the letter of the constitution to avoid provoking an uncontrollable reaction. He was little stirred by the nationalist passions of the times. The annual trips to meet his royal cousins, aunts and uncles in Denmark allowed him to keep a sense of Olympian proportion. Problems were manageable; they were after all within the family. Constantine, as he grew up in the cold, spacious palace at Tatoi under Mount Parnes, inevitably became more closely involved in the web of Greek life. The seven children – Constantine, George, Nicholas, Andrew and Christopher, Alexandra and Maria – were brought up by nannies and governesses, spoke English at home, and moved generally in the narrow circle of the cosmopolitan and rootless Athenian upper-class society. Constantine himself went to Berlin to study at the Military Academy, and conceived a lifelong admiration for the German military tradition and way of life. In 1889 this link was reinforced by his marriage to Sophia, the sister of Kaiser Wilhelm II. It was probably his military experience which involved him most closely in modern Greek life. By the closing years of the century, while still a young man of thirty, he was thought ready for military responsibilities out of the ordinary.

In 1897 one of the periodic outbursts of national sentiment among the Greeks of Crete – still a part of the Ottoman Empire – provoked a new round of the Greco-Turkish struggle. The Cretans rebelled and declared for *enosis* with the mother country. Pressure from public opinion, especially among the nationalist society in the officer corps, forced the Greek Government to take up the challenge. The Greeks mobilized. In April Greek irregulars crossed the frontier between Thessaly and Macedonia. A few days later Greece and Turkey were at war. The Greek army in the main eastern theatre was commanded by Crown Prince Constantine.

The war was a humiliating disaster for Greece. In less than a month the Turkish troops, recently reorganized by a German military mission, swept aside the Greeks in Thessaly, and occupied Larissa, putting to rout the Crown Prince's army. Under the peace terms imposed by the Great Powers, Greece paid an indemnity and an International Financial Commission was set up by the Powers to control Greek finances and see that the country made good its debts. But Thessaly did not revert to Turkey. The main effects of the war were thus financial and psychological. The army was brought to realize the futility of open confrontation with Turkey and the necessity of radical reorganization. The popularity and prestige of Crown Prince Constantine went into eclipse. As Commander he had not been equal to the responsibilities of his position.

But although in the history of nineteenth-century Greece frustration and humiliating reverses were mixed with infrequent successes, the pattern detected by the Greeks was one of success in the gradual realization of the 'Great Idea'. First, the Ionian islands and then Thessaly had been added to the kingdom. The reverse of 1897 had cost the country little in territory. The message seemed to be that, despite local and temporary reverses, a general historical tendency was at work in favour of Greece. The bastions of Turkey in Europe were crumbling, and the Turkish hordes would be rolled back into their Asian homelands. It was a question of time and patience. Nevertheless, the Greeks could not relax and wait for the fruits to fall into their hands; for inevitable as the decline of Turkey in Europe might appear to be, there were other claimants besides Greece to the inheritance of Macedonia, Thrace and Epirus. In Thrace and Macedonia most of the Greek populations were clustered near the Aegean coastline, while Slavs and Muslims predominated inland. There was no easy criterion by which to determine who should possess these areas; they had to be fought over, 'redeemed' not merely with diplomatic skill, but with Greek blood. Recognizing these truths, the Greeks set themselves to wipe out the shame of 1879. The decade which followed was a time of preparation in which, though all were conscious of the seriousness of the state of the nation, Greece's political resources did not match the needs of the time. Greek ambitions had so clearly outstripped her capabilities that radical reform of institutions and of the army were felt to be necessary. The political scene was dominated by a familiar bickering struggle between the old feudal political leaders, Theotokis, Rallis, Dragoumis, Mavromichalis and others. Below the surface new men who were to put their stamp on Greek history were waiting their turn. And away from the political hothouse of Athens, out in the frontier lands, in Macedonia and Crete, the struggle for the expansion of the kingdom was carried further.

It was during these years that the struggle for Macedonia reached its climax. Greeks from the independent kingdom went over into Macedonia to help organize guerrilla bands to counter the Bulgarian *comitadjis,** and to cultivate a spirit of nationality among the Greek Orthodox communities. Many of those who

* *Comitadjis*: bands of nationalist guerrilla fighters operative in Macedonia.

will feature in this book took part in the struggle, which absorbed most of the creative energy and virtue of Greek nationalists between 1897 and the Balkan Wars. In 1904 a young officer named Anastasios Papoulas was sent by the Greek Government on a secret mission to Macedonia to study the possibilities of Greek guerrilla activity. The chief of the mission was Captain Alexandros Kontoulis, who was later to serve under Papoulas in the Asia Minor campaign. A younger man, Georgios Kondylis, fought as a guerrilla band leader in the Kastoria area of Macedonia before being sent to a village in Eastern Thrace as a 'teacher', an incongruous profession for this crude, tough Thessalian. Ion Dragoumis, the young writer and philosopher of Greek nationalism, murdered in 1920 by Venizelist bravos, served in the consular service, which acted as a kind of general staff for the struggle, at Monastir, Serres, Philippoupolis, Dedeagatch (Alexandroupolis) and Constantinople between 1902 and 1908.

Within Greece too a new generation was being schooled during these years. Moved as so often by the desire for 'new men',* frustrated by a party political system which did not reflect the actual distribution of power, the emerging strength of the bourgeoisie and the growth of the provinces, the Greeks watched with interest the emergence in 1906 of a group of youngish radicals who were at once nicknamed the Japanese Group on account of their aggressive tactics and offensive spirit in parliament, which called to mind the tactics of the Japanese army in the recent Russo-Japanese war.

The titular leader of the ginger group was the elder statesman Stephanos Dragoumis, formerly a colleague and close collaborator of the great politician Charilaos Trikoupis. But the moving spirit within the group was a young lawyer and intellectual from Patras, Dimitrios Gounaris, who had entered parliament in 1902. Gounaris, who had studied in Germany and France, was a man of wide cultivation and progressive ideas. He had been deeply impressed by the achievements of Bismarck in the field of social welfare in Germany. Greece's ramshackle political structure seemed to him in need of a thorough overhaul.

A tall man with fair hair, beard and moustache, and a strong, slightly pendulous nose, he made an immediate impression in public by his mastery of his briefs and his beautifully modulated rhetoric. Gounaris's failing was a tendency to the arrogant and

* There is even a Greek word (*neandrismos*) for the concept.

doctrinaire which turned increasingly to narrowness of mind. But in these early days he could charm the political world of whose introverted and factional workings he was so impatient. In discussion with his friends he would chain-smoke Greek cigarettes as he expounded the new ideas from Europe which would transform the old Greek politics of small personalities and cliques belonging to the great political families of feudal land-owners and descendants of the makers of the Greek revolution. In parliament and outside Gounaris acquired a mastery over his contemporaries and was recognized as the coming man.

Petros Protopapadakis, Gounaris's closest collaborator throughout his career, was a rough-hewn bearded figure from Naxos, who had studied engineering in Paris and on his return worked on the Corinth canal and taught at the Evelpides military academy before entering parliament as member for the Cyclades. The other members of the group were Emmanuel Repoulis, a journalist with a facile and quick mind and sense of politics; Apostolos Alexandris, the youngest of the group, who was elected deputy for Karditsa in 1906 at the age of only twenty-seven, an almost unheard of thing in the gerontocratic world of Greek politics; Charilaos Vozikis, another close friend of Gounaris; and A. Panayiotopoulos.

Though their achievements were slight, these men acted as a leaven in the body politic. As a negative, destructive, critical force they impressed both parliament and the country. They suffered, however, from a lack of substance and political pro-gramme. They were six intelligent radical young men, different in temperament and background, united in dissatisfaction with the state of things. Gounaris, for example, was a doctrinaire and rationalist intellectual; Alexandris was an old-fashioned liberal.

The great failing of the group lay not in the lack of a class and party base – this was inevitable – but in the failure to try to create one. And this derived largely from a failure of nerve in Gounaris himself. Widely recognized as the natural leader of the Japanese Group, he yet choose to shelter behind the old man Dragoumis and thus to associate himself and the group to some extent with a discredited generation. Gounaris made no effort to make the group the kernel of something greater – a new mass radical party. He was content to operate within the parliamentary framework alone.

In the end it was Gounaris himself who dissolved his own

group of followers and forfeited his claim to the leadership of the radical opposition. In 1908 the Prime Minister Theotokis, who had been watching the activities of the Japanese Group with a wary eye, offered Gounaris the Finance Ministry and the chance – almost irresistible to a young, ambitious intellectual – to implement his programme of tax reform. Gounaris accepted. It was a classic case of seduction by the establishment. After a few months he was forced to resign.

In my view, Gounaris had great political courage and honesty [wrote Alexandris later]. He knew very well that Theotokis did not like him and that N. Kalogeropoulos, who was popular with the party, was already anointed heir of the Theotokan party. But Gounaris believed that his programme would be voted through in its entirety, since Theotokis had come out in favour of it ... and would achieve the economic renaissance of the country. Then he could leave the Ministry as quickly as he had entered it, but with greatly increased political stature and popularity.[2]

Gounaris had taken the job in order to achieve an end which a more experienced man would have recognized as impossible. In being tricked by Theotokis into dissolving the corporate strength of his Japanese Group by deserting it for the Government, for however worthy ends, he lost the right to claim to represent a new force free from the taint of the old political parties, a force which would attract what was most healthy and vigorous in Greek public life. The way was open for another, stronger contender.

This contender came in 1910. Eleftherios Venizelos burst onto the Greek political stage from the vigorous provincial school of Cretan politics, and within a few months dominated Greek political life as no man had done before him. He came by invitation, in order to break a deadlock. A group of officers, disenchanted with the performance of politicians and the royal family, had issued a pronunciamento at Goudi outside Athens, and succeeded in bringing the government of the country virtually to a halt. The politicians were forced to operate under the control and with the permission of soldiers who themselves were not prepared to govern and hardly knew what they wanted done. Venizelos was brought in to sort out the mess.

When he came to Athens and to metropolitan Greek politics in 1910, Venizelos was about forty-six years old – a tall, vigorous figure with rimless spectacles, moustache and beard beginning to go grey, the hair receding on his head – a man with a large reputation as nationalist and revolutionary, who had struggled successively with the Ottoman Turkish rulers of Crete, with the Great Powers, and with the first High Commissioner of the island when it achieved autonomy, Constantine's brother Prince George. Through these struggles, carried out in the name of *enosis* with Greece, Venizelos had made a name for himself on the larger Greek stage. Free from the taint of Greek petty politics, he descended onto the Greek stage with the attributes of a *deus ex machina*.

Venizelos was born in 1864 near Canea in western Crete into a family of considerable wealth and standing. His father was a merchant of impeccable nationalist credentials. Banished from Crete in the wake of the great Cretan revolution of 1866, he took his family to the island of Syra in the Cyclades, where Eleftherios ('the liberator') received his first education. Venizelos studied at Athens University and became a lawyer. Returning to Crete he entered politics in 1889, winning election to the Cretan Assembly established under the constitution squeezed out of the Turks after the 1866 revolution. From then until the final emancipation of Crete Venizelos was in the forefront of the island's turbulent politics, learning how to deal with allies, enemies and Great Powers in the intricacies of the 'Cretan Question'. Diplomacy and argument were followed by revolution. In 1897, at a time of worse than usual oppression and chaos in Crete, Venizelos set up a revolutionary headquarters on the Akrotiri peninsula near Canea and issued a manifesto calling for immediate union with Greece. The Greek Government was dragged into the event. The Great Powers sent a fleet to intervene and separate the combatants and find some compromise solution. They insisted on autonomy under Turkish sovereignty, and on the recall by Greece of her ships and men from Crete. The international fleet under the Italian Admiral Canevara blockaded the insurgents. The Cretans were divided into moderates who would accept autonomy as a basis for negotiation and extremists who would take nothing short of union with Greece. Venizelos was leader of the latter group. The Greek Government, subject to almost intolerable pressure from extremists and sympathizers with the Cretan nationalist cause within the Greek army, failed to bow to the Great Powers' demands in time. The result was that on 17 April 1897 the Ottoman Empire declared war on Greece, and the Powers stood idly by and watched the Greeks reap the rewards of their impatient nationalism in a catastrophic defeat by a stronger and better equipped power.

In the end it took an accident to force the Powers to coerce the Turks and hand over Crete to the islanders themselves. In September 1898 a band of Turks set on a detachment of British bluejackets and killed a number of them, together with the British vice-consul. Without delay the Powers took over control of the island, and within two months Turkish troops had left Crete. Prince George of Greece was appointed High Commissioner of the Powers in Crete. The fight for a genuine autonomy, though not for union, was won. Venizelos could now devote himself to political struggles, in many ways as bitter as those which went before, with the new High Commissioner, struggles which led to another armed revolution in 1905, the resignation of Prince George, and further manoeuvrings towards the inevitable end of Cretan *enosis* with Greece, which was finally achieved only in 1913.

By 1910, as a result of these activities, the name Eleftherios Venizelos was well known in Greece. It was as a politician tested in the fire of revolutionary struggles and anxious to apply his energies in a wider field that Venizelos sailed to Athens in January 1910 to see the situation, talk to the revolutionary members of the Military League, and help find a political solution to the country's problems.

The time was ripe for him. Within a few months he had broken the political deadlock, persuaded the League to dissolve itself, and imposed himself on the King and the political world. As Prime Minister he established a commanding position in the political life of the country through his newly founded Liberal Party with its network of Liberal clubs, local organizations based on the professional and commercial sections of the rising bourgeosie. Venizelos presided over an exhilarating period of constitutional reform, social legislation and military reorganization.

In 1912 at last there came the moment patriotic Greeks had awaited since 1897. In patient negotiations with Greece's neighbours Venizelos had forged a Balkan alliance that could confront Turkey with some confidence. General war was provoked by a Montenegran attack on the Turks in October. Within a fortnight Turkey was at war with Montenegro, Serbia, Bulgaria and

Greece. The main burden of the allies' offensive was shouldered by the Bulgarian forces, which defeated the Turks at Kirk Kilisse and Lule Burgas and drove eastward through Thrace to the Chatalja lines, the very gates of Constantinople. Meanwhile Serbian forces were equally successful; Old Serbia was cleared of Turkish troops and the First Army under Crown Prince Alexander pressed down into western Macedonia and defeated a Turkish army at Monastir. The squeeze was completed by a successful Greek advance northward through Thessaly into Macedonia. The Greeks sent a further army into Epirus to liberate Ioannina, and made a large contribution to the allied cause by clearing the Aegean of the Turkish fleet.

In the race for Salonika, the richest prize vacated by the Turks, the Greeks beat the Bulgarians by less than twenty-four hours. It was in this ancient city, inhabited by a good medley of Muslims, Greeks, Slavs and Spanish Jews (the largest single element), that King George I fell to an assassin's bullet in March 1913, and Constantine, who had redeemed his reputation in the recent victorious campaign of the Greek army, assumed the throne.

The war in the Balkans awakened in English Liberals passionate feelings of Gladstonian distaste for the Turks, and warm sympathy for the oppressed peoples who had thrown off the yoke.

The first successes of the Balkan allies' armies stirred up feelings of exhilaration. As the Turkish armies were rolled back rapidly through Macedonia and Thrace, it began to look as if after five centuries the Ottomans were being prised loose from their foothold in Europe and driven back to their Asian homelands. On Sunday 10 November 1912, when the issue was no longer in doubt, a young Greek expatriate in London made the first dramatic entry in a new diary:

I dined tonight at 11 Downing Street; there were present Lloyd George, Masterman, Spender, Roberts and three ladies. The conversation was all about the war. At dinner Lloyd George ordered champagne and proposed the following toast: 'I drink to the allies, the representative of one of whom we have here tonight, and may the Turk be turned out of Europe and sent to ... where he came from.'[3]

The diarist was a young solicitor of expatriate Greek origins named John Stavridi, who had struck up a friendship with

Lloyd George in the days when the Welsh politician was a prac-
tising solicitor, and had become Greek Consul General in London.
With his experience as a Reuter correspondent, his connections
with the great Greek political family of Rallis, his sound business
sense, he was ideally placed to mediate between the worlds of
Greek and British politics. He moved easily and fluently in and
between the earnest liberal world of the National Liberal Club,
the feverish world of Greek nationalist politics and the solid
prosperity of the high bourgeois London Greek community
with its shipowners, merchants and bankers.

Throughout that evening Lloyd George talked about the war
in the Balkans. It is the first glimpse we have of interests and
prejudices which were to stir him for the next ten years. He was
all for expelling the Turk from Europe bag and baggage:

Personally I don't want him even to keep Constantinople. This
latter, however, is the most difficult question we shall have to deal
with. In my opinion the best solution would be to have Constantinople and the Dardanelles internationalized.

He lectured Stavridi on the necessity of unity:

The one great thing for the allies is to stick together. If they do
so many difficulties will disappear and no one will be found to oppose
you. If you begin quarrelling among yourselves as to the division of
the spoils you will give a loophole to other powers to step in.

As to the Greeks themselves:

You have wiped out the memories of 1897 [said Lloyd George] and
shown what you can do when properly armed, trained and led, and
now nobody will be allowed to stand between you and your conquests. If the allies are in agreement they can divide up European
Turkey as they think best.... You may consider Crete as yours. The
only power that could prevent you from having it is England, and
England will not fire a shot or move a single ship to prevent you
from having it.

Stavridi pointed out that Greece was unjustly prevented from
occupying the Aegean Islands by the fact that the Italians had
occupied them during their recent war with Turkey. Lloyd
George reacted warmly:

This is a disgrace. If Italy does not clear out before the end of the
war, Greece should make it a *sine qua non* of the terms of peace
that all the islands are handed over to her. But you should assist by

creating a public opinion in England by means of the Press and public meetings, publications etc. Officially the British Government cannot help at present, but England will do nothing to oppose Greece having the Islands if she makes it a term of her peace conditions...

He asked me to see him [wrote Stavridi] as often as I liked on all questions of difficulty and he would assist me as much as he could.

Thus, without the need for recruitment and blandishment, Greece had gained a patron. Four days after this dinner party, Stavridi sent a résumé of the conversation to the Greek prime minister, Venizelos. In further conversations, Stavridi was able to build on the basis of this first meeting. It became apparent that Greece could be of use to Britain. Churchill, First Lord of the Admiralty, was interested in getting his hands on the facilities Greece could offer to a great naval power. Stavridi met Lloyd George and Churchill in the House of Commons on 18 November:

Winston Churchill went straight to the heart of the question. After a few questions as to the latest news from the seat of the war and the expression of hope for the final and complete success of the allies, he explained the organization of the British fleet in the Mediterranean and the working thereof in conjunction with the French fleet. As the powers were grouped at present, the enemies were Italy and Austria, and in any future war if they could close up the Adriatic they could bottle up the whole of the Austrian and part of the Italian fleets, and would then be able to deal with any other ships of the enemy. Provided England had a base close enough to the Adriatic it would be an easy matter to close the Adriatic. ... Of all the available spots, the one the Admiralty would prefer would be Argostoli in the Island of Cephalonia.

Churchill then suggested an agreement whereby the British Government would have the use of Cephalonia for its fleet in time of peace or war. What was Greece to get in return? Stavridi tried to link the proposed grant of facilities at Argostoli with British support for Greek aspirations at the peace negotiations which would have to take place at the end of the war. Greece would need help over Salonika and the Aegean Islands. Lloyd George pointed out the difficulties in such an arrangement. Churchill's idea, with which Lloyd George agreed, was to cede Cyprus to Greece as compensation. He told the story of his visit to Cyprus:

The people had yelled themselves hoarse and had waved Greek flags all the time. When he told the Governor how pleased he was with the enthusiastic reception given to him, he was informed that the cries raised were 'Ζήτω ἡ Ἑλλας' and 'Ζήτω ἡ Ἕνωσις';* that the enthusiasm was not for him but was raised by the hope that he would assist them in obtaining reunion to Greece. He was very much struck with this persistency of the Greek nationality; there were practically no complaints against the British Government, but only a great desire to be reunited to the mother country, and if it lay in his power he was going to see justice done.

Here was a prize worth winning indeed for Greece. Stavridi, eager to report on this conversation to Venizelos, had to contain his impatience until Lloyd George and Churchill had consulted Asquith and Sir Edward Grey. 'What a day this would have been for Byron if he was alive,' was Churchill's parting shot.

At the next meeting – one of Lloyd George's well-known breakfast parties – Stavridi tried to enlarge the prospect opened up by Churchill's proposals, suggesting that apart from the question of the naval base at Argostoli it might be to the benefit of England to have a more general understanding with Greece, which would enable the British to make use of the Aegean Islands too :

A general understanding with Greece, with Great Greece as she would be in the future, would enable them to use all their ships for fighting the enemy, leaving us to police the seas and protect their commerce. We would undertake to strengthen our navy and to build under the guidance of England and act in all matters in conjunction with England. He replied that the proposal was a good one and well worth consideration, that he would discuss it with Winston Churchill and speak also to the Prime Minister and Grey about it. In the meantime everything was to remain secret as before.

Here, expressed for the first time, was the kernel of a new outwardlooking foreign policy for Greece – the first step on the road which led, twisting and turning, to Salonika in 1916, Smyrna in 1919 and catastrophe in 1922. When Venizelos stepped on to the platform at Victoria Station on 12 December 1912, fresh from the triumphant victory celebrations in Greece, the foundations of his Anglophil policy were already laid.

Lloyd George himself had been urgent that Venizelos in person must come to London. 'The future of Greece will be

* 'Long Live Greece', and 'Long live Union with Greece'.

decided in London not at Athens,' he told Stavridi, 'it is a question of life and death to you.' On Monday 16 December the two men met for the first time, at breakfast at No. 11 Downing Street. Venizelos lost no time in stating that he approved of the negotiations that had taken place and was prepared to continue them. They discussed the Argostoli–Cyprus bargain. Stavridi reverted to the idea of a general Anglo-Greek Entente:

M. Venizelos said he was quite willing to discuss that question also, but as a separate entity quite distinct from the Cyprus–Argostoli arrangement. That all the national aspirations of Greece tended towards a closer union with England and that from the King down to the meanest subject everyone in Greece would welcome such an understanding. Both Lloyd George and Isaacs [Sir Rufus Isaacs] agreed that it would be a good thing for both countries. Lloyd George pointed out that England had no treaties with any country and that our understanding would have to be on the same lines as their entente with France; that is to say, the Foreign Offices of both countries would have to keep in constant and intimate touch with each other, and it would only be by an open and loyal understanding that either could call upon the other to assist in case of difficulties or war with other nations.

M. Venizelos quite agreed and was prepared to discuss the subject on that basis.

Over the next few days the seductive toils were drawn tighter round the flattered Greeks. Churchill strongly advised Venizelos to cancel, if it were still possible, the dreadnought that was building at that moment in the Vulcan shipyard in Germany, and order several smaller ships in her place. At another breakfast party, supported by Prince Louis of Battenberg, the First Sea Lord, he propounded his views on the role of the Greek navy in a future war in which Greece would be the ally of France and England. While the British fleet with its great capital ships operating out of Argostoli and Malta would bottle up the Austrians and Italians in the Adriatic, the Greeks with small, rapid craft would police the Eastern Mediterranean and the Islands. Asquith and Grey held that the whole arrangement would have to be made public in due course; otherwise it would be impossible to justify the surrender of Cyprus to Greece to the British public. Some time should therefore be allowed to elapse between the conclusion of the peace negotiations between the Balkan States and Turkey, and the publication of the news of the Anglo-Greek Entente.

Churchill went to Paris where he met Delcassé and discussed Greece and the Entente. A week later, on 29 January, he, Lloyd George, Prince Louis, Venizelos and Stavridi met at the House of Commons. Churchill handed out to Venizelos and Stavridi copies of a memorandum he had prepared on the role of the Greek navy. He had cut off the indication at the bottom of the memo that it originated in the Admiralty, in order to preserve absolute secrecy. Once more he urged the Greeks to concentrate on building up a fleet of small, fast ships and to avoid the delusive grandeur of dreadnoughts, despite pressure from the Greek naval chiefs, who like all sailors would prefer big ships.

Churchill told Venizelos that the more he considered the question, the more he was convinced that the Argostoli–Cyprus arrangement could not be carried out alone, but must be agreed in the context of the larger understanding. There could be an open Anglo-Greek Treaty, with secret clauses covering the sensitive aspects of military co-operation. French Ministers were in favour of the proposed arrangement. Venizelos, who was about to leave England for Salonika, was anxious to inform King George of the conversations which had taken place:

Churchill unhesitatingly refused. 'No, no, certainly not, it would endanger the whole of our negotiations, the matter would be certain to leak out and there will be an end of it.' Venizelos pointed out that the King was most discreet.... Lloyd George said, 'Well, we could not say the same in the same quarter here,' to which Churchill and Prince Louis assented.

It was agreed that Venizelos should tell the King, and only the King, that a possible basis for an Anglo-Greek entente had been found and that negotiations might be resumed after peace had been signed.

Venizelos was well satisfied with events. Before departing for Greece, he summed up his impressions for Stavridi:

He felt happy at the thought that our negotiations would result in an entente with England, and probably with France, and that Greece's future would be very different to her past, when she had to stand absolutely alone, supported by no one, with not a single friend to care what happened to her. She would now build up a strong navy, develop her railways and commerce and with the friendship of England and France would become a power in the East which no one could ignore.

Talking of Lloyd George he compared him with the old prophets of the Ancient Testament and expressed his great admiration for his splendid capacities and clear insight of people and events.

Lloyd George for his part was equally impressed. The day after Venizelos left he told Stavridi, 'He is a big man, a very big man.' Greece would be in safe hands so long as Venizelos was at the helm.

Lloyd George's sympathy for the Greek cause was not confined to midwifery of these naval discussions. He was prepared to offer his advice to Stavridi on every aspect of Greece's international problems. The most pressing of these was the status of the Aegean Islands. Those which had been occupied by Greece during the war looked safe enough. But what was to become of the islands of the Dodecanese, which had been occupied by Italy? Lloyd George insisted to Stavridi that the Italians would not be allowed to keep them. They would probably be allowed to revert to Turkey under strict guarantees of good government. Stavridi protested that this would be a calamity. Lloyd George returned an ingenious reply :

He was quite frank. He thought we could prevent it. England might arrange for the evacuation of the islands before the Turks returned. It would then be for us to organize a revolution in every island; we should have to arm the population, and they would have to declare their independence immediately and to notify the powers that they would not allow a single Turk to land. With a view to avoiding bloodshed England would then intervene and prevent the Turks from landing and the matter would then have to be settled on a different basis.

Is it fanciful to see here what made Lloyd George's ways of political thought and action so congenial to the Greeks – a speculative, dynamic, mercurial approach to problems based on lively personal sympathies; and a belief, common to both sides in the developing love affair, in the efficacy of human, and of Georgian, ingenuity. From now and for the next ten years the Greeks ignored all too easily, and to their ultimate cost, that Lloyd George, a dynamic and terrible force capable of astonishing achievements and feats of persuasion, could not alone impose for ever a policy which failed to strike resonances among the governing classes and party bosses of England.

Tension between the Balkan allies, temporarily suppressed in the common cause against the Turks, was not far beneath the surface. The Serbs and Greeks, both deeply suspicious of Bulgarian pan-Balkan ambitions, and determined to hold on to their recent gains, signed a secret defensive treaty of alliance in June 1913 which committed them to aid each other in the case of aggression by a third party.[4] Bulgaria was clearly the party in question. The war thus prudently guarded against broke out at the end of June, when the Bulgarians attacked the Serbs and Greeks along a wide front. After initial setbacks the two allies held the Bulgarians, and the Greeks, fighting a series of engagements with great panache against bitter resistance, advanced from Gevgeli through Doiran and up the Struma valley. Meanwhile the Turks took advantage of the situation to reoccupy Eastern Thrace and the Romanians entered Bulgaria from the north and annexed the Dobrudja region. A month after the outbreak of war a defeated Bulgaria sued for peace.

For Greece the gains of the two Balkan wars were a magnificent justification of Venizelos's policies: Salonika and the coastal strip of Macedonia including the rich tobacco-growing region of Kavalla; Southern Epirus with Ioannina; Crete (for *enosis* was at last formally recognized), and the islands Lesbos, Chios and Samos. The population and surface area of the country were almost doubled.

This triumph marked a temporary halt in the realization of the Great Idea. Rapid expansion had strained Greece's economic and administrative resources to the limit, and a state of precarious equilibrium was established in the Balkans by the territorial settlement of the Treaty of Bucharest of 1913. Venizelos himself recognized that the period of expansion must now be followed by peaceful reconstruction and development.

Hitherto Greece had expanded her frontiers outwards from the original core of the independent Kingdom, through Thessaly to Epirus and Macedonia. By a logical projection, now Thessaly was won and Macedonia divided among the Balkan allies, the next regions to be cultivated by Greek irridentists would be northern Epirus and Thrace. Only when these regions were integrated in the Greek Kingdom was it reasonable to look towards Constantinople and Asia Minor. To adapt a metaphor of Venizelos, territorial expansion should not proceed so fast or so haphazardly that Greece's backbone - the solid, Greek-inhabited land mass which had to support the territorial accretions – was distorted or broken.*

The expansion of Greece to this date had brought within the frontiers populations which were in their majority Greek; but even so, with her penetration into Epirus and Macedonia,† Greece embraced sizeable minorities of Albanians, Slav Macedonians and Muslims. With further expansion the problem of minorities would become more acute. The Greeks did not constitute an absolute majority in Thrace, Constantinople or western Asia Minor. Greek expansion in these areas would therefore be re-sisted by other elements in the population, and could not be expected to succeed without a prolonged period of preparation and struggle and cultivation of the terrain, such as had taken place in Macedonia in the early years of the century. There had been no such struggle in western Asia Minor.

* The origin of the 'backbone' metaphor was a speech of Venizelos in parliament on 2/15 March 1913, between the First and Second Balkan Wars; in response to an appeal from the Greek populations of East Mace-donia (including Drama and Kavalla) and Thrace, then occupied by the Bulgarian forces, for incorporation in the Greek Kingdom, Venizelos re-plied that these areas would go to Bulgaria 'because geographical reasons put us in such a position that, even if the Allies told us that they were pre-pared to allow us to extend our frontiers in that direction, so as to include those Greek populations, I at least as the responsible Minister would reject such frontiers as being too dangerous; I would recognize ... that Greece would be weaker if she were to extend in this way along the coasts without a backbone, than if her frontiers were filled out in another direction...'; I. Mallosis, *The Political History of Dimitrios P. Gounaris*, Athens 1926, pp. 255–6. Venizelos was, of course, savagely criticized for this remark, made at a time when he was intent on preserving the Balkan alliance.

† The 1913 Greek census gives the Greeks only a narrow relative majority in Greek Macedonia over the Muslims, the Greeks forming about 44 per cent of the population (Greeks 528,000; Muslims – 465,000; Bulgarians – 104,000; Jews – 98,000); A. A. Pallis, 'Racial migrations in the Balkans during the years 1912–1924', *Geographical Journal*, lxvi, no. 4, Oct. 1925.

2 | The Background in Anatolia

Church, School and Commerce kept ablaze the torch
of Greek Civilization and of the Great Idea.

G. Sakkas, *History of the Greeks of Tripolis in Pontus*,
Athens 1957, p. 26

Classical Greece had no frontiers, for it was not a state but a
collection of city states sharing certain things in common – the
most important of which was language. The frontiers of ancient
Hellenism were therefore the shifting frontiers of the language.
One of the first areas which the Greeks penetrated as colonizers,
explorers and exploiters was the Ionian coast of Asia Minor. The
main Ionian cities had formed a league by the end of the ninth
century BC. Greek colonies on the west coast and offshore island
states such as Samos and Chios grew and prospered. By the
seventh century, Greek colonies and trading posts were springing
up along the shores of the Black Sea, at Sinope, Trebizond and
elsewhere. Culturally and linguistically, the coastal cities of Asia
Minor – Smyrna, Ephesus, Halicarnassus, Miletus, Erythrae,
Phocaea, Pergamum, and others – remained Greek. The langu-
ages and cultures which had preceded the Greek, or which co-
existed with it, in Anatolia – Hittite, Lydian, Phrygian, Carian
– disappeared in the course of time. Greek civilization and culture
survived through the stormy periods of Alexander's conquests,
the Hellenistic kingdoms and the Roman imperial occupation of
Asia Minor, to the foundation of the Eastern Roman Empire and
the Turkish invasions.

Until the time of Alexander, the Greek presence in Asia was
that of a number of separate city states clustering around the
coasts of western Anatolia and the Black Sea – the diaspora of a
culturally and commercially vigorous minority. The cities fell
subject to the great Persian Empire. Alexander 'liberated' them
on his way through Asia Minor to Egypt, Persia and India.
Passing through Gordium, near the modern Eski Shehir, Alexander cut through the famous knot of which legend said that he
who untied it would conquer Asia. But though Macedonians and
Greeks followed Alexander as far as the Ganges and settled in

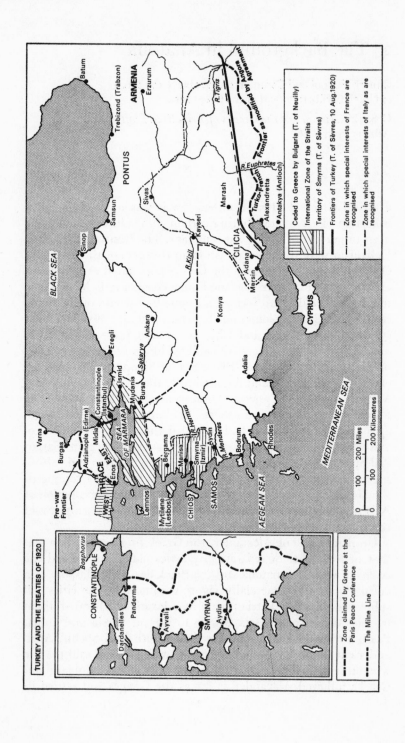

TURKEY AND THE TREATIES OF 1920

Ceded to Greece by Bulgaria (T. of Neuilly)
International Zone of the Straits
Territory of Smyrna (T. of Sèvres)
Frontiers of Turkey (T. of Sèvres, 10 Aug.1920)
Zone in which special interests of France are recognised
Zone in which special interests of Italy are recognised

BLACK SEA

Batum
Trebizond (Trabzon)
Erzurum
ARMENIA
PONTUS
Samsun
Sinop
Sivas
R. Kizil
Marash
Kayseri
R. Tigris
Turko-French Frontier as modified by Ankara Agreement
R. Euphrates
Alexandretta
Antakya (Antioch)
CILICIA
Adana
Mersin
Konya

Eregli
Ismid
Ankara
R. Sakarya
Mydania
Bursa
R. Hermus
Bergama
Menisa
Aydin
Smyrna (Izmir)
R. Menderes
Bodrum
Adalia
Rhodes
CYPRUS

Constantinople (Istanbul)
SEA OF MARMARA
Adrianople (Edirne)
Midia
Enos
Burgas
Varna
Pre-war Frontier
WEST THRACE
Lemnos
Mytilene (Lesbos)
CHIOS
SAMOS
AEGEAN SEA

MEDITERRANEAN SEA

0   100   200 Miles
0   100   200 Kilometres

Bosphorus
CONSTANTINOPLE
Dardanelles
Panderma
Ayvali
SMYRNA
Aydin

Zone claimed by Greece at the Paris Peace Conference
The Milne Line

the new Greek cities founded in the east, expanding the frontiers of Hellenism, only a thin crust of Alexander's eastern 'empire' was Greek. It was under his successors, the Seleucid kings, who inherited Alexander's Asian domains, that the Hellenization of Anatolia – interior as well as coastal regions – was achieved. In the Hellenistic period the Greek city was still regarded in theory as the 'natural' political and social unit, autonomous and complete, making its own internal and foreign policy. But in fact Alexander had made the cities subservient to his own arbitrary power. Inheriting this power, the Successors subsumed the cities in kingdoms which were more like modern nation states or absolutist regimes than classical city states – kingdoms with centralized, bureaucratic systems of government, centred on a ruler of absolute powers.

The successor kingdoms, created out of disparate linguistic, racial and cultural elements, needed a unifying principle; and the Seleucid kings found this in Hellenism. Greek was the official language; the immigration of Greeks and Macedonians was encouraged. The Greeks, although far outnumbered by the native populations of Cilicia, Babylonia, Syria, Media, etc., were the ruling class and culture. The educated natives adapted themselves to Greek customs, took Greek names and learned the language. In this way Anatolia was gradually Hellenized.

The pre-Christian history of Hellenism in Asia Minor helped to form the modern Greek view of the geographical and cultural boundaries of Hellenism; it was an element in the Greek's view of his country's destiny.

A more important element in national sentiment derived from the history of Anatolia in the Christian era and the emotional feelings evoked by Byzantium. Anatolia was the heart of the East Roman or Byzantine Empire, the source of the imperial ruling class, the main recruiting ground for its army, the granary of empire. While the Balkans were hammered and reforged by barbarian Slav invasions, Anatolia remained untouched. In these circumstances it was natural that the centre of gravity of Hellenism should move from Old Greece to Constantinople and Anatolia.

At the same time the domination of the Byzantine Empire by the Greek element made Constantinople with its magnificent Christian and imperial monuments the capital of a Greek as well as a Christian empire. In theory the Empire was universal,

Christian, and multiracial. In practice Hellenism was dominant and the Orthodox Church was identified with Greek culture, language and liturgy. Even before the fall of Constantinople in 1453, in face of the encroaching Ottoman Turks, who battered and undermined the diminished Empire like an irresistible tide from out of Asia, there were Greeks who foresaw the collapse of the Empire and took refuge in a consciousness of linguistic and national separateness as an alternative to the imperial consciousness.[1] After the fall of Constantinople to the Turks in 1453 the Orthodox Byzantines looked forward to the recovery of the City and the resurrection of the Empire through God's help in the fullness of time. A mass of legend, religious tradition, folk song and poetry arose out of this expectation,[2] which belonged in theory to all the Orthodox, but was most concentrated in the hearts of the Greeks. And by the time its realization began to seem possible, it had become thoroughly mixed with different, more modern theories of nationalism and national identity.

With the fall of Constantinople and the establishment of the Turks throughout Anatolia the Greek element was in time submerged and in danger of losing its hold except in the coastal regions. Turkish language and customs gained a grip over the peasantry in the interior, and great numbers of Christians were converted to Islam. But in the late eighteenth and nineteenth centuries the increasing power and prosperity of the Greek merchant-bourgeoisie was reflected in a development of the economic and cultural strength of Hellenism in western Anatolia. This development was assisted and accelerated by the growing interest of western capital in the possibilities of exploitation of Anatolia.

Education was at the heart of the revival of Hellenism in Asia Minor. In 1733 Pantoleon Sevastopoulos, a British subject, put the Evangelic School of Smyrna under the protection of the British Consulate, in order to protect it from the vicissitudes to which schools in the Ottoman Empire were subject. The school became the glory of Greek culture in western Asia Minor, boasting a fine library of printed books and rare manuscripts. Parallel with the growth of the Evangelic School went the foundation of Greek schools all over Anatolia. The education offered was modern, secular, calculated to encourage in the Greeks a sense of nationality, pride in their language, kinship with the ancient Greeks and the classics.

Around 1773 an imperial firman was granted to the Greek community of Ayvali, giving wide powers of local autonomy, and the privilege that no Muslim might live within the community's boundaries.[3] Ayvali henceforward served as an example of the possibilities open to Greek initiative and talents in Asia Minor. Greek colonists came from the Peloponnese and the islands. The town grew and thrived on its export trade in olive oil and soap. As a prime example of Greek enterprise, it attracted Turkish reprisals at the outbreak of the Greek war of independence and in 1917. Despite the widespread destruction of life and property on these occasions, the town recovered, was repopulated and prospered.

The establishment of the independent Greek state boosted the renaissance of Asia Minor. Greece served as an example and a lure to the still unredeemed communities. At the same time, the economic growth of the Greek communities on the west coast was partly dependent on, and helped to attract, Greek immigration from the mainland. Greeks from Lavrion and Mitylene, experienced in mining, moved to exploit the mineral resources of Bergama and Balia.[4] Much of the Erythrai peninsula flanking the bay of Smyrna was colonized after 1821 by Greeks from the offshore island of Chios. Greeks from the Zagoria came to Aydin, Maniots to Apollonia sited on a lake well stocked with fish and fringed with orchards. At Kula in 1921 Toynbee noted that about half of the Christian population of the town was indigenous, half recent immigrants from Samos and other islands.[5]

Greek immigration in the nineteenth century was due not simply to Greek enterprise and mobility, but also to the opening up of Anatolia to western trade by penetration by western capital. From the 1850s railway tracks began to snake their way inland, metal symbols of European technological and political preeminence. The Smyrna–Aydin railway, for which the concession was granted in 1856, was a British concern. Running southwards from Smyrna, it swung sharply inland to Aydin, and thence up the valley of the Meander, passing through Nazilli and north of Denizli to halt at Egridir. The effect of the railway on the economic life of Anatolia was impressive:

Smyrna is one of the few ports in Turkey where the value of the exports exceeds that of the imports, a condition of affairs largely due to the Smyrna–Aidin railways. ... Besides increasing the export trade of Smyrna, the railway has given an immense stimulus to the domestic commerce of the interior. Ten years ago * it was officially stated that the tithes [taxes on produce] from the districts near its lines had on an average doubled thirteen times over since the creation of the company. A number of factories have been erected and new industries created along its route, and there has been a notable increase of the Christian population owing to the peace and security prevailing in adjacent districts.[6]

These favourable effects were produced also by the Smyrna–Kassaba railway, the concession for which was granted in 1863. The line ran inland from Smyrna through Manisa (Magnesia), Kassaba, and Alashehir and up on to the escarpment at Ushak, running from there across the western edge of the central Anatolian plateau to Afyon Karahisar. In 1910 a concession was granted for the extension of the Smyrna–Soma branch line northwards to Panderma on the Sea of Marmara. Of this French enterprise the Foreign Office's verdict was:

The lines ... have been of the greatest service to the regions of Magnesia, Kassaba, Alashehir, and Soma, and share with the Smyrna–Aidin railway the credit for the remarkable expansion of the export trade of Smyrna. They have greatly stimulated the production of fruits, especially raisins and olives, and in the last years before the war the population near the lines, which was largely Greek, enjoyed unprecedented prosperity.[7]

The Anatolian railway from the Bosporus through Eski Shehir to Angora, with a branch from Eski Shehir through Afyon Karahisar to Konya, and the Baghdad railway from Konya through the Taurus mountains to Adana, constructed in the late nineteenth and early twentieth century, completed a system of communications in western Anatolia of vital strategic as well as economic importance. Quick to exploit the new opportunities, the Greeks penetrated inland along the railway lines, establishing trading posts, setting up as smalltime shopkeepers or agents for the great European commercial house of Smyrna.[8]

The Anatolian Greeks were not in the nineteenth and early twentieth centuries a homogeneous community. In the far northeast, there were the very ancient Greek-speaking Orthodox communities of the Pontus. In the interior, and especially in the Konya vilayet, Orthodox communities existed where the Greek language had been supplanted by the Turkish, a process which had begun with the establishment of the Turks in Anatolia and

* Ten years ago denotes 1908–09.

which only the widespread and conscious Greek nationalist and educational revival of the nineteenth century began to halt. These were the Karamanli Christians, named after Karaman, the former Turkish principality of Konya. Their knowledge of Greek was confined to the alphabet; their books were curiously produced in the Turkish language written in Greek characters.[9] In contrast with the Orthodox Greeks of the coastal regions, they were distinguishable from the Muslims neither in occupation, class, nor racial stock, but only in religion.

The disappearance of the Greek language before the Turkish began early and continued into the present century. The traveller Leake, who visited Asia Minor in 1800, wrote that 'the generality of the Cappadocian Greeks are ignorant of their own language and use the Turkish in the church-service'.[10] In 1816 a correspondent wrote to the British and Foreign Bible Society, formed twelve years earlier to promote the dissemination of the scriptures, that 'the only language in use among the Angora Christians, is the Turkish, which they are unable to read in its proper character. Some Bibles in the Turkish language, but in Armenian or Greek letters, would be very acceptable there.' [11]

In the mid-nineteenth century there were communities of Karamanli Turkish-speaking Christians in most of the towns of western Anatolia.[12] It was not from them but from the Greek-speaking bourgeois communities of the great cities – Constantinople and Smyrna – that the impetus for the nineteenth-century nationalist, educational and cultural revival came. The Karamanli communities were the raw material on which Greek-speaking Greeks could work, first and foremost by teaching them their proper language. The Karamanlides were keen to learn. A French traveller, invited to attend the class of the local school teacher in Isparta found 'des écoliers à barbe grise, des pauvres vieillards, des pères et grandpères qui venaient à l'école épeler l'alphabet de leur langue maternelle avec leurs petits enfants'.[13]

The third group of Greeks in Asia Minor was the relatively compact population of Smyrna and the western coastal strip with its historic towns. This community was variegated, ranging from the peasant farmer working in vines, currants or olives, through a large middle class of clerks, shopkeepers and salaried men, to the educated class of doctors, teachers, lawyers and prosperous traders who were at the heart of the nationalist movement and who had more in common with their counterparts in Constan-

tinople, Alexandria or Liverpool than with the Karamanli
Christians of the far interior. It was through these men, often
immigrants from the Greek kingdom, that the Greek language
and the Great Idea were propagated.

The descriptions of the Greek communities of Asia Minor left
by nineteenth-century travellers give an impression of energy,
mobility and life within a still ordered and hierarchical social and
communal structure. The basis of the Greeks' way of life was the
community, a corporate entity that was self-regulating as far as
was possible within the limits laid down by the Ottoman state
for the *Rum Milleti* or Greek nation. Under the direction and
jurisdiction of the local bishop, and through him of the Ecumenical Patriarch in Constantinople, the community had its own
representatives, its village elders or magistrates who dealt with
litigation and relations with the Ottoman administration; its
financial treasurers; its 'ephors' who administered the local
schools, selecting staff, vetting the programmes and syllabus,
administering benefactions. The nineteenth and early twentieth
century community was a self-disciplined society with faith in the
value of corporate action for the benefit of the community and
of future generations. Schools and hospitals were established and
maintained only through the generosity of rich benefactors
and the voluntary contributions of the mass of Greek inhabitants.
The *eranos* – a collection of funds for some charitable or social
cause – was a feature of the life of every Greek town or village.
As Toynbee noted, the Greeks' corporate spirit expressed itself
also in a genius for clubs.[14] Not only Smyrna but also smaller
provincial centres teemed with clubs, literary societies, and
assorted groups of do-gooders.

The Greeks impressed themselves vividly if not always favourably on foreign visitors. Murray noted that some of the Drago-
mans of Smyrna, who were commonly Greeks or Jews, 'without
principle and without instruction', carried testimonials by
foreigners they had served warning other foreigners against
them.[15] The Greeks were well established too as proprietors of
general stores :

In every town is to be found the *bakkal* or chandler's-shop keeper,
Armenian or Greek, who sells bread, cheese, onions, leeks, sugar,
coffee, coarse salt, soap, oil, native pickles or torshoon, pins, needles,
nails, string, lucifer matches, and a miscellaneous collection of
English imports and German imitations of them.[16]

The Greek grocer tended to be from the interior; he would go to Pera or Galata as a young man, practise the trade, picking up in the cosmopolitan atmosphere of the city a smattering of sophistication, national ideology and Greek language, and return eventually to his village to disseminate what he had learned.

Smyrna itself – *Ghiaour Izmir*, Infidel Smyrna, to the Turks – was the heart of Hellenism in Asia Minor. The great expansion of the port in the nineteenth century, to which the creation of the Anatolian railway system contributed so greatly, comprised a vast growth of population and trade. The Greek share in the total population moreover rose steadily from less than one third in 1800 to almost one half just before the Balkan Wars. Thus during the nineteenth century the Greeks steadily overtook the Turkish element until, by about the turn of the century, the Greeks could justly claim that Smyrna was a 'Greek' city. Smyrna's foreign trade grew along with her population. The new railways extended the commercial hinterland which had been opened up originally by the Levant Company, and by the end of the nineteenth century Smyrna's exports exceeded those of any other Turkish port including Constantinople.[17] Goods from the interior were funnelled down the great river valleys and railway lines to Smyrna for processing and dispatch abroad. The principal exports, of which Britain and France took the greatest share, were figs, raisins, barley, olive oil, valonia, opium, liquorice, wool and finished carpets, raw cotton, tobacco, hides and emery.[18] Most of the large business houses were foreign owned. But these – C. Whittall and Company, MacAndrews and Forbes in the liquorice trade, Oriental Carpet Manufacturers, etc. – though large and influential, were relatively few and could not equal the ever increasing Greek share in the city's commerce.

Between the Greek War of Independence, with its inevitable repercussions on the relations of Greeks and Turks in Anatolia, and the early years of this century, the Greeks were able to increase and multiply, colonize, penetrate inland, found new businesses and propagate nationalist ideals with little interference from the Ottomans. There were no massacres or widespread persecutions such as those suffered by the Armenians. A partial explanation of this is the fact that although the educated Greeks in Asia Minor sympathized with Greece's nationalist aspirations in theory, such sympathy did not yet extend to the concrete political demand for *enosis* with Greece. Such a demand was out-side the realm of practicable politics.

Nevertheless, the great upheaval in the Balkans between 1908 and 1914 initiated by the Young Turk revolution brought great changes in the position of the Greeks in the Smyrna area, turn-ing them into an 'issue' between Greece and Turkey, which on one occasion nearly led to war. The Young Turk revolution by its introduction of parliament and constitution awoke feelings and hopes among the Christians – visions of becoming 'co-governors' of the Empire, in Ion Dragoumis's phrase – which were soon dangerously frustrated by the Young Turks' policy of 'Ottomani-zation' of the minorities. National animosities and differences were sharpened; the militant nationalism of the Young Turks and their policy of pounding the non-Turkish elements in a Turkish mortar caused the Greeks to look hopefully towards Athens. Then came the first Balkan War, in which Greece, Serbia, Bulgaria and Montenegro set upon the Turks in Europe.

The Balkan War had psychological effects on the relationship between Turks and Greeks in Anatolia similar to those of the Greek War of Independence of 1821. The Turks naturally tended to identify the Ottoman Greeks, who sympathized ardently with their co-religionists of Old Greece, with the enemy at their gates. But even apart from this the increasing tension between Muslims and Christians in western Anatolia was exacerbated by a phenomenon which was to bedevil Greco-Turkish relations for almost two decades – the refugees.

As the armies of the Balkan allies advanced through Mace-donia and Thrace they pushed before them the first of the waves of destitute Muslim refugees which continued to pour into Con-stantinople after the conclusion of peace.* More than 100,000 Muslims fled through Eastern Thrace before the advance of the Bulgarian army in 1912; some 10,000 left Macedonia in the same year; nearly 50,000 left Western (Bulgarian) Thrace in 1913 under the terms of the Turco-Bulgarian Treaty; and after this more

---

* Toynbee cites these figures of the Ottoman Ministry of Refugees:

	1912–13	1914–15
Muslim refugees from all territories lost by Turkey in the Balkan Wars	177,352	120,566
Muslim refugees from territories lost by Turkey to Greece in Balkan Wars	68,947	53,718

(*The Western Question in Greece and Turkey*, p. 138)

than 100,000 Muslims evacuated Macedonia.[19] The upheaval of Muslim communities in Europe led to reprisals on the Anatolian Christians. One motive was desire for revenge. There was also the practical motive that for every Christian family expelled it was possible to settle a Muslim refugee family in the empty accommodation.

The Turkish reprisals fell on the Greek communities of western Anatolia in 1914. In a systematic way, through the operations of irregular bands of *chettés* (the Turkish equivalent of Macedonian *comitadjis*)[20] and with the collusion of the Ottoman authorities, Greek communities in the coastal region were uprooted, their houses and lands seized, themselves violently forced into exile. Arnold Toynbee heard of a typical incident:

One morning in the spring of 1914, the Bergama Greeks were informed by the local Ottoman authorities that they could not guarantee their safety if they remained that night in the town. Abandoning everything but what they could carry in their hands, they got down before nightfall to the skala of Dikeli, crossed over to Mitylini as soon as transport could be found for them, and remained there six years.[21]

This experience, and worse, was repeated along the western littoral of Asia Minor.

It was not a 'massacre' in the sense of the Armenian or Bulgarian massacres, though numerous incidents of murder, destruction and rape took place. It was what the Greeks call a *diogmos* – persecution. French eye-witnesses described the phenomenon as it afflicted Old Phocea, a seaside town of about 9,000 inhabitants, in June 1914: 'On 11 June the Greek inhabitants of the surrounding villages suddenly poured into Phocea with the news that their villages were being attacked by the surrounding Turks. On the next day, 12 June, the movement spread to Phocea and the massacres began.'[22] A day and night of horror and pillage followed. The Turkish *chettés* who had attacked the town were armed with old Gras rifles and cavalry muskets:

From all directions the Christians were rushing to the quays to seek boats to get away in, but since the night there were none left. Cries of terror mingled with the sound of the firing.... The panic was so great that a woman with her child was drowned in 60 cm of water.... We saw doors broken in and horses and asses laden with booty. This continued all day. Toward evening I mounted a little hill and saw a hundred camels laden with the pillage.[23]

The Greeks took refuge in Mitylene and Chios, some even further afield. Phocea was left a ghost city.

Incidents such as these, which illustrate the deteriorating relations between Greeks and Turks in Asia Minor, explain also the pressures on Greek politicians to embrace the cause of the Asia Minor Greeks, and on the Greeks themselves to opt for *enosis* as the solution to their problems. The Ottoman persecutions and expulsions of the Greeks on the coast were part of a systematic policy designed to put pressure on the Greek Government in the dispute over the possession of the Aegean islands, and to further the policy of Ottomanization. The successful Balkan Wars, the Ottomanization policy of the Young Turks, and the impression that in Venizelos Greece had found a leader capable of realizing a Greater Greece, led the more romantic and visionary of the Greeks in Asia Minor to look to Old Greece for help.

Venizelos, of course, protested strongly against the persecution of the Greeks, and inquired of Serbia how she would interpret the Greco-Serbian defensive alliance should war break out between Greece and Turkey. He was not, however, tempted by sympathy for the Asia Minor Greeks into publicly embracing the cause of *enosis* or in other ways provoking the Turks. Venizelos wanted a peaceful solution to the disputes between Greece and Turkey based on recognition by Turkey of Greek sovereignty over the Aegean islands, Mitylene, Chios and Samos,* a settlement which would allow Greece a period for reconstruction and development without foreign entanglements. In fact, so hard-headed was Venizelos over the exposed position of the Asia Minor Greeks that he went so far as to negotiate a convention which, in different circumstances, might have solved the Asia Minor question once and for all. Venizelos concluded an agreement with the Porte for a voluntary exchange of the Greek-speaking populations of Turkish Thrace and the Aydin vilayet in Asia Minor for the Muslim populations of Greek Macedonia

---

* The fate of the Aegean islands, the main issue between Greece and Turkey, was left after the Balkan Wars to the decision of the Powers, who assigned them all except for Imbros and Tenedos to Greece by a decision of Feb. 1914. Turkey refused to accept this decision for Mitylene, Chios and Samos, because of their strategic position off the coast of Asia Minor and their proximity to the large Greek populations of the mainland. Greece was in *de facto* occupation, and the outbreak of the Great War settled the issue in her favour.

and Epirus.[24] This agreement, a radical new initiative in the handling of national minorities,* provided for the interchange of the minorities in an orderly and peaceful manner under the supervision of a mixed commission, and for the valuation and liquidation of the migrants' fixed property. The negotiation of the agreement at once eased the lot of the Asia Minor Greeks; but whether the minorities would have taken advantage of it to emigrate, or would have had to be forced to go, was never determined, since Turkey's entry into the Great War interrupted the preliminary work of the Commission, and the agreement was never ratified

Thus in the space of a few years the status and treatment of the Greek communities of western Asia Minor had become an issue which could not be ignored by any Greek government. The Great War highlighted the problem. There were two possible approaches for a Greek government. It was possible to argue, with Venizelos, that the war presented a unique opportunity for the redemption of Ionian Hellenism; for Turkey's participation on the side of the Central Powers gave Greece, if she joined the Entente, all the moral and material support of Britain and France in wresting Smyrna from Turkey. For those who argued this way, the suffering and persecution that Greece's entry into the war on the opposite side to Turkey would entail for the Asia Minor Greeks was simply the price they would have to pay for the reward of eventual *enosis*.

It was possible, on the other hand, to argue that Greece could not hope, except in the most unlikely conjunction of favourable circumstances, to establish herself in Asia Minor. It was sensible, therefore, in the interests of the Asia Minor Greeks themselves, to avoid provoking Turkey to reprisals and persecution by joining in the war against her. The position of the Asia Minor Greeks could thus be used by anti-Venizelists as an argument in favour of Greek neutrality.

---

* The treaty between Turkey and Bulgaria after the second Balkan War included a protocol providing for an exchange of Bulgarians and Muslims and of their properties in a 15 km zone along their common Thracian frontier; but this convention was almost entirely retrospective, confirming and settling the details of the migrations which had already taken place during the Balkan Wars. The Greco–Turkish agreement was the first to suggest exchange of populations as a *preventive* measure, to improve inter-state relations and solve the problems arising out of minorities; Pentzopoulos, *The Balkan Exchange of Minorities*, pp. 54–5.

The effects of these two differing theories will be explored in the next chapter. It need only be noted here that after a break, the Ottoman persecution of the Greek communities recommenced on a wider and more systematic scale in early 1916. Whole communities were deported from coastal regions into the interior, with great brutality and widespread suffering and loss of life. In March 1917 the entire population of Ayvali was turned out of house and home and transported to Balikesir and other centres inland. Muslim refugees from the lost provinces of European Turkey were then settled in the town. In Ayvali, Bergama, Dikeli and other towns, Greek churches, schools, hospitals and private houses were desecrated and ransacked after the expulsions.[25] The Turks claimed that the deportations were a military measure dictated by the necessity of clearing the coastal regions of hostile and disloyal Greek populations; and it is true that Greeks engaged in intelligence work for the Entente Powers. The effect of the Turkish persecutions, in which Greeks in their thousands were deported or migrated in fear,* was to increase the desire of the Greek communities for revenge and for *enosis* with Greece, and to keep the issue alive in the minds of Venizelos and his Government.

* Mr Gounarakis, Secretary-General of the Greek High Commission in Smyrna, estimated the number of those expelled to Greece during the war at *c.* 105,000, and the number of those deported into the interior of Anatolia at *c.* 50,000; *Documents on British Foreign Policy*, first ser., xv, no. 21, pp. 182–4. But these figures apply to the Greek zone of the Treaty of Sèvres only, and the figures for all Western Anatolia must be higher. The Greeks of Eastern (Turkish) Thrace also suffered. See Pallis, 'Racial Migrations', *Geographical Journal*, lxvi, no. 4, Oct. 1925.

3 | Great War and National Schism

I have the impression that the concessions to Greece
in Asia Minor, which Sir Edward Grey
recommended, may, if of course we submit to
sacrifices to Bulgaria, be so extensive that another
equally large and not less rich Greece will be
added to the doubled Greece which emerged from
the victorious Balkan wars.

Venizelos to King Constantine
30 January 1915

On 23 January 1915 the British Foreign Secretary, Sir Edward
Grey, telegraphed to Sir Francis Elliot, the British Minister in
Athens, instructing him to offer 'most important territorial com-
pensation for Greece on the coast of Asia Minor' in return for
Greek participation in the war on the side of the Entente. 'If M.
Venizelos wishes for a definite promise,' added Grey, 'I believe
there will be no difficulty in obtaining it.' [1]

How could Grey offer Smyrna to Greece? Early in the war,
when only Serbian and Austrian troops were committed on
opposing sides in the Balkan theatre, in a grim struggle on Serbian soil, Greek cooperation was useful to the Entente allies only
provided it did not compromise Bulgarian or Turkish neutrality
or cooperation. In August 1914, on British initiative, the Allies
turned down a remarkable offer by Venizelos of cooperation with
all Greece's forces, on the grounds that the entry of Greece would
provoke Turkey and probably Bulgaria to abandon neutrality
and join the Central Powers.

The entry of Turkey into the war released the Allies from
scruples in that direction, but the problem posed by Bulgaria
remained. It was now Grey's object to induce Bulgaria, Greece
and Romania to cooperate with Serbia (which had to bear the
burden of successive Austrian offensives) against the Central
Powers – Greece actively, Bulgaria at least by a benevolent
neutrality. The consequence of this policy was that Britain could
not offer territories in Macedonia or Thrace, the natural areas
for Greek expansion, for fear of pushing Bulgaria into the opposing camp. To Bulgaria, the Allies were in a position to offer only

Eastern (Turkish) Thrace; but Bulgarian aspirations were for expansion in Macedonia. Given the priority attached by Britain to Bulgarian cooperation or neutrality, therefore, it became necessary to persuade Serbia and Greece to make concessions to Bulgaria in Macedonia. But in order to bring about an act of such unbalkan generosity, Greece must be offered compensation elsewhere.

The offer of territorial concessions can now be understood by a glance at the map. Concessions on the northern frontier of Greece were ruled out by the rival claims of Serbia and Bulgaria. Compensation around Constantinople and the Straits or in northern Asia Minor was excluded by the attitude of Russia. The Russians' secular dream was of mastery of the Straits, that narrow channel from their own domestic waters, the Black Sea, to the warm-water Mediterranean, a channel vital to Russian commercial and strategic interests. The war presented them with a chance to secure this prize. Sazonov, the Tsar's Foreign Minister, was not going to put the prize at risk by allowing the Greeks to get in the way.

There remained the islands. An admirable course would have been to offer Greece the lovely islands of the Dodecanese, with their predominantly Greek populations. But since 1912 these islands had been occupied by Italy. And the Allies were at this moment trying to persuade Italy to join the Entente. The negotiations with Italy ruled out not only the Dodecanese but also northern Epirus (now southern Albania), with its substantial Greek minority; for the Italians regarded Albania-Epirus as a sphere of influence.

Lastly there was Cyprus, where the Greeks were some 80 per cent of the population. But Cyprus was British. It was easier to offer what belonged to others. Cyprus was a card which the British Government was prepared to play only in the last resort. Before it need be played there was Smyrna and its fair hinterland – 'most important territorial compensation' which belonged to the Ottoman enemy and could therefore freely be promised away.

Venizelos's desire for an Anglo-Greek entente dated from before the war. The appointment of a French Military and a British Naval Mission to Greece had suggested that he saw Greek interests as identified with the interests of Britain and France.

The secret talks with Lloyd George and Churchill in London, arranged through Stavridi, had taken him much further in the identification of Greek aspirations with British power in the Eastern Mediterranean. As a result of them the idea of an Anglo-Greek entente in the Eastern Mediterranean took root in Lloyd George's fertile mind, and never left it thereafter. (The case was not the same with Churchill, who was at the time concerned with the specific question of the Ionian islands naval base and the potential menace of the Italian fleet, rather than the general question of an Anglo-Greek entente. Churchill was in any case less inclined to write off the Ottoman Empire, even at the time of the Balkan Wars, than was Lloyd George.) Venizelos, for his part, left the talks fortified in his conviction that Greek interests demanded the wholehearted cooperation of Greece with Britain (and, as a corollary, with France) in the Eastern Mediterranean.

Venizelos's policy was twofold: the territorial expansion of the Greek state so as to include as many as possible of the Greek people, and the making of Greece into an important Mediterranean power. These two aims were complementary, but not identical. After the Balkan Wars, the second had priority: Venizelos looked forward to a period of peace and reconstruction, an expansion of Greek resources and a development of the Greek administration which would make possible the eventual expansion of the Greek frontiers. With the outbreak of the Great War the first aim assumed priority. The war presented itself to Venizelos's mind as an opportunity which could not be ignored for territorial expansion. If the opportunity were taken, Greece would win new economic and human resources which in time would transform her from a nullity into a significant 'second-class power'.

Given the nationalist assumptions of the entire politically conscious Greek world at this time, the policy was unimpeachable in its ideal end. It was the means to an end which aroused bitter dissension.

Venizelos's opponents were an uncohesive, motley crew of politicians and soldiers whose binding principle was their opposition to Venizelos; hence, though they were called many names by their enemies – the Royalists, reactionaries, the 'old politicians' among others – the simple term 'anti-Venizelist' is the most comprehensive. They included the King's advisers and friends, such as the erudite diplomatist George Streit; the frustrated, ageing leaders of the old political faction thrust aside by the expanding irresistible tide of Venizelism – the distinguished names of Dragoumis, Rallis, Mavromichalis, Theotokis, and others; men of Venizelos's own generation such as Gounaris. (Of the old Japanese Group, Repoulis and Alexandris had joined the Venizelists. The rest remained in opposition.) An interesting case was that of Nikolaos Stratos, a clever lawyer who had joined the Venizelist Party, risen to ministerial rank, and been forced to resign after allegations of corrupt practices. He had gone into opposition and remained there, wasting his undoubted talents, until 1922. It was Stratos on whom Compton Mackenzie was moved to reflect when he saw him leaning over the rail of the *Spetsai* during a crossing to Italy in 1915:

The tragedy of Stratos was that in his heart he believed in the policy of his old leader, but that out of personal hatred he had sold his soul to thwart it by every unscrupulous device he could contrive. He was a dark-bearded, bulky man, with a sour expression in his eyes. He and I were the only two creatures on deck, and it occurred to me that, if I were a figment of my own imagination, I should have the courage to seize the legs of the big man and tip him overboard. He was an enemy of the allies, an enemy of Greece, an enemy even of himself. A moment of resolution, and he would be struggling vainly in that long line of grey foam which stretched it seemed indefinitely across the dim sea.[2]

In all this there was a melodramatic imagination at work. Stratos was shrewd, ambitious, talented, but no tragic hero.

Venizelos's opponents argued that in backing England to win the war, he was backing the wrong horse, or at least could not know that he was backing the right horse. They claimed that whether or not the Entente finally won, Venizelos did not take sufficient account of the immediate danger to Greek territorial integrity from Bulgaria. Even if the Entente won, Venizelos's diplomatic methods made it likely that the territorial compensations in Asia Minor would not be realizable, in the absence of firm, written guarantees from the Allies that they would carve up Turkey in Asia and enforce the partition. Lastly, Venizelos's policy, which was no secret to the Turks, exposed the Greek communities in Asia Minor to certain persecution in the immediate future, against the uncertain hope of *enosis* after the war.[3]

The difference in policy between Venizelists and anti-Venizelists reflected a difference of psychology between Venizelos and his opponents. Venizelos's policy arose from a deep faith in British victory and in the identity of British and Greek interests in the Eastern Mediterranean.⁴ In the blinding light of this faith, details and practical calculations, however important in deciding the timing of Greek intervention and in imposing that intervention on the country, were ultimately irrelevant. Calculation might suggest that intervention entailed the danger of Bulgarian assault on Greece and of increasing persecution of the Greeks in Asia Minor; but these disasters, even if they materialized, would be justified by the magnificent compensations to be obtained after the war. Thus Venizelos positively sought the opportunity for intervention. It was the policy of a visionary and a gambler.

Venizelos's opponents were neither visionaries nor gamblers. They approached the question of intervention with the wary suspicion of shoppers in the market place. Their attitude to the war was negative. Some of them believed in 1915 that the most probable outcome of the war was either a stalemate or a German victory. But this belief did not lead them to favour cooperation with the Central Powers, which was ruled out by Greece's vulnerability to naval pressure from the British Mediterranean fleet. The clear choice for hardheaded anti-Venizelists was neutrality, unless it became apparent that the Entente Powers could satisfy an impressive series of Greek demands. They must guarantee Greek territorial integrity (territorial concessions by Greece to Bulgaria were absolutely excluded); and further guarantee Greece militarily against the possibility of Bulgarian invasion. They must give convincing evidence that they were likely to win the war, and make the 'dissolution of the Ottoman Empire' one of their war aims.⁵ In practical terms, to ask all this in 1915 was to ask for the moon.

The positions of Venizelists and anti-Venizelists shifted from day to day in accordance with the changing fortunes of the war and the threats and bribes brought to bear on the Greeks. It would be hard to point to a single Greek politician who did not waver in his convictions at some point. Venizelos himself, while remaining unmovable on the ultimate ends of Greek policy, showed a remarkable flexibility in the first months of the war. At one of the 'Crown Councils' of politicians and elder statesmen called at critical moments in the war he went so far as to advise the King to keep Greece's options open by negotiating with

Germany.[6] On the anti-Venizelists' side, the volatility of attitudes is shown by the advice offered by the party leaders at the Crown Councils, and especially the elderly and peppery Dimitrios Rallis, who urged Greek intervention in the strongest terms.[7] The myth of a solid Royalist *bloc* pursuing a policy of Germanophil neutrality was created by the Venizelists after the events of 1915, when the country was already divided. In truth, the anti-Venizelists were torn between their suspicions of the outside world, and the nationalist passions awakened in them when Venizelos dangled such baits as Constantinople before their eyes.

Much was made by the Venizelists of the Germanophil charge. Historically the ties of Greece with the liberal western democracies were stronger than those with Germany; but the politically conscious world in Greece looked towards both France and Germany in the cultural domain. Most of the politicians prominent in this period completed their education with a spell in 'Europe', as the Greeks say. Rather more went to France than to Germany. There is no neat pattern whereby Liberals tended to go to Paris and Royalists to Berlin. In fact, rather more Venizelists than anti-Venizelists seem to have studied in Germany.[8] There are no *a priori* grounds here for expecting to find Germanophilia in the anti-Venizelist world.

With the soldiers, however, the country of study seems to bear a more significant relationship to political views – perhaps not surprisingly in view of the patriotic mystique involved in military training. Metaxas and Xenophon Stratigos, both Royalists and extreme anti-Venizelists, studied at the Berlin Military Academy, as did another Royalist and anti-Venizelist – the King. Danglis, Paraskevopoulos and Pangalos, all prominent Venizelists, studied in France.

Sympathy for Germany in itself was of course no crime, nor love of the Entente a virtue. The admiration of Gounaris for Bismarckian social insurance legislation and the cultural and philosophical achievements of nineteenth-century Germany might be compared with the attitude of Haldane in England. But sympathy for Germany affected calculations of probabilities and interests by predisposing Metaxas and others to overestimate German military power and diplomatic good faith. In this way Germanophilia affected the judgement of the anti-Venizelist world, just as Venizelos's Anglophilia led him seriously to underestimate the dangers of his own policy. The importance of the phenomenon was that two of the men whose judgement was most powerfully affected, Ioannis Metaxas and Georgios Streit, were men on whose judgement the King depended.

Luckily both Streit and Metaxas kept diaries. Their tone was very different, Streit measured and self-concealing, Metaxas passionate and unable to conceal his frustration, pride, egoism and ambition. Metaxas was a soldier, relatively inexperienced in diplomacy and politics; Streit was a learned and experienced diplomatist of the old school. A short, barrel-shaped man who took himself exceptionally seriously, Metaxas was the shrewdest of the Greek staff officers who had risen to prominence in the first decade of the century. His studies in Germany had impressed on him the virtues of Prussian discipline and the strength of German militarism, which reflected the deep yearning for order in Metaxas's own temperament. As a staff officer Metaxas was first-class. Together with Victor Dousmanis, he played a vital part in the staff work during the Balkan wars.

Metaxas's attitude to the war was complex. He saw it as a disaster which would hurt victors and vanquished alike, and recognized that Greece was well out of it; but his puritanism and dissatisfaction with the existing state of society and morals led him to believe that humanity might progress only through a disaster of such magnitude. Metaxas at first expected the war to end in stalemate, the Germans victorious on land, the English preserving their domination at sea and thus able ultimately to impose their terms. On 17 August 1914 the first signs of disagreement with Venizelos appear:

Recently he has been swept away by the innate hostility he feels for Germany, he has been swept further than he should. Certainly it is not in our interests that Germany should win.... The only positive is that we should not be on the opposite side to England. Luckily, everyone has recognized that.[9]

As the days passed, Metaxas's admiration for German moral values and military efficiency affected him more and more strongly:

The serious German spirit, which takes everything in life seriously, *ernst*, with the feeling of duty and submission to God, does not please the Greeks, who from the point of view of spiritual development are like children....

Happy are those who have understood the German spirit and

conformed to it, not exchanging our own for it, but shaping ours in conformity with the German, without throwing away our Greek talents and characteristics, our *cachet*.[10]

This view was balanced by an equal contempt for the French, whom he called 'enfants gâtés et pervertis':

Discipline and order always conquer a higher spirit and individualism. .... Individualism produces artistic races, but not races of progress and civilization. On the contrary, it is a dissolving factor, and the clever races are not the great ones. .... Clever men are never deep, nor deep men ever clever. ....

The French are characterized by fragmentation, lack of discipline, egoism: not individualism: as for cleverness, they have it, and unfortunately in large measure, but their cleverness serves only for *bons mots* and *mondanités* and *comédies*.[11]

Such views affected Metaxas's military and political judgement. On 26 August the memoirs of a nineteenth-century German staff officer inspired in him a 'brilliant thought' which he wrote down and handed to his colleagues Dousmanis and Streit. The thought was, quite simply, that 'the safety of Greece is ensured only if Germany wins'.[12] This was the counterpart of Venizelos's belief that the salvation of Greece was ensured only if she marched with the Entente. There was nothing intrinsically immoral in either view. But Metaxas's view implied the abandonment (at least temporarily) of Greece's secular aspirations for expansion at the expense of Germany's ally, Turkey. It therefore ran directly counter to the assumptions of the majority of the Greek people at this time. Metaxas's words were, in fact, a conscious adoption of what the Venizelists later categorized as the Royalist policy of a 'small but honest Greece', calling it the policy of timid, petty-minded merchants.[13]

Metaxas could not believe in, nor did he desire, total defeat of Germany; and only this would allow England a free hand in settling the affairs of the east. Admiration for Germany and military experience led him to distrust the optimistic assurances of Venizelos that ultimately the Entente would win the war and be in a position to bring about the dissolution of the Ottoman Empire. His views hardened as the German military machine proved itself in western Europe and on the Russian front (the rallies of the Entente were explained away), and as the prolonged haggling with the Entente revealed the unwillingness of allied statesmen to take Greek fears of Bulgaria seriously.

For personal reasons Metaxas was ready to dissociate himself from Venizelos. His attitude to Venizelos was nervously possessive. He treasured signs of the older man's friendship and goodwill, but regarded him as fickle and unstable, and violently resented any sign that Venizelos might encroach on his integrity and independence by 'using' him. He speaks continually of detaching himself from Venizelos and others and standing on his own feet.[14]

Venizelos for his part was never completely unmoved by the advice of Metaxas and Dousmanis, which accounted for some of his hesitations. He knew in any case that their dismissal would deprive Greece of her two most capable and experienced staff officers, but would not remove the source of their threat to his policy – their influence over the King.*

The attitude of George Streit was essentially similar. An erudite diplomatist, whose grandfather had come to Greece at the time of King Otho and taken a Greek wife, Streit looked on the King with affection approaching veneration. 'A nature sincere and without the slightest guile, a profound and fine intelligence. May God preserve him for the good of Greece.' [15] Streit found it easy to do business with the representatives of the Central Powers, having served as Greek minister in Vienna and being himself of German stock. By nature sceptical, cautious and even pedantic, Streit mistrusted the unstable genius of Venizelos, and was convinced of the King's right to impose neutrality (which Streit and his associates construed as the right to interpret the will of the majority of the Greek people). He played a predominant part in bolstering the King's sometimes wavering conviction of the rightness of neutrality, and in restraining the unreliable Gounaris government which succeeded Venizelos in March 1915 from committing Greece too far with the Entente. The foundation of Streit's policy was the realization of a pan-Balkan neutral bloc (as opposed to Venizelos's belligerent bloc), his motive the desire to avert the hostility of both the Entente and the Central Powers.

Streit defined his attitude in conversation with Demidov, the Russian Minister:

---

* Venizelos did dismiss Dousmanis, for an act of gross insubordination, in Feb. 1915, but displeased the King by so doing, and soon reinstated him.

I fear neither the one nor the other [i.e. Prussian militarism and the Slav peril].... The small nations should pray for a balance between the Great Powers, which is in any case inherent in the nature of affairs as a sort of natural law, and reestablishes itself.... It is true that I think it more probable that the Entente will win.* but I cannot forecast with certainty in face of the imponderables of war, nor do I think that Venizelos is right in considering the complete dissolution of Germany probable or even possible. Nor do I even wish it. That is the measure of my 'Germanophilia'.[16]

Finally, there was King Constantine – the only political agent with the influence and prestige to impose a policy other than that of Venizelos. The King shared the views of Streit and Metaxas, but was less consistent, and less intelligent, more subject than they to Venizelos's eloquence, more easily swayed by the vision of Constantinople, and conscious of the responsibility which weighed on him as the final arbiter of Greek policy. His two aims were to preserve Greek neutrality, and to avoid provoking a political and constitutional crisis through Venizelos's dismissal. The aims eventually proved incompatible, and Venizelos was forced to resign so that neutrality might be preserved.

If the anti-Venizelist attitude has been discussed in terms of individuals, this is because the determining of policy rested in the hands of a very few men. Metaxas wrote in August 1914 that four men only were at the helm – the King, Venizelos, Dousmanis and himself; and this was scarcely an exaggeration. None of the party leaders or elder statesmen – G. Theotokis, D. Rallis, Zaimis, S. Dragoumis – played a decisive role. Neither parliament nor 'the country' was the forum in which the issues were thrashed out. Appeals to public opinion meant little. It was only after the elections of 31 May/13 June 1915, the first for three years, that Venizelos could plausibly claim a mandate for his policy. The game was played out in Athens between the anti-Venizelist faction (the King, the Staff, Streit, Gounaris and a few others), and Venizelos, representing the great mass of voters who had entrusted the country's fate to him.

Sir Edward Grey's offer of January 1915 was prompted by Venizelos himself. On 6 January, Sir Francis Elliot had seen Venizelos and suggested that Greece come to the aid of Serbia. Venizelos replied that for Greece to enter the war solely on

* This was not always Streit's view.

account of *Serbia* was impossible; but the situation of the Greeks in Asia Minor was desperate, and if a rupture of Greece and *Turkey* were precipitated, the 'magnificent compensation' which could arise from war with Turkey would move public opinion sufficiently to enable him to bring Greece into the war on the side of the Entente. Elliot promised to consult his Government.[17]

It was in the light of this conversation that the Powers elaborated their offer to Greece of 24 January. The offer was based on suggestions from the Buxtons, tireless supporters of Bulgarian aspirations in parliament and press and through the Balkan Committee in London. Noel Buxton, whose travels in the Balkans in the late nineteenth century had awoken a lifelong interest in the politics of the region, had founded the Committee in 1903, to promote Balkan unity and liberation from Ottoman rule. With his brother C. R. Buxton he undertook an unofficial mission to the Balkans early in the war, at the suggestion of Lloyd George and Churchill, to secure Bulgarian cooperation or neutrality. The two brothers elaborated in January 1915 a series of 'Notes on the Balkan States' which foreshadowed precisely the policy adopted by Grey on 23 January, suggesting concessions to Greece in Asia Minor as the only means of securing the concessions to Bulgaria in Macedonia which might bring her round to the Entente.[18] Noel Buxton was in contact with members of the Cabinet at this time, and successfully urged on them Venizelos's views on the subject of Asia Minor, in the context of a general Balkan policy which would secure Bulgarian intervention or at least benevolent neutrality.[19] The offer of 24 January did not therefore come out of the blue to Venizelos; it was based on his own prior acceptance of Buxton's 'Balkan bloc' policy.

While the 'proposal' to Greece was being elaborated, the Russian Foreign Secretary Sazonov suggested that Greece be asked to concede Kavalla to Bulgaria in exchange for her compensations elsewhere.[20] The busy little port of Kavalla in Macedonia, looking out towards the wooded island of Thasos in the northern Aegean, had been won from the Bulgarians by the Greek army in the second Balkan war. It was and is the centre of a rich tobacco industry. But this was not the point at issue. The point was that Kavalla had been wrested by Greece from her enemies, and to talk of giving back what had once been 'redeemed' with Greek blood sounded like treason.

Sazonov's proposal was in line with the Buxton plan. But

when Grey sent his famous telegram to Elliot on 23 January, concessions to Bulgaria were not specified. Grey wrote that it was 'most desirable' for the allies to be able to assure Bulgaria that she would get adequate compensation in Macedonia for joining the Entente or for friendly neutrality. Elliot was to tell Venizelos that compensation for Bulgaria was 'primarily a matter for Servia'; Greece's role was not to oppose these Serbian concessions.* Kavalla was not mentioned. Lloyd George, who acted as a goad to the Government in all negotiations concerning Greece and the Balkans, asked Stavridi to assure Venizelos that there was no longer any question of requiring Greece to retrocede Kavalla to Bulgaria.[21]

Venizelos had extracted from the Allies the offer he desired, without promising to concede Kavalla in return to Bulgaria. But with what seems in retrospect like extraordinary rashness on 24 January he himself raised the question of Kavalla in a long memorandum to the King, in which he urged the acceptance of the offer of the Entente, subject to the realization of the Balkan bloc which was to the Greeks a condition of the offer.[22] Perhaps Venizelos realized that concessions from Serbia alone would not move Bulgaria, and therefore decided that Greece should go further than even Grey had suggested. He wrote to the King that hitherto there had been well-founded reasons for Greek neutrality:

But now the circumstances have clearly changed. At this moment when the prospects of realizing our national views on Asia Minor are opening before us, certain sacrifices in the Balkans can be made in order to secure the success of so magnificent a national policy.

Above all we should withdraw our objections to concessions being made by Serbia to Bulgaria, even if these extend to the right bank of the Vardar.

But if these concessions are not sufficient to draw Bulgaria into cooperation with her former allies, or at least to the maintenance of a benevolent neutrality towards them, I should not hesitate, however painful the operation might be, to recommend the sacrifice of Kavalla, so as to save Hellenism in Turkey and to secure the creation

* The idea was for Serbia to make concessions in the Monastir–Ochrid area, in return for her gains in the west (Dalmatia etc.). There were strong reservations in military and political circles, shared by Venizelos himself, to consenting to any Serbian concessions to Bulgaria in Macedonia which would upset the 'equilibrium' in the Balkans established after the Balkan Wars.

of a truly great Greece, including almost all the territories in which Hellenism has been active during its long history.

This sacrifice, however, would take place not just as the price of Bulgarian neutrality, but in return for her active participation in the war with the rest of the allies.

If this view of mine were accepted, it would be necessary through the intervention of the Entente Powers to secure that Bulgaria should undertake to buy the properties of all those inhabitants of the sector to be conceded to her who wished to migrate within the frontiers of Greece. Simultaneously it would be agreed that the Greek populations living within the Bulgarian frontiers should be exchanged with the Bulgarian populations within the Greek frontiers, with a mutual purchase of the vacated properties of the two states. ... In this way the ethnological settlement in the Balkans would be finally achieved and the idea of the Balkan Federation could be realized; at any rate a treaty of mutual guarantees would be signed by these states, which would permit them to devote themselves to the work of economic and other development.

This memorandum to the King (of which only a small part has been quoted) perfectly illustrates the virtues and defects of Venizelos's mind. There was on the one hand the broad vision of a final settlement in the Balkans, a Federation of friendly states; the willingness to transcend the narrow mutual suspicions of the Balkan powers; the quickness to adapt his policy to the circumstances of the war; and the recognition that there could be no permanent Balkan settlement until the problems of national minorities had been eliminated.

On the other hand, the proposals were in many ways extraordinarily unrealistic given the prevailing assumptions of the Greeks. Venizelos was proposing a complete reversal of the doctrine of a Balkan 'equilibrium'. His proposals were therefore anathema to the General Staff and the King, who held that appeasement of Bulgaria, so far from leading to a definitive Balkan settlement, would encourage expansionary Bulgarian nationalism.[23] Secondly, Venizelos's scheme would exclude the possibility of Greek expansion into Western and Eastern Thrace. His claim to be creating a greater Greece including almost all the territories historically associated with Hellenism was thus incorrect. What he proposed was the sacrifice of hopes of future expansion in the Balkans at the expense of Bulgaria, against the uncertain hopes of a still more difficult and risky expansion in Asia Minor. Thirdly, Venizelos was proposing the cession of rich and valuable Greek territories gained during the Balkan Wars. He could persuade his supporters to stomach this, but it was certain to raise the temperature of the opposition to fever pitch.

In his telegram to the Greek legations in London, Paris and Petrograd the next day, Venizelos was more circumspect.[24] Greek acceptance of Grey's offer was made contingent on the attitudes of Bulgaria and Romania. No mention was made of Kavalla. It was not surprising that the complicated and conditional plan fell through because of the attitudes of the Balkan states.

But Venizelos was not beaten. He knew that the chief threat to his policy lay in the person of the King, who was able, and by Greek precedent entitled, to play a leading role in the shaping of foreign policy. The precise limits of that role were undefined. What mattered was not the theoretical consitutional position, but the balance of power and popularity between the opposing political forces.

Venizelos therefore concentrated his powers of persuasion on the King and his trusted adviser Col. Metaxas, who was acting Chief of General Staff while his senior colleague Dousmanis was under a cloud for one of those acts of political indiscipline to which senior Greek staff officers including Metaxas were prone. On 26 January he told Metaxas of Grey's offer, and assured him that there was now 'no more talk of surrendering Kavalla to Bulgaria'.[25] Questioning the military assumptions behind the offer, Metaxas asked who was going to liquidate Turkey and how, if Greece herself campaigned in Asia Minor, her European frontiers were to be defended against Bulgaria. When Venizelos replied that Bulgarian cooperation with Greece and the Entente was an essential condition of the whole scheme, Metaxas allowed himself to admit that the operation could be considered.

The following day Metaxas drew up for Venizelos a closely reasoned memorandum [26] which concluded that it would be extremely difficult for any Power to establish itself permanently in western Asia Minor. In Metaxas's pedestrian words, Asia Minor was

a whole of which the parts are closely bound together geographically, economically, historically and ethnologically.

It is difficult to divide this territory politically, without creating anomalies which, reacting on the economic and ethnological planes, will inevitably give birth eventually to friction which will lead to struggles for the reunification of these territories through the domination of one of them.

Metaxas supported this conclusion with a number of historical allusions,[27] and pointed out the impossibility of finding a satisfactory frontier for a western zone in Anatolia. He argued that the best geographic and economic frontier would be one dividing Anatolia in two from a point between Eregli and Sinope on the Black Sea, running southwards through the mountain country round Ankara to the Mediterranean. This frontier would at least reflect the separation of eastern from western Anatolia by the central salt desert. But the Greek (western) zone would then be so large as to include an overwhelming majority of Muslim inhabitants.

Metaxas had put his finger on a serious problem. One cannot do better than cite Toynbee's description of the military geography of Anatolia. The problem, wrote Toynbee, was not so much to conquer western Anatolia, to which the railway system radiating up open valleys from Smyrna offered access, as to hold it down:

Western Anatolia has, it is true, a patch of desert in its hinterland, but this possible frontier lies at an average distance of more than 250 miles from the west coast. ... Moreover, there are gaps at each end of this desert, leading on, round its northern and its southern border, into the vast interior of Central and Eastern Anatolia. The value of the Anatolian desert as a frontier for a conqueror of the western part of the country must therefore not be overestimated.

Starting from the west coast of Smyrna or the neighbourhood and following the two main river valleys (the Hermus and Maeander, each provided with a railway) inland and eastwards, the invader first traverses a hundred miles or so of open river valley, with a landscape like that of Greece, except for the softened outlines and the greatly enlarged scale. Then he encounters a plateau with a steep escarpment, and, when he has climbed it, he has still 150 miles to go across a bleak, rolling surface not unlike the Lincolnshire wolds – especially in winter, when the great open fields are either miry or frost-bound or covered deep in snow. Scrubby oaks and irregular outcrops of rock, rising here and there into mountains, hardly break the monotony or diminish the openness of the country. Roads and railways are rare, and the soil unfavourable for transport apart from them. They are also devious. . . .[28]

A further problem facing an invader was that the central plateau which covered most of the Anatolian peninsula was rimmed by mountains which offered favourable ground to defenders to launch attacks on the invader's flanks. The mountain ranges which separate the interior from the Aegean and Black Sea 'push out westwards, outflanking the lowlands, till their last spurs plunge into the Aegean Sea'. The mountains on the north flank, Simav and Troad, overlooked the railways from Smyrna to Afyon Karahissar and from Smyrna to Panderma on the Sea of Marmara respectively. The great mass of Mount Olympus towered over Bursa and the vital road from Mudania on the Marmara up country through Bursa to Eski Shehir. The effect of these mountain masses was to block the lateral communications of an invader at points west of the escarpment of the plateau.

These geographical factors, as Toynbee observed, tend to produce a front on one of two lines whenever Anatolia is invaded:

The first line ... runs from north to south somewhere near the western escarpment of the plateau, with the right flank buttressed on the Simav and the left on the Mughla mountains. As long as this line is held by the defence, the invader is confined to the western lowlands, denied the possibility of concerted operations from Adalia or the Marmara, and harassed ... by guerrilla warfare against his communications. The second line, about 150 miles further east, also runs north and south, from the main northern to the main southern mountain-rim of the plateau, with the desert making a break in the centre.

Toynbee argued, and the Greeks were to argue in 1920, that this second line was more favourable to the invader than the first. It cut the defender's front in two, while it gave the invader a unified front which could be served from the west coast through Smyrna and from the north-west through the Marmara. It gave the invader fine lateral communications across the plateau between Eski Shehir and Afyon Karahissar by rail and road. But it created extremely grave problems at the same time by lengthening the invader's lines of communications and by presenting him with a very long frontier which is not physically easy to defend. The difference in strategic value between these two fronts was sufficient, as Toynbee writes, to make the area between them – the western strip of the plateau – the military key to Anatolia, and the focus of war and government in the peninsula. These historical considerations were amply borne out by the Greek experience after the war.

Metaxas's final choice was for the lesser of evils, a frontier running from the mountain chain round the gulf of Adalia to a point on the Sea of Marmara west of Gemlik. He admitted that this line was geographically arbitrary, cutting across the east–west valleys which connect the hinterland with the Aegean Sea; and the result of this severing of natural economic and political arteries might be to draw the Greeks further inland towards the interior.

On 28 January Venizelos saw Metaxas again. He now told him that in order to achieve the Balkan bloc which would permit Greek intervention, he would if necessary sacrifice Drama and Kavalla to the Bulgarians. Metaxas reacted strongly:

First, I developed for the Prime Minister my opinion that neither he nor anyone else has the right to make concessions of Greek territory, and that such concessions, if realized, completely destroy national solidarity and undermine the foundations of our state.

I then developed my opinion that Asia Minor has a great majority of Turkish population against a minority of Greek population. Thus the essence of the Greek Kingdom would be perceptibly changed by our establishment there, which would be desirable only after long preparatory work with a view to the attraction of these populations. Further, that the Greek state is not today ready for the government and exploitation of so extensive a territory, as a colony.* Further, that its security and protection from internal reactions will devour almost the whole of the Greek army for many years. The recruitment and formation of a sufficient army from the local inhabitants will require much time. Likewise, the rest of the state's means and resources will be devoured. Hence over a long period of time our position in Europe will be weakened, which could prove disastrous if we were hit by the Bulgarians. Only if we secure our position in

* Anti-Venizelists were charged with unpatriotically condemning the Asia Minor policy as 'colonialist'. But the use of the word 'colony' by Metaxas is justified by the fact that he recognized that any defensible frontier for Greece in Asia Minor would have to include a majority of Turks over Greeks. Count Bosdari, Italian Minister in Athens, describes a conversation with Zographos, Foreign Minister in the 1915 Gounaris Government, in which Zographos characterized the compensations offered in Asia Minor as 'illusory'. 'Li definiva comme "interessi coloniali" difficile ad acquistare e ancora piu difficile a conservare'; A. Bosdari, *Delle guerre Balcaniche, della Grande Guerra*, Milan 1917, p. 120.

Europe, by neutralizing the Bulgarians and Serbs, can we look to an extension in Asia Minor without endangering the existence of the state. And I developed to him in this context the analogous policy of Philip of Macedon.

I then developed the argument that such support from the Entente as to bring about the dissolution of the Turkish state – which would certainly entail a new campaign by us and the Entente allies after the Serbian campaign – is very unlikely. Thus we should run the risk of fighting in Serbia, of conceding Drama and Kavalla, and of getting nothing in return.[29]

In the course of these few hectic days, Metaxas had deployed the whole range of objections to Venizelos's Asia Minor policy. Venizelos remained totally unconvinced. Indeed the two men, after four years of uneasy cooperation based on unwilling mutual respect, were now divided by differences which were not to be settled in their lifetime. Neither was to deviate from the line adopted at this time. The clash served only to strengthen their convictions. The arguments for and against the Anatolian venture were never again to be put in so pure and rational a form, but were henceforward muddied and distorted in the waters of personal antipathy, factional bitterness and schism.

Having failed to convince Metaxas, Venizelos returned to the King with another memorandum:[30]

The concession of Kavalla is indeed a most painful sacrifice, and I feel the deepest mental pain in recommending it. But I do not hesitate to propose it, when once I take into account the national gains which are to be secured by this sacrifice. I have the impression that the concessions to Greece in Asia Minor, which Sir Edward Grey recommended, may, if of course we submit to sacrifices to Bulgaria, be so extensive that another equally large and not less rich Greece will be added to the doubled Greece which emerged from the victorious Balkan wars.

Venizelos speculatively defined the area in Asia Minor which Greece could reasonably hope to demand from the Entente as the whole western littoral from Cape Phineka to the gulf of Adramytteion (Edremit), with a substantial hinterland of 125,000 square kilometres. This compared with an area to be conceded (the kazas of Drama, Kavalla and Sari-Saban) amounting to only 2,000 square kilometres. The Drama-Kavalla region was rich, but could not be compared in wealth with the whole region sought in Asia Minor. As to population, Greece would gain more than 800,000 new Greek souls in Asia Minor, while the 30,000 or so in the Kavalla area would not be lost to Greece, because of the exchange of populations which Venizelos envisaged. He planned that the Greek populations leaving East Macedonia under the exchange should migrate to Asia Minor, thus strengthening the Greek element in the population of the Smyrna zone.

Venizelos argued that such an opportunity would not present itself twice. If Greece failed to enter the war Asia Minor would be lost to her for good. He drew for the King an alluring picture of a Greater Greece of fertile and prosperous regions, the dominant power in the Aegean basin. He questioned the caution of the General Staff:

The Staff appear against all expectations not to be strongly attracted by these views. They fear, they say, on the one hand the difficulty of administering so great an extent of new territories, and on the other that we may be more exhausted through participation in the war than the Bulgarians, who may take advantage of this situation after the war in order to attack us.

Venizelos admitted the first difficulty, but claimed that the administration of Asia Minor was not beyond the powers of the Greek state. He dismissed the fear of Bulgarian invasion as inherently unlikely because of Bulgarian preoccupations with the administration of their own new territories. He made one concession:

It is true that for a number of years, until we organize all our military forces on the basis of the new resources yielded by the mobilization of the greater Greece, we shall be forced in case of war in the Balkan peninsula to employ part of our forces in Asia Minor in order to avert a possible local uprising there – an uprising which is extremely unlikely, since with the complete dissolution of the Ottoman state, our Muslim subjects will be excellent and law-abiding citizens. The force to be disposed for this purpose will anyway be provided within a very short space of time by the Greek population of Asia Minor.

These breathtakingly optimistic words suggest that Venizelos was gripped by a false but seductive determinist theory of the rising power of Greece and the declining power of Turkey, a process which must end with the total dissolution of the Ottoman state.

Venizelos recognized that Bulgaria would very probably refuse to be tempted by the bait of Kavalla. In that case the value of the offer lay in the goodwill and support that Greece would gain with the Entente. The proposed concessions in Asia Minor proved that the vigour of the New Greece had won the confidence of 'certain powers' (i.e. Great Britain) who now considered her an 'important factor in the reshaping of the East at the moment when the Turkish state is dissolving', and would provide the economic and diplomatic support needed to cope with her sudden expansion.

The Ionian vision blinded Venizelos both to the military dangers of the action he proposed and to the ruinous effects of the Kavalla proposal on national unity. For Kavalla was to become one of the chief symbols of the developing schism between the Liberals and their opponents which came to be known as the 'national schism' (*ethnikos dichasmos*). When Venizelos was forced to resign on 6 March 1915, after the King had refused to sanction his attempt to bring Greece into the war by contributing a Division to the allied expeditionary force at Gallipoli, the new Gounaris government lost no opportunity of throwing Kavalla in his teeth, nor Venizelos of replying.[31]

The bitter and undignified debate helped to exacerbate relations between the two sides and to make their future cooperation impossible. But the origin of the schism lay elsewhere, in the anti-Venizelists' belief that Venizelos was determined to bring Greece into the war eventually regardless of the terms (a belief that seemed to be reinforced by his attitude to Kavalla), and the Venizelists' belief that their opponents were determined to maintain Greek neutrality under all circumstances. Neither belief was entirely correct in the first half of 1915, though both were plausible when one considers the terms that each side regarded as adequate for abandoning neutrality.

Passions were fed by the determination of the anti-Venizelists and the King to uphold their views against the elected government of the day. And the schism was fuelled by party politics – the desire of the anti-Venizelists for a share in the spoils of which they had been deprived since 1910, and the desire of the Liberal left to settle once and for all with 'reaction' in the person of the King and his acolytes. But in its origin the dispute was what it seemed – a radical difference over the issue of war or neutrality, reflecting a broad difference in psychology between those who shared Venizelos's vision of an expanding, dynamic Greece actively associated with England, and those whose attitude to the outside world was narrow, suspicious and defensive.

The fall of Venizelos was not the end of allied attempts to inveigle Greece into the war. The offer of Smyrna and its hinterland was renewed to the Gounaris Government in April 1915. The negotiations of the new Government with the Entente never looked like catching fire. The King, Streit and Gounaris, encouraged by the General Staff, insisted that Greece must stand out for guarantees of Greece's territorial integrity which the Allies were not prepared to take seriously while the attitude of Bulgaria remained uncertain.

If anything was calculated to destroy what little confidence the anti-Venizelists still retained in the good faith of the Entente, it was the Allies' almost incredible ineptitude over Kavalla. On 29 May they attempted to seduce Bulgaria by promising to try to persuade Greece to cede Kavalla to the Bulgarians in return for compensations in Asia Minor.[32] The Greek Government protested. Adding insult to injury, the Entente Powers assured Bulgaria on 3 August that the recognition of any territorial gains for Greece in Asia Minor would be 'absolutely dependent on the condition that Greece shall cede to Bulgaria Kavalla and a hinterland proportionate to her gains elsewhere'.[33] Gounaris once more rejected this line of thinking, in a strongly worded note which stated that the Greeks would not hand over to Bulgaria a portion of national territory which Greece considered flesh of her flesh – 'chair de sa chair parce que peuplée de ses frères et acquise au prix de son sang'.[34]

The Powers, with their schemes for territorial adjustment in the Balkans, never appreciated the strength of the emotional attachment of the Balkan peoples for lands so recently 'redeemed' with blood and treasure. This bungled attempt to realize a Balkan bloc brought negotiations with the Gounaris Government to a halt. Only a few days later the new Greek Chamber assembled, after almost two months' delay due to the illness of the King and the desire of the Gounarists to hold on to power as long as possible. Venizelos, who had won a reduced majority of 184 seats out of 317 in the general elections held on 13 June, returned to power.

The question of territorial compensation for Greece in Asia

Minor did not arise again during the course of the war. The focus of Greek interest shifted from the Dardanelles, Constantinople and the west coast of Asia Minor, to Salonika and the northern frontier, where the armies of Greece's ally Serbia had been in action since the outbreak of war against the Austrians and were now expecting the incursion of the Bulgarians.

In the first weeks after the assassination of the Archduke Ferdinand at Sarajevo and the outbreak of war, Austrian troops crossed the Drina into Serbia, were bravely held by the Serbs, and driven out of Serbian territory. Three months later an Austrian offensive took the Serbian capital Belgrade in early December 1914. Counterattacking fiercely along the river Kolubara, the Serbs liberated Belgrade and again drove their enemies out of Serbia. Small, courageous, ravaged by typhus, poorly equipped, the Serbian armies stood along the Danube blocking the communications of the Central Powers with their ally Turkey. The Germans decided to sweep aside this obstacle. Hitherto the Serbs had faced only the Austrians. In September 1915 the Germans and Austrians agreed with Bulgaria on joint action in the Balkan theatre. While German and Austrian armies drove down across the Danube and Sava from the north, the Bulgarians would march into Serbia from the south east. The Serbian army would be caught in a giant trap. On 22 September Bulgaria began to mobilize her army. A fortnight later the offensive began, and the long heroic retreat of the Serbian army across the mountains to the Adriatic Sea and evacuation to Corfu. These events had important repercussions in Greece.

As the intentions of Bulgaria became clear, the question for Greece became not whether to intervene on the side of the Entente against Turkey, but whether to come to the aid of Serbia when she were attacked by Bulgaria. The test of Venizelist or anti-Venizelist was thus the Greco-Serbian treaty of 1913.[35] Venizelists claimed that Bulgarian entry into the war against Serbia would constitute a *casus foederis*; anti-Venizelists claimed that the treaty was intended to apply only to Balkan entanglements, and not in the case of a general European war. The dispute over the treaty was a further token of the developing schism between Venizelists and anti-Venizelists which underpinned the subsequent history of the Asia Minor venture, and dictated the terms in which internal Greek politics were conducted until 1922 and beyond.

It was Bulgarian mobilization which provoked the second great crisis between Constantine and Venizelos in September 1915. Greece at once mobilized her army. According to the Greco-Serbian treaty, Serbia was obliged, if she wished to call upon Greece to honour the treaty, to supply 150,000 men for the Bulgarian front. She was already fully committed and clearly could not do this. Venizelos therefore suggested that the deficiency be made good by allied troops, to which Britain and France agreed. The King and the anti-Venizelist opposition objected that the landing of allied troops at Salonika would be a violation of Greek neutrality. Venizelos won a vote of confidence in the Chamber; but the King's continued disagreement with his policy led him to his second resignation on 5 October. It was too late to stop the allied forces – the 'gardeners of Salonika' – who were landing at Salonika, soon to turn the city into a vast transit camp and to dig in along a line from near Ochrid to the gulf of Orfano, successfully resisting the advance of the German and Bulgarian armies although they were too late to save the Serbian army.

The next year was one of successive and increasingly flagrant encroachments on Greek neutrality by the Allies, both by the autocratic General Sarrail in Salonika and by the Powers' representatives in Athens. Under the screen of Sarrail's armies, Pamikos Zymbrakakis, Georgios Kondylis and a few other stalwarts, launched the revolutionary Venizelist movement of National Defence (*Ethniki Amyna*) in Salonika in August 1916. They dissociated themselves from the Royalist Government in Athens and called on the Greeks to join the allied armies on the Macedonian front. With Sarrail's protection, they won over the majority of the Greek garrison. On 25 September, Venizelos left Athens for Crete in order to set his seal on the revolutionary movement. From Crete he proceeded through the Aegean islands to Salonika, arriving on 9 October. There Venizelos established the 'Provisional Government', revolutionary but not republican, which was to bring half of Greece into the war.

The physical separation of the country into two camps symbolized the deep and unbridgeable psychological schism in the nation. The establishment of the Provisional Government in Salonika meant the growth of a Venizelist administrative and political complex in northern Greece parallel to that of Athens. The fact that there were two Greek states in 1916 meant that in 1917, when the King was expelled by the Allies and Venizelos returned to Athens, one must devour the other, thus reinforcing and further exacerbating the schism.

The picture was most clearcut in the army. Venizelos's revolutionary Government was set up with the declared aim of bringing Greece into the war on the side of the Entente. For this purpose the Provisional Government's first need was an army; and it set about, speedily and sometimes ruthlessly, building up the army of National Defence into an effective fighting force. Every army officer in Greece was thus faced with the choice, whether to join the *Amyna* in Salonika, or to remain in Old Greece, loyal to the King and the Athens Government. That for those without strong convictions the choice was frequently decided on geographical or equally arbitrary grounds did not make it unimportant to the individual; for his future prospects of promotion depended on it. It was a choice rich in consequences both for the careers of individuals and for the future of Greece. The officer who made his way to Salonika to join the army of National Defence thereafter had a vested interest in the political dominance of Venizelism; the 'loyalist' officer vice versa. For both men, the dominance of the opposite party or faction would mean loss of seniority, a severe setback in professional career, perhaps dismissal. For these reasons talk of 'bridging the gap' between Venizelos and Constantine was now unrealistic. The ball of schism once set in motion was almost impossible to stop.

This thesis is perfectly illustrated by the reactions of the Venizelist regime to its opponents after the two states were reunited. Venizelos returned to Athens in June 1917, being installed in power, as his opponents jeered, by the 'foreign bayonets' of the Entente's detachments. King Constantine was forced to resign the throne, not abdicating irrevocably, but retiring to Switzerland; and his second son Alexander became King. A boy of only twenty-three, Alexander was chosen as more likely to be malleable clay in the hands of the Venizelists than the Crown Prince George, who accompanied his father into exile.

The first measures of the Venizelist Government and its allied backers were designed to remove opposition and to give the country some sort of Venizelist parliament. The current Chamber, dating from the general election of December 1915, was void of Venizelists, who had boycotted the election. Venizelos therefore insisted on recalling the Chamber of 13 June 1915, known as the 'Chamber of 31 May', or the 'Lazarus Chamber' after the peculiar manner in which it was thus raised from the dead. In this Chamber the Venizelists held a substantial majority. After the upheavals of the last two years, there was no means of telling whether it reflected the views of the country. But Venizelos rejected the course of calling for new general elections, fearing, as he later admitted, that the Liberals would lose them.[36] The Liberal Party, in its posture as guardian of the people's sovereign rights, found justification for the resuscitation of the dead Chamber in the doctrine that the Chamber of 31 May had been unconstitutionally dissolved by the King after his second dispute with Venizelos over the issue of intervention.

The Lazarus Chamber gave Venizelos a vote of confidence on 11 August 1917 by 188 out of 198 votes (the ten ministers abstained, and the opposition boycotted the proceedings). By this time the opposition had been deprived of its leading figures. A list of about thirty men whom Venizelos considered dangerously Germanophile had been prepared, including Gounaris, Dousmanis and Metaxas. Ion Dragoumis was added to the list at the last moment because of an article he wrote in a political review.[37] These men were shipped to Corsica, where they remained under French supervision for the next two or three years. Another group comprising leading anti-Venizelist politicians such as Stephanos Dragoumis, Skouloudis, Lambros and Baltazzis, and several prominent officers, including Hexadaktylos, was placed under police supervision. Streit, by going into voluntary exile with the King, avoided the humiliation of banishment or house arrest. The royal princes and their families also had to leave. Of leading anti-Venizelist figures, very few apart from the moderates N. Stratos and D. Rallis, and of course the indestructible Alexander Zaimis (who was prime minister at the time of the banishments), remained active and at large in Greece. That the men removed were powerfully and articulately anti-Venizelist was at least as important a reason for their removal as that they were 'hostile to the Entente' – a phrase, indeed, which made no sense at all when applied to men such as Ion and Stephanos Dragoumis.

These measures removed potential troublemakers and deprived the opposition of its leadership. By a thorough and radical reshaping of the machinery of government and the public services, the Venizelist regime then attempted to sink deep roots and to eradicate the 'disease' of Constantinism. The Government suspended the permanency of tenure of the judiciary, and confirmed retrospectively the dismissals of judges and prosecutors by the Provisional Government.[38] The Ministry of Justice was enabled to carry through a complete purge of the corps of the judiciary.

The purge of the civil service extended widely. A decree suspended the permanency of all public servants of whatever branch or grade. Another permitted the demotion or transfer of any civil servant. University teachers, mayors, village presidents and other officials were made subject to the purge.[39]

The Orthodox Church was not spared, being as riven by schism as any other part of the nation. Legislation was passed of doubtful constitutional validity permitting the regime to set up a new ecclesiastical court to try the Metropolitan Bishops of Athens and Larissa and a number of other bishops who had taken part in anti-Venizelist manifestations such as the notorious *anathema* of Venizelos on 25 December 1916.[40] These clerics were found guilty and degraded. Some of them were confined to remote monasteries. Meletios Metaxakis, an actively Venizelist bishop, took the place of Theoklitos as Metropolitan Archbishop of Athens.

Thus parliament, the army, the Church and the public services were purged of their more important anti-Venizelist elements. Not only leading figures such as Gounaris, Metaxas and Theoklitos were purged or banished, but large numbers of insignificant individuals were removed either to satisfy party spite or to make room for Venizelist clients in the public service.[41] The exact figures are in dispute, but by any calculation are large.

These illiberal measures were not signs of totalitarian leanings or an attempt to establish a permanent one-party state. They were rather the relapse of the Greek political mechanism into its 'natural' state in which the political party exists in order to cater for the needs of its clients and supporters.[42] This state was thrown into relief by the peculiar circumstances of the times. The dissolution of the prewar 'Old Parties' and the development of Venizelism and anti-Venizelism as the only two forces in politics gave a change of regime the entirely new character of a total upheaval in the life of the nation, involving the entire people in its indirect effects. Moreover, the existence of the two rival governments, armies and bureaucracies of Athens and Salonika made radical reorganization inevitable when the two states merged into one in 1917. Finally, the ideological conflict between the two sides and the personal and constitutional conflict between Venizelos and the King, fostered by the war and the problems it raised, added a note of bitterness to the schism which enabled the Venizelists to address themselves to their opponents with an almost religious conviction. Venizelists spoke of eradicating the 'disease' of Constantinism, and honoured their leader with the fervour of devotees.[43]

Venizelos's aim was to capture and hold the middle ground of Greek politics, isolating both the extreme right and the extreme left, and putting his party eventually to the test of a general election. In the meantime, taking as his justification the national emergency of the war, he was prepared to tolerate acts of repression and vindictiveness which, even if mild by the standards of more recent regimes, were more widespread and no milder than the acts of his opponents when in power. Some of the Venizelists' repressive measures were made necessary by the refusal of many of his opponents to accept the legitimacy of the new regime, and by opposition carried to the point of mutiny in the army. But many could not be justified on these grounds.

This was the schism which, cutting deep into the roots of society, was to embitter Greek political life for more than two decades, and still leaves its trace today.

4 | The Paris Peace Conference

Those three all-powerful, all-ignorant men sitting
there and carving continents, with only a child
to lead them.

A. J. Balfour to Harold Nicolson

With Venizelos established in Athens, Greece was able to play
her part in the war at the side of the Entente. By the autumn of
1918, with allied help in training and equipment, the old
National Defence corps of the Salonika movement had grown
into a formidable army. Greek divisions were in the forefront of
the massive allied offensive of September 1918 which broke the
Bulgarian front and led to the collapse of the Central Powers and
the sudden end of the Great War. On 30 October Admiral Calthorpe signed at Mudros an armistice with the Turks which put
the Ottoman Empire at the mercy of the Allied Powers.[1]

Venizelos hastened to western Europe to inaugurate the Greek
campaign in favour of her claims at the peace settlement. He
spent most of October and November in London, canvassing
British statesmen, journalists and philhellenes, and organizing
Greece's propaganda machine for the prolonged struggle that
lay ahead.

Propaganda was not a new game for the Balkan states, all of
which had experience in pulling the wool over the eyes of innocent Europeans. But the Greeks were perhaps more adept than
their opponents in this field, and had more natural advantages.
They had fought on the right side in the war, even though
belatedly (and a massive effort went into demonstrating to
Western opinion the value of Greece's contribution to the war
effort). Venizelos fully recognized the importance of the propaganda battle and devoted ample resources to it. But Greece's best
argument and advertisement was Venizelos himself and his reputation for statesmanship. He was ready to devote unstintingly of
his time and energy in promoting his country's 'image'.

In the capitals of Europe Greek clubs and benefactors passed
resolutions, raised money, sponsored lectures, printed maps of
the ethnography of the Balkans in which the Greeks always

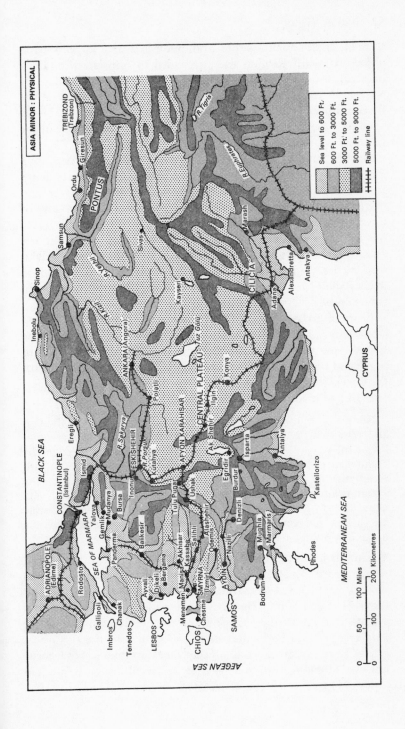

ASIA MINOR : PHYSICAL

Sea level to 600 Ft.
600 Ft. to 3000 Ft.
3000 Ft. to 5000 Ft.
5000 Ft. to 9000 Ft.
++++ Railway line

BLACK SEA

TREBIZOND (Trabzon)
Giresun
Ordu
Samsun
Sinop
Inebolu
Eregli
PONTUS
R. Yesil
R. Kizil
ANKARA (Angora)
Polatli
Sivas
Kayseri
Tuz Gölü
CENTRAL PLATEAU
Konya
R. Sakarya
ESKISHEHIR
Porsu
Kutahya
Inonu
Tulu Punar
AFYON KARAHISAR
Ak Shehir
Ilgin
Isparta
Egridir
Burdur
Ushak
R. Tigris
R. Euphrates
Marash
CILICIA
Adana
Alexandretta
Antakya
CYPRUS

CONSTANTINOPLE (Istanbul)
Ismid
SEA OF MARMARA
Yalova
Gemlik
Mudanya
Bursa
Panderma
ADRIANOPLE (Edirne)
Rodosto
Gallipoli
Imbros
Chanak
Tenedos
LESBOS
Balikesir
Bergama
Ayvali
Dikeli
Menemen
Manisa
Akhisar
Kassaba
Salihli
SMYRNA (Izmir)
Chesme
CHIOS
SAMOS
Odemis
Alashehir
Denizli
Nazilli
AYDIN
Mughla
Marmaris
Bodrum
Rhodes
Kastellorizo
Antalya

MEDITERRANEAN SEA

AEGEAN SEA

0   50   100 Miles
0   100   200 Kilometres

seemed predominant, wrote and published articles and pamphlets. Rudyard Kipling was persuaded to translate the Greek national anthem, Solomos's Hymn to Liberty, into English. It was published in the *Daily Telegraph*.[2] The philhellenes of the British liberal establishment worked for the cause – Harold Spender, Lord Bryce, Ronald Burrows of King's College London.

Having lunched with Lloyd George in London and sent him a long memorandum on the forthcoming Turkish settlement,[3] Venizelos crossed to Paris to prepare for the Peace Conference. With his own hand, he composed the formal statement of Greece's claims to put before the Conference. Assiduously he set out to win the allied statesmen to his point of view. But the allies had their own interests to pursue in the Turkish and Balkan settlements, and were constricted by obligations entered into during the Great War, some of which proved embarrassing in time of peace.

In these early days, Britain, characteristically, had no settled Anatolian policy. With Gallipoli still heavy in their minds the British saw the preservation of the freedom of the straits in peace and war as a vital interest. Lloyd George sympathized with the Greeks and disliked the Turks. In a famous speech in January 1918 he had made a number of pledges:

> Nor are we fighting to deprive Turkey of its capital, or of the rich and renowned lands of Asia Minor and Thrace, which are predominantly Turkish in race. ... While we do not challenge the maintenance of the Turkish Empire in the homelands of the Turkish race,* with its capital at Constantinople – the passage between the Mediterranean and the Black Sea being internationalized and neutralized – Arabia, Armenia, Mesopotamia, Syria and Palestine are, in our judgement, entitled to a recognition of their separate national conditions.

There was nothing binding about these statements of war aims. At the Peace Conference all was fluid and negotiable and much was for sale. A few remarks in a wartime speech did not tie Lloyd George's hands. But they were remembered against him.

Lord Curzon, sitting at his desk in the Foreign Office, making only rare trips to Paris, and then unable to dent the surface of events, knew far, far more about the Near East than Lloyd George was ever to know. Moreover he knew specifically what he wanted

* One of Lloyd George's geographical blunders!

to do – to eject the Turks forever from Constantinople and Europe. As early as January 1918 he had mapped out on paper the broad lines of a straightforward solution to the Turkish problem. The Turks – 'for nearly five centuries ... a source of distraction, intrigue and corruption in European politics' – were to be expelled from Europe. They were to lose their Arab and Armenian possessions. But they were to retain Anatolia in its integrity. Constantinople and the Straits would be internationalized.[4] This solution was fair and practicable. Curzon had no love for the Turks, whom, like many others of his epoch, he invariably named in the singular as if there was a genus 'Turk' to which the epithets corrupt, oppressive, intriguing applied. But he had no love for the Greeks either, believing them also to be administratively incompetent and corrupt. Nor for the Italians. There were few foreigners whom Curzon liked.* His evenhanded and comprehensive disdain, together with a long experience of the east, ensured a kind of justice for his proposals.

While Curzon as Acting Secretary of State sat impotent and frustrated in his backbrace in Whitehall, deprived of information and largely unconsulted, waiting impatiently for Arthur Balfour to retire from the post of Foreign Secretary, Balfour himself crossed to Paris with the cream of his permanent officials for the Peace Conference. It was thus he and not Curzon who had a chance to influence events in Paris and to act as steadying influence to the volatility of Lloyd George. But Balfour was by this time sinking into a detached lethargy in which it often seemed to matter little to him what solution was adopted. The difference between the two men's approach – Balfour cool and unflappable, Curzon nervous, overbearing and always convinced he was right – was admirably summed up in their discussion in the Eastern Committee of the Cabinet of the reply to be sent to a telegram from General Milne in Salonika, asking what were the general lines of British policy in the Caucasus:

MR BALFOUR. This unhealthy curiosity on the part of our proconsuls in distant parts of the world is embarrassing. ... I do not think it is our business to have a policy with regard to these places.
LORD CURZON. We shall get on very badly if we do not. I think we must have an idea of what we are working for.[5]

* One exception was apparently the Bulgarian politician Stambuliski, whom Curzon is alleged to have liked for his peasant origins and rough manners.

It was this sort of cool sanity in the insane world of international affairs, combined with the elegant manner, the air of flippant cynicism, that drove Curzon to regard his superior as an evil man.

France had less important long-term strategic interests in Anatolia than Britain, but equally strong emotional ties with the Near East. The French were determined to preserve their cultural predominance in the Levant and their financial interests in Ottoman institutions such as the Régie des Tabacs and the Otto-man Debt. They were determined also not to be deprived by British manoeuvres of their share in the economic pickings fore-shadowed in the wartime Sykes–Picot Agreement by which the Near and Middle East was carved up between the allies.[6]

France had the aged tiger Georges Clemenceau at the helm, a phenomenon of old ivory skin and drooping sleepy eyelids, of long silences and short, pointed interventions for the sake of France. As representative of the host country he was chairman of the Conference. An admirer of classical Greece, who had visited the country many years before, he despised the modern Greeks as corrupt and bastard descendants of the ancient. His relations were never entirely easy even with Venizelos, though the two men established a good working relationship and bonds of mutual service rendered. At the Conference table, he sat guarded and still, in his grey gloves, the warden of France's eternal interests, suspicious of Greece, yet beginning to lose interest in what was peripheral. And Greek affairs were peri-pheral, compared with Germany, the Rhine, reparations, even Syria.

The unknown factor at the Conference was the American. Everyone knew that President Wilson would support the self-determination of the subject nationalities of the Ottoman Empire. No one knew what responsibilities the Americans would take on in the Near East. Would they, for instance, take a man-date for Constantinople and the Straits, or for Armenia, which would be incapable of standing on her own as an independent nation and with which the United States had close ties of an educational and philanthropic nature? The Americans too were determined not to allow themselves to be excluded from Turkish markets by exclusive 'colonialist' deals by the Old World powers.

Venizelos needed the support of these big three leaders, and set out to win it.

Charming his guests at the Hotel Mercedes, finding time to

cultivate the friendship of even relatively junior members of important delegations, always available, always persuasive, Venizelos was one of the stars of the Conference who seemed to have risen above the petty level at which affairs were conducted by most delegates. 'I can't tell you the position that Venizelos has here!' wrote Harold Nicolson to his father, 'He and Lenin are the only two really great men in Europe.'[7] His talk was 'a strange medley of charm, brigandage, welt-politik, patriotism, courage, literature – and above all this large muscular smiling man, with his eyes glinting through spectacles and on his head a square skull-cap of black silk'.[8]

Venizelos quickly won a reputation for moderation, wisdom and statesmanship. This reputation, founded on passionate sincerity and strength of will coupled with charm of manner and political tact, enabled him to press Greece's claims to the utmost. By showing every appearance of cooperation with the United States, Britain and France on side issues (the League of Nations in the case of the Americans, the French entanglement in south Russia in the case of France, Cyprus in the case of the British) he hoped to engage them to support Greek claims in their fullness against Italy and others. A young American delegate, Charles Seymour, described his technique:

> I can see how he got his reputation for great statesmanship. In this way: I think he found out very soon that Clive [Day] knew the difference between truth and fiction; realizing that his strongest asset would be *our* belief in his honesty, he determined to lay his cards on the table and speak with absolute frankness, and I think that he did. This policy was almost Bismarckian in its cleverness. Any double-dealing of the kind others are trying would have been useless; now he has our sympathy. His policy is one of moderation.[9]

In 1963 Seymour noted against this passage, 'Venizelos – "Moderation"!?' And it is true that the moderation was more of style than substance. In a curiously opaque passage Harold Nicolson came near to admitting this in his defence of Venizelos, whom he described as undoubtedly an imperialist, but at the same time a man 'humane above all others, an intelligence always ready for the assault, a gentleness almost virulent in its applicability'; meaning presumably an imperialist with a gentleman's style.

Venizelos's attitude to the French expedition to South Russia is important to an understanding of his priorities and methods. When the French Government decided to send a large expeditionary force to help Denikin's White Russians against the Bolsheviks in the Ukraine, and found themselves short of men, Clemenceau turned to the Greeks. Unhesitatingly Venizelos promised his support. French troops landed at Odessa in December 1918 and the two Greek divisions followed in January. The expedition was a disaster and broke up in confusion within a few months. The French troops were not prepared to fight in this cause so long after the war in western Europe was over. The Greeks fought creditably. But although there were Greek communities in the Crimea, there was no Greek interest at stake in the campaign. In so far as Greek intervention affected the Greeks of Russia it made their lives more difficult. Venizelos threw in the Greek army purely to raise his stock with the French in Paris in the important negotiations at the Peace Conference.

There remained the Italians, represented in Paris by their Prime Minister Orlando and the sombre architect of their foreign policy, Baron Sonnino. Unlike the Great Powers, Italy had staked out colonialist claims in Asia Minor which directly conflicted with those of the Greeks. It was this direct clash of Greek and Italian ambitions and interest which made the support of the Big Three statesmen so important to Venizelos.

Italy's claims derived from secret agreements reached during the war. Since long before the war Italian nationalists had seen the Adalia region in southern Anatolia as a sphere of interest, and from 1912 on there had been a considerable extension of Italian commercial and financial activities in Anatolia. The British Minister in Athens commented wittily on Italian intrigues during the war:

> They mustn't keep Rhodes nor Stampalia,
> So they've sent a young man to Adalia,
>   Where he's now hard at work
>   At cajoling the Turk
> To cry 'Viva, evviva Italia!' [10]

The haggling which preceded Italy's entry into the war on the side of the Entente enabled her to stake her claim to a share in the land grab which would follow the eventual defeat of Turkey. In the Treaty of London of April 1915, which defined the spoils Italy stood to win, she was promised 'a just share in the Mediterranean region adjacent to the province of Adalia' in the event of partition of Turkey in Asia.[11]

A year later, without the knowledge of the Italians, Sir Mark

Sykes and the Frenchman Georges Picot negotiated the secret agreement which bears their name, and which defined the post-war zones of influence and territorial acquisitions of Britain, France and Russia in Asiatic Turkey. Russia was assigned the provinces of Trebizond, Bitlis, Van and Erzurum, and a part of southern Kurdistan. (She had already been assigned Constantinople and the zone of the Bosphorus under the 1915 Constantinople Agreement.) France was to obtain the coastal strip of Syria, Adana vilayet, and the portion of Turkey in Asia between Syria/Mesopotamia and the newly defined Russian zone. England was to obtain southern Mesopotamia with Baghdad.

There was nothing in the Sykes–Picot agreement which necessarily conflicted with Italy's promised just share of Turkey. But when Grey finally revealed to the Italians the terms of the secret agreements, Sonnino demanded Smyrna, Konya, Adana and Mersina as well as Adalia. All these could – at a pinch – be defined as lying within the 'Mediterranean region adjacent to the province of Adalia' of the Treaty of London.

The conflicting claims were reconciled in the settlement known as the agreement of St Jean de Maurienne, a little town in the French Savoy where Lloyd George and Ribot, the French prime minister, met Sonnino and the Italian prime minister Boselli in April 1917. The talks at St Jean de Maurienne laid the basis for a later agreement by which Italy renounced her claim to Adana and Mersina, and was thus able to recognize the Sykes–Picot agreement. In return for this concession, and for Sonnino's previous agreement to the ejection of King Constantine from the Greek throne, Italy was assigned a clearly defined zone in Asia Minor including not only Konya but also Smyrna.[12] As Boselli observed: 'We gave them a King in return for Smyrna.'[13]

Italian policy over Asia Minor, though to a large extent based on feelings of national pride and kept alive by nationalist pressures, had an economic and social foundation in the need for foreign possessions as a receptacle for surplus manpower, and in the need for coal and wheat. Asia Minor took the place in the minds of the Italians held by Africa before the Great War; the vilayets of Konya and Aydin came to be seen as fertile granaries, lands of untapped resources:

The climate there is suitable for our emigrants, the fertility is well known, as the corn bears fiftyfold; finally the existence of immense uncultivated areas is proved by the population density, which, including the towns, is at present less than twenty-seven persons per square km; the population itself would then have everything to gain and nothing to lose by Italian colonization.[14]

Greek and Italian interests clashed at two other points besides Smyrna. The Italian occupation of the Dodecanese (ratified incidentally by the Treaty of London) was in direct conflict with the just Greek claim to these islands. And the Greek claim to 'northern Epirus' was endangered by Italian ambitions and Italian troops in Albania, where on 3 June 1917, General Ferraro, commander of the Italian army of occupation, proclaimed the 'unity and independence' of Albania under the aegis of Italy.*

Venizelos was anxious for an accommodation with the Italians, but was prepared to negotiate only over Epirus and the Dodecanese and not over Smyrna. On his way through Rome in December 1918, and in Paris a month later, he argued for a bilateral understanding in advance of the Peace Conference. Except for Sonnino, the Italians were impressed. 'Sonnino however held to his point.'[15] He stood for the letter of the Treaty of London and the August 1917 Agreement. Greek relations with Italy sharply deteriorated as it became clear that neither country would yield over Smyrna.

Italy's designs on Anatolia were, at least initially, viewed with some sympathy by the British. Balfour in April 1917 wrote to the Italian Ambassador painting an idyllic picture of a southern Anatolian region populated by industrious Italian farmers:

Italy has a large surplus population, well skilled in the practice of Mediterranean agriculture. In the south-west of Anatolia, this population will find a soil and a climate admirably suited to its needs. ... If colonization be one of the main ends which Italian statesmen have in view, there is no part of the world (as it seems to me) it could be more successfully secured than in the proposed Italian sphere....

Before the Byzantine Empire was overwhelmed by the Ottoman invader Italian cities led western civilization in Eastern waters. If this war should break the power of the Turk, I should rejoice that a united Italy should bear a great share in restoring to civilization the neighbouring lands which the Turk has so long laid waste.[16]

Balfour's lyricism had a purpose in that he was trying to persuade the Italians to withdraw their claim to areas (including Mersina and Adana) which had been assigned to France under

* This was a violation of the Treaty of London; see an attempted Italian justification in *D.B.F.P.*, iv, 19–20 (7 July 1919).

the Sykes–Picot agreement. Curzon, when he saw the letter in the different circumstances of November 1919, minuted: 'I find myself in the unhappy position of disagreeing with almost every proposition in Mr Balfour's letter which I consider to have been both uncalled for and deplorable.' Curzon believed in British, but not Italian, imperialism.

Lloyd George too was not in principle averse to Italian colonization of southern Anatolia. But two rival nations could not both have Smyrna. Who was to get the prize depended not on the justice of the claim and the wisdom of the peacemakers, but on the conjunction of circumstances and the interplay of personalities in the corridors of the Peace Conference. And here Venizelos was in his element.

Venizelos's views on the Turkish peace settlement were set out in a long memorandum he had sent to Lloyd George while he was in London.[17] The memorandum contained his plans for the dismemberment of the Ottoman Empire. Taking for granted the detachment of Syria, Palestine and Mesopotamia, he argued in favour of a threefold settlement in Asiatic Turkey, comprising the creation of an independent Armenian state; the creation under the auspices of the League of Nations of an independent state of Constantinople and Eastern Thrace, to assure the freedom of the Straits; and the annexation of western Asia Minor to Greece.

With superb confidence, Venizelos wrote that the very large area he claimed in Asia Minor could be delimited 'without the slightest difficulty': 800,000 Greeks would still remain in Asia Minor outside the Greek zone; but the zone 'might be made to include an Ottoman population appreciably equal in number', and the peace treaty should then be drafted so as to encourage mutual and voluntary intermigration of Greeks from outside the zone and Turks from within it.

Thus Venizelos pictured an Asia Minor divided into Turkish, Greek and Armenian sections in which the population would eventually be homogeneous. He had groped for a similar solution in 1914.[18] His aim was to abolish the causes of friction in Asiatic Turkey, and to create a strong, defensible Greek zone which would not be subverted from within.

Venizelos appeared before the Council of Ten to explain and justify Greece's claims on 3 and 4 February. His exposition was based on the long, formal statement, *Greece before the Peace*

Congress,[19] composed by Venizelos himself, in Greek, in about
twelve hours of almost uninterrupted work,[20] and published in
English and French in December 1918.

In this pamphlet Venizelos pitched his claims high. With
every justification he claimed the islands which remained to
Turkey in the Aegean, and the Dodecanese which had been
under Italian occupation for six years. On cultural and historical
grounds he claimed almost the whole of northern Epirus with
its mixed population of about 200,000, of whom the majority
were Albanian-speaking. He claimed both western (Bulgarian)
and eastern (Turkish) Thrace, despite the majority of Muslims
over Greeks recognized in Greek statistics. Venizelos laid no
formal claim to Cyprus, out of delicacy for British susceptibilities,
nor to Constantinople, because of the vital international interests
in the city. Later, before the Council of Ten, he both claimed
and did not claim Cyprus:

It might be asked why no specific claim had been put forward to
the island of Cyprus. He had not done so for various reasons, the
most important of these being that he was convinced that the British
Government ... would at the end of the war be sufficiently mag-
nanimous to surrender Cyprus to Greece. To sum up, Greece
claimed all the islands of the Eastern Mediterranean, including ...
Cyprus.[21]

In Asia Minor, Venizelos proposed to solve the problem posed
by the Greeks of Pontus by incorporating the vilayet of Trebizond, where the Greeks were most densely concentrated, in the
new state of Armenia. This solution would disengage Greek
responsibility for a population too distant for Greece to protect
and too weak to protect itself against the Turks. Venizelos wisely
refused to endorse the demands of the Pontine Greeks that
Pontus should become an independent Greek Republic.[22]

In western Asia Minor, Greece claimed the strip lying west of
a line running from near Panderma on the Marmara to a point
on the south coast opposite Kastellorizo. The strip included
Smyrna and most of the Aydin vilayet.

According to Venizelos's figures, which were those of the
Ecumenical Patriarchate's census of 1912, the zone claimed by
Greece contained just over 800,000 Greeks as against just over
one million Turks and just over 100,000 Armenians, Jews and
others. Venizelos got round these inconvenient figures by incorporating in the zone for statistical purposes the neighbouring

islands of Imbros, Tenedos, Mitylene, Chios, Samos, Ikaria, Rhodes and the Dodecanese, and Kastellorizo, where the Greeks easily outnumbered the Turks (by about 370,000 to 25,000). He justified this manoeuvre on the grounds that these islands were from the economic and geographical points of view a part of mainland Turkey, an argument which the Turks themselves had invoked in arguing against the cession of the Aegean islands to Greece after the Balkan Wars. (Venizelos did not observe the awkward corollary of this argument, that if Greece's claim to western Asia Minor were rejected, the Turks would have had grounds for taking the words out of his mouth and asking for the offshore islands back!)

Thus fortified, Venizelos was able to argue for the cession of western Asia Minor to Greece on the grounds that the Greeks were the preponderant element in the area claimed, once the offshore islands were included. He argued also that western Asia Minor was an area historically and geographically distinct from the central Anatolian plateau. Climatically and physically it formed part of the Aegean basin – a land of olives and vines, with a mild Mediterranean climate and vegetation utterly distinct from those of the harsh windswept steppes of Anatolia. Venizelos invoked further the necessity of making just restitution to those 450,000 Greeks deported and expelled during the war. He argued that the reestablishment of the survivors in their homes and confiscated lands entailed the abolition of Ottoman sovereignty.

This combination of arguments enabled Venizelos to claim a larger zone than could be justified on grounds of population alone. For the ethnological argument on its own would have justified a claim to the sandjak of Smyrna alone, and then only if the population statistics adopted were not the *actual* figures of 1918–19, but figures for the period before the 1914–16 persecutions. The historical and geographical arguments on their own were of course inconclusive. There were unromantic but compelling counter-arguments.* But Venizelos's arguments

* e.g. that Smyrna was the natural outlet for the products of Anatolia, so that the cession of Smyrna and its hinterland to Greece would choke the economy of the interior. This was the argument of the Americans on the Territorial Commission set up to examine Greek claims. Venizelos answered it by promising to create a Free Port on the west coast (i.e. at Smyrna); *F.R.U.S. 1919*, iii, p. 837.

added up to a sweeping vision, supported by statistical data no more suspect than those of any other interested party, of a Great Greece stretching from the Adriatic to the Euxine, a Mediterranean area of vines and olives and classical temples, a foyer of Hellenism from time immemorial, reverting to its historical owners. For those who wished to be convinced, this vision was overwhelming.

And what of Turkey in this scheme? Turkey was to be reduced to a pitifully small Anatolian kernel of Kastamouni, Angora and Konya vilayets. The Turks, as defeated enemies, did not take part in the Peace Conference. It sometimes seemed they had been entirely forgotten. Yet even as Venizelos was presenting his case in Paris, it was becoming clear to the small band of allied control officers who traversed the vast spaces of Anatolia policing the armistice and supervising the collection and surrender of armaments that this armistice was a fragile thing based on the passive consent of the defeated. Beneath the crust of acquiescence there lay resentful nationalist passions ready to burst out. In the uncontrollable interior of Anatolia the hidden guns would be brought out, and a new Turkish phoenix would arise from the ashes of war.

Venizelos made a good impression in his exposition of the Greek claims before the Council of Ten. He flattered Lloyd George with a reference to his Welsh speaking, complimented Wilson on the virtues of American teachers in northern Epirus, and put the Council in a good mood by showing them photographs of sponge fishing in the Dodecanese.[23] But the whole farcical procedure, gone through by the leaders of most of the small claimant nations, was of a ritual nature. Decisions were not made on the basis of these presentations.

In a letter to Repoulis, his deputy in Greece, Venizelos reported the favourable impression of the Big Four and for the first time allowed himself to speculate optimistically on the outcome of the negotiations in Paris:

What I can regard as almost certain is that we shall be given Smyrna and Kydonies [Ayvali] with a corresponding hinterland, which I cannot yet define accurately. Also Cyprus and the Dodecanese, at the sacrifice of one or two islands and half of northern Epirus.... The partial sacrifices in northern Epirus and the Dodecanese are the necessary price for the normalization of our relations with Italy and the ending of her reaction after our establishment in Asia Minor.[24]

At the session of the Council of Ten on 4 February, at Lloyd George's suggestion, the Greek claims were submitted to an expert committee, charged 'to reduce the questions for decision within the narrowest possible limits and make recommendations for a just settlement'.[25] These terms of reference were both narrow and vague – vague in that they gave no indication of the criteria to be adopted in assessing the 'justice' of Greek claims, narrow in that they gave the committee the task of assessing Greek claims outside the general framework of the Turkish and Bulgarian settlements.[26] Alone among territorial commissions appointed by the Conference, the committee completed its work within the prescribed time, but only at the expense of unanimity. Broadly speaking, the British and French delegates did well by Greece; the Americans were less generous, and dissented from the Greek claim in Asia Minor; and the Italians strenuously opposed almost every Greek claim.*

In Asia Minor, France and Britain were agreed that Greece should obtain a substantial zone, though smaller than that claimed by Venizelos. The Americans disagreed; their statistics showed the Greeks to be in a minority in every sandjak except that of Smyrna itself, and they found the separation of the Smyrna zone from the interior to be undesirable on economic grounds. The Italians refused to discuss the claim at all. They argued with justice that the Smyrna zone could not be taken in isolation from the general political settlement in Anatolia. They held also that Smyrna was the subject of commitments (the Treaty of London and the St Jean de Maurienne agreement) which conflicted with the Greek claim and which had priority.

The report of the Territorial Committee brought Greek claims no nearer to realization. The coordinating committee appointed to consider the various reports of the territorial committees could only reflect the lack of unanimity in the original report, and indeed went further in the direction of disagreement, since the Americans withdrew their assent to Greek claims in Thrace.[27]

* The French, interestingly in view of their later attitude to Greek claims, took a line very favourable to Greece in the committee; it was they who, for instance, took the initiative in assigning Korytsa in Northern Epirus to Greece even against British objections. See the committee's final report of 30 March in Lloyd George Papers, F 92/12/8.

In late March however it began to look as if the Americans would assent to a Greek zone in Asia Minor.[28]

Thus in the spring of 1919 all was fluid and unsettled. No final decisions could be reached until the Supreme Council addressed itself seriously to the Turkish Treaty. Greece's claim to a Smyrna zone had been accepted in principle by the British and French delegates to the territorial committee. Clemenceau had told Venizelos that though France could not take the initiative in assigning Smyrna to Greece because of her relations with Italy, he personally sympathized with Greek aspirations in Asia Minor and would follow the lead of other powers.[29] But doubts supervened as the confident young expert peacemakers realized the practical difficulties which a Greek zone would create.

In mid-April, for instance, Harold Nicolson and Arnold Toynbee, two experts on the British staff, got together to cook up a solution to the problem. They agreed:

(1) That no mandatory will be able to run Constantinople without a fairly large zone behind him. On the other hand a big zone will include Greek populations, while cutting the future Turkey off from all communication with the Marmara. (2) That as we have demobilized so quickly, and as people at home are bored by the future settlement, we shall be unable to put the Greeks into Smyrna. I mean keep them there. They can't hold it without allied support or unless the whole of Turkey behind them is split up among the Allied Powers. Yet if they do not get Smyrna Venizelos will fall from power. (3) We agree, therefore, to propose to cut the Gordian knot. Let the Turks have Anatolia as their own. Give the Greeks European Turkey only. And let the Straits be kept open by a 'Commission Fluviale' with powers analogous to those of the Danube Commission.

Such a solution would at least have the merit of finality. All other solutions would entail trouble for the future. We put this down on paper; we sign it with our names; we send it in. It will not be considered.[30]

This was good sense. Sir Eyre Crowe sent the scheme on to Balfour with his blessing. While British officials were beginning to see the light over Anatolia, American resistance to the Greek claims in Thrace (which was due to American sympathy for Bulgaria) and Italian irreconcilability made an agreed settlement of the Greek claims seem a remote prospect. But in the first fortnight of May all was suddenly and startlingly changed.

It was the Italians who precipitated the crisis. They began to make moves in the Anatolian theatre which looked like an attempt to preempt the Conference's decisions about the area. At the same time their dispute with President Wilson over the fate of Fiume in the Adriatic came to the boil. On 24 April Orlando and his team walked out of the Conference and left Paris in protest against the handling of the Adriatic question by the Big Three. In due course the Italians were bound to return. But while they were absent, the suspicion and hostility with which the allied leaders, and especially Wilson, regarded their ambitions came close to hysteria. It was in this heated atmosphere of peevish doctrinal indignation that President Wilson spoke on 2 May, following a report that Italy had sent two cruisers to Smyrna:

I see also that they are sending ships to Fiume and Smyrna. I can send our largest cruiser, the *George Washington*, to either Fiume or Smyrna.... If I do that, it could produce a result – and far be it from me to desire that this result should be war. But the attitude of Italy is indubitably aggressive; she is a menace to the peace....

MR LLOYD GEORGE. A dispatch received from Mr Venizelos ... indicates that there is an understanding in Asia Minor between the Italians and the Turks, who are resuming their policy of terrorism against the Greeks. Mr Venizelos asks us to send a warship to Smyrna and proposes to send a Greek ship himself.... My opinion is that we should all three of us send ships to Smyrna.

M. CLEMENCEAU. A fine start for the League of Nations![31]

That same evening, Venizelos dined with Harold Nicolson, and discussed the effect of the Italian crisis on Greece's claims. Nicolson was afraid that Italy would be given 'compensation' in Anatolia for what she had to give up in the Adriatic. Venizelos sighed deeply, and reported that he had received assurances of support and comfort from Lloyd George and Wilson. Nicolson saw that by trying to steal a march on the Asia Minor coast the Italians had unwittingly helped the Greeks. Venizelos talked expansively of his future plans in anticipation of the triumph. 'Aucun homme politique,' he told Nicolson, 'n'a le prestige que moi je possède.'[32]

The Italians' activities in Anatolia came up again in the Supreme Council on 5 May. President Wilson announced that he had received a petition from the Greek population of Rhodes, who complained of Italian brutality and massacre on that island. It was Lloyd George's turn to launch into a diatribe against the Italians and their 'large plan of action in the eastern Mediterranean'. He accused them of inciting the Bulgarians to attack their neighbours and of extending their occupation of Adalia by sending troops inland and landing also at Marmaris:

> We are going to find ourselves in the presence of a *fait accompli*; the Italians will be in Anatolia. The only way to stop it is to settle the question of mandates as soon as possible and to settle the question of the occupation of Asia Minor at once. That will allow us to get out of the Caucasus and to send troops to Bulgaria; the Americans will occupy Constantinople and the French Syria. We should let the Greeks occupy Smyrna. There are massacres starting there and no one to protect the Greek population.
>
> M. CLEMENCEAU. Do you know how many ships Italy has off Smyrna at the moment? She has seven.
>
> MR LLOYD GEORGE. The best thing is for us to decide all this between ourselves before the Italians come back. Otherwise I am convinced they will beat us to it.
>
> M. CLEMENCEAU. I am quite willing to do so.[33]

The Chief of Imperial General Staff, Sir Henry Wilson, who attended this meeting, commented in his diary: 'I don't believe half these things, but Lloyd George greatly excited.'[34] No doubt the excitement was partly factitious, designed to exploit the aggrieved malevolence of President Wilson against the Italians and thus to secure his approval for a Greek occupation of Smyrna to which in calmer frame of mind he might have demurred. On other occasions (indeed, less than ten days later) Lloyd George viewed with equanimity the prospect of the Italians obtaining a large zone in southern Asia Minor.

The matter was taken further at the meeting of the Big Three on 6 May. Time was running out, for Orlando and Sonnino would be present again the next day. In the middle of a long and inconclusive discussion of Italian perfidy, the injustice of the 1915 Treaty of London which gave Italy the Dodecanese, and the impossibility of American troops occupying any part of Turkey, Lloyd George suddenly chipped in:

> I must insist again that we do not let Italy confront us with a *fait accompli* in Asia. We must allow the Greeks to land troops at Smyrna.

PRESIDENT WILSON. The best means of stopping the Italians' ventures are financial. . . .

MR LLOYD GEORGE. Have we ever prevented the Turks and the Balkan powers from making war, although they have always suffered from lack of money? My opinion is that we should tell Mr Venizelos to send troops to Smyrna. We will instruct our admirals to let the Greeks land wherever there is a threat of trouble or massacre.

PRESIDENT WILSON. Why not tell them to land as of now? Have you any objection to that?

MR LLOYD GEORGE. None.

M. CLEMENCEAU. Nor have I. But should we warn the Italians?

MR LLOYD GEORGE. In my opinion, no.[35]

So casually was the fateful decision taken. President Wilson would have put the devil into Smyrna if that would have kept the Italians out. Lloyd George would happily have allowed the Italians in if he had not felt a deeper sympathy with the aspirations of the Greeks. Clemenceau felt less strongly. He gave his word but was to qualify and regret it.

The fateful meeting of the Supreme Council took place at 11 a.m. After lunch Lloyd George telephoned Venizelos and asked him to come round to the Quai d'Orsay before the afternoon session, at which the Conference in plenary session was to approve the terms of the German treaty. Venizelos arrived at 2.45 p.m. He described in his diary how Lloyd George approached him with these words: [36]

'Do you have troops available?'
'We do. For what purpose?'
'President Wilson, M. Clemenceau and I decided today that you should occupy Smyrna.'
'We are ready.'

Lloyd George told Venizelos that it was the Italian machinations which had provoked this decision. The two men entered the Conference Hall and the session was declared open. Venizelos watched fascinated as the decision began to be clothed with flesh. General Sir Henry Wilson approached Lloyd George and sat down behind him, and the two men talked for some time. (The General was making the first, and vigorous, protest against the decision, asking Lloyd George if he realized that this was starting another war. Lloyd George brushed the protest aside.[37]) Wilson approached Admiral Hope. Hope spoke with Lloyd George. President Wilson spoke to General Bliss. Thus the word went round. The military and naval experts left the Conference room, followed by Venizelos, to meet in the Astoria Hotel and settle the details of the Greek landing.

General Wilson insisted on the fact that it was a Greek affair, under Greek command, that there was danger of opposition both from the Italians and from the Turks, and that both these Governments should be warned. Bitterly distrustful of any scheme cooked up in secret by three politicians, or 'Frocks' as he called them, he commented in his diary: 'Of course, the whole thing is mad.'[38]

The decision had been taken and the details were on the way to being settled. The two architects of the scheme could now allow themselves to relax a little and consider the longer term. Lloyd George dined with Venizelos on 9 May. He spoke expansively:

Greece has *great possibilities* in the Near East and you must be as powerful as possible in the military sense in order to take advantage of them. We are trying to get America to take the mandate for Constantinople, and her presence there will in no way prevent Constantinople from coming under Greek sovereignty in the fullness of time. President Wilson is not against the idea, but he doubts whether American public opinion and therefore the Senate will approve it. If they don't approve it the only solution which England will accept for Constantinople is for it to go to Greece.[39]

It was after his dinner that Venizelos decided to keep a diary throughout the critical period.[40] The spare, bony sentences in which these days of drama and emotion are recorded give away nothing of the man and his secret life.

The important question of what to say to the Italians and the Turks remained. President Wilson, Lloyd George and Venizelos were in favour of presenting the Italians with a *fait accompli*.[41] At the morning session of the Council on 12 May Clemenceau finally told Orlando of the decision, inviting the Italians to take part in an interallied landing at Smyrna, but making clear that it would be the Greeks who would land in force and remain as a garrison of the town. The fact that the main motive of the decision was the desire to keep the Italians out of Smyrna lent a certain hypocrisy to the discussion. In order to secure Italian consent, Clemenceau emphasized that the landing did not prejudice the final decisions of the Peace Conference as to the fate of Smyrna. 'It is not a question of occupying or sharing out territories in Asia Minor, but only of protecting the population.'[42] Orlando asked for time to consult with Sonnino. When the Supreme Council met again that same afternoon, Orlando gave in. Clemenceau repeated his pledge: 'Today Smyrna belongs to no one; it is not a question of deciding the fate of this town, but of executing a temporary operation with a defined aim.'[43] Thus there now remained no further reservations or objections to the Greek landing.

'Those three all-powerful, all-ignorant men sitting there and carving continents, with only a child to lead them': thus Balfour on the attitude of the Big Three to Asia Minor.[44] The decision to send the Greeks into Asia Minor was taken suddenly, casually and in great secrecy by the Big Three, with Venizelos's encouragement, but on their own initiative, without serious consultations with the expert advisers or thought for the consequences. Lloyd George, acting on Venizelos's information, engineered the decision. President Wilson, disregarding the views of the American experts on the Greek Territorial Committee, fell in with the scheme in order to frustrate Italy. Clemenceau played a subsidiary role.

The decision was not a part of a comprehensive plan for Asiatic Turkey, as has been implied.[45] The Big Three did not seriously address themselves to the question of mandates and zones of influence in Anatolia until *after* the decision had been taken, on 13 May.[46] Harold Nicolson's description of the scene in the Rue Nitot that day well conveys the casual ignorance with which they went about their business:

As I expected, the idea of 'compensations' [for the Italians] in Asia Minor is much to the fore.... I spread out my big map on the dinner table and they all gather round. Lloyd George, A. J. Balfour, Milner, Henry Wilson, Mallet and myself. Lloyd George explains that Orlando and Sonnino are due in a few minutes and he wants to know what he can offer them. I suggest the Adalia zone, with the rest of Asia Minor to France. Milner, Mallet and Henry Wilson oppose it: A. J. Balfour neutral.
We are still discussing when the flabby Orlando and the sturdy Sonnino are shown into the dining-room. They all sit round the map. The appearance of a pie about to be distributed is thus enhanced. Lloyd George shows them what he suggests. They ask for Scala Nova as well. 'Oh, no!' says Lloyd George, 'you can't have that – it's full of Greeks!' He goes on to point out that there are further

Greeks at Makri, and a whole wedge of them along the coast towards Alexandretta. 'Oh, no,' I whisper to him, 'there are not many
Greeks there.' 'But yes,' he answers, 'don't you see it's coloured
green?' I then realize that he mistakes my map for an ethnological
map, and thinks the green means Greeks instead of valleys, and
the brown means Turks instead of mountains. Lloyd George makes
this correction with great good humour. He is as quick as a king-
fisher.

Meanwhile Orlando and Sonnino chatter to themselves in Italian.
They ask for the coal-mines at Eregli. Lloyd George who really
knows something about his subject by now, says, 'But it's rotten coal,
and not much of it in any case.' Sonnino translates this remark to
Orlando. 'Si, si,' replies the latter, 'ma, l'effetto morale, sa!'[47]

Finally the Italians appeared ready to accept the Adalia mandate. Someone pointed out that the Covenant of the League of
Nations regarding Mandates provided for the 'consent and wishes
of the people concerned'. This caused great amusement. Nicolson,
young, idealistic and shocked, observed Orlando's cheeks wobble
with laughter and his puffy eyes fill with tears of mirth.

This first attempt to work out a general Turkish Anatolian
settlement owed much to the inspiration of the moment. After
lunch the same day the Big Three consolidated the morning's
work in President Wilson's house. Lloyd George explained their
decisions to Harold Nicolson, while Clemenceau sat silently on
the edge of his chair leaning his blue-gloved hands on the map,
like a yellowish ivory gorilla.[48] Nicolson dashed back to the
Astoria and dictated the necessary resolutions.

The situation by 14 May was therefore as follows. Greece was
to get the Smyrna-Ayvali zone including the lower Meander
valley. Turkish Anatolia was to be divided into three mandates:
Greek over the rest of the Aydin vilayet, Italian over the south,
and French over north and central Anatolia. America was to
take the Armenian mandate.

Isn't it terrible [wrote Nicolson to his wife], the happiness of
millions being decided in that way, while for the last two months
we were praying and begging the Council to give us time to work
out a scheme?

Their decisions are immoral and impracticable. 'Mais voyez-vous,
jeune homme, que voulez-vous qu'on fasse? Il faut aboutir!'

The funny thing is that the only part where I do come in is the
Greek part, and here they have gone beyond, and dangerously
beyond, what I suggested in my wildest moments.[49]

When Nicolson voiced these thoughts to A. J. Balfour, the great man was tiresome and bland: 'All that', he admitted, 'is quite true. But, my dear young man, you forget that we are now at the Paris Conference. All you say is pure aesthetics.'[50] Despite this Balfour argued against the Lloyd George proposals, which were soon superseded.* Indeed, for all Nicolson's anxiety about the immoral haste of the proceedings, it was to be almost a year before the broad lines of a Turkish settlement were worked out.

So Lloyd George, with no clear picture in his mind of a general Anatolian settlement, exploited the Italian fracas to achieve a result which in other circumstances might have foundered on American and French objections. He pressed through the decision on the Greek landing in secrecy and haste in order to anticipate the acrimonious negotiations over Anatolia which otherwise might have made a Greek landing impossible. Venizelos was instigator and willing accomplice, 'entitled to plead', in Churchill's words, 'that in going to Smyrna he acted as mandatory for the four greatest Powers. But he went as readily as a duck will swim.'[51] His motives were transparent, his actions open. But what moved Lloyd George to the impetuous and fateful decision?

Lloyd George knew and was not dismayed by the contrary views of his advisers. Curzon had expressed himself strongly against the attribution of a Smyrna zone to Greece.[52] General Sir

---

* On 17 May Lloyd George began to back-pedal over the partition of Anatolia. Balfour had submitted a critical memo, and Montagu and an Indian Muslim delegation argued strongly against partition before the Supreme Council that day. Mantoux, *Les Délibérations du Conseil des Quatre*, nos. 81, 82; Nicolson, *Peacemaking 1919*, pp. 273–4.

On 19 May, Lloyd George argued that to put the Italians into Asia Minor would simply create trouble; he suggested a French mandate over all Anatolia; Mantoux, ii, no. 83. A Cabinet meeting the same day revealed differences between Balfour, Montagu, Milner, Curzon and Churchill, and reinforced Lloyd George's new-found dislike of partition; Nicolson, *Peacemaking 1919*, p. 281.

On 21 May, in a long statement in the Supreme Council, Lloyd George definitely rejected partition, attributing his change of mind to the importance of the Indian Muslim views, and to the formal decision of the British Cabinet. He proposed not France, but the U.S. as mandatory for the whole of Turkish Anatolia. (This new change of mind did not of course affect the Greek zone, nor Armenia, which were not regarded as part of Turkish Anatolia.) Mantoux, ii, no. 86.

Henry Wilson, when told of the decision to send in the Greeks, warned Lloyd George of the consequences in forthright terms. Sir Maurice Hankey, the *éminence grise* of the Cabinet Secretariat, who had been present at the meeting of the Supreme Council on 7 May, spent a sleepless night and rose at 5 in the morning to write a letter to Lloyd George expressing his grave doubts over the Greek enterprise. The letter was transmitted at once by Lloyd George to Venizelos, who was unconvinced.[53] Winston Churchill, Secretary of State for War, heard of the decision with bewilderment and alarm.[54]

The warnings were in vain. The secrecy of the Supreme Council's processes allowed the decision to be taken without serious consideration of the consequences. The military experts, who disapproved of the decision,* were presented with a *fait accompli*. Lloyd George wished to send the Greeks into Asia Minor, and therefore did not wish to hear arguments to the contrary.

Lloyd George found some faint support in the sympathy of Balfour, Eyre Crowe and the junior experts such as Harold Nicolson for Greek aspirations. His support of the Greeks was based on a sense that Greece was the coming power in the Eastern Mediterranean, a virile, vigorous and expanding nation, opposed to a feeble, moribund and untrustworthy Turkey. Given this conception of a Greek renaissance, which was encouraged by Venizelos at every turn, it was possible to ignore the warnings of military advisers and politicians as prejudiced and Turcophil. If forced to rationalize his support for the Greeks, Lloyd George could have argued that the new Greece was to be the carrier of British interests in the Eastern Mediterranean, the power on which Britain could rely for support if imperial communications with India or the freedom of the Straits were threatened.[55] This dangerously attractive vision was based on a premature assumption of the impotence of Turkey.

In that first hectic and delirious fortnight of May Lloyd George conceived of a Greece greater than even his critics have hitherto supposed, including Cyprus and Constantinople,[56] commanding the Straits, circling the Aegean in a great arc from the Corfu channel to Smyrna. If there was something superb in this

* Gen. Wilson's diary for 10 May: 'the whole thing is mad and bad ... Venizelos is using the three Frocks for his own ends. After the three Frocks had gone, Bliss, Le Bon, Fuller and I ... all agreed we were doing a stupid thing.' Callwell, *Field-Marshal Sir Henry Wilson*, ii, p. 192.

shared vision of Lloyd George and Venizelos, there was also something frightening in the isolation of the two men. The scruples of Clemenceau, the unreliability of the Americans, the resentment of the Italians, the caution of the military advisers, should have given warning that trouble was on its way.

5 | The Occupation of Smyrna

I cannot understand to this day how the eminent
statesmen in Paris, Wilson, Lloyd George,
Clemenceau and Venizelos, whose wisdom,
prudence, and address had raised them under the
severest tests so much above their fellows, could
have been betrayed into so rash and fatal a step.

Winston Churchill, *The World Crisis: the
Aftermath*, p. 369

The Greeks had been actively making propaganda in Smyrna
since the armistice. The Greek journalist Michael Rodas, himself active in the propaganda exercise, described the jockeying for
position between Greeks, Italians and Turks:

Smyrna at this time began to present the aspect of a secret war.
The English grasped the situation, and were clearly on our side. The
British Consul ... came to Smyrna and released all the Christians,
and visited Erythrai ... and saw the ruined Christian towns and
villages, and on his return spoke harshly to the Turkish leaders and
held them responsible for the treatment of the Christians. The
French ... did not deny us any help. And the Italians – the Italians
fought alongside the Young Turk elements and did their best to
slander us and eject us from Smyrna.[1]

There was in the Smyrna area a large colony of Turcocretans,
Greek-speaking Muslims who had left Crete around the time
that the island was united with the Greek Kingdom. Venizelos
sent a Cretan politician called Makrakis to win them over to the
idea of Greek government in Asia Minor. The mission was a
success. Little groups of Turcocretans were to be seen sitting in
village squares smoking their *nargileh* pipes and recalling nos-
talgically with Makrakis the old life in Crete.

A Greek Mission in Smyrna was set up, responsible to the
Foreign Ministry in Athens. The Mission claimed to have won
the support of Armenian and Jewish leaders, but to have made
no headway with the Levantines – those of European descent
who had been born and bred in the Levant – nor with the Turks
themselves. Subsidies to the Turkish newspaper *Kiuli* and the

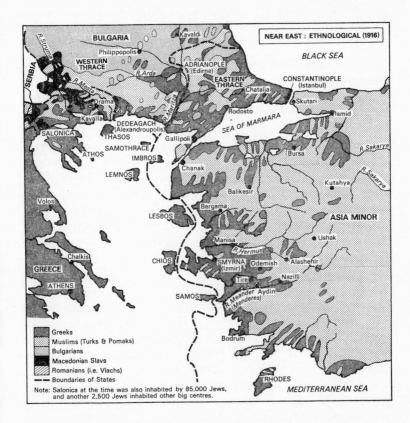

French *Liberté* had yielded little result. The Levantines were well aware that their economic interests would be better served by a continuation of the old regime of capitulations and commercial and economic privileges for foreign interests in Turkey than by the untried experiment of a Greek regime which could be expected to favour Greek capital.

In its report to Athens, the Greek Mission presented a naïve picture of the incorrigible Turks:

The Turks have not yet realized that whatever the solution of the territorial question may be (and the solution depends neither on them nor on us), the piling up of old and recent passions and the widening of the already almost unbridgeable gap by the continuation of the struggle against us through the press and through various organizations which include the worst elements among the Turco-

Albanians, Turcocretans, Laz and other alleged escaped convicts, is disastrous and inexpedient for both races.... The Turks do not believe in the liberalism and justice of our political system.[2]

It is not surprising that the Mission was a failure. Its very presence was a token of Greece's annexationist designs.

Suddenly, strange movements by the Allies were observed and rumours began to circulate that important developments were imminent.

On 14 May 1919 allied detachments under the orders of Admiral Calthorpe landed to take possession of the Smyrna forts, after Izzet Bey, the Turkish Vali, had been informed of the allies' intentions. The word went round that the town was to be occupied by the Greeks. During the afternoon Captain Mavroudis, commander of the *Leon* and Greece's representative in Smyrna since the armistice, called together the leaders of the Greek community and announced the news that the Greek army was on its way, reading to the people a proclamation by Venizelos which was received with great emotion.[3] The news spread rapidly. During the night several thousand Turks met together on the heights of Bachri-Baba near the Jewish cemetery, where they lit fires and beat drums in a great demonstration of protest.* That night too several hundred prisoners, mostly Turks, were permitted to escape from the prisons, with the complicity of the Turkish authorities and the Italian major who headed the allied prison control. Some of them succeeded in procuring arms from a depot near the barracks.

The next morning, 15 May, dawned fine and clear. Thousands of chattering Greeks converged on the seafront. Blue and white Greek flags waved on the quayside and fluttered on the houses along the front. For the Greeks of Smyrna it was an infinitely moving occasion, the accomplishment of a dream. Not one of them doubted that the occupation was to be permanent. With the flags and streamers waving in the early morning sun, the atmo-

---

* The Greeks claimed that this gathering was intended to drum up resistance to the occupation, while the Interallied Commission of Enquiry into the events which followed the landing found that the gathering was intended to prove the predominance of the Turkish over the foreign element in Smyrna; see the report of the Commission in *D.B.F.P.*, 1st Series, ii, no. 17, app. A; Toynbee, pp. 404–5, with translations of proclamations issued by the Turks on this occasion, tending to show that the intention was pacific resistance.

sphere was that of a public holiday. A small detachment of Greek troops, landed in advance to guard the points of debarkation, tried ineffectively to hold back the crowds. The first sign of the approaching ships was wisps of smoke on the horizon. At seven o'clock the transports came in sight at the far end of the gulf. Half an hour later the liner *Patris* was approaching the quay. A bugle sounded from the bridge. The steamers hooted and whistled.

As the Greek troops began to land, Metropolitan Chrysostom came forward to bless them. The first men off the ships stacked arms and did a little dance on the shore. The crowds cheered and wept. By about nine thirty, all three regiments of the 1st Division composing the army of occupation had landed.

Despite the landing of allied detachments the previous day, the Greeks now had sole command on land. The 4th and 5th Infantry Regiments marched off to occupy the areas north and east of the city. Owing to a conflict of orders, the 1/38 Regiment of Evzones, which was to have disembarked at Karantina to the south and proceeded from there through the suburbs to occupy the town, landed in the middle of the quay. It was thus obliged to march southwards along the broad seafront road in front of the excited crowds to take up its intended position. This route took the regiment past the *Konak* (Government House) and the barracks in which regular Turkish troops were confined. At about 10 a.m. the 1/38 Evzones set off along the front, flanked and followed by delirious Greek civilians. Just as the regiment passed the barracks, someone fired a shot.*

Pandemonium broke loose. The Greek troops in the gardens of the Konak Square started up a brisk fusillade, and kept the barracks under concentrated fire for over half an hour, until the Turkish officers inside surrendered.

The Turks began to come out of the barracks, holding up their hands in surrender. Donald Whittall, who had been standing on the balcony of the Whittall Co. office when the firing began, was one of the few neutral observers. 'They were made to go through no end of humiliation and received a good deal of knocking

---

* No one knows who fired the first shot. Toynbee (*The Western Question*, pp. 396–400) made exhaustive investigations. The Interallied Commission found that it was impossible to establish who fired first, but that the Greek *troops* did not open fire, simply responding to the first shot.

about', he wrote of the Turkish prisoners. When the Greeks had collected together all the Turks from the barracks and the surrounding buildings, they marched them back from the Konak Square along the quay to the *Patris*, which served as a prison ship.

Whittall left his office and followed the procession. Somewhere along the route discipline broke down. Whittall estimated that thirty unarmed prisoners were butchered. Most of the atrocities were committed by the crowds of Greek civilians who followed the procession, but Greek soldiers were straining at the leash, and 'the officers could with difficulty prevent their men from shooting the prisoners'.

Allied officers on board their warships saw the Turks being marched along, their hands above their heads, with Greek soldiers prodding the stragglers with their bayonets. Some were knocked down, bayoneted or shot, stripped of their valuables, and thrown into the sea. The Captain of H.M.S. *Adventure* saw a Turkish officer, marching with his hands up, veer out of line. A Greek soldier struck him on the head with his rifle butt. When the Turk rose, he was struck again and then bayoneted. Finally the top of his head was blown off. Greek troops surrounded a Turkish gunboat tied to the quay next to the *Adventure* and riddled it with fire, wounding two of the crew severely. Prisoners were forced to shout 'Long live Venizelos' and 'Long live Greece'. Finally they were shut up on the *Patris*.[4]

In other parts of the town order had broken down. Many Turks had procured arms. Bands of civilians, not all of them Greek, took advantage of the disorder to plunder and loot the Turkish houses. A mob of Greeks carried off thousands of pounds worth of hides from a Turkish tannery. A Greek patrol which happened to be passing ordered them to stop; as soon as the patrol had gone, they continued to plunder. The next day order had still not been restored. American witnesses in the American Collegiate Institute for girls saw all the Turkish houses in the neighbourhood looted before their eyes.

During the first day, the Turks suffered 300 to 400 casualties, killed and wounded, and the Greeks about 100, including two Evzones among the killed.[5] Before long the killing and looting spread through the town into the surrounding villages.

These deplorable events were due not only to Greek indiscipline and provocative nationalist fervour, but also to the hypocrisy of the Allies as to the nature of the Greek occupation. If the object were really to keep the peace and prevent massacre, then the occupation should have been genuinely and not nominally interallied. As it was, both Venizelos and the allied politicians and military advisers in Paris had insisted, each for his own reason, that the Greeks should have a free hand on 15 May. The occupation of the forts was a symbolic gesture. A proposal of the U.S. Senior Naval Officer in Smyrna that the town be physically occupied by British, French, American and Italian detachments on the 14th and handed over to the Greeks on the 15th, was rejected.[6]

On their side, the Greeks failed to take adequate precautions. The occupation was entrusted to a colonel, who had neither the prestige nor the will to impose himself ruthlessly on his men. It was six days before the Greek High Commissioner arrived – a delay which filled Venizelos with dismay[7] – and no Greek general set foot in Smyrna until a month after the landing. By that time the Greeks had consolidated their position by fanning out from Smyrna and occupying Aydin, Ayvali and other important provincial towns. The extension of the occupation was attended by massacres and excesses on the part of both Turks and Greeks. Aydin was occupied by the Greeks on 27 May, evacuated after horrible scenes on 29–30 May, and reoccupied on 4 July. The town was left a smoking ruin, two-thirds destroyed.

Back in February Venizelos had chosen a governor for Smyrna. It was known that at least one Liberal party politician, Themistocles Sophoulis from Samos, wanted the job. Traditionally in the Greek political system provincial governorships had gone to men of political ambition – Sophoulis himself had been Governor General of Macedonia – and were therefore too often exercised by men who were continually looking over their shoulders at the political scene in Athens. Venizelos rejected this tradition and made a surprising choice – Aristeidis Stergiadis, a fifty-eight-year-old lawyer and civil servant who was then serving as Governor General of Epirus.

Stergiadis was a friend of Venizelos from Cretan revolutionary days. An acknowledged expert in Muslim law, he had helped the Liberal government in drafting the clauses concerning Muslim questions in the prewar Treaty of Athens. In Epirus he had won a reputation for firm and impartial government, and scored a notable success in the suppression of the brigandage which flourished in the area.

On his arrival in Smyrna, Stergiadis had two immediate aims: to reimpose law and order, and efface the damaging effect of the events of 15–16 May; and to build up, from scratch, an effective administration in the circumstances of a military occupation. He tackled these tasks with a mixture of threats, bullying and common sense, aided by a 'kindergarten' of young administrators whom he brought with him from Athens and Epirus.*

The first task, the imposition of order, was quickly accomplished in Smyrna itself. The main offenders of 15–16 May were sternly punished by court martial. And Stergiadis promptly announced that Greece would compensate the victims on the basis of damages estimated by a mixed commission including allied representatives. These measures had an immediate effect.

Stergiadis struck hard at any discrimination against the Turks which might disturb order or complicate his delicate relationship with the allied representatives. Having instructed the censorship of the local press, for instance, to avoid any form of provocation of the Turks, he sacked the chief of the department when a satirical poem about the Young Turks appeared in the weekly *Kopanos*, appointing a new chief censor with even stricter instructions.[8]

The second task, the creation of an efficient and impartial administration, took longer. In theory, since Turkish sovereignty was not impaired by the occupation, the Turkish administration continued to exist. In practice, it immediately came under Greek control. Stergiadis retained Turkish functionaries in lesser executive posts, subordinating them to the administrative machinery of the Greek High Commission, which was located in the old Greek Consulate. Of the fourteen departments in the High Commission, only one, that of Muslim Affairs, was headed by a Muslim – Ali Naip Zade, a Turcocretan who had been Nomarch of Drama. Most of the important administrative posts were filled by civil servants from Athens, under whose supervision the locally recruited Greeks learned their business. The Greek administration had to be built up from nothing at a time

* e.g. P. Gounarakis, who had served under Stergiadis in Epirus, and became Secretary General at the Smyrna High Commission; Toynbee refers to two others who impressed him favourably – G. Vasilikos at Aydin, and I. Nabouris at Soma (p. 166).

when poor conditions and lack of trained personnel were straining Greece's administrative resources to the breaking point even in Old Greece. The most immediate problem was lack of trained gendarmerie to police the new territories. Venizelos recognized the problem,[9] and the priority of Asia Minor in his thinking undoubtedly enabled Stergiadis to choose his staff very freely.

Stergiadis was a man of harsh and ungovernable temper. Physically he was not imposing. Surveying the world from behind gold-rimmed spectacles, conventionally and rather shabbily dressed, he gave an impression of remoteness and intellectual arrogance. He abhorred the social scene and kept to his own rooms when not on duty, making no attempt to ingratiate himself with local Smyrniot society. When forced into company, he was abrupt and domineering, though from time to time he would unburden himself to younger colleagues in monologues of great charm and brilliance.[10] He admired Venizelos, finding in him a certain 'moral beauty',[11] but had no time for the self-seeking intrigues of many of his colleagues. In 1913 when asked by a young journalist his opinion of Venizelos's political worth, he replied after a few moments thought, 'I'll say just this; Venizelos has a star, a great star!', perhaps inventing what later became a common metaphor for Venizelos's *daemon*.[12]

Stergiadis resisted every temptation to enter politics, recognizing that he was temperamentally unsuited to the game. When he was told of Venizelos's desire that he should stand for Heraklion in the elections of June 1915, Stergiadis replied: 'The only way of preserving my friendship with Venizelos, whose limitless intellectual and spiritual gifts I appreciate, is for me not to become a politician; for if I did, we should soon be at loggerheads.'[13] It was a wise assessment. When Metaxas met Stergiadis in 1914, he had the impression of 'an intelligent man, and master of himself ... preparing himself, studying the services in all their details'.[14]

Stergiadis recognized the weakness and immaturity of the political and administrative machinery of Greece. He held that the state should send its best servants, especially the younger men, to the new territories, so as to establish the administration on the right lines. There they should stay long enough to see the job through. This was an important problem in a rapidly expanding country. Alexander Pallis, who served as a Financial

Inspector in newly liberated Macedonia in 1913–14, saw the same problem from below in similar terms:

The New Territories also suffered much then from the frequent changes of Governors. This was the fault not only of the governments but also of the persons who were appointed to these posts. A Governor who wishes to do real work in some province must take the decision to pass several years of his life there. But the various politicians who were usually sent to govern the New Territories were interested only in getting the title of Governor General, and then looked for a way of getting back to Athens as fast as possible. I remember one such, an old politician from Patras, who had been appointed Governor General of Eastern Macedonia, with Drama as his base, in 1918, and who on his way through Salonika told us in the plaintive tone of a wronged man how much it cost him to abandon his political clientèle in Patras in order to concern himself with the 'problems of the Turks' (the phrase was his own) of Drama and Kavalla! What could one expect with that sort of mind?[15]

Stergiadis would have agreed. 'He condemned the Nomarchs and Governor Generals who go to a place and proceed to create a local party, such as Argyropoulos in Salonika and George Papandreou in Lesbos.'[16] He told Michael Rodas that Andreas Michalakopoulos, who as Minister of Agriculture had introduced agrarian legislation to break up the great estates, should go and live in Macedonia for five years to ensure that his legislation was effectively implemented. These views were good portents for his tenure of the Smyrna job.

To the qualities of industry, personal force, long experience of Muslim affairs and impartiality between Muslim and Christian (in so far as that was possible for a Greek), Stergiadis added, in the early period of the occupation, a positive vision of Greco-Muslim cooperation, and of a Greek cultural and social renaissance. His dearest project was the 'Ionian University' of Smyrna, which Professor K. Karatheodoris, an enlightened professor of mathematics at Göttingen University, came to Smyrna to direct.[17] More than once he was heard to claim that Greece in Asia Minor would create the 'third or fourth Hellenic civilization'.

Arnold Toynbee, who was sent by C. P. Scott to report on the situation in Anatolia for the *Manchester Guardian*, saw Stergiadis's work at close quarters, and interviewed him several times. He left a useful description of his methods:

He is highly strung – resourceful and courageous but capricious and hot-tempered – and his method of administration was to strike unexpectedly and hard, as if he were pleading a weak case or fighting a desperate duel. This fencing style of government, with its lunges, feints, and dexterous avoidance of hostile thrusts, is un-Western and particularly un-English, but then Mr Stergiadis did not command the means of an Indian lieutenant-governor. To begin with, he was perpetually in financial straits, for he had to pay his own way without assistance from the Greek Government; the local revenues had dwindled with the commercial isolation of Smyrna from the hinterland; and the Capitulations (which remained provisionally in force) made it difficult to tap new sources. He had no judicial system and no civil service. He had to hold his own against the military, who became less amenable as the military situation grew more grave. He was not sure of backing from Athens. . . . He had to improvise everything, pending the inauguration of the Sèvres regime. . . .

People with a case against his administration in Smyrna certainly did not find Stergiadis easy to tackle. He was not loved either by Western consuls or by unofficial petitioners of any nationality, whom he had an unlimited capacity for ignoring, unless he chose to embarrass them by doing them more than justice, in order to choke off future applications. This was his favourite sleight-of-hand in holding the balance between the different elements in the local population. He gained some unpopularity among the Smyrna Greeks, but more credit among Western visitors and even among residents who ought to have known better, by occasional spectacular acts of partiality towards Turks, when Turks and Greeks were in conflict. He could not or would not prevent or redress the far more frequent injustices, great or small, which were done to Turks by the Greek military or gendarmerie or subordinate members of his own civil administration, or still more frequently by the Greek population with local official connivance. . . . Probably, however, these gestures were the most effective that he could make in the circumstances.

Toynbee fairly concluded that

he could hardly have had a worse start or performed a more brilliant acrobatic feat than to keep afloat as he did in such a sea of troubles. . . . National animosity stultified his efforts as inexorably as if he had been a well-meaning Ottoman Vali of Salonika in 1912 or a liberal-minded English Viceroy of Ireland in 1921.[18]

Stergiadis's swiftness to crush any outburst of nationalist enthusiasm, his arbitrary methods and his austerity of character soon brought him into conflict with the local Greeks, the army command and the Church. His relations with the Archbishopric were particularly strained. On one notorious occasion at an official doxology attended by all the leading figures of Smyrna including the allied consuls, he interrupted Metropolitan Chrysostom's sermon, which he regarded as trespassing on dangerous political ground, and brought the service to an abrupt close.[19] The incident was not merely a tactless outburst of temper; it marked Stergiadis's determination to be subject to no restraints within his new domain even from the Church, with its traditional function of political leadership, its powerful hold over the people's loyalties and its equally powerful nationalist fervour. In view of the prestige and status of the Orthodox Bishops in Turkey, this was a dangerous attitude to adopt.

In his relations with the local Greeks, Stergiadis was apt when he lost his temper to use physical violence. He carried a stick with which to beat the stupid or intransigent, and frequently boasted of his intention to govern by means of it.

More important at this stage than Stergiadis's brushes with the civilian populations were his disputes with the military. Tension between the civil and military arms was inevitable in view of their utterly different aims. The High Commission was concerned with good government, good relations with the Allies, a favourable 'image' of Greece. The soldiers were concerned with the security of the Smyrna zone, and covertly with its extension, and were not over-scrupulous about how they achieved these ends. Apart from the acknowledged atrocities of 15–16 May in Smyrna and later at Aidin, there were many occasions when Greek troops in the normal course of duty fell foul of the instructions of Venizelos and Stergiadis. Such incidents, for obvious reasons, do not often appear in Greek sources unless they show Stergiadis in an unfavourable light. But Saraphis, then a Major in the 5/42 Evzones, later Commander of ELAS, the communist dominated resistance army of the Second World War, tells how he had his men beat up some Turks after Greek barbed wire defences were found cut through:

The Turks had been called on to surrender weapons of war but only surrendered useless ones. The episode of the wire made me realize that the Turkish population was hostile and in case of serious operations would stab me in the back. I preferred to be punished for breaking an order than to suffer as Schinas [Commanding Officer of the Greek troops which occupied Aydin] did.[20]

In another incident, contrary to Stergiadis's orders, Greek troops shelled and brought down a minaret which they suspected was being used as a lookout post by Turkish *chettés*.

Relations were complicated by the interdependence of the civil and military arms. For instance, the High Commissioner was forced to make use of the courts martial, because he was not prepared to entrust sensitive cases to the Turkish courts, but could not establish Greek courts until the final annexation of Smyrna.[21] His interference with the workings of the court martial annoyed the army.[22] When General Miliotis – a character as mild as the sound of his name – took over the Asia Minor command, Stergiadis went so far as to interfere with military appointments.[23] Even Paraskevopoulos, C. in C. of the Greek army, suspected that Stergiadis was working to engineer his replacement, and the removal of his Chief of Staff, Theodoros Pangalos, an arch-intriguer and agent of Venizelism, later to become dictator.[24] At one time or another almost everybody wanted to get rid of the odious but undoubtedly powerful Pangalos. Venizelos was forced to intervene and define the precise limits of the authority of High Commission and army command.[25]

The resentment aroused by Stergiadis's methods and temper culminated in an incident demanding Venizelos's personal intervention, only two months after the Greek landing. On 14 July 1919, in suspiciously similar terms, Repoulis and Alexander Diomedis, the acting Foreign Minister while Politis was away in Paris, telegraphed to Venizelos and Politis about Stergiadis.[26] They accused him of insulting and humiliating the Greek community in Smyrna, and asked Venizelos to intervene. The telegrams were strongly worded, insisting on the high-handed methods of the High Commissioner. Repoulis feared that Stergiadis's condition might be a 'pathological phenomenon'. He described how Stergiadis had insulted journalists without cause, offended the workers of the Bank of Athens by forbidding them to strike in sympathy with their colleagues in Athens, and threatened beatings right and left.

With great regret [wrote Diomedis] I am forced to send you painful information about the activities of Mr Stergiadis in Smyrna.

His sick neuroticism has reached a climax. No one dares speak to him or complain or give any informataion to the High Commission.... He is at odds with almost all the delegates of the powers and communicates with them in writing. Even the American delegate, who is the best disposed towards us, is almost at odds with him.* In general Greeks and foreigners have a most unfortunate impression of him which reflects on Greece. He insults the Greeks even in front of foreigners with the intention, one would say, of humiliating them. At least that is the impression given. Whenever our authorities in the discharge of their functions find a Turk or a Jew in the wrong, they incur the High Commissioner's displeasure.... He terrorizes all with open threats of whippings and beatings.

And Diomedis went on to describe a series of incidents in support of his case, including Stergiadis's curt interruption of Bishop Chrysostom's full flow of rhetoric in the church. He ended:

Greeks coming here [i.e. to Athens] speak very harshly telling the facts, and adding that they do not react to this behaviour in Smyrna because our cause there is still unsettled. The situation is critical, and should be dealt with all the more immediately in that I suspect we are dealing with a pathological phenomenon.† I bring all this to your attention out of the highest sense of duty after a painful struggle in the exercise of this duty.

Neither Repoulis nor Diomedis asked directly that Stergiadis be replaced; but it was clear that, along with many other Greeks in Smyrna,[27] they would have been happy to see him go.

Venizelos took these outbursts as personal attacks on Stergiadis, arising from the resentment of the military, whose excesses Stergiadis was trying to prevent, and the frustrated ambitions of petty-minded politicians. He replied to Diomedis in a long letter which shows how well he understood that the Greek occupation was being compromised by the very nationalism which had inspired it:

When I received Repoulis's telegram, and before I received yours, I was very anxious lest Stergiadis might really have suffered some mental disturbance under the pressure of events. But as soon as your telegram arrived, then I understood what is happening. What is happening is that of all our military men and politicians in

* But Horton, the United States Consul, wrote later that Stergiadis was 'a great man who made a supreme effort to perform a superhuman task', (*The Blight of Asia*, p. 82).

† Exactly the same phrase as that used by Repoulis.

1 Venizelos's Greater Greece. This popular map of 1920 reflects the settlement of the Treaty of Sèvres, and includes as parts of 'present-day Greece' the Smyrna zone, North Epirus, East and West Thrace, and the Dodecanese apart from Rhodes. The legend traces the expansion of Greece from a territory of 64,679 square kilometres and population of 2,632,000 in 1911, to 173,779 square kilometres and 7,156,000 in 1920. The maiden holds a blue and white Greek flag and a shield proclaiming: 'Greece is destined to live and will live.'

2 George I on horseback, about [to]
lead the official entry into libera[ted]
Salonika in 1912; he fell to an as[sas]
sin's bullet four months later. V[en]
zelos is behind in top hat and ta[ils,]
Metaxas in plumed helmet.

3 Constantine as Crown Prince with [his]
wife Sophia and two elder s[ons]
George (standing) and Alexa[nder]
(sitting). Both of them became k[ings;]
so did Paul, the third son, not [yet]
born at the date of this photo (18[ ])

Smyrna, only Stergiadis has retained a clear conception of the situation, trying to save it from shipwreck ... protesting, very likely losing his temper from time to time, and regarded as unbalanced by men who are themselves genuinely disturbed. I realize full well that your telegraphic outburst is based on information coming from Paraskevopoulos.... Note that from Stergiadis I have not received *any* indication of a clash with Paraskevopoulos.... You telegraph that 'whenever our authorities in the course of their duties find a Turk or a Jew in the wrong they fall victim to the displeasure of the High Commissioner'. This charge alone does not convict Stergiadis of being an organ of the Turks and the Jews. And I perceive that the unfortunate High Commissioner has often found himself in circumstances where our authorities have sought unjustly to throw the blame on the Turks or Jews and must have risen up against this tendency.

But that is not all. I can see and I realize from far off that there are men in Athens who claim that this difficult task should have been entrusted to them. These men – of whom the President of the Chamber is probably one – exploit all the difficulties of Stergiadis's position and seek to create a current of public opinion against him in Athens, in order to bring about his replacement. When I see such examples of petty mindedness, at a time when our position in Smyrna is becoming politically more dangerous every day, not because of Stergiadis's incapacity but because of the excesses of our army and the ruined brains of the rest of his colleagues, who provide ammunition for our innumerable enemies there of various nations, then I almost despair and I begin to wonder whether those who mock our Asia Minor policy may not be right, whether our stature may not be too small for so colossal a task.

The unfortunate Stergiadis saw and felt from far off, as I saw from close quarters, that a storm was about to break over our heads. Only you in Athens seem to have seen nothing – and the military men in Smyrna even less. The storm broke today, when I was called before the Supreme Council, to hear the news that the Great Powers have decided to send a *Commissaire* to Smyrna, to conduct an enquiry into the alleged excesses of the Greek army.* At the same time I was told that General Milne is being sent there, and will have the right to give orders to the Greek army.... The military occupation which was initially conceived as *purely Greek* now loses that character and becomes substantially interallied.... I tell you that if we do not show wisdom and if in particular our military men in Smyrna do not pull themselves together from their intoxication and do not prevent any new excess, and punish with the necessary

---

* These events are described below, ch. 6.

166243

severity all those that have occurred, we shall end by being driven out of Smyrna, humiliated and degraded. And the purely Greek occupation of Smyrna decided by the Powers only about sixty days ago, and rightly considered then as the beginning of a new era of Greek greatness, will prove to have been but a transitory moment of brilliance, which merely illuminated the wretchedness of Greece.[28]

Venizelos ended by asking Diomedis to visit Smyrna and 'ring the warning bell' to Paraskevopoulos. He had already sent his personal secretary K. Markantonakis on a similar mission, with instructions to speak in the strongest terms to the leaders of the Greek community in Smyrna.

This passionate and uncompromising letter reveals the strain Venizelos felt from the continual pressure to justify the Greek army in the face of allied criticisms. But although it was probably true that envious and ambitious colleagues were out to undermine Stergiadis's position, so far as the accusations related to his manners and temper rather than his policy they were justified. To Venizelos, who did not have to work with or under Stergiadis, it was the policy and not the manners which mattered; hence his total support and confidence in Stergiadis. His instinct that no one else could be relied on to carry through unflinchingly and if necessary ruthlessly the policy of firmness with the Greeks, and fairness to the Muslims, was probably correct. The qualities for which he had selected Stergiadis could be matched by none of his colleagues. If a price had to be paid for these qualities in the dissatisfaction of the Smyrniot Greek community, the price was in Venizelos's view worth paying.

Stergiadis stayed. His achievements in the early months were substantial. One of the first tasks of the High Commission was to assist the resettlement of the thousands of Greeks who had been forced to leave their homes in the persecutions of 1914–16 and take refuge in Greece. More than 100,000 were settled, and given the opportunity to make good by generous credit and the distribution of farm implements, as well as advice in agricultural methods. An experimental farm was set up for research and practice in mechanized methods. Toynbee, who visited the farm and spoke with its director, was impressed. The man had

found the house dilapidated, the cattle-sheds choked with dung, the currant bushes suffocated with undergrowth and unpruned, the fig trees left to degenerate. He brought with him two old tractors. ... He reckons that, with tractors, one man can perform all the agricultural operations for ten hectares in the year.... In the director's mind (and in the mind of Mr Sterghiadhis who appointed him) the real importance of Tepé Keui is educational. By this example, the peasantry – Turks and Greeks alike – are to learn to exploit the agricultural riches of the Smyrna Zone. But the experiment at Tepé Keui is of more than local significance. For all Anatolia it may mark the turn of the tide.[29]

In the field of public health, the Greeks established a microbiological laboratory and a Pasteur Institute which waged vigorous war on malaria, syphilis, rabies, smallpox and other diseases which ravaged Anatolia. The Department of Health was the first department of the new university to come into operation.[30] The High Commission supervised the distribution of medical and economic relief to both Christian and Muslim destitute. For the first time, the municipal administration of Smyrna was effectively organized.

These and other works were Stergiadis's contribution to Greece's 'civilizing mission'. But the factors working against such an ideal were too great to permit more than the semblance of order and progress. The repatriation of Greek refugees and the harsh measures of the Greek army in the early period of the occupation caused great numbers of Muslims to leave the Greek zone, swelling the Turkish refugee population.[31] Numerous small injustices inflicted on the Turks by the lower ranks of the administration and by the indigenous Greeks helped to keep Muslim hostility alive, if temporarily suppressed. In one observer's view, the Greek administrative operations 'reveal a deficit when one strikes a balance'.[32] But no balance can be struck in situations of this kind. The achievements of the administration were nullified by the intractability of the situation, in which Greeks undertook to rule over Turks in a climate of suspicion and rampant nationalism on both sides.

6 | Turkey Alive

Nevertheless the whole attitude of the Peace
Conference towards Turkey was so harsh that
Right had now changed sides. Justice, that eternal
fugitive from the councils of the conquerors, had
gone over to the opposite camp. . . . In the tapestried
and gilded chambers of Paris were assembled the
law-givers of the world. In Constantinople, under
the guns of the Allied Fleets there functioned a
puppet Government of Turkey. But among the
stern hills and valleys of 'the Turkish Homelands'
in Anatolia, there dwelt that company of poor men
. . . who would not see it settled so; and at their
bivouac fires at this moment sate in the rags of a
refugee the august Spirit of Fair Play.

Winston Churchill, *The World Crisis: The
Aftermath*, p. 368

While Stergiadis grappled with the problems of establishing
Greek government over a multiracial society, Venizelos was hard
put to it to defend by diplomacy the position which the Greek
army had extended and consolidated by force of arms. Though
often downcast by the burden laid on him by his colleagues and
his army, he was forced to be confident before the Allies, who
might otherwise be tempted to revoke Greece's 'provisional' mandate. Venizelos was thus led to depreciate the Turks' will to
resist and overestimate Greece's capacity to 'go it alone' in Asia
Minor. In this way he encouraged the Allies to leave Greece to
her own resources and ignore the reports of their diplomatic and
military advisers that the Greek occupation was ruining the prospects of a stable Turkish peace settlement.

For the Turks were no longer a submissive enemy on whom
the Allies could impose their will. The flame of nationalism,
briefly damped down by catastrophic defeat, flared again in the
summer of 1919. The Turks had resigned themselves to accept a
period of stringent allied controls and the loss of the non-
Turkish portions of their empire. They were not prepared to
tolerate the loss of parts of the Anatolian heartlands, still less
invasion by their secular enemies.

And they had found a new leader. Mustapha Kemal was now thirty-eight – an experienced, war-hardened officer of the regular army, a stern, controlled figure with fair hair and chilling blue eyes. Born in Salonika, he had passed through the Ottoman War College and joined in the underground subversive politics which preceded the Young Turk revolution in 1908. He won a reputation as a tough fighting soldier commanding a division at Gallipoli, and served later on the Russian front and in Syria. After the war Kemal joined the mass of disillusioned and demoralized officers in Constantinople who were forced to stand by and watch while the allies inflicted on Turkey the humiliation of disarmament and occupation. Suspect in the eyes of Damad Ferid's pro-allied Government, deprived of troops, Kemal, like many others, seemed to have run out of luck.

Then came a stroke of fortune. The Government offered him the post of Inspector in the Eastern Provinces, perhaps on the grounds that even if he failed in his mandate of keeping law and order and disbanding unofficial armies, he would at least be well out of the way. For Kemal it was a chance to get out into the country and rally support for a nationalist movement of resistance to a humiliating imposed peace. Since late in 1918 local Nationalist groups for the defence of Turkish rights had sprung up throughout Anatolia and in eastern Thrace. The kindling wood was there. It needed the spark of leadership.

Mustapha Kemal left Constantinople on his mission at the same time almost to the day as the Greeks landed in Smyrna.

On 19 May he landed at Samsun on the Black Sea and set himself to organize the National movement to defend Turkish rights and territory against foreign intrusion. From this moment there were two centres of power in Turkey, that of the Sultan's Government in Constantinople under the guns and control of the Allies, and the shifting centre of the Nationalist movement in the interior.* As the first waned so the second waxed in confidence and strength.

The victory of the Nationalists over the Sultan's Government was not assured from the start; indeed the Kemalists passed through a number of desperate crises. Nevertheless the existence of a growing Nationalist movement was from the early summer of 1919 a fact to be reckoned with by the peacemakers. The

* The centre shifted from Erzurum (Nationalist Congress, July/Aug. 1919) and Sivas (Nationalist Congress, Sept. 1919) to Angora (Dec. 1919).

British in Whitehall – not least Lord Curzon – tended to mis-interpret Turkish nationalism as 'Kemalism', hoping that re-sistance to the allies would disappear once the movement were crushed by the Constantinople Government or the Greeks. The Italians quickly realized that Kemal was a dynamic new factor, and took steps to come to unwritten terms with the Nationalists, hoping to secure the economic concessions they coveted in Ana-tolia without having to fight for them. The French, deeply sus-picious of British activities in the Levant, inclined more to the Italian view than the British. But there was a complication in that France wanted a part of what Kemal's Nationalists pro-claimed to be sacred and inalienable Turkish soil – Cilicia in the south east corner of Anatolia. After the armistice Cilicia with Syria fell under the authority of Allenby and was occupied by British troops. By an agreement between Lloyd George and Clemenceau of September 1919, the French replaced the British. General Gouraud became French High Commissioner for Syria and Cilicia. Towards the end of 1919, Kemal began to put pres-sure on the French occupying forces, and in January 1920 launched a full-scale Nationalist attack on Marash. So long as France took seriously her colonial mission in Cilicia there could be no terms with Turkish nationalism.

This growing Turkish intransigence first posed a direct chal-lenge to the allies over the implementation of the armistice. In the eastern vilayets, for instance, Colonel 'Toby' Rawlinson's experiences illustrated the problems faced by the allied control officers charged with supervising the demobilization and dis-armament of the Turkish troops. Furnished with an impressive sheaf of documents, including the Sultan's firman authorizing him to visit the eastern army headquarters, Rawlinson had pro-ceeded from Trebizond up country along rugged roads to Erzu-rum, arriving at the end of April 1919. The town stands in the shelter of mountains at a height of almost 7,000 feet and in May is all mud from the melting snows:

The winds there blow with terrific force, and the piercing cold defies all furs. . . . No tree or shrub of any sort can be found within over 50 miles, either to afford fuel when cut or shelter of any kind, and the words 'dismal', 'dreary', 'desolate', and 'damnable', suggest themselves irresistibly as a concise description of the whole locality. Our work in this delectable retreat was important, as on its result depended the estimate to be formed of the future intentions of the

Turks. Though every facility was afforded to me in my inspections, I early understood and reported that no real progress towards disarmament was being made, or was, indeed, intended.[1]

Rawlinson's instructions were to render the Turkish artillery unserviceable, with a few exceptions, and correspondingly to reduce the quantities of machine guns, small arms and ammunition. Of 100,000 or more rifles, only about 15,000 (3,300 per division) were to be left to the Turks. Merely to locate the arms was a problem. The discovery of a cache of over forty unreported modern guns near Trebizond was encouraging, but confirmed the suspected inaccuracy of the Turkish returns. With the aid of his small party of men, and a bearhound called George – 'of gigantic size and the greatest possible enterprise' – whom Rawlinson had picked up in Georgia, he began the impossible task of collecting and classifying the breech-blocks and breech-bolts in the hope eventually of evacuating them along the largely destroyed Decauville railway line which led out of Turkey over the eastern frontier.

Guns, breech-blocks and rifle-bolts were collected and packed, some sent down to Trebizond by camel, others loaded into the still immobile trains while repairs were made to the railway. The work seemed to be proceeding at good speed. But as time passed Rawlinson noticed that a suspiciously large number of 'accidents' were occuring on the railway. He decided that the Turks had no intention of finally surrendering the bulk of their armaments, but wished to postpone a crisis with the allies as long as possible.

Meanwhile Mustapha Kemal had arrived in Erzurum and was organizing a Nationalist Congress there, having refused the Sultan's orders to return to Constantinople and therefore been deprived of his military rank. Like Kiazim Karabekir, the commander of the local Turkish IXth Army in the East, he impressed Rawlinson.

Matters came to the crisis in late July. The railway was almost repaired. Rawlinson's collection of arms had been taken by rail to a point near the Turkish-Armenian frontier where the line was blocked by a rock fall. Trains were already waiting on the Armenian side of the frontier. All that remained was to carry the arms across the final stretch of the journey where the line was blocked. Rawlinson telegraphed Kiazim Karabekir to request his cooperation in the final transfer of the arms out of

Turkey. Kiazim politely refused. Against the background of Kemal's Erzurum Congress, which was in progress and at which the Nationalists were defining their revolutionary identity and their territorial claims, this refusal was not surprising. Rawlinson immediately told him that this action, if persisted in, must bring the armistice to an end. But this was bluff. The arms were lost to the allies, but the armistice remained in being, ignored by the Turkish Nationalists. After further hair-raising adventures and an interview with Mustapha Kemal at the close of the Erzurum Congress, at which he was given the news of the adoption of the Turkish 'National Pact', Rawlinson returned to Constantinople and London to report.

It took some time for the reports of control officers such as Rawlinson to reach London. Nevertheless, from the early summer of 1919 onwards British representatives on the spot in Asia Minor and Constantinople were impressing on the British Government, with gradually increasing urgency and force, the dangers of anarchy and revolution in Anatolia, the threat of an anti-Entente Nationalist revival feeding on the Greek invasion for its moral strength, and the importance of an early peace settlement. On 23 June Admiral Calthorpe made what seems to be the first reference to Mustapha Kemal Pasha's mission to the eastern vilayets and his becoming a 'centre for National and anti-foreign feeling'.[2] Soon after, his deputy Admiral Webb wrote describing the dangerous increase of friction between Greeks and Turks:

It has now become most serious, and of course it all dates back to the time of the occupation of Smyrna by the Greek troops.... Up to the time of the Smyrna landing we were getting on quite well. The Turk was, of course, somewhat troublesome, but we were gradually getting the bad Valis, Mutessarifs, &c, removed, and I think we could have got along very well without any big trouble until the peace.... But now things are quite changed. Greeks and Turks are killing one another wholesale in the Aydin Vilayet. Mustapha Kemal is busy round Samsoun, and so far refuses to come to heel. Raouf Bey and one or two others are getting very busy down Panderma way, and there are symptoms which seem to point to the Ministry of War here at Constantinople being the organizing centre of the disturbances.[3]

On 27 July Calthorpe, resuming for Lord Curzon the course of events since the armistice in similar terms, warned him that Kemalism posed the danger of 'the establishment of an independent, and probably intensely fanatical and anti-European Government in Asia Minor rejecting authority of Constantinople and sovereignty of Sultan'.[4]

Thus according to the reports arriving in Whitehall from Turkey, up till May 1919 all had been well in Anatolia. 'The situation was not only generally satisfactory but was, moreover, steadily improving.'[5] The terms of the armistice were generally accepted by the Turks. The allied control officers were obeyed, or at any rate not molested. 'The authority of the central government was, in fact, fairly well established.'[6] The British attributed this phase of Turkish docility, correctly, to the numbness of defeat, and incorrectly to Turkish willingness to accept the dictates of the British themselves.

Then came the Smyrna landing, and following this a period of depression in which the Turks awaited some definite decision of the Allies to put an end to the uncertainty of the armistice. Nothing came out of Paris, and in the early summer the Nationalist movement really began to take root, led by nationalist officers and groups who were able to exploit the Greek occupation in order to work up a movement of resistance to Greek rule and allied dictation. 'The Greek occupation of Smyrna,' wrote the British High Commissioner, 'stimulated a Turkish patriotism probably more real than any which the war was able to evoke.'[7]

The recommendations of the British on the spot followed from this analysis. First, a quick peace settlement. 'Each day's delay is making the ultimate settlement more difficult.'[8] The quicker the peace, the more easily the Turks would accept severe terms. Secondly, the withdrawal of the Greeks so that no part of Anatolia was left under Greek control. As Webb reported, peace terms involving a Greek zone in Asia Minor or the division of Anatolia into spheres under foreign administration would lead to the repudiation by the provinces of the Constantinople Government's authority. The execution of any peace terms would then entail 'the undertaking of military measures on a very considerable scale' by the allies.[9] No one could say the British Government were not fairly warned, both of the growth of power of Kemal's movement and of the consequences of allowing the Greek occupation to determine the shape of the 'peace'. But now and for a long time to come the lessons of Kemal's success were too difficult for most of the allied statesmen to learn. They continued to conceive of Turkey, like Germany, as a defeated enemy subject to their unfettered will.

Meanwhile Venizelos was having trouble with his allies. Friction between the Greeks and Italians on the ground in Asia Minor spilled over into the Conference in Paris. The Italians complained that the Greeks had violated the limits to the Greek occupation laid down by the Council of Four,[10] and that Greek artillery had fired on their positions in the Meander valley.

Venizelos in turn complained that the Italians in Asia Minor were encouraging the Turks in their resistance to the Greek occupation. With the connivance of the Italian military authorities, the Turks were using the Italian zone as a base for aggressive sorties into the Greek zone, confident that they could retire south of the Meander unmolested. To reinforce his point that the Turks should be stamped on quickly, Venizelos added some alarming information about the Turkish military resurgence, already so far advanced that there was a risk of war flaring up again through the whole East and making a settlement of eastern affairs impossible. He wrote of 'nearly 60,000 men' already concentrated near Konya, and alleged that an army of 300,000 would probably soon be on a war footing.[11] These claims were wildly exaggerated.

Summoned before the Council on 16 July, Venizelos asked for either a definite line limiting the Greek occupation, or liberty of action for the Greek troops.[12] He insisted that if there were real collaboration between the Greeks and the Italians, and the Turks saw that this was so, they would give no more trouble. Venizelos suggested that small detachments of allied troops should be placed between the Greek and Turkish advance posts. 'The moral effect of this would be great and would probably render any conflict unlikely.' This was a tacit admission of the absurdity of the pretext put forward by the Supreme Council, that the Greek landing in Smyrna was a peace-keeping operation; for Venizelos was now admitting that a company of allied troops could do the job of several Greek divisions. The Council rejected the suggestion that they should provide troops. But it was agreed that Venizelos and Tittoni, the Italian foreign minister, should agree together on the limits of the Greek and Italian zones in the south.

It took only a fortnight for Venizelos and Tittoni to resolve their problems on a much wider scale. At the end of July they reached a comprehensive understanding on the conflicting Greek and Italian territorial claims.[13] Italy undertook to support Greek claims in Thrace and Northern Epirus, and to cede the Aegean islands under her occupation, with the exception of Rhodes. Under a separate understanding of the same date it was agreed that Rhodes would have self-determination (i.e. could opt for *enosis*) on the day that Great Britain decided to cede Cyprus to Greece. Greece undertook to support an Italian mandate over Albania, and, provided her claims in Thrace and Epirus were satisfied, to concede to Italy a part of her Asia Minor claim including the Meander valley. This was a satisfactory arrangement for Greece, but a fragile one.

But it was not only with the Italians that Venizelos had to contend. The first signs of French doubts over the wisdom of the Greek occupation soon appeared. It was Clemenceau, recognizing the responsibility of the Supreme Council for the atrocities of 15 May who proposed the dispatch of an Interallied Commission of Enquiry to Smyrna.[14] It was Clemenceau again who in early August put Venizelos through a searching cross examination on Greece's military capacity and made it brusquely clear that the Greeks were on their own in Asia Minor. France had no intention of embarking on a new Balkan campaign.[15]

Venizelos was optimistic. 'He fully understood that the Great Powers could not undertake to enforce the Peace for him.' Clemenceau had asked whether Greece could if necessary undertake simultaneous defensive action in Asia Minor and Thrace. Venizelos admitted that this was impossible, but claimed that it would not be required of her. He concluded with a curious historical argument:

It had often been alleged that the shape of Greece towards the east was such as to render her eastern frontier untenable.

He showed by the help of an atlas the persistence throughout the centuries of a territorial distribution of the Hellenic world very similar to the territorial claims of the Greek Delegation.

The Council was doubtless enlightened. But the argument perverted the realities of the postwar settlement. In the multi-religious Ottoman Empire before the establishment of the Greek kingdom, there was no reason why Orthodox Greeks should not continue to inhabit the territories they had inhabited for centuries. Their presence in western Asia Minor was no support for the proposition that *now*, when the Kemalists were intent on ejecting the Greek army of occupation, the historic frontier of Hellenism (which was in any case a shifting one) was militarily defensible. But Venizelos did not at this time consider the question of a satisfactory frontier for the Greek zone in Asia Minor with the seriousness it deserved. He put his faith in the solution of intermigration of those Greeks and Turks who found themselves outside the limits of the Greek and Turkish portions of Anatolia respectively. Whether by this means the Smyrna zone could be made solidly Greek and defensible before the paper of the peace settlement was consumed in the fires of Turkish nationalism was a gamble on which Venizelos staked his reputation and the lives and happiness of Greek soldiers and the Orthodox of Asia Minor.

Greece's difficulties were brought to a head by two separate investigations carried out during the summer by the Interallied Commission of Enquiry and by General Milne, commander of the British forces in Turkey. The Milne enquiry arose from the Supreme Council's attempt to reduce friction between Greeks and Italians in the Meander valley by defining the limits of their respective zones of operations. Milne sent officers to confer with the Greek and Italian generals on the spot. The investigation inevitably touched on the wider issue of the strategic position of the Greeks. Milne's final report made clear that a state of active warfare existed between the Turkish and Greek forces:

The greater portion of the Turkish forces is composed of organized bands of brigands, reinforced by armed peasants driven from the villages by the Greeks and determined to prevent further advance of the Greeks. These armed forces which are secretly receiving reinforcements from the regular units are in considerable strength....

The Turkish Government has no control over these forces, which are pledged to drive the Greeks out of Asia, and hence cannot insist on their withdrawal from any stipulated line....

The Greek forces having advanced in many places to a purely Turkish area and an extremely difficult country, are from a tactical point of view badly placed but ... any further advance to gain better positions will be resisted to the utmost and can succeed only after severe fighting.[16]

Milne recommended that the Greeks should remain in

their present positions, with only minor rectifications to improve their tactical position. Reading between the lines of his report, one can see that he regarded the Greek occupation as a regrettable and dangerous mistake. 'Guerrilla warfare', he wrote, 'will continue so long as Greek troops remain in Sanjak, and any further advance will tend to create greater difficulties.'[17] The Supreme Council, however, when it considered the report on 7 October, ignored these warning implications, and adopted the 'Milne Line' defining the entire Greek zone.

If, as General Milne wrote, the Greeks and the Turks were in a state of active warfare, the Supreme Council's injunction on the Greeks not to penetrate beyond an arbitrary line was hard on the Greeks, who were being kept on a maddeningly tight leash. But the Supreme Council, fearing to unleash a force which might prove uncontrollable, was determined to place limits on the Greek occupation. All that was conceded to the Greeks was the right to counterattack in defending themselves against Turkish attacks, and pursue the enemy to a distance of three kilometres beyond the Milne Line, provided they returned afterwards to their original positions.[18] This concession could not solve the problem of the Turkish irregulars.

The Interallied Commission of Enquiry into the events of May was still more important to the Greeks than the Milne inquiry. Its subject matter was politically highly charged; an unfavourable report by the Commission could prejudice the Greek claim to Smyrna in the final Turkish peace treaty.

The Commission, consisting of Admiral Bristol for the United States, General Bunoust for France, General Hare for England, General Dall'olio for Italy, and Colonel Mazarakis as the Greek non-voting observer, began its work in August.* It held forty-six meetings, hearing 175 witnesses from all nationalities, and visiting Smyrna, Aydin, Nazilli, Odemish, Menemen, Manisa, Ayvali, and Girova in the Italian zone. Its investigations had ranged widely, and in the frequent cases where Greeks and Turks

---

* Mazarakis, who was appointed on Venizelos's insistence, was excluded from the Commission's meetings on the grounds that Turkish witnesses might be intimidated by his presence. Venizelos twice complained to the Supreme Council over these procedures. Mazarakis disagreed with the Commission's findings and submitted a minority report. *D.B.F.P.*, i, 165, 446, 837; Mazarakis, *Memoirs*, pp. 263–5.

gave contradictory testimony, it had tried to ensure reliability by hearing French, English and Italian witnesses. This was the only possible procedure. But, as Venizelos later pointed out, it did not guarantee the truth; for 'many Europeans in Smyrna preferred the continuance of the Turkish regime which, with respect to strangers, was a regime of special privileges, rather than the establishment of the Greek regime, which was a regime of equality'.[19] This was especially true of the Italians.

The Commission submitted its report in October. It was highly unfavourable to the Greeks.[20] As well as finding the Greeks responsible for the incidents which followed the landing, and the disorder and bloodshed in the interior during the Greek advance, the Commissioners questioned the whole basis of the Greek occupation, which they found to have 'assumed all the forms of an annexation'.[21] Their main conclusions were as follows:

(a) That if the military occupation of the country is to have as its sole purpose the maintenance of security and public welfare, this occupation should not be intrusted to Greek troops, but to Allied troops, under the authority of the Supreme Allied Commander in Asia Minor.

(b) That the occupation by the Greeks alone should not be maintained unless the Peace Conference is resolved to announce the complete and definite annexation of the country to Greece. . . .

(c) That the pure and simple annexation as above stated would be contrary to the principle proclaiming the respect for nationalities, because in the occupied regions, outside of the cities of Smyrna and Aivali, the predominance of the Turkish element over the Greek is incontestable.

It is the duty of the Commission to observe the fact that the Turkish national sentiment, which has already manifested its resistance, will never accept this annexation. It will submit only to force, that is to say, before a military expedition which Greece alone could not carry out with any chance of success.[22]

The Commission therefore proposed that as soon as possible all or part of the Greek troops should be replaced by allied troops much fewer in number. When this had been done, the Turkish gendarmerie should be reorganized under the direction of allied officers, so as to assure order throughout the region when allied troops were finally withdrawn.

What the Commission recommended (like the British High Commission in Constantinople) was nothing less than the termination of the Greek occupation, and the rejection of Greek claims in Asia Minor. This was perhaps the only occasion after the landing on which the Greeks might have been extracted from Asia Minor; for this report offered the Allies a pretext for kicking them out of Asia Minor without too much loss of face. And when the Council considered the report on 8 November,[23] Clemenceau for the first time questioned the desirability of the Greek presence in Asia Minor. Noting the Commission's opinion that the Greeks would not be able to maintain themselves in Smyrna of their own efforts, he asked Venizelos whether Greece could, without the support of the Allies, make the necessary military and financial efforts until Turkey was completely pacified. Venizelos's reply was that, with an army of twelve divisions, Greece had nothing to fear from Kemal's men, who did not exceed 70,000. The confidence was by now a little forced; Venizelos already recognized, and had told Lloyd George, how serious the situation was.* But Clemenceau took the matter no further; and Eyre Crowe supported the Greek case by arguing that the Commission had exceeded its instructions in questioning the whole basis of the Greek occupation.

The Commission of Enquiry directly, and Milne by implication, had questioned the wisdom of the allowing the Greeks to remain in Smyrna. Clemenceau also now regretted the decision to send the Greeks to Smyrna, and took the opportunity of his note to Venizelos containing the Council's views on the Commission's report to re-emphasize the provisional nature of the occupation.[24]

Venizelos reacted sharply. Anxious to chivvy the Supreme Council into making a rapid peace with Turkey, he argued in his reply that the disorder and incidents on the borders of the Greek zone were not due to the Greek occupation at all, but to uncertainty as to the final decisions of the Peace Conference. Good order would be assured 'as soon as the Turks, deprived of the hope of finding support in instigating trouble, will really become conscious of their defeat'.[25] This was an instance of Venizelos's refusal publicly to recognize the nature of Turkish resistance to the Greek occupation. But he went on to expose with a just and merciless clarity the difficulty in which the Supreme Council had landed itself:

* See below, p. 115.

The Supreme Council notices that the occupation of Smyrna was only decided for political reasons, and constitutes no new right in the future. May I point out that, whatever be the reasons for the decision to send Greek troops to Smyrna, the Supreme Council could not be mistaken as to the interpretation given it, with good reasons, by the Greek Government and people. The Greek claims on Smyrna and the neighbouring region were not only well known, but they had been officially formulated to the Conference, defended at length before the Supreme Council, and frankly approved by the Committee on Greek Territorial Claims.* In occupying Smyrna, Greece knew that [?if] she was not yet legally, she was at least morally, entitled to it. She did not simply send her troops as executive instruments to a foreign country, as she had previously done in Russia, but as organs most interested in the success of an international mandate, with a view to maintaining order in an essentially great country. Therefore, although the occupation of Smyrna did not constitute, from a strictly juridical point of view, a new right to the benefit of Greece, in fact, it has created a new situation which should not be disregarded. It does not extend the rights which Greece previously had in Smyrna, and already recognized by the Committee on Greek Affairs, but at least it corroborates them and strengthens the legitimate confidence of the Greek nation in the final decision of the Peace Conference.[26]

The dispute, crucial to Greek prospects in Asia Minor, remained unsettled. Clemenceau held to his point of view.[27] Venizelos invoked British support. Writing to Crowe, he argued that the decision to send the Greeks into Smyrna was 'the first step towards giving Greece part of western Asia Minor'.[28] He was of course right. But so was Clemenceau. The explanation was simple. Lloyd George said one thing to Venizelos, and Clemenceau another to the Italians. Crowe wrote to Curzon and endorsed Venizelos's version of events.[29] Greece still had one ally morally at least beside her.

By the autumn of 1919, the administrative and military base of the Greek occupation was firmly laid. Venizelos had ridden the storm raised by the Commission of Enquiry, whose report remained secret. By the Venizelos-Tittoni Agreement of July 1919 he had secured a provisional and fragile understanding with Italy. But the questions of Thrace and northern Epirus were unresolved, and Greece's difficulties in Asia Minor were aggra-

* Only by the British and French; see above, ch. iv.

King Constantine with his Staff during the Second Balkan War. Sitting at the table, *left to right*, Xenophon Stratigos, Constantine, Victor Dousmanis and Metaxas. Standing, *left to right*, the king's brothers Nicholas (father of Princess Marina, the late Duchess of Kent); Andrew (father of Prince Philip, Duke of Edinburgh); Christopher; and the king's second son Alexander.

5 General Paraskevopoulos

6 King Alexander at the wheel of his Packard in 1919, with Fritz; the dog was involv
the next year in the King's fatal encounter with a monkey.

7 Dimitrios Gounaris

8 Colonel Stylianos Gonatas

vated by the Allies' delay in tackling the Turkish treaty. Delay increased the burden of mobilization on Greece, and undermined the position of the Liberal Party in Greece.

These problems now began to weigh on Venizelos,[30] who unburdened himself to Lloyd George in a long letter on 27 October.[31] 'A whole year has now elasped since the signature of the Armistice with Turkey', he wrote; and even now there was no prospect of a speedy Peace Treaty, because of the delay caused by the United States in deciding whether or not to accept mandates in Turkey. This delay created serious dangers. Within four or five months, if not prevented, Nationalist Turkey could dispose of a worthwhile army. The allies should therefore wait no longer, but make peace with Turkey. As to the nature of the settlement, Venizelos now had no objections to an Italian (or French) mandate over southern Anatolia; indeed he recommended it as a means of protecting the Christian populations. Otherwise, as earlier, he proposed the ejection of the Turks from Constantinople and the Straits; an independent Armenia, including the Pontus, under the mandate of one of the Powers; and a voluntary exchange of populations between the small surviving Turkey and the new Greek and Armenian areas in Anatolia.*

Venizelos warned Lloyd George that anything less severe than the settlement he proposed would land the Conference with the moral responsibility for the extermination of millions of Christians in Turkey; the Young Turks would resume their destructive work, war between Greece and Turkey would inevitably follow, and the situation thus created would be a permanent danger to the liberated Arab areas such as Mesopotamia.

Finally, he gave two pressing reasons for hastening the Turkish settlement. The first was the presence at the head of the French Government of Clemenceau, who was alone capable of resisting

---

* Although Venizelos wrote that such an exchange would be voluntary there is little doubt that he was determined that nothing should prevent it. In conversation with Paraskevopoulos and Stergiadis in 1920 he toyed with another idea: 'For further security, Venizelos thought to set up on the limits of the Greek state, in the prosperous areas of the interior of Asia Minor, an ethnological wall formed out of the most healthy and the most profoundly Greek representatives of the race. The Acarnanians, the Aetolians and Arcadians, tortured by the struggle to win a livelihood for themselves and their families in their infertile homelands, would find in these prosperous areas land which would be given to them free, and every means necessary for cultivation'; Paraskevopoulos, *Memoirs*, p. 362.

the systematic efforts of financial circles in France to engineer a settlement favourable to Turkey.* The second was the existence of a Greek army of twelve divisions on a war footing, which could be used to impose the decisions of the Peace Conference on Turkey. If the Turkish settlement were further postponed, Venizelos would be forced after the signature of the Bulgarian Treaty † to demobilize half of this army so as to relieve the financial burden on Greece. The new military balance thus created in the east would allow the Turks effectively to resist the eventual decisions of the Conference.

The alarmist language of this letter shows that despite the confidence he was obliged to show in public, Venizelos now appreciated the menace of the Turkish Nationalists to Greece's position in Asia Minor. A creature of strong emotions, sunk occasionally in the darkest depression, buoyed up more often by an elated optimism, he seems at this time to have come close to despair. The day after he had written this letter, Sir Henry Wilson tackled him:

I told him straight out that he had ruined his country and himself by going to Smyrna; and the poor man agreed, but said the reason was because Paris had not finished off the Turk and had made peace with him. . . . Venizelos was very bitter against the Turk, and said the whole twelve divisions were available if we would finish the Turk off. He realizes that he is in a hopeless position, and is now trying to sell his twelve divisions. He begged me to tell Lloyd George that both he [Venizelos] and Greece were *done*. I said I would. The old boy is *done*.[32]

The first plank in Venizelos's policy was cooperation with Britain and her allies. The Greek army could not therefore be launched into the interior to seek out and destroy the Kemalist forces without allied permission. It was in any case too small and deficient in means of transport and shipping to deal with the Kemalists on three fronts, in Western Asia Minor, Armenia and

* Venizelos returned to this point the following March, claiming that Millerand, the new President of the Council, was subject to the influence of these financial circles; Frangulis, *La Grèce, son Statut* etc., ii, p. 140.

† Treaty of Neuilly, signed 27 Nov. 1919, which fixed Bulgaria's southern frontier, excluding her from the Aegean but providing for an economic outlet to the sea. Western Thrace was conceded to the allies to dispose of, and occupied by the Greeks (replacing allied troops) in May 1920.

Cicilia. Venizelos had originally hoped that the presence of allied garrisons and the effective disarmament of the Turkish army would induce the Turks to offer no resistance. This hope had now vanished. Therefore they must be 'finished off'. This meant determination on the part of the allies to enforce severe peace terms. It would probably have demanded tough simultaneous campaigns at three points – determined resistance to the Kemalists by the French in Cilicia, an advance by the Greeks from the Smyrna zone, and the launching of a powerful allied expedition to defend the new Armenia. The Allies had neither the will nor the desire to approve such energetic measures. But nothing less would reduce the Kemalists to impotence.

The six Greek divisions in the Smyrna zone, if given the word to advance, could clear the ground in front of the Greek lines and win a respite of months or years for Greece. But the Greeks alone could not destroy the Nationalists' will to resist, nor occupy all Anatolia. The problem could therefore not be solved by Greece alone. For the first time, in October 1919, Venizelos began to appreciate these hard truths. The logic of events was leading him towards the attempt to cajole the Allies into that 'serious effort with a view to the dissolution of the Ottoman Empire' which his opponents had regarded in 1915 as an essential condition for Greek participation in the war.

For Greece there could now be no going back. The die was cast when Greek troops landed in Smyrna on 15 May. Venizelos's internal position in Greece depended on a successful outcome to the Asia Minor venture. It was not, of course, that he went into Asia Minor for narrow political reasons; but once committed he could not withdraw without destroying his credit at home. In any case, it was not in his nature to consider withdrawal from an enterprise which had been his main political motive since 1915, involving his whole heart and mind. The tension between an irrevocable commitment and a growing realization of its difficulties and dangers accounts for the inconsistencies in Venizelos's position, the seesaw between optimism and public confidence* on the one hand, pessimism and appeals to Lloyd George on the other.

It was to be ten months yet before Venizelos got his peace treaty. Negotiations dragged on over the winter of 1919–20 and

* See above, p. 113 for his posture ten days later before the Supreme Council.

the following spring. In the United States President Wilson had fallen victim to a paralysing stroke and no longer exercised any influence over events. It was by now clear that the United States in its new mood of isolation would not undertake any major responsibility in Turkey; yet this was not yet openly admitted, and the Americans' hesitation was a convenient excuse as well as a reason for the delay in making a settlement. The intractability of the problems themselves, the differing interests involved, the waste of time and spirit which attended diplomacy by conferences of prime ministers, ensured that the negotiations would be drawn out.

Late in the year 1919 the British and French at last made a serious attempt to get to grips with the problems of the Turkish settlement. Lord Curzon in person presided over a series of businesslike talks at the Foreign Office, at which the basis of a settlement was agreed.[33] The Turks were to be ejected from Europe, and an international state of Constantinople established. The Italians and Greeks were to be persuaded by economic and other concessions to withdraw their troops from Asia Minor, which would be confirmed in Turkish sovereignty.

Left to themselves, no doubt senior officials could now have drafted an adequate treaty without delay. But others must have their say. In the British Cabinet Edwin Montagu, the youngish, intelligent Secretary of State for India, took the strongest line in favour of the Turks. A combative debater, not afraid to encroach on the territory of his colleagues, he argued with force and to Curzon's fury against the ejection of the Turks from Constantinople, provoking Curzon to a reply of extreme length and magisterial style.[34] The arguments on both sides, at this distance in time, have a curiously unreal quality. On the one hand Montagu urged the bad effects on Indian Muslim opinion of the expulsion of the Sultan, and the unrest that would arise to Britain's detriment throughout the East from a sullen and dangerously provoked Islam. Lord Curzon ridiculed the Indian argument. But in turn he advanced the equally ridiculous propositions that if Turkey were not to lose Constantinople it would be held throughout the East as evidence that she had not been beaten in the war, and that decisive action by the Allies at decisive points (such as Constantinople) could cause the Nationalist movement to disappear. Both, in other words, misunderstood the force and the quality of Kemal's Turkish Nationalism, seeing it in outdated terms.[35] But at least Montagu saw that if Britain wanted a lasting settlement with Turkey the loss of Constantinople was not the way to go about achieving it.

The argument was brought to the Cabinet on 6 January, along with the Curzon-Berthelot scheme for a Near East settlement. The future of Constantinople was the sort of tangible and easily comprehensible issue on which all could have views, and which for that reason occupy a disproportionate amount of any committee's time, not excluding the British Cabinet. One man's view could be held to be as good as another's on such weighty political issues as whether the capital of the future Turkish state, assuming the Turks' exclusion from Constantinople, should be Konya or Bursa (there were sound precedents for both); whether the Sultan should be allowed to retain an enclave, an Islamic Vatican, in Constantinople, and the political and spiritual centres of Turkish Muslim feeling be thus separated; or what should be the status of the great mosque of Sancta Sophia, which had been the Christian cathedral of the Orthodox Byzantine Empire before the Turks had come in 1453 – Christian church, Islamic mosque, or a non-denominational museum? Montagu had done his work well. Despite the support of Lloyd George and Balfour for the Curzon scheme, the Cabinet rejected it.

An extraordinary situation was thus brought about. It was the French who had earlier insisted on leaving the Turks their capital city; Clemenceau had put the case at a Conference in Downing Street to Lloyd George, Balfour and Curzon. The French had then accepted Curzon's view in working out the package of proposals for a settlement. And now the British Cabinet had rejected its own Foreign Secretary's proposals. The wheel had come full circle. Lord Curzon complained bitterly to his colleagues that their decision was short sighted and imprudent. But it was clear that Montagu and the War Office between them were a match for Curzon, Lloyd George and Venizelos.

The aged Clemenceau had now fallen, and when the Eastern question was discussed in London on 12 February it was the radical Alexandre Millerand who spoke for France as President of the Council. The decision to allow the Turks to retain Constantinople was confirmed. Apart from this, the talks centred on Armenia, financial control of Turkey, and zones of influence in Anatolia. Throughout the negotiations, Lloyd George sustained the Greek cause against French or Italian pressures. In

December Clemenceau had wanted both Greeks and Italians excluded from Asia Minor.[36] Now Millerand, the new President of the Council, proposed on 14 February that if there was to be a stable peace with Turkey, the Greeks must leave Smyrna.[37] Between them Venizelos and Lloyd George succeeded in over-bearing this French attitude. The Conference decided to assign a Smyrna zone to the Greeks, but to retain nominal Turkish sovereignty over it.[38]

The discussions were interrupted by the sudden news of a serious defeat of General Gouraud's French troops in Cilicia by Turkish Nationalist forces, and of the massacre of some thous-ands of Armenians in the Marash area.[39] The news showed con-clusively that it would be difficult, if not impossible, to impose on the Turks the sort of peace treaty that was under discussion. French pride was touched in the raw, and the British were glad of the opportunity to exact guarantees from Turkey. The Con-ference therefore decided to occupy Constantinople and take over the War Office, as a means of exerting pressure on the official Turkish government. The occupation took place on 16 March.[40] So far from weakening the Kemalist movement, it strengthened it, since Turkish Nationalists in Constantinople fled to join Kemal in the interior.[41]

Venizelos urged the allies to go even further in intimidating the Turks. He asked that the Turkish government be given one week to disband the Kemalist forces (a quite impossible stipula-tion), and that if it failed, the Greek army should advance to search out and destroy them. He did not, of course, contemplate invading Cilicia, but meant simply to disband the Nationalist troops opposite the Greek lines. Despite his assurance that such an advance would not prejudice the territorial decisions of the Conference, his proposal was not accepted.[42]

Writing to Lloyd George later, Curzon complained that in his 'eloquent appeal to the Supreme Council to let his troops go ahead' Venizelos had exaggerated the Turkish threat to the Greek zone, as was proved by intercepted telegrams from Ster-giadis and General Paraskevopoulos.

The events in Marash and Cilicia, and the occupation of Constantinople, at last brought home to the allies what had been impressed on them repeatedly by their expert advisers, especially the High Commissioners in Constantinople, namely, that the Turks would resist the treaty if it provided for a Greek Smyrna and an independent Armenia.[43] It was therefore decided to ask Marshal Foch's Military and Naval Commission at Versailles for advice on the means that would suffice to enforce the treaty on an unwilling Turkey. Foch's report, of 30 March, concluded that not less than twenty-seven divisions would be required, a force that could by no stretch of the imagination be conjured up.

Shortly before the Conference of San Remo, which was to decide the final terms of the Turkish Treaty, Churchill, Wilson and Curzon all made attempts to point out the dangers which the Foch report confirmed. On 19 March Churchill and Wilson tackled Venizelos in London. Churchill told him that England could not help him with troops, either in Thrace or in Asia Minor, but would be prepared to give what help she could in arms and munitions.[44] Wilson was even more direct: 'We made it clear to him that neither in men *nor in money* ... would we help the Greeks, as we already had taken on more than our small army could do. I told him that he was going to ruin his small country.... He said that he did not agree with a word I said.'[45] Wilson told Venizelos that there would be war between Greece and Turkey which might last ten to fifteen years, and cripple Greece. The two men clearly suspected that Venizelos was relying on hopes that in the last resort Britain would help Greece out by intervention. Venizelos was unruffled by these warnings. As well as stating his confidence that Greece could take over Smyrna and Thrace, he made the strange prophesy that 'owing to the breeding qualities of the Greeks his Smyrna population before the end of the century would exceed the total population of the Turkish Empire'. He interpreted the conversation as an encouragement. And with some justification. Churchill had sought the interview on Lloyd George's account, to ask whether, if Turkey refused to accept the treaty, Greece could undertake to enforce it in Thrace and Asia Minor. Thus, while Wilson and Churchill were trying to warn Venizelos, Venizelos assumed that the very posing of this question by Lloyd George implied that he was seeking *reassurance* as to Greece's power and will to enforce the treaty. Venizelos relied, as usual, on Lloyd George's interest and sympathy overcoming the views of his advisers. He wrote: 'There is no need for me to explain that it is a question of Anglo-Greek cooperation to impose the terms of the treaty and that if the Turks refuse to sign it ... the terms as finally imposed will be much more severe than was originally proposed.'[46]

The Advisers in Constantinople, too, did their best to point out the dangers inherent in the drastic peace terms the allies were known to be contemplating. In fact de Robeck could hardly conceal his impatience with the peacemakers. He applied three criteria: that the peace terms should (a) be compatible with the principles for which the allies were supposed to have fought; (b) pave the way for a lasting peace; and (c) be feasible without further bloodshed and sacrifice on the part of the allies. The Allies' peace terms failed on all three counts. They meant putting 'territories overwhelmingly Turkish in population' under the rule of the Turks' secular enemies – 'a flagrant violation of the principle of self-determination, to which I was under the impression that the Supreme Council had given its adherence'. As to (b), the provisional Greek occupation of Smyrna had been the canker in the Near East since May 1919. 'How much more so will definite annexation be the canker,' wrote de Robeck, 'the constant irritant which will perpetuate bloodshed in Asia Minor for years to come.' As to (c), the Supreme Council apparently realized that the terms they proposed would have to be imposed by force:

They are quite right. The terms are such that no Turks ... can very well accept. The Supreme Council, thus, are prepared for a resumption of general warfare; they are prepared to do violence to their own declared and cherished principles; they are prepared to perpetuate bloodshed indefinitely in the Near East; and for what? To maintain M. Venizelos in power in Greece for what cannot in the nature of things be more than a few years at the outside.* I cannot help wondering if the game is worth the candle. I should wonder, even if M. Venizelos were immortal; he is not immortal, but ephemeral, and he is not only ephemeral, but as regards Greece, a phenomenon. By that I mean that he has no successors of his own calibre. In other words, he is not Greece.[47]

De Robeck pointed out that the proposal to dismember the Ottoman provinces of Turkey in the interests of Greece would drive the remaining Turks into the arms of the Bolsheviks – 'men who have instigated the killing, flaying alive, and otherwise torturing of probably hundreds of thousands' of the kith and kin of the British people. This argument could be relied on

* A gross simplification of the Council's motives.

to impress the War Office, and Lord Curzon circulated this eloquent letter to the Cabinet. Finally he himself had a crack at Lloyd George, who was about to leave for San Remo to settle the final peace terms. Writing from his bed of sickness, he warned Lloyd George that to go against the French and the Foch report, the General Staff,[48] and the local experts, required very strong grounds.[49] Curzon described himself as 'an unswerving critic and opponent' of the Turks: 'But I do want to get something like peace in Asia Minor: and with the Greeks in Smyrna and Greek divisions carrying out Venizelos's plan of marching about Asia Minor and fighting the Turks everywhere I know this to be impossible.' Curzon soon rose from his bed and crossed the channel to keep his critical and resentful eye on the Prime Minister.

The terms of the Turkish settlement were settled at San Remo in April.[50] They were drastic in their effects on Turkish sovereignty and unrealistic in their conception of what was within the Allies' capability to enforce. They dismayed not only the Turkish Government, to whom they were presented on 11 May, but also Britain's representatives in Turkey. They ignored the Foch report. But before the treaty embodying them could be signed, the situation in Asia Minor suddenly changed.

The Greek army was champing at the bit. It had now been sitting for a whole year within the restricted Smyrna zone, unable to do more than cross the Milne line for a few kilometres to pursue Turkish irregulars, and then return to quarters. The situation was frustrating and bad for morale.

While the Turkish Nationalists had been flexing their muscles and the Greeks remained immobile, General Milne's British Army of the Black Sea had steadily decreased in strength since the armistice. At the end of 1919 Milne had reported the strength of his troops in Turkey as 4,469 rifles in the Constantinople area, 2,272 along the Anatolian railway from Ismid to Afyon Karahisar, and 657 at the Dardanelles.[51] These were supplemented by six French battalions in Constantinople and Thrace as well as one Division which did not fall under Milne's command. As British advisers were not slow to point out, peace could not be imposed on an unwilling Turkey with forces such as these.

Now, on the night of 14–15 June 1920, the Nationalists for the first time directly challenged the British army. Nationalist troops attacked a British battalion stationed in the Ismid region. For the first time, the allied position in Constantinople and the Straits zone was threatened. A few battalions supported by the guns of the big ships lying in the Bosphorus stood between the Nationalists and the city. None of the Allies wished to re-inforce this exiguous garrison if it could be avoided.

Arriving in London on the 14th, Venizelos was immediately summoned by Lloyd George, who warned him that Greece could expect no help from the Allies in imposing the treaty on the Turks. Italy would be pleased if the treaty were *not* executed. French public opinion would not accept the dispatch of an expeditionary force to Turkey. And Lloyd George himself had difficulties with the Turcophil spirit of Foreign Office and milit-ary circles. He therefore asked Venizelos if Greece could impose the treaty. Venizelos 'replied, without showing any hesitation, that Greece had the necessary force, and, I believed, would have the will to make the necessary effort, in so far as she were co-operating in this with the two Western Powers, or at least with England'.[52] Lloyd George asked Venizelos to see Churchill and try to persuade him of this view. The two prime ministers agreed that the possibilities of Turkish resistance were greatly exag-gerated by the military.

Venizelos hoped for a cooperative venture in Turkey, despite Churchill's, and now Lloyd George's warnings. He was also gambling on the chances of better terms for Greece should the treaty be so severe as to be rejected by Turkey. He saw an en-larged Asia Minor zone and even an independent Pontus-Armenia federation, this last a totally unrealistic hope, as the possible spoils.[53]

Thus it is no exaggeration to say that Venizelos now desired the harshest possible terms for the Turkish treaty in order to justify war with Nationalist Turkey. Greece was already in a state of intermittent warfare with Turkish irregulars. Venizelos had by now realized that there was no prospect of these hostilities ceasing or of the Turks accepting the Greek presence in Asia Minor on the mere signature of a Peace Treaty backed by the moral authority of the allies. He saw only one way out of the impasse – to deal the Turks a crushing blow. It was in Greece's interests to ensure that the treaty was so harsh as to be rejected by Turkey, so that the Greeks might be authorized to impose it while still stronger than the Nationalists and while the war could be justified as an operation undertaken by Venizelos on behalf of the Allies. As 'mandatory' of the Allies, Greece could hope for material and financial support from England, even though her armies would be on their own. If the Allies themselves were drawn into the war, so much the better for Greece.

What had held the Greeks back so far was the reluctance of the Allies to permit an advance which might complicate the peace settlement by stiffening Turkish nationalist resistance and putting up Greece's price in territorial gains.[54] But Lloyd George would willingly have permitted an advance had he been able to justify it on military grounds to the Foreign Office and the Staff. He was now able to do so. The Turkish attack on the Ismid peninsula, tentative though it was, posed a threat to the weak allied contingents in the Straits zone. General Milne telegraphed at once for reinforcements. Sir Henry Wilson, the C.I.G.S., realized (but with the greatest reluctance) that the only troops available were Greek.* In Cabinet on 18 June, Wilson proposed that a Greek division be used for the defence of Constantinople. Venizelos was called for, and offered one of his divisions from western Thrace.

The *quid pro quo* for this loan was permission to advance in Asia Minor. On Sunday 20 June, at Lympne, Lloyd George and Millerand, in informal conversation, decided to authorize the advance.[55] The next day, despite ironic murmurs about the Foch report from Count Sforza, Italian Foreign Minister, the decision was confirmed by the Supreme Council. The Greeks were to lend one division to General Milne; at the same time they were authorized to engage in 'concerted action ... in the Smyrna area'.[56] It was understood that this was to be an advance northeastwards out of the Smyrna zone up the Smyrna–Panderma railway, and the occupation of Panderma on the Sea of Marmara. What was agreed was therefore a limited advance to new positions which would ease the strain on the allied garrison in the Straits zone, not a great drive by the Greek army eastwards into

---

* 15 June: 'Lloyd George is persuaded that the Greeks are the coming power in the Mediterranean both on land and on sea, and wants to befriend them. The whole of Lloyd George's foreign policy is chaotic, and based on totally fallacious values of men and affairs.' 17 June: 'I will urge that the Greeks be allowed to take Eastern Thrace and to threaten from Smyrna towards Panderma. But I will point out that all this means war with Turkey and Russia.' (Callwell, *Sir Henry Wilson*, ii, p. 243–4).

Anatolia, nor a 'knock-out blow' at the Kemalists.* Nevertheless, Venizelos was relieved and exhilarated; for there could be no question now of a last minute softening of the terms of the treaty.

In a much-quoted telegram of 23 June to the Foreign Ministry, Venizelos reported on the decision taken at Boulogne. He described the issue as a choice between undertaking to impose the terms of the treaty, and seeing Greece's claims whittled away in response to pressure from the French, Italians and British military circles. Therefore, 'at this critical point in the history of the nation', he had undertaken to lend the British one division for Ismid, and to smash the Turkish concentrations opposite the Greek lines, without seeking any aid, even economic, from the Allies. He had added that if even this lesson would not induce the Turks to sign and execute the treaty, he would undertake to increase the strength of the Greek army to such a point that it could, together with the British troops presently in Turkey, impose the treaty. But in this case he would need British economic aid and war materials, and an undertaking that Turkey would be reduced to the central Anatolian plateau (i.e. would lose Constantinople, and presumably Pontus). 'I succeeded in getting Mr Lloyd George to accept these proposals, and it was thanks to him that we succeeded in getting the permission given at Boulogne.'[57]

On 22 June Greek troops fanned out of the Smyrna zone in a three-pronged advance across the Milne Line.[58] The I Army Corps pushed up the Hermus and Cayster valleys as far as Alashehir. There was a parallel and supporting advance in the south up the Meander valley. In the north, the Smyrna Army Corps drove northwards from Manisa up the railway line to Axarios and Soma. Panderma was occupied. Finally, Paraskevopoulos sent the Archipelago division, with the Cavalry Brigade

* On 25 June Venizelos specifically warned Paraskevopoulos against being drawn too far eastwards; Greek General Staff, *The Asia Minor Expedition*, ii, appendix 13. His reasons seem to have been first a new-found nervousness of the effects of extending the Greek lines of communication too far, and second, the anxiety to keep sufficient forces available for a subsidiary operation in Eastern Thrace. The operation was conceived from the start as a limited one, and the widespread myth that the French and Italians, alarmed by the Greeks' success, insisted that the advance be brought to a halt seems to be unfounded (for this, see Nicolson, *Curzon: the Last Phase*, p. 251).

ranging ahead, east of Panderma to Bursa, which was captured on 8 July. The advance was called to a halt with Greece occupying a greatly extended front (or series of fronts) enclosing Bursa, the Panderma railway, and Alashehir. The Greeks rounded off this operation in August, by pushing on up the escarpment and occupying Ushak on the edge of the Anatolian plateau.

Paraskevopoulos telegraphed to Venizelos on 1 July, when the end of the operations was in sight, outlining two further possibilities: first, to stand fast on the lines occupied to date, and to detach forces from Asia Minor to occupy eastern Thrace, then to resume the Asia Minor campaign with a 'more general operation for the total liquidation of the Kemalist Turkish Nationalist movement'; second, to ignore Thrace and continue the operations in Asia Minor until the enemy were totally destroyed.[59] Paraskevopoulos preferred the second course. Venizelos was eager to put the Turks in the wrong before resuming the advance in Asia Minor, and thus to be able to ask Lloyd George's aid in stiffening the terms of the treaty; he therefore preferred the first. On 7 July he told the Supreme Council at Spa that the Greek troops, having completed their successful attack, should stay where they were until the Peace Treaty were signed.[60]

Ultimately, Venizelos now hoped for great things. He told Wilson that the Greeks would occupy Eastern Thrace; then, later, if necessary, Bursa, Eski Shehir, Afyon Karahisar, Constantinople, and even Trebizond.[61] When Wilson suggested that operations based on Smyrna should be under Greek command, and operations based on Constantinople under Milne, Venizelos of course agreed. Nothing suited Greek interests better than to involve Greek troops in operations under British command, consolidating the entente and making it harder for the British to deny support at a later date.

Venizelos envisaged a further advance up to the Eski Shehir-Afyon Karahisar line, should the Turks refuse to execute the treaty.[62] He understood Wilson to have agreed that Milne and Paraskevopoulos should produce plans respectively for an advance under British command on Eski Shehir, and under Greek command on Afyon Karahisar.* He told Wilson that he would

* There seems to have been a misunderstanding. Three weeks later Wilson reacted with irritated disapproval to a report that the Greeks were planning a new advance on Eski Shehir and Afyon Karahisar; Venizelos Papers, 315, Wilson to Stavridi, 30 July 1920.

call up three more divisions for these operations, and asked
Paraskevopoulos to submit a list of supplies required for the
equipment of these divisions and for the operation in general.[63]

This was the nearest Venizelos came to his dream of intimate
Anglo-Greek cooperation. Once the immediate crisis provoked
by the Kemalist threat to Ismid in June passed, he lost his bar-
gaining power with the British General Staff. The Greek operations now moved to Thrace. In late July the Smyrna division and
G. Kondylis's 3rd Infantry Regiment were shipped from Panderma to Rodosto. The weak and disorganized irregular forces
of Jafar Tayar, the Turkish Nationalist leader in Eastern Thrace,
were pinched between the Greek forces and easily dispersed.
Tayar himself was captured. Greek troops entered Adrianople
on 26 July. In Athens the flags were hung out, a salute of 101
guns was fired, and the event was celebrated by a solemn Te
Deum in the cathedral.[64]

At last, on 10 August 1920, the treaty which had been so
long delayed was signed at Sèvres.[65] A last minute quarrel between Greece and Italy which threatened to cause new delays
was hastily patched up by an agreement between Venizelos and
the Italians.[66] The dour French lawyer-politician Raymond
Poincaré was one of the first to observe the symbolism of the
name Sèvres, the home of fine and fragile porcelain.[67]

Under this fragile instrument, signed under moral duress by
the Sultan's Government and unrecognized by Ankara, the
Ottoman Empire ceased to exist. Turkey was reduced to her
Anatolian kernel and a strip of Europe extending to the Chatalja
lines. The treaty provided for a free and independent Armenian
state and an autonomous Kurdistan in the east. Smyrna and its
hinterland were taken away from the Turks. As a sop to Turkish
sentiment, the Smyrna zone was to remain under nominal
Turkish sovereignty for five years, administered by Greece. At
the end of this period it would be annexed to Greece if the local
parliament or a plebiscite so decided.

The Straits were internationalized, their freedom guaranteed
by a controlling Commission on which the Great Powers would
have the dominant voice. The Powers' hold over Turkish
finances, built up during the nineteenth century, was now in-
stitutionalized in a set of stringent provisions. A Tripartite
Agreement which accompanied the Treaty carved up Anatolia

into zones of economic influence, France receiving Cilicia, Italy
Adalia and the south-west, and rights of exploitation over the
coal of Eregli.[68] A further treaty of the same day annexed Thrace
to Greece.[69]

This should have been Venizelos's finest hour. The series of
instruments signed at Sèvres on 10 August 1920 won for Greece
almost the whole of Thrace, the islands of the Aegean including
Imbros and Tenedos off the mouth of the Dardanelles, the
Dodecanese except for Rhodes (and a good prospect of securing
even Rhodes), and a generous Smyrna zone which would definitely fall to Greece after a five years' delay. Of the regions
in which Greece had a major interest, only northern Epirus,
Cyprus, Constantinople and the Straits zone, and the Pontus fell
outside this settlement, and of these Venizelos had advanced a
serious claim only to northern Epirus. But the pieces of paper
signed at Sèvres, the climax of almost two years of patient weary-
ing diplomacy by Venizelos himself, were paper victories which
brought a lasting Turkish settlement not one inch nearer. The
Turkish Nationalist forces remained in the field, determined to
resist the dictates of the Powers in Paris. It was the Greek army
which, if Greece was to reap the fruits of Venizelos's diplomacy,
must enforce the terms of the treaty. Venizelos well knew by now
the magnitude of this task.

On the signing of the Treaty of Sèvres, Stergiadis formally
took over the government of the Smyrna zone from the Turks.[70]
For the Greeks it was an emotional ceremony. Confidence within the Greek community was high, and favourable reports on
Stergiadis's administration reached Western Europe from western visitors and representatives. A senior naval officer who visited
Smyrna and had discussions with Stergiadis in September 1920
reported typically that Greek rule was not, and never could be,
popular in Smyrna: 'None the less one and all bear testimony to
the success of M. Stergiadis's rule of toleration and fair play for
all. . . . Greek administration now appears to be firmly established
in Smyrna.' The writer referred to Stergiadis's 'paroxysms of
ungovernable temper', and called him 'probably as honest as it is
possible for a Greek to be'.[71]

Within thirty-five days, Greek troops had cleaned up eastern
Thrace and western Asia Minor as far as the Bursa-Alashehir
line. Paraskevopoulos quickly began shipping troops back from

Thrace, anxious to press home his advantage with a great drive up to the Anatolian railway. Milne and de Robeck advised against the plan; Milne feared that it might lead to 'Greek troops getting compromised in interior, thus requiring us to give military assistance to extract them'.[72]

Towards the end of August, Paraskevopoulos sent Venizelos a long report urging action.[73] He argued that Kemal was not going to recognize the treaty. The Kemalist movement must therefore be crushed by a great campaign in two stages: first the capture of Eski Shehir and Afyon Karahisar, and then an advance on Ankara and perhaps even Konya. The possession of these important railway junctions would deprive Kemal of his essential means of supply, and the capture of Ankara would be a 'colossal moral blow to the enemy'. The central Anatolian salt desert would divide the Kemalists into two widely separated bodies with poor and lengthy communications. Kemal would therefore be forced to give up the struggle; or, if he continued to resist, his troops would be reduced to small disorganized bands which could quickly be broken up by the Greek army.

The advantages of the forward front were certainly considerable. Nevertheless the report rested on false assumptions. Paraskevopoulos contemptuously underestimated the nationalist will to endure and resist. He drew from the correct assumption that the Kemalists were unpopular with large numbers of the Anatolian peasantry because of their financial exactions the fallacious inference that the liberating Greek army would be welcomed wherever it went. He therefore ignored the problem of resistance and sabotage behind the Greeks' vastly extended lines of communications. (Greek generals were consistently deceived by the gratitude and enthusiasm with which they claimed to be received by the indigenous populations, Orthodox and Muslim, in each successive advance; Balkan and Anatolian peoples had long experience of 'welcoming' liberating armies and authorities.) Nor did Paraskevopoulos explain how the Greeks were to crush the Kemalists if the latter were to retire eastwards towards Sivas.

As Paraskevopoulos recognized, the Nationalist forces on the western front still consisted of unreliable bands of irregulars. If the plan were to be implemented therefore, the sooner the better. But Venizelos, preoccupied with problems of internal politics and anxious to demobilize rather than to mobilize new divisions, did no more than promise to act on it if Turkey did not execute the treaty within six months. Then, suddenly, he changed his mind. The hesitations of the last few months were swept away. On 5 October he sent a long telegram to Lloyd George:

Obliged to take decisions very soon about the demobilization of the army whose indefinite maintenance on war footing becomes henceforward impossible from a political and financial point of view and useless if an immediate utilization were not foreseen. . . .

I am convinced that the Turkish Government will be unable to reduce Mustapha Kemal, and that it would be extremely dangerous to grant the permission requested by them to form new divisions, for these would fatally reinforce the nationalists. The prolongation of the actual state of affairs in Anatolia would be full of menaces of the future. The Allies' inaction would embolden Kemal, complete the destruction of the Christian populations, and leave a free hand to the intrigues of certain Powers, desirous of using Kemal and Bolshevism in order to hinder the pacification of the East.

The only radical remedy would be a new campaign with the object of destroying definitely the nationalist forces around Angora and the Pontus, with the following double consequences:

1. Of driving the Turks out of Constantinople which would form, together with the zone of the Straits, a separate state the existence of which would constitute a unique efficacious guarantee of the liberty of the Straits.

2. Constitution of a separate state at the Pontus with the Greeks that have remained there, and those who having emigrated to escape from the Turkish persecution during the last fifty years are dispersed in the south of Russia, and whose total number amounts to 800,000. This state, collaborating with Armenia and Georgia, would form a solid barrier against Islamism and eventually against Russian imperialism. The forces which Greece now disposes of would be sufficient to ensure the complete success of this expedition, but for political and financial reasons the Hellenic Government would be unable to assume the exclusive initiative and responsibility thereof, as in June last. They would nevertheless be ready to collaborate with all their forces with England if she were willing to take such an initiative in order to arrive at the aforesaid objects, and if she were willing to give Greece the necessary financial assistance to that effect.[74]

Venizelos ended by appealing for a very prompt decision, since in a few weeks' time the winter season would set in and make a campaign almost impossible. Failing a favourable decision, the Greek government would be forced for political reasons to execute their plan for demobilization, after which a new mobilization would be impossible within the next few months.

This highly interesting appeal was Venizelos's response to the conflicting pressures of his civilian and military friends in an increasingly intractable situation. Paraskevopoulos and the military, dissatisfied with the present Greek front, wished to push on into Anatolia in a hopeful attempt to search out the elusive Nationalists and destroy them. But with a general election approaching, Venizelist politicians were eager for at least partial demobilization. These two demands were irreconcilable, since a campaign on the scale here envisaged would have ruled out demobilization for months if not years. But demobilization at this time would have exposed the Greek front to Nationalist attacks and ultimately endangered the whole Greek position in Asia Minor.

Now Venizelos went boldly for the military solution. Demobilization would have to be postponed; but to compensate for this there was the nationalist fervour which would have greeted a new holy war for the destruction of the enemy, the redemption of the Pontus, and the possible acquisition of Constantinople.* The long term military and political problems would, however, have been enormously aggravated by such a vast extension of Greece's involvement in Asia Minor.

Venizelos's démarche demanded a swift and clearcut reply. Perhaps luckily for his reputation, no such reply was given. The matter was pursued in a desultory way, but with no outcome before the Greek general election. A copy of Venizelos's telegram was forwarded to Crowe at the Foreign Office on 12 October, with a letter from Sir Maurice Hankey stating that Lloyd George regarded it as 'rather specially secret because if anything were to come of it, it would be important not to let Mustapha

---

* Venizelos may have had in mind also that the action he proposed would enable him to postpone the elections for a further indefinite period. I put forward this suggestion very tentatively, since there is no concrete evidence for it. But it is certain that this vast campaign, involving the recognition that an active state of war with Nationalist Turkey existed, and that the peace settlement was not final, would have given him grounds for postponement. This is, at any rate, a more reasonable supposition than the fantastic theory put forward by some anti-Venizelist writers, that Venizelos held the elections only because, knowing that he would lose them, he could thus escape the responsibility for a disaster in Asia Minor which he now saw to be inevitable.

Kemal have time to prepare for the attack'.[75] Sir Henry Wilson's requests for further information evoked the explanation that the Greek Staff required ten days to reach Eski-Shehir and Afyon Karahisar, and a further three weeks to advance on Ankara.[76] Within this same period of one month, the Pontus could also be occupied. Venizelos asked that the British troops at Ismid, together with the Manissa Division under Milne's command, should cover the line of the Sakarya river during the Greek advance. In the matter of equipment he was more exigent, asking for a variety of war materials, 200,000 pairs of woollen pants and socks ('absolutely essential'), and an average of £3 million a month. It seems unlikely that these supplies could have arrived before winter set in.

Finally, on 16 October, Venizelos sent a last message to Lloyd George, in answer to the questions and doubts which his démarche had raised.[77] He admitted that the Nationalists would probably withdraw before the advance of the Greek troops. 'Our arrival at Ankara would therefore not constitute a definite success, for it would be necessary to maintain the occupation for a fairly long time.' This being the case, if the Allies were not prepared to consider his radical solution, Venizelos proposed, as an indispensable measure, the rapid formation of an interallied commission for the organization of the Turkish army and gendarmerie as provided for in the Treaty of Sèvres.

As early as the summer of 1919 Turkish Nationalists had been ignoring, or interning, allied military control officers. In January 1920 they successfully raided a valuable dump of Ottoman war materials under French guard on the Gallipoli peninsula.[78] In February they inflicted a severe defeat on French troops in Cilicia. The threat they posed to foreign interests on Turkish soil had not diminished since then. Yet Venizelos was reduced to proposing the creation of an interallied commission to organize Turkish forces which, once organized, would very likely have deserted to join the Nationalists. (Venizelos himself recognized this danger in his telegram of 5 October.) What he now suggested was no more a solution than the vast campaign which it was to replace. Yet, in words which betray his tragic incomprehension of the forces arrayed against Greece in Anatolia, and of the temper of the postwar East, he ended his appeal:

The pacification of Anatolia can thus be arrived at shortly for these forces [i.e. forces organized by an interallied commission] would be amply sufficient to disperse the Kemalist troops. The Musulman populations of Anatolia are tired of the means used by the nationalists and they only long to have peace for a while. This is easily proved by the fact that our troops are received everywhere as saviours by the native populations of Anatolia who do not cease to request their advance in order to be protected by them against the exactions and tyranny of a movement which calls itself nationalistic but has nothing common with nationalism.

Even this appeal evoked no response. Four weeks later, on 14 November, Venizelos fell from power.

7 | The Monkey's Bite

I happened to be with Mr Lloyd George in the
Cabinet Room at the time the telegram announcing
the results of the Greek election arrived. He was
very much shocked, and still more puzzled. But with
his natural buoyancy, and hardened by the
experiences we had all passed through in the Great
War, he contented himself with remarking, with
a grin, 'Now I am the only one left'.

Winston Churchill, *The World Crisis:
the Aftermath*, p. 387

The life of the 'Lazarus' Chamber of 1915 had been prolonged
three times beyond its natural life of four years, so that the
government of Venizelos might see the peace settlement through
to a successful conclusion. Venizelos had pledged himself to hold
general elections as soon as the Turkish treaty were signed.[1] On
his triumphant return to Greece, when Venizelos presented the
Treaty of Sèvres to parliament on 7 September 1920, he explained
that he would dissolve the Chamber forthwith and hold elections
on 7 November, under the supervision of his own and not a
service government.[2] Martial law and the censorship were raised.[3]
The electoral campaign was already under way when an unexpected event raised the old issue of the monarchy in a new and
dangerous form. For the first and last time, the unfortunate young
King Alexander was brought out into the centre of the Greek
political stage.

Ever since he was raised to the throne, Alexander's relations
with the Liberals had been strained. He had to listen to long
lectures on constitutional practice from Venizelos, who lost no
opportunity of pointing out the ex-king's failings to his son.[4]
The King complained to friends that he was virtually a prisoner
in the palace, prevented by the regime from communicating
with his father's old associates and friends. He frequently
threatened to resign, and retire to private life. The truth was that
Alexander had none of the interest in public affairs and politics
of his uncle Nicholas and of most other members of his family;
his passion was fast motor cars.

Since the King's abdication would have raised the dynastic issue once more, Venizelos and his colleagues had taken pains to soothe his feelings where possible. Alexander's chief weapon against the Government was to refuse to sign or to delay in signing the decrees which came to him for signature. In May 1918, the King's objections to the new Civil List bill, and refusal to sign it, almost led to an 'immediate and fatal explosion'.[5]

The main cause of dissension between King and Government was an unexpected one – his proposed marriage to Aspasia Manos, an attractive and strongwilled young lady from a Royalist family. Already in 1917 his love affair with Miss Manos was known to Venizelos and his colleagues and to the ambassadors of the powers. Lord Granville favoured it on the grounds that opposition to the marriage, by provoking the King to resign, could destroy the monarchy; and the British favoured monarchy.[6] (It was moreover difficult to see among the crowned or nearly crowned heads of Europe any suitable bride for Alexander.) But the Greek government disapproved of the match.

The question arises why this should have been so, when the recurrent complaints of the Venizelists against Constantine were of his 'Prussian methods' and his German wife. The simplest way for a party committed, as was the official Liberal Party, to the monarchy as an institution, to put an end once and for all to the complaints that the monarchy was a foreign institution, never wholly Hellenized, would have been to allow the King to marry a Greek wife. This was not how the Venizelists saw the issue. The marriage would have opened a channel of communication between the King and the Royalists, through Miss Manos and her relations. Besides, neither Athenian 'society', whether Constantinist or Venizelist, nor even the republicans in the Venizelist party, were prepared to accept the notion of the King marrying a commoner.[7] The manners and conceptions of the time were such that republicanism, with its respectable ideological history, was more tolerable than such a royal match. Venizelos therefore told the King that the country was not yet ready to accept the marriage.

Britain fostered the monarchy as an element of 'stability' and out of fear that a republican Greece would naturally fall under French influence. Lord Granville was therefore authorized by London to take 'active steps in favour of the King's marriage',[8] and intervened with Venizelos. At a two-hour cabinet meeting on 17 May 1918 Venizelos asked his colleagues

not whether they approved of the marriage (he knew they all disliked it) but which they preferred of two evils – to allow the marriage under the conditions suggested [i.e. that it be 'semi-morganatic'] or to run the risk ... of the position becoming quite impossible and the King having to go, leaving the Government to be carried on by a regency pending the decision of an eventual National Assembly.

Venizelos insisted on putting the question to them one by one. Three men (Koundouriotis, Negropontis and Spyridis) voted for a regency. All the rest preferred the marriage; but the whole Cabinet insisted that the marriage must be postponed. The result was that Granville was asked to act as mediator between the Government and the young couple, to calm them down and make them see the reasons for delay; and Aspasia left for the front to submerge her troubles in hard work as a nurse.

Seven months later Granville reported rumours that the marriage was off. The King was about to go to Paris; and the trip was interpreted as an opportunity for 'widening his amatory experiences' and plucking up courage to jilt Aspasia.

The general idea here is that the hot summer months spent under the same roof were too much for the young couple and that he got what he wanted with the result that his ardour has cooled. ... It is devilish hard luck on the girl and the King has behaved like a young skunk; but I am afraid that events have proved that Venizelos was right and I was wrong.[9]

It was Granville who was wrong. The King had not changed his mind. In May 1919 he was writing to Venizelos in Paris, 'I desire to combine the national rejoicing [i.e. over the occupation of Smyrna] with what is for me especially a happy event, and which is also moreover in accordance with the ideas which you have repeatedly expressed about making the dynasty a "national" institution.' This was a subtle approach. The King announced that he intended to marry Aspasia unofficially the following month.[10]

Venizelos begged him to do nothing rash. He promised to examine the situation on his return to Athens with the greatest goodwill towards the King.[11] The King must have suspected that the Venizelists were giving him enough rope to prevent him from resignation, with no intention of allowing the marriage in the foreseeable future. His response was to call their bluff. In November 1919, in great secrecy, he and Aspasia were married. Venizelos's reaction was not generous acceptance of the *fait accompli*, but to 'allow the news to leak out very gradually and see if the people get used to it'.[12]

The trials of the young couple were not yet over. They were not even allowed, as man and wife, to live together at Tatoi. The government, on the pretext that there was a dangerous 'effervescence' in the officer corps, advised Aspasia to leave. From Paris she wrote to Venizelos asking to be allowed to talk to him: 'Vous comprenez n'est-ce pas, cher monsieur Venizelos, combien cette séparation nous a fait souffrir tous les deux.'[13]

Such remained the situation in September 1920. The secret of the marriage had begun to seep out only in the spring of 1920.[14] The grudging acquiescence of the Venizelists never softened into approval. The whole episode is an interesting commentary on the Liberals' attitude to the monarchy. Presented with the opportunity, in Granville's words, to 'solidify the King and make him more reasonable',[15] to 'Hellenize' the institution of monarchy in Greece, they chose to thwart his strongest desire, reducing him to a mere cipher. What the consequences of this attitude might have been, we cannot know. For at this moment Fate took a hand, saving the Venizelists from these consequences and relieving the King in an unprecedented way of a burden he had never sought.

In the morning of 30 September, a fine sunny day, King Alexander took a walk in the grounds of the palace at Tatoi with his wolfhound, Fritz. During the walk, the dog jumped suddenly into a clump of bushes. Hearing barks and the sounds of a scuffle, Alexander followed, and found him vigorously shaking a pet Spanish monkey in his teeth. While he was trying to free the monkey, the King was attacked by its mate, the male of the pair, and severely bitten in the calf. The wounds were cleaned and dressed, but two days later severe fever set in. After a three-week struggle for life, Alexander died of blood-poisoning on 25 October.[16] The young King's grandmother, Queen Olga, arrived just too late, having been delayed by bad weather in the Adriatic. She was the only member of the royal family permitted by the Venizelist government to visit the dying King.

Venizelos's immediate reaction to the death of Alexander was to recall the Chamber, which elected Admiral Koundouriotis to the Regency. The elections were postponed for a week, until 14

November. The constitutional issue then had to be faced. Alexander left no heir, and even if he had, the attitude of the Liberals to his marriage with Aspasia Manos (who was five months pregnant) would have precluded the adoption of their son as king. The positive choices before Venizelos were therefore the proclamation of a Republic, the abandonment of the Glucksberg dynasty in favour of a new king from perhaps the British royal house, and an invitation to one of Alexander's brothers to assume the throne.

In the short term, the choice was between an invitation to Prince George or Prince Paul, and a decision to leave the issue in suspense until after the elections. In his anxiety to settle the issue at once so as to exclude the return of King Constantine from debate, Venizelos decided even before Alexander's death to invite Prince Paul, Constantine's younger son, to assume the throne.[17]

Prince Paul was in exile in Switzerland with his father. He rejected Venizelos's overtures on the grounds that his father and elder brother had never renounced their prior rights to the throne.

This refusal made Venizelos's dilemma painfully clear. He wanted a constitutional monarchy. He did not wish to offend the British by declaring a Republic,[18] and could not do so before the elections for fear of provoking a massive Royalist vote. (Venizelos was aware that there was little popular support for republican ideas, and was always against attempts to establish a Republic before the Greek people were 'educated' to accept it.)* With Alexander dead, he could not prevent his opponents from turning the electoral campaign into a campaign for the return of the ex-King without assuming the dictatorial powers which he deplored. In this way Venizelos was driven to escape from the swarm of difficulties by posing the stark question 'Constantine or Venizelos' as the issue of the elections.

It was generally assumed, both in Greece and abroad, that the

* He advised Politis in November 1922 that the new Republican Party would be 'making a capital political error if they thought to change the regime and achieve a Republic on the basis of only a simple majority against a strong opposing minority.... The chief mission of the Republican Party should be the education of the people.' Venizelos Papers, 268, Venizelos to Politis, 3 Nov. 1922.

Venizelists would win the elections. In the early summer of 1920 Whitehall had not been so confident. Sir Eyre Crowe revealed the orthodox Foreign Office view of Venizelos:

M. Venizelos is well aware of the unsatisfactory state of things in Greece. He is anxiously awaiting the definite conclusion of peace in order to be able to give to the internal affairs of his country the attention which he has [been] compelled so far to devote almost entirely to questions of foreign policy. He has more than once told me that if he could have seven to ten years in which to tackle the problem of internal government, he felt confident he would establish Greek administration both in the old and in the new Greek territories on a sound and satisfactory basis.[19]

Curzon's minute on this showed that he had doubts. He had never liked the Greeks:

Personally I do not look forward to the Hellenic regeneration we are promised, for (1) I believe the Greeks to be administratively corrupt and incompetent and (2) so far from believing that M. Venizelos will be given eight to ten years to achieve the administrative reform of his country, I gather from all indications that the Greeks would even now be only too willing to exchange him for the ex-king.

Granville too had his doubts in Athens:

I have always felt confident that, provided the decisions of the Peace Conference were favourable to Greece, Monsieur Venizelos was safe to secure a majority – and probably a big majority – at the elections. I confess that during the last few days my confidence has been a good deal shaken: any number of people have told me stories of the strong feeling existing in the country against him, and especially against his colleagues in the government.[20]

All doubts were stilled, however, by the persuasive charm of Venizelos himself: the inexhaustible eloquence, as Curzon once called it, which left no chink for a reply.

Venizelos improved his chances in two ways. In February 1920 Politis advised him that it was absolutely necessary for the new territories to take part in the forthcoming elections; it would not be impossible within two or three months from the ratification of the Turkish Peace Treaty to draw up provisional lists in Smyrna and Thrace, registering all the Greeks and those Muslims who wished to become Greek citizens.[21] The Greek populations of Thrace and Asia Minor regarded Venizelos as their liberator.

Moreover, since these were militarily occupied areas, there was no question of the opposition mounting a serious campaign there. This was shrewd advice. Thrace was duly annexed to Greece in September 1920, so that the Greek population might enjoy the franchise.[22]

The second Venizelist measure to improve the party's prospects was the introduction of the army vote,[23] on the grounds that a group so large and so intimately affected by the Government's policy should not be disfranchised. The decision was criticized by civilian moderates and some army officers as a grave error tending to encourage divisive political activity among an already overpoliticized officer corps.[24] Already in 1919 a group of middle-ranking officers had planned a Military League to keep the opposition in its place.[25] Now the decision to hold elections and extend the vote to the army raised political feelings to a fever pitch. High-ranking Venizelist officers were freely accused of exerting pressure on their troops to vote for the Government.[26] A divisional commander in Thrace who put in a report to Venizelos recommending postponement of the elections or at least the abandonment of the army vote, was told that he ought to be able to ensure the 'right' result.[27] The egregious Pangalos, Chief of General Staff and future dictator, offered General A. Mazarakis the Ministry of the Interior in the military government which was to be formed if the Venizelists were inconveniently beaten at the polls.[28] Spyridonos, a senior staff officer and a 'neutralist', described the upheaval created in Asia Minor:

> These elections were conducted in such a way that one colonel, in command of an infantry regiment (and a future Regent of Greece at that!), was forced to run away from his regiment by night so as to escape the anger of his men who had discovered the falsification of the results of the vote which had taken place on his orders in the regiment.* During the period before the elections, when representatives of the parties were visiting the companies and addressing them, the nuclei of groups favouring the opposition were formed; many Venizelists, having been mobilized for many years and suffered hardships and wishing an end at last to their endless mobilization, agreed with them. These men by their vote or by their abstention swelled the ranks of the opposition to Venizelos. The attempt at falsifying the results provoked uproar in the army units and for a time there was a threat that discipline might break down.[29]

* Georgios Kondylis, i/c 3rd Infantry Regiment.

The Venizelist campaign turned on two main propositions. The first was that the 'National Question', thanks to the policy and genius of Venizelos, had been triumphantly settled. The second was that whatever mistakes had been made in internal affairs were pardonable if not inevitable at a time of war and acute political division.

Venizelist orators touched on the internal situation, but in muted tones. General Danglis encapsulated the entire Venizelist approach in a short passage from a campaign speech in Epirus:

I admit that the internal situation has not been, and could not be rosy in this stormy period; I admit that profiteering has raised its ugly head, and that the prices of all sorts of goods have risen excessively; I admit that the administration has not been able to satisfy completely all the needs of the country. I admit that many functionaries in various branches of the administration have not risen to the demands of their position. But if you consider that these evils have occurred not only in Greece, but in all the belligerent and even neutral states, and in some of them indeed to a much greater degree; if you consider that they were an unavoidable consequence of the terrible world war; if you consider that the Prime Minister was almost continuously absent from the country, engaged in the handling of the main national question, and that the Ministries were surrounded by so many departments of one sort or another, organized and staffed by a mass of civil servants lacking the necessary experience, you will be charitable in your judgments and will thank God that such great gains have been won in the National question for such relatively slight disadvantages.[30]

Venizelos's own vision of the issues was more complex, and in some respects irrelevant to the immediate struggle. Impressed by the Bolshevik revolution, preoccupied by the tensions within the Liberal Party between socialists such as Papanastasiou and the bourgeois centre, he was anxious to define the proper function of a liberal Centre party, and the 'general social and political interest' to be served by liberalism. In a set of notes on the land question and the relations between capital and labour, written some time in 1918–19, Venizelos defined a philosophy of 'social interdependence' opposed to the Bolshevik theory of relentless class warfare.[31] Having outlined a moderate reformist approach to industrial relations and the land question, he concluded:

I am well aware that by not accepting to diverge either to the right or to the left I risk seeing both the right and the left wings of the party break away. I hope that this applies only to the extreme right and left. And I believe that the trunk which remains will still be capable of securing a great majority of the Greek people....

Here is an early formulation of the philosophy of the Greek centre, with its commitment to the middle road. As Venizelos himself recognized, his philosophy was ultimately a conservative one, appealing to the mass of small businessmen, salaried workers and smallholders (once the land question had been settled). It was also rooted in the realization – shared by Gounaris – that the exploited classes in Greece were incapable of supporting political parties representing their sectional interests. The industrial working class was too small and disorganized; the peasantry was too fragmented, and dependent on strong local patrons of whatever ideology to protect its interests.

It was as the exponent of this philosophy that Venizelos campaigned in the elections of November 1920. Allowing it to be assumed that the national question was settled in Greece's favour, he concentrated on giving a lengthy and dry account of his party's stewardship.[32] Perhaps he hoped to transcend the divisions of the *dichasmos*, attracting votes by an exposition of the party's achievements in agrarian policy, social welfare and labour legislation, and shifting attention from the embarrassing dynastic issue. If so the attempt was doomed to failure. The determining issues of the election were those recognized by Venizelos's supporters such as Danglis, and by the opposition – the dynastic question, and the internal administration of the country, which, while sincerely debated in moral terms of justice and injustice, concealed also the all-important material question of what the government had offered to its clients.

The Venizelists offered to the electorate the Treaty of Sèvres as compensation for disappointment and hardship at home. If there was dishonesty in the Venizelist campaign, it was the failure to allow even a hint that the national question was other than definitively solved, although Venizelos well knew the difficulties which remained to be faced in Asia Minor. For their own reasons the opposition did not choose to underline this weakness in the Venizelist case. The electorate was therefore encouraged in the dangerous belief that the Asia Minor question was a settled issue.

In March 1920 the anti-Venizelist leaders had formed a sixteen-man committee of the 'United Opposition',[33] the fruit of several months of efforts by Kalogeropoulos, Stratos, Tsaldaris and others to unite the various factions of anti-Venizelist and Royalist feeling in a broad front from which only the small socialist and communist groups to the left of the Liberal party were excluded. The ageing D. Rallis and the exiled Gounaris were represented on the Committee by colleagues. It was a warning to the Venizelists that the opposition would not waste its substance in factional disputes, but would enter the elections united, with agreed lists of parliamentary candidates. The presence of Ion Dragoumis and G. Bousios, both heroes of the Macedonian struggle, was a further warning that the Venizelists could not plausibly claim a monopoly of patriotism in the forthcoming struggle.

The strength of the Committee was soon diminished by a tragic event. On 12 August 1920, two days after the signature of the Treaty of Sèvres, as Venizelos was about to embark at the Gare de Lyon on a train for Greece, he was shot at and wounded by two disaffected Royalist Greek officers. Venizelos escaped with light injuries. But the consequences in Athens were immediate and alarming. When the news came through, Venizelist crowds went on the rampage, breaking up the offices of opposition newspapers, a common phenomenon at times of tension. But there was worse. Ion Dragoumis, coming down from his home in Kiphissia to Athens by car, was stopped by the security forces, taken out and shot dead. It was the least forgivable crime of the years of schism.

The United Opposition fought the campaign on two main issues, the Venizelist 'tyranny' and the return of King Constantine. At the same time the opposition sensibly tried to convince the Powers of its reliable attitude to Greece's national claims and the Treaty of Sèvres. They knew that French and British statesmen regarded them as Germanophile 'traitors' to the allied cause. These statesmen now seemed all-powerful in European and Near Eastern affairs. It was time to mend fences, if that were possible, without admitting that either Venizelos or the Entente had been right during the war.

In an open letter to President Wilson in April 1919, Stratos and Kalogeropoulos had endorsed the Greek Government's claims at the Peace Conference as representing the views of all the Greeks:

The Greek people as a whole, independently of any divergence of opinion exclusively related to internal politics, solely aim to promote national claims, and believe that the only right solution of the eastern problems concerning Hellenism lies in the re-establishment of a single national Greek State – constituted from the lands of the present kingdom, of Northern Epirus, Thrace including Constantinople with the peninsula of Gallipoli, of the vilayets of Aidin and Broussa, the cazas of Nicomedia and Dardanells [sic], the Dodecanese and the isle of Cyprus – and assuring the Greeks of the Pont an independent political life. . . .[34]

Similar points had been made by Ion Dragoumis in two memos which he addressed to the Peace Conference from his exile in Corsica and Skopelos.[35]

Such notes and memoranda were not well calculated to dissolve the suspicion with which the Entente regarded the anti-Venizelists, even if they had reached the statesmen for whom they were intended (which is unlikely). They contained violent attacks on Entente policy in Greece during the war and on the resulting Venizelist 'tyranny'. These were not subjects of which the Entente wished to be reminded. And the grounds on which these authors based their support of Greece's claims were not such as to carry weight with the Entente. These were the rights of small nations and of the ethnic groups within the Ottoman Empire, recognized in President Wilson's Fourteen Points. There is no hint of the welcome Venizelist thesis of the identity of Greek and British interests and the willingness of Greece, in return for territorial compensation, to act as carrier of British interests in the east.

The anti-Venizelists, many of them isolated by exile or imprisonment from the mainstream of events, had only a slender grasp on postwar realities. Carried away, as were almost all the Greeks (except Metaxas) by the Wilsonian conception of self-determination, and aware of what this conception, favourably interpreted, meant for Greek aspirations, they nevertheless could not restrain themselves from preaching to the Allies the evils of foreign intervention in Greek affairs, and of the Venizelist regime which issued from it.[36]

The United Opposition clarified its position on foreign policy shortly after its formation, issuing an official declaration to the ministers of the Entente Powers in Athens on 4 June 1920. The declaration assured the Powers of the 'unity of views of the Greek Nation' over the national claims, and the 'unchangeable sentiments of friendship and interdependence which the Greek People feels for the Allied and Associated Powers'.[37]

But these assurances did not imply wholehearted endorsement of Venizelos's foreign policy within Greece. The burden of the opposition's criticism of Venizelist foreign policy continued to be that it was 'opportunist'; Venizelos had thrown Greece into the war without exacting firm guarantees and written undertakings from the allies as to the rewards to be won. Now that the rewards were visible to all, anti-Venizelists argued that they were due not to the policy and wisdom of Venizelos, but to the virtues of the Greek army and people* and the recognition by the Peace Conference of the rights of that people to self-determination.

Gounaris himself had been in exile for more than three years. In June 1917, on the establishment of Venizelos in Athens, with the Allies' help, he and Metaxas, Dousmanis, Ion Dragoumis, G. Pesmazoglou and other leading spirits in the anti-Venizelist world had been shipped off to Corsica. There they lived in frustrated idleness, but not discomfort, as the unwilling guests of the French Government at the Grand Hotel Continental in Ajaccio. Gounaris's first care was to buy a bookcase and recreate a comfortable booklined environment. A part of his time was spent composing memoranda of protest to Clemenceau. Late in 1918, suspecting that the French were going to repatriate the exiles forcibly to Greece to face show-trials at the hands of the Venizelist regime, Gounaris, Metaxas and Pesmazoglou made a dramatic escape by fishing boat to Sardinia, and thence to Italy. There Gounaris was able to resume his political activities and contacts with Royalist circles in Switzerland and in Greece itself. Exile had completed that process of embittering which had begun some years earlier. Gounaris was now filled with a deep and unreasoning loathing for Venizelos and his regime, and a rigid conviction of his own rightness.

Gounaris, now free to return without fear of arrest, landed in Corfu on 23 October, and proceeded from there through his home constituency of Patras to Athens, where he arrived shortly after King Alexander's death.

* Markezinis acutely compares this attitude to the attitude of Metaxas's opponents in 1940, in attributing Greece's successes in Albania to the army and people, and ignoring the role of Metaxas and George II in laying the foundations for these successes; Markezinis, *Political History of Modern Greece*, iv, app., p. 88, n. 853.

In his first speech, in Corfu, he touched on foreign policy in only the vaguest and most rhetorical of terms, picturing Greece 'opening her arms to her children who are about to live in freedom, thanks to the magnificent work of our glorious heroes'.[38] Such remarks were an acknowledgement of a subject which could not be entirely ignored; but throughout the election campaign Royalist politicians played down the issues of foreign policy, since a full airing of the Asia Minor question would raise the embarrassing extent of Venizelos's success in negotiating the Treaty of Sèvres.

The two great issues on which the opposition based its appeal to the country were the constitutional, or dynastic, question, and the government's dictatorial tendencies. The return of King Constantine had been the main demand of anti-Venizelists ever since his enforced departure from Greece; but the government had been able to exclude the subject from public discussion through the notorious Law 755 'concerning hostility to the prevailing regime', backed up by martial law and the press censorship. The situation was changed by the raising of martial law and the death of King Alexander. Gounaris defined the attitude of the opposition to the dynastic issue in a statement to the press on 31 October, in which he opposed Venizelos's intention to invite Prince Paul to assume the throne, and called for a referendum on the issue.[39]

Venizelos's reply, offering 'consultations' if the opposition would accept a swift solution of the problem and an immediate summons to Prince Paul, was rejected by the opposition.[40] Thus the dynastic question immediately became the burning issue. Gounaris made it one of the two themes of the speech he gave on 7 November at the opposition's main rally in Athens:

Actually there is no dynastic question. The throne has its lawful occupant. The king of the Hellenes is Constantine. . . .
Here are the reasons why I consider it essential that the people should give its decision. The leader of our opponents says: the people, in its great majority, does not want King Constantine. We reply: then let the people be asked. He rejects this in a strange fashion, saying that the Constitution says nothing about putting such a question to the people. That is true. But it is equally true that the Constitution says nothing about doubting the rights of the king. . . . Rejecting a referendum, they demand that the question be solved by the elections. Quite simply these men are demanding the

establishment of the doctrine that the vote at the elections gives the elected politician the power to dispose of the throne, that is to depose the king or to impose conditions on the king.

Because this is what they declare they will do, if they succeed in the elections. They will depose Constantine and impose conditions on their own king. We have a duty to oppose with all our force this pitiful doctrine, which would reduce the king to a mere servant of whichever party were victorious in the elections.[41]

It would have been more logical to argue that since Constantine had never resigned his rights to the throne, no question of a referendum would arise if the opposition won the elections; the king would simply be invited to resume his throne without further ado. But it was now clear that the fate of the Greek monarchy depended on the results of the election.

The opposition's second theme was the Venizelist 'tyranny' – the exiles, deportations and trials by court martial, the injustices associated with censorship, martial law and 'Law 755', the illegality of the Venizelist regime and its 'Lazarus Chamber'. Gounaris's speech in Athens conveys the flavour of the attack:

Three and a half years have passed since I was forcibly removed from you. Throughout these years violence and arbitrary rule have been rampant. All personal and political liberties have been shamelessly trampled on in a manner unexampled in history. The constitutional charter has been torn up. ... The concepts of justice and law have been dissolved. ... The Church, guardian for centuries of the national ideals, has been torn down. ... Justice, the bastion of every free society, despite all the constitutional guarantees of its independence, has been dragged into the whirlpool of the corybantic passions of tyranny. ... The press whose freedom is guaranteed by the Constitution has become the object of a ruthless persecution.... The prisons have been filled with citizens unaware of why they have been dragged there. ... In their tens and hundreds, even in their thousands, those excellent citizens who were displeasing to the tyrants were sent away to the islands of the Aegean.... All those civil servants and officers who were suspect for their views were dismissed from their posts.... These are facts known to all of you.[42]

This was the platform on which the United Opposition fought the elections – the overthrow by the long-suffering people of the Venizelist tyranny, and the return of the rightful king. The only politicians who occasionally rose above the simplicities of the campaign were Venizelos, in his attempt to stake out for his party a claim to the centre ground of Greek politics, and Gounaris, who in a long speech at Patras on 10 October,[43] outlined a programme of procedural reform of Greek politics, recommending proportional representation (which would assure representation to minority agrarian and labour sections of society), votes for women, and reform of the electoral procedure.* But even this speech contained not a political programme in the usual sense, but a prepolitical programme – a set of proposals for constitutional reform which would revise the framework within which Greek politics took place. It was of course irrelevant to the passions of October 1920.

The electoral period began. Candidates left Athens for their constituencies. Alexander Pallis, a young man who had gone out to Greece after education at Eton and Balliol College, Oxford, and stayed to work for the Venizelist regime in Salonika on refugee problems, stood as candidate in the Salonika region. He wrote an account which throws light on the deficiencies of the Venizelist campaign:

Such was the spirit of optimism which prevailed, that most of the candidates did not even take the trouble to make tours of the countryside. Going from village to village almost on my own, I found everywhere a hidden reaction, whose exact force it was impossible to estimate. The opposition avoided holding mass meetings, and organized their campaign with great secrecy. The people hid their true feelings on account of terrorism by organs of the gendarmerie, who had got into bad habits owing to their immunity from control during the long period of war. They all came to the Liberal party meetings and listened to the speeches without making the least interruption. At the very most, some lawyer or retired officer, usually from Old Greece, would get up at the end of the speech and ask a question or start a discussion.

In one village only – Drimynklava near Langada – the inhabitants left us in no doubt as to their feelings. We knew that the atmosphere in this village was hostile, because in 1917, after the Salonika revolution, the inhabitants had refused to be mobilized, and Kondylis, to punish them, had sent a detachment which burnt all the barns in the village. We arrived in the evening, five or six candidates, and asked that the people gather in the school to hear us. When all the inhabitants were gathered together, one of the candidates, Alexander

* It was after this speech, on N. Kampanis's recommendations, that the name of Gounaris's party was changed from *Ethnikophron* ('National-minded') to *Laikon* ('Populist').

Letsas, a popular and eloquent speaker, made a speech whose main theme was the successes of Venizelos's foreign policy. The audience followed it to the end in dead silence. But as soon as he finished, they all got up together, shouting 'Long live Constantine', and left the hall in a body.[44]

The Venizelists paid a heavy price in Macedonia for the effects of the war. Merchants and contractors in Salonika had profited from the allied armies; but the mass of the peasantry had been subject to requisitions and forced mobilization by Kondylis and his bravos, as well as the usual governmental neglect. In general, where local issues played a part in the election they tended to favour the anti-Venizelists, simply because every economic grievance arising out of the war and the blockade, every personal grievance arising out of mobilization, requisition or interference by the bureaucracy or the military authorities, was put down to the debit of the party which had been in power, with only short interruptions, for ten years.

Election day was 14 November – as always in Greece, a Sunday. The people began to stream through the polling stations in an orderly manner to throw their ballots, in the traditional way, into the ballot boxes. There was one box for each candidate, divided into two compartments marked YES and NO. The day passed quietly enough, as the Royalists with their emblems of olive branches and the confident Venizelists waited for the first results to trickle in that evening.

They were startling. The British ambassador, Lord Granville, dropped in on an election night party given by Negropontis, the Finance Minister, and thought at first that the Minister must be joking when he said that things were not going well. To the amazement of the diplomatic and most of the political world, successive returns confirmed the initial picture. Only one foreigner, a humble Second Secretary named Hudson in the British Legation, is known to have correctly predicted the result, and his opinion was of course disregarded.[45] And now the day after the election the news was that all Attico-Boeotia had gone anti-Venizelist, that not one Venizelist candidate had been successful in the entire Peloponnese. That evening Granville telegraphed London, 'Monsieur Venizelos is hopelessly beaten'.[46]

The Venizelists won only 118 out of 369 seats. Liberal candidates won all the seats in Venizelos's home ground, Crete; in the

islands of Lesbos, Chios, Spetsai* and Hydra (where the Venizelists stood unopposed); and in the west of Greece in Arta, Preveza
and Ioannina, where General Danglis led the Venizelist ticket.
In the six new electoral districts of eastern and western Thrace,
the Venizelists stood unopposed, and thus captured fifty-two
seats. The only other success was five out of thirteen seats in the
Drama area of Macedonia.[47]

The results were geographically significant. The Venizelists
had won only three electoral districts (Hydra, Arta and Spetsai)
in the Old Greece of before the Balkan wars. Venizelism was
reduced to its original core in Crete, a few pockets in Epirus, the
Aegean islands of Chios and Lesbos, and Thrace.

But though the Venizelists won less than one-third of the seats,
their share of the total vote was considerably greater than 33 per
cent.† There can be no precision about the figures, because of the
lack of adequate electoral statistics for Greek elections of this
period. The elections of November 1920 were conducted according to the electoral law of 1864 as modified in 1887.[48] This system
provided for multimembered electoral districts in which as many
candidates were elected as seats were assigned to that district. The
electorate voted by lead ballots and were obliged to vote 'yes' or
'no' to *every* candidate in their district. It was thus possible to
vote *for* more candidates than there were seats available – indeed
to vote for (or against) *all* the candidates. Under a perfect
system of party organization and party loyalty on the part of the
voters, one would expect any individual voter to vote *for* all the
candidates on one party's ticket, and *against* all the other candidates. But the reality did not correspond to this ideal, because
of the still primitive sense of party loyalty and because the
pattern was disrupted by the candidature of socialists and other
representatives of minority groups, and by local notabilities

---

* The Spetsai result was annulled owing to alleged irregularities and
the three seats were lost to the Venizelists in the subsequent by-election.

† Daphnis, p. 132, cites the following figures, which he accepts with
reservations, from Papanastasiou, *Democracy and Electoral System,*
Athens 1923:

Old Greece:

Venizelists	172.717 votes	(40.3%)
United Opposition	255.437 votes	(59.7%)

New territories which had voted in the elections of 1915:

Venizelists	292.822 votes	(44.1%)
United Opposition	368.678 votes	(55.9%)

(standing either as independents or on one of the party tickets) whose ties of patronage or influence transcended party lines.* Because of this system, and because electoral statistics covered only the number of those who actually cast votes, and not the numbers of registered voters, the interpretation of results in other than general terms is impossible.

It will be seen from this account that the electoral struggle was asymmetrical, the Venizelists seeking re-election on the strength of their successful foreign policy, the opposition campaigning on the issue of Venizelist tyranny at home. The two sides therefore never met head-on except over the dynastic issue. In interpreting the vote of 1 November 1920, the difficulty lies in this lack of a head-on clash. Venizelos himself attributed the result to war-weariness. He wrote to Lloyd George that 'one must not condemn the Greek people who were clearly war-weary, because, after all, it is a fact that I found myself in the necessity to continue mobilization for two years after the armistice and there was no certain sign in view of an immediate demobilization'.[49]

According to this interpretation 'the vote of November 14 was a vote for peace'.[50] But if this is so, it is extraordinary that after the elections there is no evidence of popular discontent with the decision to continue the war in Asia Minor, and at least curious that the issue of war or peace played so little part in the electoral campaign.

According to Venizelist mythology, the opposition campaigned actively for an end to the war, taking 'Demobilization' as their slogan:

* An example is the candidature of K. Zavitsianos in 1920 in Corfu. Out of 21,721 voters, 10,842 voted for Zavitsianos; an average of about 13,000 voted for each of the Royalist candidates; and an average of about 8,000 voted for each of the Venizelists. Thus the United Opposition candidates were elected. Zavitsianos, a former colleague of Venizelos, had broken with the Venizelists over their internal policy, and stood as an independent. He admits that most of the votes cast for him were votes of 'personal respect' and did not indicate agreement with his views. And just as it is impossible to tell how many of the votes for him on this occasion were cast on ideological and how many on personal grounds, so it is impossible to calculate on those occasions when a notability like Zavitsianos stood for a major party how many of his votes were for the party and how many for the person: Zavitsianos, *Recollections of the Historic Dispute of King Constantine and E. Venizelos*, ii, p. 87.

The majority of the new Chamber [wrote Zavitsianos] in the pre-election period, had attacked the whole policy of Venizelos, both foreign and internal, with exceptional harshness. They stood for the programme of a 'small but honest Greece' as they put it. They would not want Asia Minor even if it were offered to them. They would never have made war in order to win it, because according to them Asia Minor was a burden on Greece. They said it was a colony, and they were not disposed to pursue a colonialist policy. It was inhabited for the most part by foreign populations hostile to Greece. Greece, they said, had not the strength to govern so extensive a tract of territory, however rich and productive, if it were inhabited by enemies. The frontiers which the new Greece would obtain, mainly because they would be very extended, would be easily attacked. Therefore Greece would not be able to hold them. With the first war the whole structure called Great Greece would collapse. Moreover the Greeks were exhausted. They had fought now almost continuously for eight years. And so they [the anti-Venizelists] arrived at the popular slogan of demobilization which so electrified the masses and especially the army.[51]

This account faithfully reproduces the doubts felt by anti-Venizelists at various times over Venizelos's policy, but gives a seriously misleading picture of the opposition's views in 1920 when Venizelos's policy seemed to have become realizable. As we have seen, the official policy of the opposition was to accept the Greek claims as formulated by Venizelos at the Peace Conference.

The Greek occupation of Smyrna in May 1919 placed the opposition in a delicate and difficult position. Tempted to seize every stick at hand with which to beat Venizelos, they nevertheless could not disguise from themselves that the Smyrna landing was a national triumph and a realization of Greece's irredentist dreams. Even Metaxas, for a brief period, revoked his earlier criticisms when he heard the news: 'The Greeks have occupied Smyrna. Military occupation. Greece will certainly get it [i.e. in the final peace settlement]. It's all over. We are definitely beaten politically, but may Greece be enlarged and prosper.... Political life is over for good.'[52] And Gounaris, who was with Metaxas in Sardinia when the news arrived, was apparently still more generous in his reaction.[53]

The desire of the anti-Venizelists to attack Venizelos's government on every possible count seems to have resulted in a gap between the official policy of the United Opposition and the unofficial attitudes of certain extreme anti-Venizelists. Officially the United Opposition made no pledge to demobilize or to liquidate the war. But it is indubitable that many Greeks, particularly in the army, voted against Venizelos in the hope that this would mean a rapid end to the war.* They may have done so on the inference that the opposition's traditional policy of caution over foreign entanglements, and its bad relationship with the Entente, would force it to make peace. But it is possible that unofficially representatives of the opposition irresponsibly promised demobilization. All that can be said is that there is no concrete evidence of such a promise.

It seems likely that the majority of the electorate voted against Venizelos primarily because of their dissatisfaction with his internal policy and their desire to see Constantine come home – perhaps also because of their memories of the effects of the Great War within Greece, rather than their determination to stop the present war. What determined the result of the election was, in a word, the schism which, starting as an ideological and personal dispute between Venizelos and the King, had become a rift which divided the entire nation. As the years passed, more and more voters drifted away from Venizelos. He disappointed potential supporters through the repressive measures of his lieutenants, the failure of Venizelist patronage to live up to expectations in the hard economic circumstances of war and postwar years, and the favouritism shown to Venizelist extremists.

The process can be observed most clearly in the army officer corps, which was divided by the schism into three categories – the Venizelists of the National Defence movement, the Royalists who were retired in 1917 (known as the *apotaktoi*), and the neutralists in between the two extremes (the *parameinantes*, 'those who remained').[54] This latter group represents a block of 'floating voters'. The preference shown to committed officers of the National Defence, such as Kondylis and Plastiras, in the question of promotion, and the partisan activities of Pangalos as Chief of Personnel at the War Ministry, pushed more and more of these neutralists into the opposite camp; just as Royalist favouritism of the War Ministry in 1921–22 was to push them back into sympathy with Venizelism. This pattern observable in

---

* Theodore Stephanides told me of a Venizelist friend serving with him in Asia Minor who admitted shamefacedly to voting against Venizelos on these grounds; Argyropoulos, File 7, p. 1, tells of a similar case.

the army was probably a microcosm of the change of sympathies occurring throughout the public services and in any situation where voters were brought into close contact with government patronage. The Venizelists thus fell victim to 'the cumulative dissatisfaction of personal grievances and unrealized hopes of patronage which in Greece inevitably erodes the popularity of a party long in power'.[55]

The war in Asia Minor must have worked against Venizelos in so far as it had an effect on the result. For despite the official policy of the opposition, it remained true that the name of Venizelos had become associated with war, whereas the anti-Venizelist forces had always stood for the avoidance of foreign adventures without firm guarantees ensuring their practicability. The electorate knew this, and those voters whose primary interest, because their relatives were mobilized, was a quick end to the war, would have looked to the opposition and not the Venizelists to achieve it.

Many of Venizelos's friends and collaborators, with the benefit of hindsight, charged it against him that he held the elections of November 1920 at a time when the crucial questions of Asia Minor, northern Epirus and Thrace were still unsettled:

In proclaiming and holding elections before the great issue of foreign policy was settled, Venizelos failed to see that in the life of peoples there arise certain questions which cannot be settled according to the decision of a transient majority. . . .
Above even the constitutional charter stand the Nation, the people, the race. . . . Nations live for ever, while persons come and go.[56]

Venizelos answered these critics many years later in a letter to his friend George Ventiris:

When the treaty of Sèvres was signed, I judged that there was no longer any justification for my postponing the elections further. The results of my policy were faithfully reflected in the treaties which had been signed and which had brought the war to an end; the people therefore had the means whereby to see what were the fruits of my policy, and, without denying that I felt a certain uneasiness about the probable result of the elections, I nevertheless had good hopes, along with Repoulis and the majority of my colleagues, that the people would approve what had been done.
It was necessary for me to be certain that the people approved my

policies, before I could proceed to those further actions which were necessary for the implementation of the Treaty of Sèvres.[57]

Venizelos's argument, supported by the analogy from Great Britain and France, which had held elections after the war had ended, depended on the proposition that the peace treaties marked the end of a state of war and a return to normality. The contention of his critics was that normality did not exist: the Greek Army was mobilized and engaged in important operations in Asia Minor; therefore this was no time to open the door to a possible change of regime.

Despite his habitual optimism, Venizelos knew well that there was no state of 'normality'. But other, psychological reasons prevented him from drawing the conclusion drawn by Ventiris. He was accused of tyranny. He was repeatedly challenged by the opposition to put his alleged popularity to the test of public opinion. The implication behind the challenge was that, as a tyrant, he would not dare to do so. The accusations hurt Venizelos. Even if the circumstances of war, the division of the nation and the petty animosities of his lieutenants had entailed harshness and injustice, he knew that he was no tyrant. 'I have explained to you repeatedly,' he told Ventiris, 'that I am not made of the stuff of which dictators are made.... I would loathe myself, if against the will of the people I had continued to govern because I considered myself better than the rest.' [58] Therefore he accepted the challenge.

Nevertheless, Venizelos accepted the justice of the criticism that he had mishandled the dynastic issue:

My mistake was quite other than that with which I am charged. It was not a mistake that I did not abolish the monarchy. My mistake was that when the death of Alexander occurred I failed to postpone the elections in order to negotiate with Constantine and the Powers for the accession to the throne of the constitutional heir, George. This solution might have been accepted by Constantine. Nor would I perhaps have met insuperable opposition from the Powers, who at the time when they enforced the resignation of Constantine, excluded George from the succession. But this view, when put to those of my colleagues in whose opinions I had the greatest confidence, was received coldly. I was informed at the same time that this solution would arouse great discontent in the army. I had already written a letter to Take Ionesco, inviting his intervention with the Royal Family of Romania, who might have persuaded

Constantine to accept such a solution; but all these factors caused me to tear up the letter.

This was my great and, you might say, unforgivable error. Because this solution, if it had been achieved, would have restored national unity, and the result of the elections would very probably have been totally different. But even if the elections had gone the same way as in fact they did, the acute disagreement with the Entente arising from the return of King Constantine to the throne would not have occurred.[59]

This explanation seems to be a rationalization produced in later years to satisfy Venizelos's feeling that there must have been a way out of his dilemma. The presumption must be that George would have given the same negative answer as Paul. But Venizelos also ignored the attitudes of the opposition. To them, George was not the 'constitutional heir' any more than Paul was; the throne was not vacant. Constantine had simply stepped down, temporarily, bowing to *force majeure*. The opposition would therefore not have accepted any such compromise as the accession of George – and not merely on principle, but because they knew that Constantine was their strongest electoral weapon. The death of Alexander therefore allowed Venizelos no possibility of manoeuvre, negotiation or compromise. He was forced by the logic of the opposition's attitude to the dynastic issue since 1917 either to proceed with the elections, knowing that a major issue would be the return of King Constantine from exile, or to postpone the elections once more, laying himself open to those accusations of dictatorship and arbitrary rule which he deplored.

Proposals were made at various times for a 'reconciliation' of Royalists and Venizelists based on the resignation of King Alexander, the accession of Prince George, and the definitive abdication of King Constantine. All these had fallen to the ground. One such attempt was made in late 1918 by Queen Marie of Romania through the mediation of Apostolos Alexandris, the Venizelist politician.[60] Venizelos imputed his rejection of it to the objections of his closest colleagues and the anti-Constantinist feelings of the army. Among the Royalists, Streit, Nikolaos Theotokis and D. Maximos at various times made similar unsuccessful overtures.[61] Equally unproductive was the attempt of a group of distinguished moderates including E. Demertzis, A. Christomanos, G. Christakis Zographos, Leonidas

Embireikos and K. Zavitsianos to found a 'third party' with a programme of national unity.[62] Most of these men had strong ties with Venizelism. But still Venizelos would not defer to their views.

These proposals came either from those closely associated with the fortunes of the Royal House, or from disenchanted Liberals who continued to believe in Venizelos's foreign policy but had lost confidence in his conduct of affairs at home and saw the dangers of the schism. Neither group carried the political weight to influence him. There was no reason for Venizelos to look for compromise unless he accepted the premise that the bitterness of the schism actually threatened his foreign policy and electoral prospects. But he did not believe this. Only once, in May–June 1920, did Venizelos toy with the idea of a very limited and partial reconciliation.*

The Venizelists knew how strong was the Constantinist myth and how slender the popular basis of Alexander's reign. They had tried by every means to prevent the dynastic issue from being raised. The risk of compromise was that it would reopen the dynastic question with unpredictable results. It would in any case have been difficult for Venizelos consistently to turn his 'own' king, Alexander, off the throne.

Venizelos disingenuously blamed his refusal to compromise on the army.[64] But he himself did not stand outside the mythology of the schism and deplore it. He shared the assumptions of his subordinates. When Joseph Koundouros, the rabidly anti-Royalist public prosecutor at the show trials of these years, publicly insulted King Constantine, calling him a 'royal brute',[65] Venizelos's reaction to Alexander's demand for an apology was characteristic. He formally rebuked Koundouros, but simul-

---

* Venizelos suggested that a move towards a 'national front' over foreign policy be made by dropping the impending charges against D. Rallis and bringing him into the government as Minister without Portfolio, allowing him to support the government's foreign policy while maintaining his independence over internal policies. Venizelos also indicated that he might invite the opposition to elect a three-man committee to consult with the government over the 'national questions'. These suggestions came at a time when Venizelos feared that the attitude of the opposition, unless placated, might prevent him from calling up those classes of reservists demanded by the situation in Asia Minor, and that England might therefore recommend that Greek claims be limited in the final peace treaty.[63]

taneously sent a private assurance that he understood and sympathized with the 'anger which the memory of the ex-king's crimes provokes'. 'I am not sure,' wrote Venizelos to Repoulis, 'that in his position I could have restrained myself either.' [66]

The two sides were therefore too far apart for compromise. Neither Venizelists nor Gounarists believed that the common interest of a united approach to foreign policy should override their party political differences over the dynastic question.

Suggestions that if Venizelos had played his cards more skilfully his party could have won the elections are implausible.* The Liberals were beaten fairly and squarely. They were caught in a trap sprung by the uneasy mixture of liberal theory and illiberal practice in the difficult circumstances of divided postwar Greece. Too dictatorial and repressive to win widespread popularity, the Venizelists were not repressive enough to ensure electoral victory by modern totalitarian methods. However unfortunate the 14th of November may have been for Greece's foreign ambitions, it was a vindication of the still primitive workings of an open social and political system.

* Zavitsianos (ii, pp. 84–5) writes that had Atticoboeotia been divided into two electoral districts, as he suggested to Venizelos, the Liberals could have won some sixteen seats (including that of Venizelos himself) in the metropolitan area, leaving the rural area to the opposition. As it was, the opposition won all twenty-two seats in the single district. Pericles Argyropoulos, unpublished Memoirs, File 7, pp. 3–4, suggests another manoeuvre whereby Atticoboeotia might have been won. He also argues implausibly that by legislating that Muslims and Jews should vote their own representatives in separate electoral colleges (as a draft bill of 1915 had provided), the Venizelists could have won all the seats in 'Greek' Macedonia, thus obtaining an overall majority. Greek elections almost invariably provide opportunities, and excite charges, of jerrymandering and fiddling by the party in power.

8 | The New Regime: Constantine Returns

Here was a potentate who, as we saw it, against
the wishes and the interests of his people, had for
personal and family reasons thrown his country, or
tried to throw it, on the enemy side, which had
also turned out to be the losing side. . . . The
return of Constantine therefore dissolved all Allied
loyalties to Greece and cancelled all but legal
obligations. . . . Greece had in fact become a
liberator. Just at the moment when her needs were
greatest and her commitments were becoming
most embarrassing to herself and to others, she
had of her own free will sponged the slate. It is
not every day that moral creditors are so
accommodating.

Winston Churchill, *The World Crisis:
the Aftermath*, pp. 387–8

Treaty of Sèvres must be saved at all costs.

Venizelos in Nice, November 1920

As soon as the results of the election were clear, Venizelos decided to resign without waiting to be defeated in the new
Chamber. The United Opposition had no formally recognized
'leader'. This fact allowed the Regent, Admiral Koundouriotis,
to influence the choice of a new prime minister. While the opposition leaders were discussing the implications of their victory,
the Regent, with Venizelos's approval, coolly determined to send
for Dimitrios Rallis, despite his relatively small following among
the deputies, on the grounds that with his long experience and
moderate views he would be more acceptable to the allies than
the dominant figures in the opposition coalition. The opposition
were content to accept this solution. Rallis and his Cabinet were
sworn in by Koundouriotis,[1] who was then told to submit his
own resignation from the office of Regent. Queen Olga, widow
of King George I, was invited to assume the Regency and the
Cabinet was sworn in all over again by her.[2]

This farcical procedure was consistent with the Royalists' total
rejection of the previous regime's unconstitutional basis. If Con-

stantine were king, Koundouriotis could not constitutionally have been Regent; *ergo* he could not validly have sworn in a new government. There followed the procedures which typify a change of régime in a politically undeveloped country. Portraits of Constantine and Sophia were restored to their places on the walls of public offices, and the courts were told to issue their decrees in the name of the King. A referendum to settle the question of the King's return was proclaimed for Sunday 5 December. The Rallis government lost no time in declaring that there would be no change in Greece's foreign policy, no reprisals against Venizelists, and an amnesty for political offences.

Meanwhile in the streets of Athens everyone seemed to have gone quite mad:

From morning to night enormous crowds paraded the streets and organized demonstrations in favour of Constantine. In the Rue du Stade and Place de la Concorde every shop that could produce photographs of the ex-King and ex-Queen Sophie did a roaring trade, and in front of practically every shop the pictures of M. Venizelos, which had adorned it for the past week, were replaced by that of Constantine. Carriages and motors paraded the streets, the occupants holding up immense pictures of the ex-King wreathed in flowers and olive-branches, and the crowds that thronged the sidewalks shouted enthusiastic greetings and pelted the carriages with flowers. In the afternoon an enormous crowd collected in the Place de la Concorde and formed itself into a procession, parading through all the principal streets singing the 'Hymn to the Son of the Eagle', and shouting 'Viva, Constantine!' Conspicuous among the procession were whole companies of soldiers, fully armed, and many officers, who joined in the march. Soldiers and sailors fired off their rifles and revolvers into the air as token of rejoicing and the civil population was not slow to imitate them, so that the whole town was in an immense uproar.[3]

The atmosphere was one of excitement and rejoicing, in which violence and revenge were muted. There were some shooting incidents and frequent scuffles in the streets. The windows of Politis's house were smashed by bravos. The Venizelists quietly disappeared from the streets and left the Royalists to their demonstrations. The Government, conscious of the effects of reprisals on the attitude of the Powers,[4] was able quickly to restore order.

The change of regime in Greece, utterly unexpected by the Allies, brought into the open for the first time the serious divergence of view between France and Great Britain on the eastern question.

The French took a strong and uninhibited line. Since 1916, when French marines had been shot in Athens by Royalist troops at the time of the heaviest Anglo-French pressure on the Greek Government, Constantine had been a bogeyman comparable to the Kaiser to the French. As soon as the news of Venizelos's defeat came through, the French press began to campaign for the revision of the Treaty of Sèvres. Within a few days the French Government made proposals for discussions with the British, and suggested a joint declaration that the two Governments would in no case allow the return of the ex-King.[5] It was soon apparent that the French wanted not only to prevent the return of Constantine (or failing that to punish the Greeks if they recalled him) but also to take this opportunity to improve their standing in Turkey by revising the Treaty.

In England the news of Venizelos's fall from power threw into relief the differences of opinion between Lloyd George and the Foreign Office on the one hand, and Churchill and the War Office on the other. The War Office was quick to produce a memorandum on the military situation in the east, which reflected a growing fear of a rapprochement between the Turkish Nationalists and the Russian Bolsheviks.[6] The Russians had begun cautiously to treat with Kemal during the summer. The two sides had a common interest in driving out the Entente powers which eventually overrode their local disputes over their common border areas. The fate of Georgia, Azerbaijan and Armenia was settled on the spot by a mixture of force and negotiation. Armenia was divided between the two. The oil port of Batum went to Russia, the Kars and Ardahan districts to Turkey. With the elimination of independent Armenia, the direct route from Soviet Russia to Turkey was opened up again, and a Soviet-Turkish treaty of friendship of March 1921 prepared the ground for the eventual arrival of a Soviet military mission under General Frunze, and for the flow of Russian arms and gold to Kemal in 1922.[7]

In November 1920, though these developments could be foreseen, the Russians and Turks were still eyeing each other warily over the ruins of independent Armenia.

But the fears of Churchill and the British General Staff were increased by the successes of the Bolsheviks in eliminating the White Russian movements of resistance despite the intervention of the Allies. Kolchak, Yudenich and Denikin were crushed. Now in November 1920 General Wrangel, the last of these forlorn commanders, was forced to abandon Russian soil. With the hungry, unkempt remnants of his White army, he sailed from the Crimea to Constantinople, posing a vast problem of relief for the allied administration, and leaving south Russia to the Red Army.

In their appreciation the British General Staff argued correctly that the Kemalists, though anxious to secure Russian arms and ammunition, were 'not unanimously in favour of allowing the Bolsheviks to penetrate into Anatolia'. It was therefore necessary to play on the differences between Bolsheviks and Kemalists rather than to throw them into one another's arms. The Staff argued that 'the disappearance of Wrangel, the capitulation of Armenia, the imminent threat to Georgia and the downfall of Venizelos confront us with a situation in the Middle East with which it may be beyond our power to cope without a change of policy'. Since it was now 'unsafe to rely upon the Greek Army to cover the Allied position in Turkey', the British Government must either reinforce its position in Constantinople, or withdraw from Constantinople, or readjust its whole policy in the Near East. The General Staff favoured the third course: 'A drastic revision of the territorial terms of the Turkish Treaty in respect of Smyrna, the province of Kars, and possibly of Thrace, would induce the Turkish Nationalists to break with the Russian Soviet Government.'

The memorandum reflected Churchill's passionate view that the basis of Britain's Near Eastern policy must be the containment of Soviet Russia. Commending the memorandum to the Cabinet, Churchill specifically argued for a closer entente with France, which would enable Britain to get a 'good peace' with Kemal, and to recreate that 'Turkish barrier to Russian ambitions' which had always been a key to British policy in the Near East.[8] Peace with Kemal would secure British interests in Constantinople and at the same time ease the position in Egypt, Mesopotamia, Persia and India. Thus Churchill neatly reversed Lord Curzon's refrain – that giving in to Kemal over Smyrna would lead to attacks all along the line against the British position in the east. Seeing that the nature of Kemalism was not expansionist (outside the area claimed by the Turks in their National Pact), he understood that the classic objections to appeasement did not here apply.

Lloyd George and the Foreign Office resisted all such persuasion. The Foreign Office was prepared to go along with the French in measures thought necessary to deal with Constantine, provided they did not affect the Treaty of Sèvres. Curzon wrote:

There is one party that says, 'Break with the Greeks. Throw them over in Thrace and Smyrna. Make friends with Mr Kemal. Tear up the Treaty and make a new one based on a relatively powerful and contented Turkey.'* But can we do this at this date, and supposing that Constantine is invited back to the throne by the Greeks and as regards his foreign policy is more Venizelist than Venizelos and is supported by his troops, he then becomes – No paper I cannot go on.[9]

Perhaps Curzon was going to write 'a martyr'. The question 'can we?' was not entirely rhetorical; Curzon was torn between his belief that the Greek occupation of Smyrna was a terrible mistake, and his desire not to disturb the treaty settlement which had been negotiated with such toil, nor to give in to the French, whom he had once called 'the most imperialistic people in the world'.[10] The effect of these divided feelings was a policy of inaction.

Sir Eyre Crowe, the Permanent Under Secretary, was fond of Venizelos, but saw the impossibility of preventing King Constantine's return:

I see grave objections to threatening Greece with the withdrawal of an allied support if Constantine returns. This would be bound to lead to Turkish and probably Bulgarian attacks on Greece all along the line, from Smyrna to Salonika. We have everything to gain from maintaining Greece in Western and Eastern Thrace at least....

Crowe therefore recommended no interference over the Greek referendum, but a declaration by Britain and France that

the attitude of England and France towards Constantinist Greece will entirely depend on the policy she will follow; but it will obviously require time and unswervingly straight-forward conduct as well as wise and effective government on the part of the new regime if it is to recover the Allies' confidence.[11]

---

* Bonar Law had taken this line, as well as Churchill: Roskill, *Hankey, Man of Secrets*, ii, pp. 199–200.

In other and less patronizing words, Crowe stood for the maintenance of the *status quo*, and allied support for Greece, provided she continued to uphold the Treaty of Sèvres. Curzon held to the same line with the French.[12]

The fallen King and fallen prime minister meanwhile were sitting in their tents in Lucerne and Nice respectively. Constantine in Lucerne had declared that his attitude was identical with that of the Government in Athens – no change in foreign policy, and strict and loyal collaboration with the two Powers.[13] On the eve of the Anglo-French Conference, Sir John Stavridi, who had been sent by Curzon to Nice to discover Venizelos's views, telegraphed that Venizelos advised the recognition of Prince George and abdication of Constantine, but if this was impossible, would prefer that Constantine be recognized in return for binding himself to carry out the Treaty. In Venizelos's view 'Treaty of Sèvres must be saved at all costs'.[14]

The Conference met in Downing Street on 26 November.[15] The French immediately made their position clear. Among the four preventive measures which they suggested the Allies might take to stop Constantine's return, one was a notification to the Greek government that 'the Allies could not entrust important strategical positions in the Near East to an unfriendly Government'.[16] Smyrna was such a position. Lloyd George and Curzon argued strongly against this first move towards a revision of the Treaty of Sèvres.

Lord Curzon circulated a long note to the Conference the next day. Curzon's note envisaged, not measures to prevent the King's return to Greece, but conditions on which his return would be permitted by the Allies.[17] These included 'an absolute undertaking to refrain from persecution or prosecution of Venizelists and an amnesty for all political prisoners', and restrictions on Greece's political and economic freedom of action in the form of an allied veto over the contraction of loans or conclusion of diplomatic or military conventions. The substance of the note was leaked to the press, and a slightly garbled version of the conditions was published in the Athens press.[18] They were well received in Greece, even by sections of the Venizelist press. They were lenient beyond expectation. The message was clear: provided the Greeks behaved with reasonable moderation at home, and upheld the Treaty of Sèvres abroad, they could hope for British support.

Curzon ended his note with a strangely muted and defensive argument against revising the Treaty of Sèvres:

Will it not be better to stand by the treaty for the present and to press for its ratification, but, if owing to the failure of Greece to fulfil her obligations, or to maintain her troops, the treaty is broken or crumbles at any point, to seize the occasion to make better terms with the Turk at the point concerned. For instance, if Greece were voluntarily to withdraw from Smyrna, she would then have broken the treaty herself, and we could repair the damage with the Turks. In this way, if the Greeks be as feeble or treacherous or war-weary as is supposed by some, the treaty will be almost automatically re-vised step by step, without the prolonged delay and convulsion of a complete reconstruction now.[19]

The policy here envisaged is one of deliberate inactivity; the treaty was to be maintained, if the Greeks proved capable of maintaining it, and French susceptibilities were to be smoothed by the 'conditions' suggested by Curzon, which would not materially damage Greek military or economic capabilities. But having gained his point on the maintenance of the treaty, Curzon was forced to yield to the French on other points including the withdrawal of financial support from Greece.

At their session of 2 December, the three Allies agreed on a joint declaration which at once acquired notoriety as marking the change of status brought about by the fall of Venizelos:

The British, French, and Italian Governments have constantly in the past given proof of their good-will towards the Greek people [the declaration ran, hypocritically]. They have therefore been all the more painfully surprised by the events which have just occurred in Greece.

They have no wish to interfere in the internal affairs of Greece. But they feel bound to declare publicly that the restoration to the throne of Greece of a King, whose disloyal attitude and conduct towards the Allies during the war caused them great embarrassment and loss, could only be regarded by them as a ratification by Greece of his hostile acts. This step would create a new and unfavourable situation in the relations between Greece and the Allies, and in that case the three Governments reserve to themselves complete liberty in dealing with the situation thus created.[20]

This declaration was handed to Rallis in Athens by the three allied representatives on 3 December. It was followed by formal notification that in the event of King Constantine's return no further financial assistance would be given to Greece.[21]

These notes represented a compromise between the French and British viewpoints. The treaty was to be maintained; but Greece was to be damaged and her capacity to maintain and enforce the treaty undermined by the withdrawal of allied financial and moral support.

The 'moral' effects of the Allies' notes were of great importance in a country which had always depended on the Great Powers in its foreign relations and whose people were accustomed to think that success or failure in any enterprise depended on the Powers' whims. They added more fuel to the fire of the schism. It was argued by the Venizelists that the return of the King and the 'freedom of action' which the Allies reserved to themselves led as a direct consequence to all the diplomatic and military reverses suffered by Greece after November 1920.[22] We shall see the effects of this attitude work themselves out over the next two years. At the time, Venizelists argued that after the allied démarche the government should have cancelled the referendum, postponing the King's return, either indefinitely, or at least until good relations with the Allies had been restored.[23] Even after the mistake had been made, it was argued, the Government should have realized how gravely the presence of the King (still unrecognized by allied governments) was damaging Greece's cause, and advised him to withdraw from Greece for the good of the nation. It was hopefully assumed that Greece would then have been 'restored' to her position in the alliance, and regained the material and moral support denied her by the allied démarches of November 1920.

This was an implausible thesis. The views of France and England on the Near Eastern settlement were not determined solely or mainly by the presence or absence of King Constantine from the throne of Greece. But the return of Constantine did have a catalytic effect on allied policy. The events of November 1920 helped to *crystallize* the French conception of their Near Eastern interests, and brought to a head the increasing French dissatisfaction with Entente policy. They enabled the French with relief to press for a revision of the treaty at Greece's expense; to do openly and suddenly what could have been done only gradually and with difficulty had Venizelos remained in power.

And they caused Great Britain, in the interests of allied solidarity, and because of a genuine mistrust of the intentions and military capacity of the new regime, to lose confidence in the practicability of her Near Eastern policy, so that British support for Greece was hereafter still more hesitant and uncertain than before.

The Allies' second note introducing a limited 'financial blockade' of Greece had significant practical effects. By blocking the allied credits opened for Greece in 1918–19[24] to enable her to play her part in the war effort, England and France deprived about 600 million drachmas of their 'cover', transforming them into paper money of forced circulation. The result was a gradual loss of confidence in the drachma and an accelerating fall in the exchange rate. The blockade also put an end to Greek hopes of further military aid on long-term credit. Finally, by strictly interpreting Greece's obligations under the 1918–19 financial agreements, the Allies could make it impossible for Greece to raise a new foreign loan, as the new government was to discover.

This withdrawal of financial support came at the worst possible time for Greece, since warning symptoms of inflation and a fall in the exchange rate had already begun to appear in the last months of the Venizelist government. In the financial climate of 1921–22, any government would have found it difficult to procure substantial aid and support from the Allies. For Constantine's regime it was impossible. The blocking of the remaining allied credits had an important effect on Greek confidence, and hastened the approach of financial and economic exhaustion of which the main cause was the colossal drain on Greek resources caused by the war in Asia Minor.

The Allies thus adopted, most nearly, the course which Harold Nicolson predicted would 'permanently destroy the fabric of the peace treaties and reduce Greece to the proportions of a third class power'.[25] Torn between his regret that the Greeks had been sent into Asia Minor, and his desire that the great settlement of Sèvres should not be tampered with, genuinely doubtful of the wisdom and efficacy of the new regime in Greece, reluctant to insist on the British viewpoint to the point of rupture with the French, Curzon was persuaded to accept the substance of French demands in return for the temporary provisional agreement not to demolish the Sèvres settlement. The hard decisions were thus postponed.

The ostensible purpose of the allied notes to Greece was to prevent the return of King Constantine. But the first note was published in the press only on 4 December, and had no time to filter through to the masses before the vote the next day.[26] The Venizelist press urged the Government to avert the King's return by cancelling the referendum. But after their initial depression over the Allies' first note, the Royalists recovered their spirits, arguing that the declaration was a bluff, and that Great Britain had joined in it only in order to please the French.

The referendum was held on Sunday 5 December. It resulted, as everyone knew it would, in a massive vote for the return of the King from exile. As preparations were made in Greece to welcome the King home, the Allies tussled with the knotty problem of how to treat him when he arrived – withdraw their ministers from the court, send them quietly away on leave, or carry on as usual and enter into full relations with the King. After agonizing appraisals, it was decided that the ministers should remain, but enter into no official or personal relations with Constantine or his court. The allied missions to the Greek navy, army and gendarmerie also remained. These difficult decisions of protocol soon led to farcical results.

The King travelled down from Lucerne to Venice and from there sailed on the *Averoff* to Greece. He reached Athens by train from Corinth on 19 December, amid scenes of great enthusiasm. Members of the allied missions were able to avoid the reception and Te Deum for the King's return without difficulty since they were not formally invited. The Italian head of the Gendarmerie Mission went along in 'plain clothes' to observe.

Granville and his colleagues were agreed that the heads of the allied missions – technically Greek functionaries – must in all decency write their names in the King's book.[27] It was decided that the British head of the Naval Mission, Admiral Kelly, would 'write his name' and then ask the Minister of Marine to use tact to see that, having done their immediate duty by the King, they were not 'unnecessarily brought into prominence'. With Machiavellian ingenuity the Greeks called this bluff. Within an hour of speaking to the Minister in this sense, Admiral Kelly was summoned to the Palace and received by the King: 'His Majesty was most gracious and expressed his devotion to Great Britain. At close of interview he handed to Admiral Kelly Grand Cross of Redeemer.'[28] This subtle move threw the British

Legation into confusion. Granville immediately called on Rallis and complained bitterly. It was customary to seek the consent of the foreign government concerned before decorating a foreign national. The Greek Government had indeed asked permission to decorate Kelly but had jumped the gun in awarding the medal. Granville protested that the award was 'an obvious trick to try and show that our relations were friendly instead of strained or hostile as they were and also to make difficulties between us and French'. Rallis said it was absolutely impossible to take back or not to publish the decoration. All he would agree to do was ensure that General Gramat, Head of the French Military Mission, would if he wished be received with exactly the same civility and awarded the same decoration.

London telegraphed waspishly: 'It is very regrettable that incident was ever allowed to take place. Permission cannot be granted to Admiral Kelly to accept this decoration which must therefore be returned by him.'[29]

Granville himself returned the Grand Cross to Rallis, who was much upset and said he would at once offer his resignation. Admiral Kelly also felt his best course would be to resign at once or at least go on leave. Ruffled feathers were smoothed, and no one in the event resigned. The British Legation began to establish a working relationship with the new regime.

On 20 December, the day after King Constantine arrived in Athens, Harold Nicolson summed up the policies of the three allied powers in an interesting memorandum.[30] The French and the Italians wished to destroy the Greater Greece of the Treaty of Sèvres, the British to maintain it:

The idea which prompted our support of Greece was no emotional impulse but the natural expression of our historical policy: the protection of India and the Suez canal. For a century we had supported Turkey as the first line of defence in the Eastern Mediterranean. Turkey proved a broken reed and we fell back on the second line, the line from Salamis to Smyrna. Geographically the position of Greece was unique for our purpose: politically she was strong enough to save us expense in peace, and weak enough to be completely subservient in war. The Treaty of Sèvres was thus an immense asset had it succeeded. It is not too early at present to conclude that it has failed?

Nicolson concluded that Britain should adjust her policy and openly support King Constantine so long as he supported the

Treaty of Sèvres, rather than leave him in Athens and subject
him to a 'series of intermittent pinpricks'. It was too late. Both
Crowe and Curzon defended the policy of the 'waiting attitude',
which was entailed by the demands of allied solidarity.[31] In
Curzon's view, it was necessary before taking any policy decisions
to wait and see how the military situation in Asia Minor developed, how Greece would get on without money, whether the
troops would fight if unpaid. It seemed indeed that, in Churchill's
phrase, 'the war was to be fought by proxy. Wars fought this
way by great nations are very dangerous for the proxy'.[32]

The upheaval of November 1920 mirrored the revolution
following Venizelos's return to Athens in 1917. By 1917 per-
manence of tenure in the civil service, enshrined in the 1911 constitution, had broken down. In the public services as in the
army, the Venizelists had removed opponents and installed
supporters, as they were bound to in order to reward their own
faithful clientele. The ideal of security of tenure could only
have been preserved after the merging of the two Greeces in 1917
at the cost of a gross inflation of numbers and consequent increase in costs and loss of efficiency. A purge was cheaper and
more satisfying to the party.

The anti-Venizelists set out to reverse the process, removing
Venizelists and installing or reinstalling their own men. On 22
November twenty-seven Venizelist nomarchs (the Government's
provincial representatives or *préfets*) were sacked, and a few days
later twenty-nine new nomarchs were appointed.[33] The appointments and dismissals affected the whole country except Thrace
and a few islands. At one stroke the Government thus asserted
its control over the provinces. Mayors of major towns such as
Salonika and Edessa were sacked or resigned. The changes in
provincial government extended downwards in some cases even
as far as the position of village president, or headman.

In the Athens ministries the senior 'political' appointees of
the Venizelists were of course removed. On 30 November the
Gazette announced the dismissal of Sir John Stavridi as honorary
Consul General in London, and a series of high level resignations
in the Foreign Service, including the ministers Dimitrios Kakla-
manos from London and Apostolos Alexandris from Berlin. The
general secretaries weeded out from the Ministries included
Nikos Kazantzakis in the Ministry of Relief.[34]

The educational experts D. Glinos, A. Delmouzos and Manolis Triantaphyllidis resigned from the Ministry of Education.[35] On 29 November a royal decree reinstated the Metropolitans of Athens and Larissa and twenty other bishops to the thrones they had occupied before 1917. Among the resulting dismissals was that of the Venizelist prelate Meletios Metaxakis, Metropolitan of Athens since 1917.

The four main areas affected by the purge were the civil service, the courts, education and the armed services. In the delicate area of justice, the new regime cancelled the dismissals of judges and prosecutors which had followed Venizelos's suspension of the constitutional provisions of life tenure for the judiciary.[36] Venizelist appointments to the higher ranks of the judiciary (e.g. President and Prosecutor of the Court of First Instance) were cancelled, but lesser appointments were allowed to stand.

A decree was published allowing the restoration to their posts of those established civil servants dismissed or demoted as a result of the Venizelists' suspension of permanency of tenure.[37] In the field of education, Venizelist appointments to university chairs were cancelled, and the dismissals of university and polytechnic teaching staff between 1917 and 1920 were declared null and void.[38]

The declared intention of the new regime was to 'restore normality'. One of the first acts of the new Government was therefore to declare an amnesty. A decree of 21 November amnestied 'all political misdemeanours' except for crimes related to the events of 31 July (Old Style), i.e. the day of the murder of Ion Dragoumis – and after.[39] The purpose of this amnesty was more to enable the Government to release anti-Venizelists from goal and the stigma of prosecution than to show generosity to opponents.[40]

The area in which the change of regime had the most far-reaching effect was the army. It was here that the schism had been most acute in 1916–17. The reason was not that the army officer corps was naturally more inclined to political dissension and fratricidal struggle than other sectors of society (though it was certainly not less), but that the nature of the schism was such as to force the officer corps to make a choice for one side or the other in the political struggle.

The new regime's first loyalty was to its own men who had been dismissed under the Venizelist regime, known as the *apotaktoi*. About 1,500 army officers who had been dismissed or forcibly put on the reserve list, or who had resigned their commissions, between 1917 and 1920, were now reinstated by Royal Decree.[41]

The mere recalling of the *apotaktoi* was only the first step. The crucial problem remained what to do about their relationship to their old colleagues, the National Defence Officers and the 'neutrals', in terms of seniority and rank, subjects about which the Greek officer corps is as sensitive as any in the world. Not only had the rest of the officer corps three years' active service to their credit for purposes of promotion and seniority, while the *apotaktoi* had languished in enforced inactivity; the notorious Law 927 of 1917 had added to the records of the National Defence officers as war service the ten month period of 'unofficial' service in Salonika from September 1916 to July 1917.[42] Thus men like Pangalos, Kondylis and Plastiras had leapt ahead of their old classmates. The *apotaktoi* regarded this as an injustice, and demanded their old position in the hierarchy, if not better.

The new regime's solution to this problem was not to reverse the coin by creating thousands of Venizelist *apotaktoi* – this, with the Greek army involved in war with Turkey, would have been suicidal – but, by a complicated series of measures, to attempt to restore the old order of seniority.[43] Law 927 was cancelled, and every change in seniority consequent on it. Thus those who had remained on active service between 1917 and 1920 reverted to their seniority as it had been before Law 927; those who had been dismissed or retired or who had resigned between June 1917 and November 1920, and were now recalled, regained the seniority they had had before leaving the army. This would restore the *ideal* order of seniority, but *actual rank* did not correspond to this order. The War Minister was therefore given powers to make the promotions necessary to restore the *apotaktoi* to the rank considered appropriate. For instance, officers holding a rank higher than their own seniors in the same arm or corps could be put in a state of 'suspension' on three-quarter's pay, until the proper order was restored; and the War Minister might promote officers by royal decree over and above the fixed number of posts for each rank where there were officers junior to them holding higher rank.

All these measures enabled justice and more than justice to be done to the *apotaktoi*. In effect, the *apotaktoi* could be promoted to the rank appropriate to their positions in the order of seniority, while the promotion of Venizelist officers could be held up. That the *apotaktoi* should be reinstated was politically inevitable, and it was certainly preferable that they be reinstated in this way rather than that large numbers of Venizelist National Defence Officers be dismissed the service. But the procedure had two great disadvantages. First, it caused resentment and anger in the ranks of the National Defence and the neutrals, who saw their promotion prospects spoiled by the reinstatement of these men who had not fought for the country (for whatever reason) during the past three years. Second, the reinstatement of these officers and their promotion without a correspondingly widespread purge of Venizelist officers created an inflation of the higher ranks of the officer corps.

The return of the *apotaktoi* therefore caused a very considerable upheaval in the ranks of the army, bringing the divisions and dissensions within the officer corps into the open. The area where the upheaval could do the most damage was Asia Minor.

The Greek population of Smyrna, Constantinople and the off-shore islands Chios and Mitylene, was predominantly Venizelist in sympathy. So before the elections were many of the officer corps and all commanders at divisional level in Asia Minor. The news of the fall of Venizelos therefore created an electric sense of expectation in the Smyrna zone. Feelings were already running high as a result of the army vote. There was now general uncertainty as to the future and doubt whether the Venizelist commanders would accept the popular verdict.

Alarmist rumours in Smyrna were soon quelled by the firm attitude of the High Commission, which emphasized the continuity of Greek policy.[44] Stergiadis submitted his resignation but the new Government asked him to stay on. Of all high-ranking Venizelist appointees, he with his resolute indifference to party politics was perhaps the most capable of bridging the gap between Venizelist and Royalist regime.

General Paraskevopoulos was, however, known to be Venizelos's man, and his resignation was accepted. In his place the Government appointed General Anastasios Papoulas, a bluff, courageous Royalist who had spent the last years in prison after conviction at one of the Venizelist show trials for his attitude during the war. The period between the Royalist victory and

Papoulas's arrival in Smyrna was one of dangerous tension in the army. Some Royalists took matters into their own hands, giving orders as if the civil and military command structure had broken down.[45] In the Cavalry Brigade especially there was serious indiscipline. Ordered to proceed to Akhissar on 27 November to the assistance of General Nider's First Army Corps, which had reported alarming Turkish concentrations on the Ushak front, the Brigade refused to move from its positions at Kassaba, claiming that the order was a ruse on the part of the G.H.Q. to remove it from the vicinity of Smyrna, and thus facilitate a Venizelist *coup d'état*.[46] On 21 November, Stergiadis attributed the 'partial disaffection of Greek troops' to a 'passing ebullition of feeling', holding that morale was basically sound.[47] But the next day the British Vice-Consul reported that 'lack of discipline in army is beginning to be admitted even by Greek G.H.Q. Kondylis, Officer Commanding Third Regiment, was mobbed by troops at Salihli and only escaped by hiding under coal in tender of train.'[48]

The arrival of Papoulas and the firmness of the High Commission soon restored order. Papoulas is generally accepted to have worked for reconciliation within the army.[49] Conceited, gullible, not blessed with a penetrating intelligence, he nevertheless did his best to treat his officers on equal terms regardless of their political affiliations. But there were limits to such tolerance: Papoulas wrote later: 'I decided to remove immediately from the Asia Minor army, and I did so, those elements which were irreconcilable and in my view incapable of putting the general interest of the country above all else.'[50] This meant men, such as Kondylis, whose history made it likely that they would actively intrigue against the new regime.

Because of Papoulas's cautious attitude, the full effects of the change of regime were not felt for some time in Asia Minor. In the immediate aftermath of the elections, however, a number of Venizelist officers who were either genuinely irreconcilable, like Kondylis, or simply did not wish to work with the new regime, deserted their posts in Asia Minor and fled to Constantinople. There were perhaps 150 such officers, of whom four were generals.[51] They formed the military core of a Venizelist movement of National Defence (*Ethniki Amyna*) in Constantinople.

Other senior Venizelist officers submitted their resignations and were retired at their own request, including, apart from Paraskevopoulos, Generals Othonaios, Hatzimichalis, Mazarakis and

Nider.[52] The fact that there were not enough high posts – divisional commands etc. – to satisfy both Venizelists and *apotaktoi* inevitably meant that for many of the former the choice was either to resign or to be put *en disponibilité* or assigned to unsatisfactory jobs in the interior.

The result was that by the operations of spring 1921 only two of the old Army Corps and Divisional commanders remained, Trikoupis commanding the Third Division and Leonardopoulos commanding the Tenth. The Commander-in-Chief, all three corps commanders, and seven out of nine divisional commanders had been changed. Changes in other senior positions on the staff and in regimental commands were also widespread, many of them occurring shortly before the March operations.

The majority of Venizelist officers remained in the army and continued to serve under the new regime. Those who left, either by desertion or retirement, were, however, the most senior and those with political connections or reputations as irreconcilable Venizelists; among others, Generals Paraskevopoulos, Ioannou, P. and E. Zymbrakakis, Miliotis-Komninos, A. Mazarakis-Ainian, K. Mazarakis, Tseroulis, Kalomenopoulos and Othonaios; and Colonels Pangalos, Kondylis, N. Zapheiriou, Loukas Sakellaropoulos. They were few in number but of high reputation.

As well as these, there were Venizelist officers who remained in the army but were for all practical purposes removed from active service by being assigned to some unimportant sector of the home front. The experience of Saraphis is illuminating. He had been Chief of Staff of Othonaios's Kydonies Division which had garrisoned Athens during the elections. After the elections, Saraphis was appointed to the 36th Infantry Regiment in Florina, but soon recalled to Athens and given a travel warrant for Kalamata. There he found about thirty high-ranking Venizelist officers of the *Amyna*, in an enforced idleness equivalent to exile, since they were forbidden to leave the city.[53] Shortly after his arrival in Kalamata Saraphis was put *en disponibilité* on two-third's pay. A request of Plastiras that Saraphis should be returned to his regiment in the 13th Division was refused by the Ministry. In such ways officers suspect for their political views were kept from the front.

It is impossible in the absence of a prosopographical study of the Greek officer corps in this period to assess the numbers of

Venizelists removed from the Asia Minor army and the numbers of *apotaktoi* who replaced them.[54] It is certain that almost all divisional and corps commanders and most regimental commanders were replaced between November 1920 and summer 1921. Perhaps some 300 higher officers were 'neutralized' like Saraphis by exile to towns in Old Greece.[55] This (very speculative) number, in relation to the total strength of the officer corps at this time – about 3,000 – is small but not negligible. If we add the officers who moved to Constantinople there to form the National Defence movement, we have about 500 Venizelist officers removed from active service. These included not only experienced and efficient senior commanders such as Alexandros Mazarakis and K. Manettas, but the more dynamic and drastic of the younger generation, Othonaios, Kondylis and Pangalos – men who would have been useful to Greece in the campaigns of 1921 but whose military virtues were more than cancelled by the threat they posed to the new state of affairs in the army and in the country at large.

Two separate charges are brought against the post-November regime by Venizelist critics for its handling of the officer corps. The first, which was widely disseminated in 1921, picked up by British G.H.Q. at Constantinople and relayed back to England, is that the *apotaktoi* were incompetents, lacking in experience of modern warfare, who superseded experienced Venizelist officers and thereby destroyed the Greek army's cohesion, fighting spirit and effectiveness.[56] It was true that the *apotaktoi* had no military experience subsequent to the Balkan Wars, while the National Defence officers and the neutrals had fought in Macedonia and some of them in Russia. This inexperience must have affected the general efficiency of the officer corps after November 1920, but was not so important a factor as critics made out, since the Asia Minor war was not only trench warfare for which Macedonian experience would have been valuable, but also a war of sweeping, open campaigns and rapid forced marches for which the Balkan Wars and the prewar training of a Greek officer were adequate preparation. The return of the *apotaktoi* contributed to the botching of the Greek campaign of March 1921, not only because of their inexperience but also because of the general upheaval caused by their recent arrival, and their unfamiliarity with their troops and with the military situation.[57] But by the summer campaign they had gained experience. It was natural that the Venizelists should consider themselves irreplaceable; but in war, as in business, the truth seems to be that executives are in general fairly easy to replace. It was generally acknowledged that the staff work and the execution of the summer 1921 campaign were surprisingly efficient for an army strained to the limits of its resources.

The second charge against the *apotaktoi* (and the regime), which seems inconsistent with the first, is that they deliberately avoided the front, skulking in Athens, reserving to themselves the 'cushy' jobs. There is in fact no inconsistency. There was competition for the better positions in Asia Minor but there were not enough of these posts to go around; and many of the *apotaktoi* were not prepared to take a post at the front which did not match their new rank. The change of regime of November 1920 therefore caused little upheaval at the level of Captain and below. There were, of course, a number of deliberate shirkers, and convincing charges of favouritism were levelled at the new Director of Personnel at the War Ministry, I. Makrykostas, as they had been at his Venizelist predecessors.

The return of the *apotaktoi* should not therefore be seen as decisively influencing the performance of the army on the field of battle, but as an inevitable phase in the schism which kept alive dissensions within the officer corps, aggravating the feelings of certain officers that they were being discriminated against, and renewing the propensity of the officer corps to play politics. These bad effects could have been mitigated but not completely averted by the new regime; for the problem faced in November 1920 was insoluble. The return of the *apotaktoi* was bound to offend and disenchant both Venizelist and neutral officers who saw the promotion and advancement of the last three years going for nothing; and Papoulas's conciliatory policy dissatisfied those extremists who would gladly have seen all the National Defence officers purged as the *apotaktoi* had been three years before. The Government thus offended both enemies and supporters. But once the dust had settled after the upheaval of November 1920, the tensions and disagreements between Venizelists and Royalists in Asia Minor tended to be subsumed in a more general feeling of isolation, a solidarity of all those serving in Asia Minor as against the civilians in Old Greece and the officers (many of them *apotaktoi*) of the War Ministry and the home front.

This is not to say that even in early 1921 there were no plots and conspiracies in the army. Kondylis from Constantinople was secretly in touch with officers at the front, and Plastiras was on the lookout for signs of a 'movement' in the army by March.* But except for Plastiras, the most likely centres and sources of revolutionary action against the new regime had either resigned or deserted or been rendered harmless by posting to Old Greece. Thus even when, after the military failure of summer 1921, discontent became rife in the officer corps and 'protocols' began circulating among groups of like-minded officers proposing various sorts of action, the movements did not have a coherent Venizelist political slant, and were easily contained by Papoulas and the army leadership. Though officers at the front talked much of change, and signed petitions, their frustrations throughout 1921 and most of 1922 were dissipated in idle talk, lacking a revolutionary focus. In the last resort, until the disaster of 1922, their loyalty to the fighting country came before the fissile tendencies of faction and clique.

* A. Zannas, one of the originators of the Salonika National Defence (*Amyna*) described in *Vima* of 22 Feb. 1959 how he visited Smyrna in March 1921 and saw Plastiras. They agreed that the situation since the fall of Venizelos was desperate, the army leadership inadequate, but that the old Amynites could not move, both because they lacked the means, and because if they did the responsibility for the imminent catastrophe would be thrown onto their shoulders. It was agreed therefore that the initiative for a *Kinima* (Movement) must be left to Royalists and neutralists who were disenchanted with the new regime, as many were: *Vima*, 22 Feb. 1959, cited in Malainos, *History of Foreign Intervention*, vi, p. 87.

9 | The London Conference

England, under the present conditions, cannot
advise an attack, but all the military will understand
that once enemy concentrations begin they must
be broken up.

Sir Maurice Hankey to the Greeks during
the London Conference

Dimitrios Rallis, the new prime minister, was old, emotional, hot-tempered, and acceptable both to the British Government and to the Greek political world as a whole. Rallis's following in the new Chamber was small, and he wielded little political power. The main force of the new regime was Gounaris, who had maintained his hold on his followers' loyalty through the long years of exile and now commanded the great majority of the 250 or so anti-Venizelists in the Chamber of 350 deputies. His only potential rival was Stratos, the one-time Venizelist minister who had kept alive in himself enough of the old Liberal to dissociate himself from Gounaris and more than enough ambition to wish passionately to become prime minister. But Stratos could command only some 30–40 votes.

King Constantine inaugurated the Third National Assembly on 5 January 1921, delivering his speech from the throne in a voice which was weak and husky, whether from emotion or a bad cold. The new Chamber was an unimpressive body, joined in fragile unity only on the question of the Greek claim to Asia Minor. Royalist deputies spent long and unproductive hours self-righteously mulling over the evils of the Venizelist regime and their own virtue in enduring it. Starting with a very reasonable motion to erect a memorial column to Ion Dragoumis, they went on to propose compensation for other 'victims of Venizelist tyranny'; to demand the publication of lists of those condemned to death by Venizelist courts martial;* to vote the erection of memorial statues to other Royalist 'martyrs'; to recommend substantial increases in the Royal Family's civil lists; and to vote for the criminal prosecution of Venizelist deputies such as Joseph

---

* The War Minister replied that 261 had been condemned to death and 140 executed.

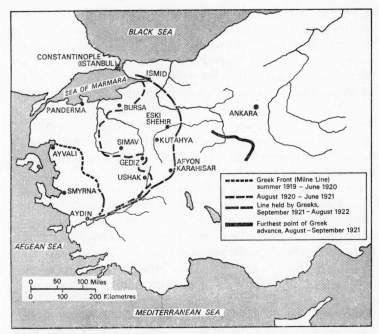

Limits of the Greek Occupation, 1919–1922

Koundouros, the crown prosecutor, who had taken the wise precaution of fleeing to Egypt after the elections.[1] The Assembly declared itself a Constituent Body, and was thus enabled to devote its spare hours to the intellectually satisfying, but in these harsh times irrelevant task of devising a new constitution for the country.

Senior ministers were calmer and wiser than their colleagues, some of whom thirsted for revenge on the Venizelists. Within the chamber Gounaris was usually though not always able to restrain his wild backbenchers. Outside parliament it was less easy to control the extremists whose passions erupted in sporadic violence. In January 1921 a Venizelist President of the Court Martial was murdered. Admiral Koundouriotis and Alexander Pallis were luckier. The two men were doling out aid to the war wounded in a little office in the Plaka district one day in January, when two ruffians slipped in among the crowds of ex-servicemen, drew pistols, and shot at them. By extraordinary good fortune the two escaped with light injuries.[2] Later in 1921, the Venizelist newspaper editor Andreas Kavafakis was killed. These were isolated incidents. The level of violence was tolerable. But the atmosphere in Athens was strained. The 'Political Clubs', the successors of the old 'Reservists Leagues' which had been the paramilitary organ of Royalist policy during the Great War, led by bullies such as General Constantinopoulos, became more and more blatant in their attempts to influence justice, intimidate the Venizelist opposition (and sometimes even the Government), and advance the careers of their members.[3] Except in certain country districts, the Government was just in control of affairs. But the thread of control was thin and stretched tight.

However much the new Government and Chamber might affect a preoccupation with compensation or constitution, the war was and was seen to be the great, burdensome issue which would not give the country or Government peace of mind. Theoretically there were several possibilities open to the Government. They could order the evacuation of Asia Minor by the Greek army; but this course, which seems so tempting in retrospect, was never seriously considered. Psychologically it was an impossible decision for a Greek Government to make. The Greeks could remain on the defensive within the present front, or a contracted front farther west. They could order an advance and try to annihilate the enemy. They could try to negotiate a compromise peace with the Turks based on total or partial removal of the official Greek presence from Anatolia.

The defensive policy – now recommended by Venizelos and later urged by Metaxas – was negative, unpopular with the military, and politically unattractive. Of these choices, therefore, the Government inclined to the military offensive. The temptation to listen to those military men who were confident they could settle the issue by force of arms was irresistible. At the same time, negotiations could not be avoided. The Allies invited Greeks and Turks (including the Kemalists) to a Conference in London to discuss a settlement on the basis of the Treaty of Sèvres.[4] This was an invitation the Greeks could not refuse if they wished to retain British support, and Rallis lost no time in replying that he would lead the Greek delegation in person.* This and

* *D.B.F.P.*, xvii, no. 23; he also told Granville that he would ask Politis to assist him at the Conference. Rallis died in August of the same year. On his position at this time, and the dispute over the question of his resignation, see the evidence of his son, G. Rallis, and Gounaris, in *Trial*

the old man's readiness to listen to Venizelos's views were too much for the Gounarist leaders; he was eased out of power and succeeded by the undistinguished Kalogeropoulos. Gounaris himself continued as Minister of War.

Before the Conference assembled, the Greek army tested the ground in Asia Minor. The new Greek Commander-in-Chief, anxious to test the strength of the Kemalist concentrations, and to demonstrate the aggressive spirit of the Royalist regime, sent the Northern Army Group forward in a reconnaissance in force from Bursa towards Eski Shehir.* Thrusting up over the broken, difficult ridges in the hard winter weather, the Greeks mounted the escarpment and came within striking distance of the upland plain of Eski Shehir, only to meet determined resistance from the Turkish troops under Ismet, Mustapha Kemal's trusted colleague, in a valley near the little village of Inonu. The Turks were still inferior in numbers and equipment, but fought with a new spirit. The wild bands of irregular troops were now merged in a regular army under dour discipline. The Greeks retired to their original lines to prepare for a larger and more determined campaign. The Turks' performance impressed Papoulas sufficiently to bring him to demand reinforcements; it did not lead him to doubt the Greek ability to capture Eski Shehir in the spring.

While the Greek Government fought its internal squabbles and prepared for the London Conference, Venizelos too was involved in the preparations for negotiations on the British side. By this time he had begun to look critically at the strategy pursued by the Government (and earlier by himself) in Asia Minor.

---

of the Six, pp. 240–4, 257–62. G. Rallis claimed that his father was strongly impressed by Venizelos's letter of 30 January describing his talks with Kerr and Lloyd George in London, and recommending a defensive posture for the Greek army. He wished to lead the Greek delegation to the London Conference in order to be able to urge these views. Gounaris argued in reply that D. Rallis was already suffering in January from the cancer that was shortly to kill him, and was therefore rightly prevented from going to London.

* Papoulas described how he put the plan for a reconnaissance in force to Rallis and Gounaris during his trip to Athens in December to welcome the return of the King from exile. Both Ministers welcomed the scheme as a means of demonstrating to England in a practical manner their determination not to abandon the Asia Minor campaign; Passas, The Agony of a Nation, p. 24.

Summoned from Nice to Paris to consult with Lloyd George, he argued strongly with Philip Kerr for the maintenance of Greek claims, on the grounds that 'the most important result for humanity of the great war was not the dissolution of the Austro-Hungarian Empire nor the limitation of the German, but the disappearance of the Turkish Empire'.[5] The Allies should provide the Greeks with economic assistance, since the Greek army was defending not only Greek but allied interests. Kerr answered that such assistance was impossible with Constantine on the throne again. Venizelos replied that he did not dare

make suggestions to the Athens Government, for fear that it might do exactly the opposite of what he suggested.

But if I were in the position of the present Greek Government, and saw that the economic situation had reached an impasse, I would abandon all the other territories occupied at present by our army, and limit myself to the occupation and defence of those territories alone which were conceded to us by the Treaty of Sèvres, together with the Meander valley. The defence of this region could be handled by a force of three divisions, or 45,000 men.

Venizelos argued that such a concentration would enable the government to demobilize the Reserve classes, and rely on volunteers and the two classes of military servicemen. This was the first appearance of the idea which was to dominate arguments over strategy in 1921 and 1922 – concentration within a defensible zone, if such could be found.[6]

It is clear that, apart from his recommendations of a concentration within the Smyrna zone, Venizelos's views on Asia Minor had not changed. The letter was a gesture of cooperation from Venizelos over the 'national' question. The gesture was ignored by the Royalists (except for Rallis) who could not admit the need for advice from their greatest political enemy.

Despite this gesture, Venizelos was already in contact with supporters who saw no reason for loyalty to the new regime and were planning to dissociate themselves from it. Like Lloyd George, he wished to keep his options open.

On 29 December, in a letter from France, Venizelos had warmly introduced to Sir John Stavridi three Greeks from Constantinople, Spanoudis, Stavridis and Iasonidis, and asked Sir

John to put them in touch with Lloyd George.[7] He endorsed their claim to represent Hellenism in Turkey. They were come

to declare that Hellenism is a force much broader than the confines of the Greek Kingdom, and that if the latter does not wish or is unable to hold Smyrna with its surrounding district, it is possible for Hellenism in Turkey itself to undertake this duty, provided the allies, or to speak more precisely England, are disposed to support this task both diplomatically and economically.

After long discussions Venizelos had concluded that the thing could be done:

The gentlemen of the Committee will explain to you that it is not a question of action directed against the Athens regime. In so far as Greece even under Constantine wishes and is able to hold Smyrna, we will all applaud, reserving to ourselves to settle our accounts with Constantine later, when our national work is consolidated. But as soon as Constantine decides to evacuate Smyrna, because he does not wish, or is unable through lack of money, to preserve it, at that moment there will be autonomous action by Hellenism in Turkey.

Despite this important reservation Venizelos hereby endorsed faction in Asia Minor; for the contingency planning against the possibility of an evacuation could not but divide the separatists from those who wished wholeheartedly to support the new government's efforts.

Sir John Stavridi put the Greeks in touch with Philip Kerr, who saw them on 14 January.[8] He found them 'intelligent and trustworthy men, but rather talkative':

I first asked them whether in the event of a crisis arising and Constantine having to abandon Smyrna, they and their friends could produce the troops necessary to hold Smyrna without any military assistance from the Allies. They replied they were confident that they could do so. I then asked them if in addition they could secure the maintenance at Ismid of the existing Greek Division. To this they replied that their estimate of the military situation was as follows:
That there were two Venizelist Divisions, the Ismid Division, and one other on which they could rely en bloc; that, in addition, there were certain Venizelist regiments which would come over, and that in any case there would be a large flow of volunteers from Pontus, Constantinople and the Islands, and that they had ample Venizelist officers to organize them into efficient troops provided they had

notice to begin their organization. They said that the total forces they could raise would be about 45,000 men.*

I then asked what they meant by requiring diplomatic and financial support from the Allies. As to diplomacy, they said that neither Venizelos nor anybody else would initiate the movement unless Venizelos was certain that as soon as a government was formed at Smyrna it would be recognized at least by Great Britain, if not by the allies. . . . As to economic assistance, they said that they required no arms, but they would require financial assistance. I asked for an estimate of the maximum which they thought would be necessary per month and for how long, and they promised to give me such an estimate in a day or two. They added, however, that if the movement got the support of the Allies it would rapidly be quite successful throughout all Greece, but that if the allies did not support it effectively it might drag on for a long time before Venizelos was back in Athens.

I then asked about Thrace, and they said that in their opinion, both Thrace and the Islands would immediately join the Smyrna Government as soon as it was formed and secede from Greece. I pointed out that Thrace was a very much more dangerous proposition than Smyrna, because of Bulgaria, but their enthusiasm was such that they were confident that if the movement got started, Thrace would rise and a similar movement would take place in Old Greece that would expel Constantine and restore Venizelos once more.

In conclusion, I said that you were favourably disposed to the consideration of the idea, always on the understanding that nothing was to be attempted until Constantine had failed to maintain the Treaty of Sèvres. For the moment, however, you could give no definite opinion, because you had to consider, first, the practicability of the proposal itself, second, the international situation it would create; and third, whether it would be possible for Great Britain to undertake the financial liabilities it might involve.[9]

This interesting account shows the dangers of Lloyd George's independent foreign policy. The reservations put forward in the last paragraph were formidable; but the impression left in the minds of the three Greeks that Lloyd George was favourably disposed to consider the idea can only have been construed by them as encouragement. What Lloyd George ignored in his dangerous facility for keeping more than one ball in the air at the same time, was that his readiness to give Constantine a chance to de-

* Precisely the number stated by Venizelos to be adequate for the defence of the Sèvres zone after shortening the front.

fend the Treaty of Sèvres and to keep these separatists in reserve, could put at risk the whole Greek effort in Asia Minor. For the very encouragement offered to the separatists would undermine the props on which Constantine's efforts depended – morale in the army, and unity in pursuit of a 'national' policy over Asia Minor. But Lloyd George saw the Constantine regime as conducting a simple holding operation in defence of the treaty, until such time as the Greek people came to its senses and restored Venizelos to power.[10] There was therefore no inconsistency in his mind between encouraging the separatists on this occasion, and soon afterwards encouraging Gounaris and Kalogeropoulos at the London Conference to impose the treaty on Kemal by force of arms.

The attitude of Venizelos was in some ways similar to that of Lloyd George. To all appearances he too was prepared to support Constantine, or preferably a Royalist regime without Constantine, in the defence of the Treaty. He warned Commander Talbot in Nice that the return of Constantine might lead to separatist movements in various parts of Greece.[11] He condemned recourse to violence by his extreme supporters, and offered no positive encouragement to conspiracy.* But effective *discouragement* was ruled out by his temperament and his pledge of non-involvement in internal politics.

The three Greeks sent by Venizelos left a memorandum with Kerr.[12] They claimed that 'the political system of Monsieur Venizelos' had not fallen. The elections could not be considered to be a fair indication of the true feelings of the Greek people, since if northern Epirus, the Dodecanese, Asia Minor and all Hellenism outside Old Greece had taken part, Venizelos would have received an overwhelming majority of the votes. Thus the fate of Hellenism in Turkey should not be determined by 'the momen-

* Cf. the memo of the Constantinople *Amyna* of 10 February 1922: 'The scheme of the separate Asia Minor state existed in the mind (*eis to pnevma*) of Lloyd George and the other English politicians after the 1st November 1920. If it was not implemented then, this was due to the stubborn insistence of Eleftherios Venizelos, who opposed any change so long as the Greek Government was continuing to pursue the struggle.' This implies that Venizelos, like Lloyd George, was playing the dangerous game of keeping the *Amyna* in reserve in case Constantine failed. The 'other English politicians' of the memo were apparently figments of the imagination. Text of the memo in Passas, *The Agony of a Nation*, pp. 177–84.

tary manifestation of bad humour on the part of a certain not-wholly Greek [sic] portion of the kingdom'.

The memorandum stated that given the necessary diplomatic and financial support, the movement could call on 25,000 soldiers at the front who were 'absolutely ready to serve the policy of M. Venizelos'; 2,500 officers of the Army of the National Defence;* and 15,000 men who had at some time done military service and were currently in Constantinople and Asia Minor. These forces would be sufficient to assure 'a definite settlement'.

The political implications of the movement were barely concealed. 'Hellenism is determined to struggle both to save herself from the catastrophe ... and to save the state from danger', just as the Salonika National Defence movement had saved the state in 1916–17. The clear implication was that underlying the patriotic scheme for the salvation of Asia Minor were Venizelist revolutionary forces which would inevitably be drawn towards the ejection of the King and the overturning of the regime. The timing of the approach to Lloyd George belies the impression given by most of the literature on the *Amyna*,[13] that the movement sprang up after the campaigns of summer 1921 as a response to the increasingly desperate military and diplomatic situation of Greece.

The separatists' revolutionary schemes were predicated on false assumptions, as a result of which they believed that the British would welcome and support the movement. The implied parallel with the Venizelist revolution of 1916 was dangerously misleading. In 1916–17 Venizelos had been able to divide Greece, raise the standard of war, and organize the National Defence army under the protective canopy of the allied army of Salonika. His enterprise was gain for the allied war effort. In 1921, on the contrary, it was the *Greek* army which held the front against the Kemalists and protected the positions of *British* troops. A Venizelist *coup d'état* at this time would therefore expose the Greek positions at the front – and risk exposing British positions. But even supposing that the army could be 'taken over' by the Venizelists comparatively smoothly and efficiently, the upheaval in Old Greece (leading possibly to civil war) could hardly have failed to affect the war effort. The Royalists were now in control

* The reference is presumably to both those officers of the old Salonika *Amyna* who were still serving at the Asia Minor front, and those, much fewer in number, who had retired to Constantinople.

of Old Greece and the machinery of government; there were no allied troops or ships to persuade them to step down.

The Venizelists, however, affected to consider the danger from Kemal as negligible. On this assumption, the coup was a purely internal matter after which they could turn their attention once more to the Turkish problem and 'impose the peace' on Kemal. What in the first instance they demanded of Britain was money. Sir John Stavridi, who was asked by Kerr to go into the plans submitted by the two Greeks, reported after a long interview with them that the new organization needed about £1 million for the first month. 'This would enable the whole matter to be reorganized and the new people to get into the saddle.' Thereafter £400,000 a month would be sufficient, for a period of six to nine months at the outside, after which the movement would be self-supporting, having presumably constituted itself the official government of Greece.[14] In view of Lloyd George's proviso that nothing was to be attempted until Constantine had tried and failed to maintain the treaty, no further action appears to have been taken. Nor was the Foreign Office informed of the soundings which had occurred.

The London Conference met on 21 February.[15] The prospects of negotiations for the Greeks were not wholly unfavourable. Aristide Briand, the shaggy, subtle socialist now in power in France, was more sympathetic to Greek aspirations and to King Constantine and the Royalists than his predecessors. He was a close friend of Prince George of Greece (the brother of King Constantine) and was rumoured to be on intimate terms with the Prince's wife Princess Marie Bonaparte. On the British side, neither Lloyd George nor Curzon had given up hope of a settlement substantially on the lines of the Treaty of Sèvres, and Lloyd George tended to disapprove of the financial blockade of Greece.[16] The Allies' invitation to a Nationalist delegation from Ankara as well as a delegation from Constantinople, meant that serious negotiations were at least conceivable. The British had considered a way of finding an understanding with France based on a linkage between eastern and western problems. Sir Eyre Crowe, after discussions with Curzon's political secretary, Robert Vansittart, Lord Hardinge and Sir W. Tyrrell, urged such an understanding based on British support for France in the west in the form of a guarantee against German aggression, in return for French support for British policy in the east where the Bolsheviks posed a serious threat to British interests.[17] This bold and imaginative conception remained unrealized.

The Greek delegation arrived in London on 17 February, led by Kalogeropoulos. Lloyd George told him the following day that 'he relied upon the spirit of the Greek people not to surrender legitimate rights'.[18] At the same time, he urged the Greeks to show themselves conciliatory over the *form* of a Smyrna settlement, accepting, for example, a proposal of autonomy under a Christian governor. In this way, if the Conference broke down it would be through Turkish intransigence, and the Greeks would have the support of the Allies. This remained Lloyd George's attitude throughout the Conference.

The Greek delegation bombarded the Conference with paper on the Greek army, repatriation of refugees, agriculture, and the administration of the Smyrna zone. Their aim was to show the Allies that they were worth supporting:

The Greek army in Asia Minor, 121,000 strong, is in a position to scatter the Kemalist forces and to impose the will of the Powers as embodied in the Treaty of Sèvres. In every respect the Greek army is overwhelmingly superior to the Kemalist levies, which along the Greek front attain a total of 30,000 to 34,000 men, including irregulars.

The objective of the Greek army in the above case would be, in the first instance, to occupy the railway line Adapazar–Eskishehir–Afioun–Karahissar, and establish itself firmly to the east of this line. ... After the break-up of the Kemalist army three divisions on a peace footing would be sufficient for the zone allotted to Greece by the Treaty of Sèvres. ... However, the necessity of guarding the freedom of the Straits imposes on the Allied Powers, including Greece, an obligation to maintain adequate forces for this purpose. These forces should, it is clear, be maintained until such time as the clauses of the treaty relative to the disarmament of Turkey shall have been executed.[19]

In their private communications with Lloyd George, the Greeks went further, arguing that the withdrawal of the Greek army would necessitate the raising of an army of 100,000 men to defend the extensive Straits zone against the Kemalists. Since this was out of the question, only Greece could bear Europe's burden. The Greeks must therefore remain on their present lines pending the complete execution of the Treaty of Sèvres. The present occupied zone was deep enough to allow them to prevent the Turkish forces from reaching the Straits. The maintenance of the present Greek front therefore protected the British interest of the Freedom of the Straits.[20]

This memorandum provides clear evidence that the policy of Greece's new Government was to offer the services of the Greek army to Great Britain in return for British diplomatic and, it was hoped, financial support. This was the policy of Venizelos, with the superficial difference that the new Government was forced by the open hostility of France to depend on Britain alone; whereas Venizelos could claim at least in the early stages of the occupation to be acting on behalf of both allies.

There was no alternative to this policy if the Greeks were determined to remain in Smyrna; for to secure French and Italian approval for the occupation was now out of the question. The only room for manoeuvre for the Greeks was over the terms on which they offered to cover the British position at the Straits. One approach would have been to threaten withdrawal of the Greek troops from Asia Minor (including the 11th Division, which was still under British orders at Ismid) unless the British would raise the financial blockade or in other ways help Greece. But the Greek politicians were accustomed to negotiate with the Great Powers from a position of weakness, and adopted the opposite course of offering their services unconditionally. In a curious sense, also, the anti-Venizelist Greeks, moved by the doubts of the western Powers as to Royalist Greece's capacity and endurance, felt a need to justify themselves and their nation to the west; in Gounaris's words, they had to prove that Greece was a 'serious nation' on whom a Great Power like Britain could rely.[21]

A necessary condition of the new Government's attitude was the view of the military that a successful advance was possible. Papoulas had stated earlier that an offensive was feasible if certain requirements were met. Colonel Sariyannis, the military member of the Greek delegation, had been Deputy Chief of the Asia Minor Staff under Venizelos and remained so under the new regime. Sariyannis was a dynamic and energetic figure and the main element of continuity in the Staff. He carried weight with Papoulas and the government, and seems to have convinced them that the advance on Ankara would be a simple matter. Kalogeropoulos described the Turkish troops to the Conference as 'a rabble worthy of little or no consideration'.[22]

On 21 February, at the first full session of the Conference, Lloyd George cross-examined Kalogeropoulos and Sariyannis on Greece's intentions and prospects. The Greeks claimed that their army could annihilate the forces of Kemal and sweep the whole country clear within three months.[23] Lloyd George was content with this optimistic account of Greek prospects. He helped Sariyannis throw doubt on the testimony of General Gouraud, French commander in Syria and Cilicia, who argued from personal experience that the Greeks' account of Turkish Nationalist fighting capacity was unsound.

The Greeks' belief that they could defeat Kemal and its grateful acceptance by Lloyd George doomed the Conference to failure. Indeed, so long as the Allies were divided over the eastern question, there was no prospect of a negotiated peace. The Ankara Turks were not prepared to settle for less than the evacuation of the Greek army; they would reject a 'fake' solution which left the Greeks dominant in a Smyrna zone which was nominally Turkish. In this determination they were encouraged by the French and Italians, who took advantage of the London Conference to negotiate separate local agreements with Nationalist Turkey.* Although these agreements were subsequently repudiated by the Grand National Assembly in Ankara, the mere fact of separate negotiations was an encouragement to the Nationalist delegation to hold out over the Smyrna issue. Bekir Sami, leader of the Ankara delegation and a 'moderate', wished to settle with Britain, and to wind up the war, on the right terms; but the right terms involved the withdrawal of the Greeks from Smyrna. On their side the Greeks were conciliatory only to the extent that they would agree to some form of autonomous regime for Smyrna which would leave the Greek communities dominant in the region's administration, and a Greek military presence in the area. Total evacuation they would not accept, and in this they were encouraged by Lloyd George.† There was therefore no possibility, yet, of compromise.

---

* The Franco–Turkish armistice, concluded on 10 March, provided for French military evacuation of Cilicia in return for economic concessions. For both agreements see Frangulis, *La Grèce*, ii, pp. 205–7.

† Whether, if Lloyd George had sincerely urged the Greeks to give up Asia Minor, they would have listened, it is impossible to say.

Since the Allies were not prepared to unite in urging the Greeks to withdraw from Smyrna, the Conference prevaricated. On 23 and 24 February, the Turkish delegates argued their claims for the return of Smyrna and Eastern Thrace. A statistical battle developed, the Turkish and Greek delegations putting forward irreconcilable figures for the populations of the disputed areas. Although population statistics had been considered at length by the Paris Peace Conference, the Allies now proposed to get off an awkward hook by sending an international Commission of Enquiry to investigate the populations of the Smyrna zone and of Eastern Thrace on the spot, both Greece and Turkey binding themselves in advance to accept the results of this arbitration, along with the rest of the Treaty of Sèvres.[24] Briand and Sforza saw in this proposal a way of easing the Greeks out of Smyrna after which it would be easy to settle with Kemal on other questions. Lloyd George explicitly refused to regard the Enquiry as a face-saving means of getting the Greeks out of Asia Minor.

The Ankara delegation accepted the proposed Enquiry subject to conditions.[25] Kalogeropoulos asked for time to consult the Greek Cabinet and National Assembly. He gave Lloyd George the Assembly's reply on 4 March.[26] It was an uncompromising refusal, endorsed by all the political parties including the Venizelists, to accept an international commission, on the grounds that there was nothing for them to investigate. The question of populations had already been decided, and the Treaty of Sèvres was Greece's irreducible claim.

Though Lloyd George had urged the Greeks to adopt a superficially conciliatory attitude over Smyrna, he refused to *deter* them from launching an offensive against the Nationalists. And the Greeks obtained the impression that he was actually encouraging them to seek a military solution. On 28 February Philip Kerr had given them a startlingly interesting account of his master's views:

Kerr declared confidentially that the Prime Minister thinks that 'Greece's consent to the decision of the Conference would be equivalent to signing a blank contract; but before one signs a contract, one should know for how much one is signing'. Kerr added that *we should not hesitate to refuse the proposal;** but that it would be preferable if the Turks were to be the first to refuse to conform with the Conference's decision.[27]

* i.e. the proposal of a Commission of Enquiry into population statistics.

Philip Kerr went on to examine Sariyannis closely on Greece's military plans and prospects. With the aid of a map, the Colonel took him through the Greek Staff's plans for a march on Ankara, supported possibly by a landing in the Pontus and descent from there on the Turks' eastern strongholds of Sivas and Erzurum. Kerr inquired about the costs of such a campaign, but made no promises of aid. The Greeks were convinced that he favoured their plans, at least for an advance on Eski Shehir and Afyon Karahisar.

This conversation has been taken as proof that Lloyd George secretly encouraged the Greeks to ignore the diplomatic efforts of Curzon and the Foreign Office and to take matters into their own hands by attacking the Turkish army.[28] Curzon himself, who was able by courtesy of the Foreign Office's intercepts to read what was in the Greeks' minds, accepted this interpretation of Lloyd George's behaviour and was angered by it.[29]

The Commission of Enquiry, weighted two to one against the Greeks, might well find for the return of Smyrna to Turkey. This would mean evacuation and the end of Greek usefulness to Britain in Asia Minor. Lloyd George was not ready to accept such a conclusion to the Greek adventure until the Greeks had lost the will to defend their claims, or the Greek army were defeated. But he was too cautious and skilful an operator to commit himself personally to a Greek offensive. Such encouragement as there was consisted of no more than hints, inflections and loaded questions. In one important sense, Lloyd George's operations were the opposite of clandestine: he told his allies and both Greeks and Turks, that neither he nor the Conference could take the responsibility of deterring the Greeks from attacking if they thought fit.[30]

The Franco-Kemalist negotiations in London, of which the Greeks were well aware, were taken by the Greeks as foreshadowing an imminent change in the military balance in Kemal's favour; for the liquidation of hostilities in Cilicia would free Turkish troops and war materials for the western front. Greek Staff Officers therefore argued that an attack should be launched at once, so as to interrupt the Turks' railway communications before they could profit by the new situation.[31] Sir Maurice Hankey, when sounded, stated that 'England, under the present conditions, cannot advise an attack, but all the military will understand that once enemy concentrations begin they must be broken up'.[32] There seems little doubt that Lloyd George, desiring to support the Greeks so far as in him lay without formally committing Britain, wished the Greeks to attack provided their chances of success were better than even, but would not take the responsibility of saying so while negotiations were in progress. On the record, he urged a spirit of compromise – but only over the inessentials of Greece's claims.

When he told Lloyd George of Greece's rejection of the proposed Commission of Enquiry, Kalogeropoulos asked for his advice as to the attitude Greece should now adopt.[33] Lloyd George suggested

that the Turks should be given the formal sovereignty over Smyrna, but that the Greeks should administer Smyrna, and in return hand over to Turkey a proportion of the revenues. ... In addition, he thought it would probably be necessary to alter the boundaries of the Smyrna zone in certain respects by retransferring to Turkey certain kazas which were predominantly Mohammedan in population. ... He thought it was essential that Greece should make peace without further delay. It would thus be possible for her to demobilize her army and put her finances in order.

Since these suggestions were put forward in private, not in the full glare of the conference, there is no reason to doubt their sincerity. Later the same day Lloyd George pressed the same solution on Bekir Sami Bey at another private meeting.[34] Bekir Sami rejected it on the grounds that to allow the Greeks to remain in occupation was contrary to his formal instructions over Smyrna. As Lloyd George had told Kalogeropoulos, he was looking for 'how a compromise could be reached in regard to Smyrna without forcing Greece to withdraw'.[35] And when Bekir Sami rejected the proposed 'compromise', Lloyd George seems to have accepted that the war must go on.* He was not prepared to press the Greeks to concede more to the Turks.

The Allies proceeded, for the form's sake, to elaborate a scheme for an autonomous Smyrna region, to be submitted to the Greek and Turkish delegations together with the recommendation of an armistice, so that the onus of prolonging the war should be seen to rest on the two belligerents and not on the Great Powers.

* At the next session of the Conference on the afternoon of 4 March, he opposed Sforza's view that the 'exercise of a little pressure by the Allied Powers' on Greece would suffice to bring the Greeks into line; D.B.F.P., xv, no. 35, p. 280.

At the session of 9 March the Greeks were told that restrictions on the movements of their armed forces were removed.[36] According to the French Secretary's notes, Briand did not formally agree. Lloyd George wished there to be no doubt on this score. He sent Hankey round to Claridges that evening to tell Kalogeropoulos that if it was of vital importance – *importanza vitale e primordiale* – to the safety of the Greek army to attack Kemal, Lloyd George as President of the Conference could not take the responsibility of restraining them. No one could of course in practice stop the Greeks if they decided to advance; but the psychological restraints on them deriving for the necessity of allied or at least British approval for their actions in Asia Minor and dating from 1919 were none the less powerful for that, and Kalogeropoulos was delighted:

The old boy, who had been very depressed when I came in, showed every sign of intense relief, declared that he would never have sanctioned an attack without authority, and that the recovery of his freedom was a great relief. He was so keen about it that I took occasion to warn him that Lloyd George was not encouraging him to attack but only removing a ban that had been placed on him.[37]

Meanwhile Gounaris had arrived in London to strengthen the Greek delegation. Lloyd George, quick to recognize where the power lay, described him as the Bekir Sami of the Greek delegation. Bekir Sami himself, the capable representative of the Turkish Nationalists, he described in more forthright terms to King George V:

A little while ago I had to shake hands with Sami Bey, a ruffian who was missing for the whole of one day, and finally traced to a sodomy house in the East End. He was the representative of Mustapha Kemal, a man who I understand has grown tired of affairs with women and has lately taken up unnatural sexual intercourse. I must confess I do not think there is very much to choose between these persons whom I am forced to meet from time to time in Your Majesty's service.[38]

On 10 March Gounaris and Kalogeropoulos were given the Foreign Office's compromise proposals for the Smyrna region.[39] They accepted the Smyrna scheme that same afternoon, subject to important modifications.[40] But acceptance was by now of only theoretical interest, for the Greeks had already decided to launch their attack. Only the strongest warning from the united Allies on the consequences of renewing hostilities might now have deterred them, and no such warning came. On the contrary, after the meeting of 10 March between Lloyd George, Curzon and the Greeks, and (significantly) after Lord Curzon had withdrawn, Kalogeropoulos received confirmation of Lloyd George's message the previous evening via Hankey, that the Greeks could not be restrained from attacking if circumstances dictated an attack.[41]

To all intents and purposes the Greeks were committed to war. By 18 March, when Gounaris and Kalogeropoulos held their last meeting with Lloyd George, Bekir Sami Bey had departed for Ankara, bearing with him the Allies' proposals for modifications of the Treaty of Sèvres to be put before the Grand National Assembly. Despite his friendly manner, nothing suggested before his departure that the Turks would compromise over Smyrna. The Greeks at any rate believed that the Turks were merely playing for time, with the intention eventually of rejecting the proposals. Gounaris therefore told Lloyd George at this last meeting that the Greek attack was to start at once.[42] The Commander-in-Chief had already left for the front.

For the first time, Gounaris seriously raised the question of Greece's dwindling financial resources. Lloyd George appeared sympathetic, and referred him to the Treasury for discussions. He ended with a little lecture:

He wished to make it quite clear to the Greek delegation that if the Greek army thought it necessary to take steps to provide for its safety in view of the increase of Mustapha Kemal's forces, the conference could not take the responsibility for forbidding them. . . . His colleagues had quite accepted this. He would add, on his own account, however, that presumably the Greek Ministry had taken into consideration the fact that if the Greek army sustained a reverse it would make the Angora Government impossible to deal with.

M. Kalogeropoulos and M. Gounaris replied that this had been taken into account.[43]

Thus Lloyd George protected his position, and the Conference ended. Five days later, the Greek army moved forward into the attack.

Summer Offensive

Only pity must be felt for the mass of the Greek
people at this point in their history. They were set
tasks beyond their strength; they were asked questions
which they were not competent to answer; they
had no knowledge of the consequences inherent
in the decisions they were led to take. They had
endured a longer strain of war, mobilization,
and war government than almost any other people
in a war-wearied world. They were torn and
baffled by faction; there were two hostile nations in
the bosom of one small harassed state; and even
under these distracting conditions their armies
maintained for a long period remarkable
discipline and constancy. They were now to be
launched upon an adventure at once more
ambitious and more forlorn than any which
we have yet described.

Winston Churchill, *The World Crisis:
the Aftermath*, p. 390

The new Greek attack was launched on 23 March 1921.[1] The
Greek army advanced on two fronts, the Southern Group pushing forward from Ushak towards Afyon Karahisar, the Northern
setting out from Bursa over the same route it had taken in
January. Afyon was captured on 27 March. But in the north the
Greek troops encountered more effective resistance than at any
time since the landing in May 1919. Ismet's troops had used the
two months since the Greeks' previous advance well. For the first
time, the Greeks faced regular troops, well entrenched in fortified positions, with all the advantages of modern defensive warfare. Furthermore, the Greek staff work was perfunctory, and
based on faulty intelligence of Turkish formations and defences.[2]
Sariyannis, the Deputy Chief of Staff, was in London throughout
the critical planning stage and had not returned in time for the
operations. Pallis, the Chief of Staff, fell ill shortly before the
attack and remained in Smyrna when Papoulas left for the front.

The Northern Army Group, consisting of the 3rd, 7th and

10th Divisions, trudged once more up long slopes and over broken ridges towards the Anatolian plateau and Eski Shehir. Arnold Toynbee, reporting on the war for C. P. Scott's *Manchester Guardian*, followed them forward, climbing slowly up to the Pazarjik plateau behind the northern front in an ambulance which, like most of the Greek motor transport, was suffering from service on the rough roads of Macedonia and Anatolia. From the corps headquarters at Pazarjik, he travelled on past dumps of material and oxcarts, and then between low hills and through a deep defile alongside river and railway :

The place was infested with the atmosphere of war, which makes inanimate hills and valleys seem malevolent and adds something sinister to the most ordinary landscape. But this place was haunted by history as well. That railway, with its magnificent embankment and culverts and bridges intact, and even its telegraph wires uncut, but with neither rolling-stock nor staff, was the Anatolian Railway – the first section of the Baghdad line. In its derelict condition it seemed symbolic of a great nation's frustrated ambitions. The giant had fallen, and smaller people were fighting for a fragment of the heritage which the German had marked out as his own. But that smoke rising above the hill to our left front as we dipped into the ravine was symbolic too. It marked the site of Soyud, the first Anatolian village possessed by the ancestor of the Ottoman Dynasty, and now the Osmanlis were fighting for their national existence on the very spot where that existence had begun.[3]

The Greek troops were stopped on the edge of the escarpment by heavy fire. A bitter struggle developed, again near Inonu. Finally the 7th Division on the right of the Greek line broke through and carried with the bayonet the magnificent Turkish positions on the Kovalyja ridge which ringed the plain of Eski Shehir to the north. The Turkish trenches faced north, and commanded the southern exits of the defile in the hills through which the Greek troops had to come from the plateau of Pazarjik. All along the northern rim of the ridge was a tilted outcrop of limestone, which turned the slope for a few yards into a precipice; and it was here on the open slope that Toynbee saw the Greek dead lying when he visited the front. The Turkish dead, killed by shell-fire, lay in their trenches.

From the captured ridges the Greek troops could look down on the plain stretching all the way to Eski Shehir. To their rear the snow-capped summit of the Mysian Mount Olympus loomed through a gap in the hills. It was a superb position. By day the troops could feel the warmth of the spring sun awakening the Anatolian hills and plateau. When dusk fell, and the light faded, the warmth quickly drained out of the stones and earth and it became suddenly chill. The guns were silenced. Plumes of smoke hung in the sky reflecting invisible fires below from villages burning behind the front line. The dawn too was intensely cold and a clinging mist hung over the front. Stretchers moved very slowly down towards the front.

The 7th Division held the ridges for only four days. The Greek centre and left were unable to resist steady Turkish pressure, and were pushed back over the escarpment. The 10th Division was the first to break, on 31 March, and the Greeks were forced to order a general retreat to their old lines near Bursa.

Arnold Toynbee witnessed the retreat of the 7th Division from beginning to end. After a series of false starts and alarms, without knowing his destination or the situation at the front, he accompanied the baggage train and mules of the divisional staff up the defile towards the Pazarjik plateau, through the burning village of Boz Oyuk: a 'weird march, between 4 a.m. and dawn, in choking dust transfused with moonlight and reeking with the odour of animals and men'. They had emerged from the defile, left the road and unloaded the mules in a field by the railway ready to take up a position for the day, when the urgent order came to start again. The men were tired and impatient. Once back on the road they realized that it was to be a general retreat. The field artillery had already overtaken them, the heavy guns were approaching, and the divisional infantry were coming out of the defile.

Toynbee overtook the entire column during the day, and was able to observe their bearing:

The men were angry – angry at spending so much blood and labour in vain, but even more humiliated at a defeat which broke a long record of victory of which they had been intensely proud. ... Certainly the quality of this veteran division came out in adversity more than when they were still confident of success. Heavy guns, field guns, mountain artillery, lorries, ox-carts, and mules – all were safely brought away, and such ammunition as could not be transported was blown up.[4]

The features were those of any well-ordered retreat across

difficult terrain. The one road was not made for a continuous stream of heavy traffic, and its surface was now broken up. Lorries and even the ox-carts broke down. But somehow they were quickly repaired and the steady stream kept flowing. Greek officers were posted at bridges and fords to direct the traffic. The comparatively nimble mules moved across the fields parallel with the road.

There was no panic. The column was well-disciplined, but also lucky. In the course of the retreat they had to describe the arc of a circle from Kovalyja back to the positions near Bursa from which they had set out a fortnight before. If Turkish troops, moving along their interior lines, had cut off the retreat from the south the Greeks would have been very hard pressed. But the northern column was spared serious assault. Turkish units had been sent instead south to cut the railway lines between Afyon Karahisar and Ushak and cut off the southern group. It was only with the skin of their teeth that the southern group escaped this net cast for them. The Turkish troops, arriving piecemeal because of the difficulties of transport, were held off at Tulu Punar by the Greek 34th Infantry Regiment in twenty-four hours of desperate fighting, before the retreating First Army Corps could bring relief. Having beaten off this dangerous attack, the Southern Group retired to its base at Ushak. Meanwhile the Northern Group retired weary, disillusioned but virtually un-scathed through the barbed wire and trenches from which the offensive had been launched and settled once more into their old positions.

This was the Greeks' first serious reverse in Asia Minor. The vaunted offensive had failed, and a fine Greek army had lost its first bloom, its innocent assumption of success. The confident assurances given to Lloyd George in London now seemed like empty bragging. What was there to do now but *reculer pour mieux sauter*? The Greeks settled down to prepare for a new round.

The reverse was due to overconfidence, inadequate planning, and excessive haste.* The lessons had been learned. 'Leaders and troops alike,' wrote the British military attaché, 'realized that

* The haste was caused partly by the desire to strike at Kemal before he could exploit the new situation in Cilicia, and before the time limit for the Turkish answer to the allies' peace proposals expired on 9 April; Stratigos, *Greece in Asia Minor*, pp. 196–7.

they no longer had in front of them the disorganized Nationalist hordes of 1920.'[5] They now threw themselves into intensive preparations for the summer campaign.

It does not seem to have occurred to the Government or the Staff to do other than attack again. But the failure of the limited operations of January and March caused the government to doubt the capabilities of Papoulas and his staff. Gounaris had lost confidence in Papoulas's offensive spirit. He thought that Papoulas would try to evade the summer campaign by putting even more extensive demands for men and equipment – demands which would eventually have to be refused, giving him the opportunity to cancel the offensive. Sitting on the sidelines, in sullen and prickly mood, was one man who could perhaps help them out of their difficulties – Metaxas, who had returned from exile after the victory of the Gounarists and promptly retired from the army with the rank of General. Without party ties, with a history of opposition to a forward policy in Asia Minor, he was now well placed to criticize the new Government's ineptitude. A dangerous man to have outside the Government as a critic, but a difficult colleague inside. Gounaris decided to turn to him now.

On 7 April Gounaris and Protopapadakis, in a five hour talk at Protopapadakis's house, put the military situation before Metaxas and urged him to join Papoulas's staff.[6] Metaxas refused to 'control' Papoulas from below in this way. He was then asked whether he would become Commander in Chief himself. Here was the test of the strength and sincerity of his views on the Asia Minor campaign. He refused to rise to the bait.

Four days later the two ministers and Theotokis returned to the attack.[7] The Government had decided to resuscitate the old 'Royal Command' of the Balkan Wars, and wished to entrust to this Command, consisting of the King advised by Dousmanis and Metaxas, the general supervision of the entire Greek army throughout the kingdom. It is clear from Metaxas's account of the discussion that the ministers had not worked out fully the implications of their proposal, and the divisions of responsibility between the King and his Staff and the Asia Minor Command under Papoulas; but the Government's chief reason for reviving the Royal Command was its propaganda value. The presence of the King at the head of the armed forces was expected to have a good effect on morale and recruitment, and the participation of

Metaxas in the 'Royal Staff' would revive public confidence in the prosecution of the war.[8]

Metaxas deployed a number of arguments against the idea of the Royal Command, objecting especially to the confusion of responsibilities that would result. He lectured Theotokis on the proper duties of War Minister.* He refused to become Chief of General Staff himself or under any circumstances to serve with Dousmanis on any form of staff. All three ministers put heavy pressure on him to change his mind; and Metaxas was forced to defend his position by defining his views on the war. He argued that should he join the Staff, as the Government wished, in order to stiffen public confidence in the government and the war, he would be deceiving the Greek people by supporting a war in which he had no confidence himself.

To Theotokis's question, why Metaxas did not believe in the policy of war, he replied:

Because in fact you are seeking the conquest of Asia Minor, and without preparing for it through the Hellenization of the country. It is only superficially a question of the Treaty of Sèvres. It is really a question of the dissolution of Turkey and the establishment of our state on Turkish soil. But even if it were only a question of the Treaty of Sèvres, we are an ethnological minority even in the area round Smyrna. In the interior of Asia Minor our own population is minute. And the Turks realize what we want. If they had no national feeling, perhaps such a policy would be possible. But they have proved that they have, not a religious, but a national feeling. And they mean to fight for their freedom and independence – precisely the things for which we have been fighting against them. They realize that Asia Minor is their country and that we are invaders. For them, for their national feelings, the historical rights on which we base our claims have no influence. Whether they are right or wrong is another question. What matters is how they feel.[9]

Metaxas concluded that victory was impossible. Even if the

* Spice is added to the whole discussion by the fact that this is the period of Metaxas's incipient political ambitions, and the hope of becoming War Minister was always at the back of his mind. By forcing Theotokis to admit his ignorance and need for expert advice, while at the same time refusing to provide that advice as a Staff Officer, Metaxas hoped to push Theotokis into saying, 'If you know all the answers why don't you try the job?' Metaxas recognized, however, that he was unlikely to win a portfolio while Gounaris was Prime Minister.

Greek army's summer campaign were successful, and Kemal and
the Turks were induced to sign the Treaty of Sèvres, the Greeks
would have to evacuate Asia Minor and demobilize the army
except for a strong garrison for the Smyrna zone. They would
be powerless to prevent the inevitable new uprising of Turkish
nationalism, the formation of new guerrilla bands, and the beginning of a new war.

The analysis is familiar. What lends it new interest is the reactions of Metaxas's interlocutors – the doubts and conflicting
desires of the Gounarist Ministers:

You see [said Metaxas] where your policy is leading us. It is a
policy of conquest of a people which does not mean to submit to
conquest – conquest for which the ground has not been prepared by
the infiltration of our civilization, our influence, Hellenism, as in
antiquity.

It is not our policy, Gounaris says. It was never our policy. It was
Venizelos who brought us to this point. We inherited the war.

You could have compromised, I answered.

I tried, he said. In London, after consultations with Lloyd George,
I agreed to make great concessions over Smyrna. I did this so as to
finish the campaign and have done with it. The Aga Khan acted as
mediator. Suddenly the Turks changed their minds and refused to
accept anything. So what could I do then?*

Not attack, I replied. The army was not ready, in any case. There
had been no preparations since November. But even if it had been
ready, we should still have avoided getting embroiled further in the
military impasse.

I know, answered Gounaris. And I admit that I was deceived. I
was deceived by the assurances of the military, that the attack would
certainly be victorious and that it would be a short campaign. Trust-
ing their assurances, I myself assured the English of the certain
success of the campaign.

At least you needn't have hurried, I said. Couldn't you have
waited to get home before starting the campaign?

Papoulas insisted, he answered emphatically. He insistently demanded permission to attack as soon as possible, since otherwise
Kemal would be reinforced from Cilicia. What could I do?

And what would have happened if we had not attacked? asked
Protopapadakis. What should we have done?

What even now perhaps we ought to be doing. Withdraw roughly
within the bounds of the Treaty of Sèvres, fortify them well and

* This is a misleading précis of the London negotiations.

dispose ourselves defensively. Instead of breaking our heads on Kemal's defences, let him break his nose on ours.*

In the meantime the Greeks would seek a settlement with Turkey enabling them to evacuate Asia Minor in return for some sort of autonomous regime for Smyrna which would allow 'friendly cooperation' with the Turks, and the free development of Hellenism in Asia Minor.

Protopapadakis said: But you must realize also that if we give up Asia Minor we should lose Thrace as well.

How so? I answered. I don't understand that. We can defend Thrace militarily with small forces for an indefinite period of time.

That's not the point, he said. We should lose Thrace because England would force us to give up Thrace as well. For us to get England's support over Thrace, England must be persuaded that we can crush Kemal and impose the Treaty of Sèvres....†

It is not a question of the policy to be followed, said Gounaris. All right, we have made mistakes, we have got ourselves involved. But what are we to do today? We cannot change policy, we are obliged to continue the war until the end, even if we risk catastrophe. Otherwise the English will cease to regard us as a serious Nation, if we do not fulfil what we promise, and will abandon us and support Turkey. We must prove that we are a Nation on which a Great Power can depend.

For a Great Power to depend on us, we must at any rate not be destroyed, I answered. We must measure the struggle in accordance with the forces at our disposal....

And another thing, said Protopapadakis. If we withdraw from the Asia Minor war, what will be the impression in Greece? Will

---

* Four days earlier, on 25 March, Metaxas had implicitly accepted the government's offensive posture. Every Greek strategist was torn between the two strategies, but the offensive, as the more positive policy, always won in the end.

† Gounaris confirmed this view, stating that the English had pre-arranged with the Greeks in London that the Greeks should reject the proposal of the London Conference for ethnological Commissions of Enquiry – i.e. had encouraged the Greeks in an intransigent posture – and had 'given us no hope that Thrace would remain Greek' if Greece were to withdraw from Asia Minor. Gounaris and Protopapadakis seem to have greatly exaggerated the significance of some remark made in London in order to bolster up the Greek attitude to Asia Minor. The truth was, as Metaxas recognized, that if the Greeks decided to get out of Asia Minor but to hold on to Thrace, no one could stop them, and England would certainly not have had the will to do so.

we not be swept away by the anger of the people? I don't mean the Government, I mean the regime. Do you imagine that the King will escape?

To this Metaxas replied that if the Government told the truth to the people – that Greece had entered on a war which was beyond her strength, and must withdraw from it – no harm would come to the regime, the Crown and the state, although doubtless the Government itself would fall. Protopapadakis argued that the loss of national self-confidence which would follow withdrawal from Asia Minor would be ruinous to the state, and would lay open even Macedonia to enemy attack. Even defeat in his view was preferable to withdrawal in the middle of the struggle. Metaxas strongly disagreed. When he repeated to Gounaris his view that the Government would do best to remain on the defensive within the Smyrna zone, Protopapadakis interrupted with a new objection: 'How long are we to remain on the defensive? We do not have the money for a long time. We must be finished in two or three months.' Lack of money and supplies was forcing the Government to seek instant, military solutions. Metaxas therefore suggested that the Government leave the Asia Minor army on the defensive, and send the Thracian army forward to occupy Constantinople. The great moral prestige of the occupation of Constantinople would enable the government to justify to the Greek people the abandonment of Smyrna and the Smyrna zone, and thus avert revolution or threats to the throne.

GOUNARIS. We cannot.
SELF. Why not?
GOUNARIS. Any operation against Constantinople is banned by the Allies. The Allies consider Constantinople as in their possession. They are in a state of armistice. So they will not allow us to do it.
SELF. Can't we try it?
GOUNARIS. No, it is out of the question.

The Ministers made one further attempt to get Metaxas to return to the Staff, so as to contribute to an immediate military success, regardless of the long-term military prospects. Protopapadakis asked him for one battle only:

Give us victory now, and we will conclude peace at once. Isn't that right, Dimitraki?
Certainly, said Gounaris.

SELF. How can you conclude peace at once? Do you imagine that Kemal will give in over Smyrna? ...

PROTOPAPADAKIS. We won't insist on Smyrna. We will make concessions. But the compromises which now, after the defeat at Eski Shehir, would be ruinous for the morale of the Greek people, and would perhaps stir up revolution in Greece, would at once become acceptable to the people after a victory.

SELF. You are dreaming! Can you imagine what the Venizelists would demand of you after a victory? Or the opposition of Stratos and the rest? They would demand the whole of Asia Minor! Do you imagine you could restrain the maddened people then?

Faced with Metaxas's refusal to cooperate, the Government continued to put its faith in Papoulas and his staff. On 28 April Papoulas advised them that the rapid and formidable increase and improvement of the Kemalist forces made it desirable that the Greeks should attack with all the forces they could command by 28 May at the latest, aiming to destroy the Kemalist army.[10]

The first need was for men. Papoulas had called for only a few thousand reinforcements for the March offensive, and had not insisted on waiting for the three new classes which the Government had decided to mobilize. But it was now clear that the Greek army in Asia Minor was too small to undertake a major offensive which would take it still further than at present from its bases. The three classes called up in late March yielded rather less than 40,000 men.[11] The Government later called up two further classes of reservists. The Asia Minor army was brought up to a new peak of more than 200,000 men, twice the numbers of a year earlier.[12] Finally, in an effort to improve morale, and despite the absence of Metaxas, the Government resuscitated the 'Royal Command' of the Balkan Wars, appointing King Constantine Commander in Chief of the army, with Dousmanis as his Chief of Staff.

These preparations were impressive. The British military attaché, who inspected the Greek army in June, called it a 'more efficient fighting machine than I have ever seen it'.[13] He wrote later: 'The Greek Army of Asia Minor, which now stood ready and eager to advance, was the most formidable force the nation had ever put into the field. Its morale was high. Judged by Balkan standards, its staff was capable, its discipline and organization good.'[14]

The increase in intensity and seriousness of the war in 1921 was matched by a deterioration in the conduct of the belligerents. From the first the Greek occupation had been marred by brutalities. It could not be otherwise when two secular enemies were suddenly brought face to face in a startling reversal of a relationship which had obtained for the last 500 years. There were Greeks whose attitude was 'We are the masters now!' Inevitably there were Turks who retaliated.

The few days which succeeded the Greek landing in May 1919 had seen arbitrary violence, killing and looting in the streets of Smyrna as Ottoman Greeks, tasting a new and exhilarating draught of liberation, and taking their cue from the Greek soldiery who had humiliated the Turkish officers that first day on the quayside, turned on their Muslim neighbours. The violence and looting were repeated sporadically throughout the occupied zone until Stergiadis established his administration and clamped his iron fist down on the malefactors. Violence flared again horribly in the prosperous town of Aydin, from which the Vilayet took its name, a few weeks after the landing.

Aydin was occupied by Greek troops in July 1919. The Greek inhabitants welcomed their 'liberators'. But the young commander of the Greek detachment which took Aydin and his men neglected the threat to their position from the Muslims who had fled the town and taken to the hills before the conquering army arrived. These *chettés* drove out the Greek troops and recaptured the town. There followed terrible scenes of carnage as the Muslims took their vengeance. The Greek quarter was demolished.

Women and children were hunted like rats from house to house, and civilians caught alive were slaughtered in batches – shot or knifed or hurled over a cliff. The houses and public buildings were plundered, the machinery in the factories wrecked, safes blown open or burst open, and the whole quarter finally burnt to the ground.[15]

The Turks did not long remain masters in their own house. Within a few days Greek reinforcements arrived, the town was retaken, and the ghastly scenes of reprisal began again. When Arnold Toynbee visited Aydin in February 1921, he found a large part of the Turkish quarter burnt, the mosques ruined and abandoned, and almost no Turks left in the town. Alongside the railway to Aydin from Smyrna stood ruins and desolated farms for miles.

The destruction of Aydin was perhaps the most spectacular and wasteful example of the ravages of this war. Similar scenes were repeated on a smaller scale elsewhere. But as Stergiadis's attitudes began to take effect throughout the occupied zone, and Greek administration became established, a semblance of good order was maintained. The high point of Greek administration was in the latter half of 1920, around the time of the signature of the Treaty of Sèvres and the formal assumption of the administration of the Sèvres zone by the Greek High Commission.

In contrast to the picture painted above of an improvement in the public order, the advance of the Greek army out of the restricted zone in June–July 1920 brought in its train renewed violence perpetrated by both Greek and Turkish regular and irregular troops in the Ismid district.[16] Turkish Nationalist bands savaged the Christian populations of the villages east of Yalova, and in the Iznik region, outside the zone occupied by the Greek army. Within the newly occupied territory Greek troops burned villages, and individual soldiers committed numerous acts of barbarity in searching the Muslims for weapons.

As if by a spontaneous process, each military move brought in its train renewed outbreaks of irregular violence; each shifting of the military frontier put the wretched peasantry, whether Muslim or Christian, which had been transferred from one administration to the other, at the mercy of hostile, envious or brutal neighbours. But because of the artificial restrictions under which the Greek army had laboured for most of 1919 and 1920, and the lack of movement at the front, the violence was itself limited. It was not until the war expanded and opened out in 1921 that the atrocities took on the proportions of an epidemic. As the war became more savage, so the armies and the irregular *chetté* bands which operated with their connivance and sometimes under their orders turned on the civilian peoples under their control in ever more savage ways.

Ever since summer 1920 the Greeks had held an extensive and largely Muslim area, in which there were nationalist Turks engaged in espionage on behalf of Kemal, and guerrilla bands operating against the Greeks' lines of communication. In the aftermath of the failure of the spring attack, the Greek troops took their vengeance on Turkish villages which they suspected of harbouring such irregulars. At the same time bands of Christian irregulars, Greek Armenian and Circassian, looted, burned and murdered in the Yalova-Gemlik peninsula. Sometimes, but rarely, local commanders were persuaded by the Greek civilian administration to put a stop to these practices. Often the irregulars acted with the connivance and even encouragement of the authorities.

Brigandage was an inevitable concomitant of the war. Even without the war Anatolia of those days was an unsettled place where authority battled not always successfully against brigandage and violence. But the Greek occupation and the war had brought with them the ingredients of a greater violence. The return of the Greek refugees who had been driven from their Anatolian homes during the Great War, and the consequent expulsion of many thousands of Muslims from the houses they had been occupying, created a rural proletariat apt for brigandage and irregular warfare. Turkish nationalist bands operated from 1919 onwards. In the words of the Interallied Commission of Enquiry into atrocities in the Ismid district in 1921, 'Where either side is in the ascendancy, the survivors of the other in many cases become fugitive; the men often become brigands.' [17]

Toynbee described the nature of these *chetté* bands:

There had always been 'economic' brigands in Anatolia – a straightforward profession, in which people of all denominations and nationalities had engaged. They were the enemies of constituted authority, which had done its ineffective best to put them down. But these new 'political' *chettés*, though they were partly recruited from the professionals, and though their personal incentive was still loot, were in quite other relations with the civil and military authorities of their respective nations. So far from discouraging them, the authorities armed them, organized them, and gave them a free hand to accomplish results which they desired to see accomplished but preferred not to obtain openly for themselves.

These bands were similar to the bands of *Comitadjis* in Macedonia who during the period of the 'Macedonian Question' had tried through terrorism and political indoctrination to influence the political decision of the question on behalf of their own nation, Greek or Bulgarian. Their existence and their activities were strenuously denied by the Greek and Turkish authorities – more successfully in the case of the Greeks than the Turkish Nationalists. Everyone in the west knew the reputation of the Turks for savage treatment of minorities within the Ottoman Empire. The Bulgarian massacres of the late nineteenth century

Greek Evzones march past the Arc de Triomphe in Paris, in the great celebration of 14 July 1919.

Greek troops land in Smyrna, 15 May 1919: the 1/38 Regiment of Evzones.

11

The attempted assassination of
Venizelos at the Gare de Lyon,
Paris, by the Royalist extremists
Kyriakis and Tserepis (who are
shown inset at the bottom corners
of the picture) on 12 August 1920.
The heavenly inscription on this
popular lithograph reads: 'He Who
is everywhere present saves the
Prime Minister of Greater Greece.'

12

Elections in Salonika. The photo
(of 1915) shows clearly the electoral
system used up to and including
November 1920 in operation. Each
voter voted for or against each candidate by putting a token through
the tube assigned to each candidate
into a box divided into two compartments marked YES (NAI) and NO
(OXI). The candidates' agents stand
behind the ballot boxes, issuing
ballots and trying to detect whether
the voter has pushed his token into
the black compartment (for NO) or
the white (for YES). The small
photo serves to remind voters of the
candidate's face.

had blackened their name in liberal circles in western Europe. The Armenian massacres and deportations of 1915–16 had aroused the horror of the western world. Thus when, in the summer of 1921, the Turkish Nationalists began to persecute the Greek communities in Pontus, that remote, beautiful and ancient centre of Hellenism fronting the Black Sea in north-eastern Anatolia, it was no surprise to observers of the war, and no Turkish denial was likely to be believed. The Turks claimed, correctly, that there were revolutionary and separatist elements in the Pontus who were a potential threat to the rear of their army in the event of a Greek offensive. It was true that certain Pontine Greeks nourished ambitious plans of raising irregular troops with the aid of regular officers from the Greek army for the liberation of the province. They wrote long and unconvincing letters to Venizelos soliciting his help in launching their projects. But the extent of the threat was slight, and in no way justified the Turkish oppression. It was true also that the Greek forces did their best to invite Turkish reprisals by bombarding some of the Turkish Black Sea ports from the sea. These bombardments were linked in the minds of the Greeks with the fact that the Turks were gun-running across the Black Sea from Russian ports; for which arbitrary and inaccurate bombardment was no cure.

The situation was quite other with the Greeks. Enrolled by history in the part of the persecuted, and now puffed up by their own propaganda effort into chivalrous liberators, they were widely regarded in western circles as in some way intrinsically averse to brutality of the Ottoman sort. The events of May 1919, acutely embarrassing to their liberal supporters, were regarded as a momentary aberration due to an excess of enthusiasm at a unique moment in their history. On the whole, the Greeks' image of themselves remained convincing in European circles until the end.

One of the techniques practised by the Greeks – copied, like other techniques, from their opponents – was deportation. Muslim religious and civil notables who proved seditious or uncooperative were deported from their home towns and villages all over the occupied territory. In the days of the Armenian massacres, the Ottoman authorities had deported entire villages and townships up-country into central and eastern Anatolia; en route to the labour camps of the interior many thousands died or were massacred by *chetté* bands. The Greek authorities were more discriminating. Such wholesale operations were beyond their means and administrative resources, and besides they had no stomach for wholesale massacre of the Muslim element. Picked Muslims were deported by the Greeks to other parts of the zone, or down country to Smyrna and there shipped to the islands. Not all reached their destinations. The Greeks were attempting to deprive the Nationalist fish of the friendly environment in which they moved – an impossible task; but the task of Nationalist spies and irregulars could be complicated and the Muslim villagers cowed by these tactics.

These deportations were a weapon consciously deployed by the Greek authorities in their attempts to deprive the Turkish Nationalists of their support in the countryside. The Greeks persisted in believing – had to believe, if they were to retain their self-respect – that the peasantry, if separated from intellectual troublemakers and nationalist agitators, would accept Greek government without regret. Stergiadis believed this to the end. But as the war became more fierce and more widely extended, hopes of winning the hearts and minds of the Muslims, for all but the most obstinate or committed (such as Stergiadis) vanished. Deportations then became simply one element in the struggle to protect public order and the security of the Greeks' lines of communications within the zone.

The deterioration of public order, and of the conduct of the war, which took place in 1921 was very marked in the army itself. As Greek resources were strained ever tighter and tighter by the need to pour more and more men into Asia Minor for the campaigns of summer 1921, the quality of the drafts sharply deteriorated. Western observers reported on the undisciplined behaviour of the drafts on their way through Smyrna city to their base. The Greek troops did not have the experience in colonial operations which might have allowed them to behave with restraint towards the Muslims. On the contrary, they were raw, often only barely trained owing to the imperious necessity of the front for manpower, and predisposed to mistrust and hate the Turks. The war and the extension of the occupation in 1921 brutalized the combatants and led to a deterioration in the treatment of minorities and of prisoners of war. That same gap between the picture of the war which was presented to the outside world and the Greek public at home, and the harsh reality of the front, which had been a feature of the Great War in Western Europe, now opened up in Asia Minor.

The complaisance and connivance of the Greek military authorities in the operations of irregular bands against the Muslim villagers was remarked on by two separate independent enquiries.[18] An Interallied Commission of Enquiry was appointed to investigate the destruction and evacuation of Muslim villages in the Yalova-Gemlik peninsula and the Ismid area at the eastern end of the Sea of Marmara between March and May 1921. It reported that the agelong hatred between Christian Greek and Armenian and Muslim Turk, and the presence of numerous Armenian and Greek refugees in the area, were insufficient to explain the rapidity and thoroughness of the reprisals taken on the Turks in the area:

There is a systematic plan of destruction of Turkish villages and extinction of the Moslem population. This plan is being carried out by Greek and Armenian bands, which appear to operate under Greek instructions and sometimes even with the assistance of detachments of regular troops.

This destruction of villages and the disappearance of the Moslem population consequent thereon doubtless has as its object to guard the flanks and rear of the Greek army against any possible attack by the population in the event of an early offensive, and perhaps even to create in this region a political situation favourable to the Greek Government.

It so happened that events in the Yalova and Gemlik peninsula and the Ismid region were fairly closely followed by western observers. The region was close to Constantinople and the neutral zone, and of military significance in that it flanked the zone on one side and the Greeks' line of advance on the other, from the railhead at Mudania on the Sea of Marmara south eastward through Bursa and up to Eski Shehir. The area could thus serve as a refuge for Turkish irregulars to make incursions against the Greeks' communications and especially the vital Mudania–Bursa–Eski Shehir railway. Such were the military reasons for an often ruthless 'pacification' programme.

M. Gehri, the Red Cross representative, surveyed the scenes of death and destruction wrought by the Greeks in May 1921 from the deck of the British warship *Bryony*; at Kapakli

... here and there among the smoking ruins, a few inhabitants.

The rest had fled into the mountains. Eight corpses, four being those of women.... Some had been mutilated.

The survivors declared that the assassins had been Greek soldiers. The staff officer (attached by the Greek command at Gemlik to the Commission) contested their statements, and, noticing a little girl, demanded that the question should be put to her, because 'in the mouths of children the truth is found'. The child declared quietly and categorically that the criminals had been Greek soldiers....

The Red Cross Commission interrogated the Greek lieutenant and adjutant of the 28th Infantry Regiment who had commanded a detachment sent to make a reconnaissance in the south of the peninsula between 12 and 15 May:

Their itinerary coincided at almost every point with the information supplied by the people of Koumla and of the burnt villages. Lieutenant Kostas admitted the possibility of his soldiers having been the incendiaries.... At Koumla landing-place, he had had four armed Turks arrested and shot.... Asked why he had shot them when he had only had orders to arrest them, he replied: 'Because I chose.'

Riding in the vicinity of Koumla with Lieutenant Kostas in order to identify these corpses, Gehri found nine corpses. That evening his group was surprisingly visited by a *chetté* leader, Yorgo of Gemlik, armed to the teeth. The man boasted of having followed Lieutenant Kostas's troops around the peninsula, and having fired the villages in his path. The next day, at the orders of the Divisional Commander General Leonardopoulos, Yorgo was brought back to deny his story. Some shame at least remained to the Greek military authorities.

Throughout the area, it was the same story. Toynbee himself, who closely questioned the surviving Muslims in the area in order to establish the pattern of violence and the responsibility for it, witnessed startling scenes when the Greek 11th Division evacuated Ismid at the end of June, prior to concentration in new positions for the great summer assault on Eski Shehir. Cruising up the gulf of Ismid in a Red Crescent ship, which was able to penetrate the cordon of Greek warships owing to the presence of a representative of the Allied High Commissioners on board, he was able to watch the Greek troops, which had evacuated Ismid the previous day, retiring along the shore in a westerly direction towards Yalova. Two colums of smoke suddenly rose into the air from the shore ahead of the ship. A little later a village burst into flames. Greek soldiers could be seen with the naked eye setting fire to the houses. Later, as the Greek column continued on its way, the group on shipboard saw new and larger columns of smoke rising from Eregli and Karamursal further westwards down the peninsula. Thus the Greek troops destroyed and burned what they evacuated. The work was completed by the Christian populations, who prudently departed at the same time as the troops. When Toynbee landed at Ismid three days after the completion of the evacuation, the Turkish shops in the town were in ruins, systematically looted; the streets leading to the water front were piled with the wreckage of the Turkish ox-carts which the departing Greeks had commandeered to carry their plunder to the boats; the water was speckled with the remains of the oxen which had been slaughtered on the jetty so that the Greeks could ship the flesh and hides with them; the mosques had been looted and defiled. The smoking ruins were haunted by tortured, half burnt cats. When the fresh mass graves in the cemetery were opened, they were found to be full of the corpses of Muslims who had been shot before the Greeks left the town. Such was the fate of Ismid.

Since King Constantine's return, the Allies had begun to turn the screws on the Greeks. The status of the belligerents had never been defined. But in April 1921 the Allies proclaimed their strict neutrality in the war. The British cut off the supply of war materials to Greece, the French and Italians concurring. As Vansittart explained to Philip Kerr, since Britain was preventing the supply of munitions to Kemal, and protestingly strongly to the Italians for permitting such supplies to get through, 'it was felt at the Foreign Office that we must adopt a consistent attitude'.[19] The consistent attitude tended to favour the Turkish Nationalists, since the French and Italians were less scrupulous than Curzon in the denial of war materials to the warring parties.

At the same time the Allies took steps to deny Greece the rights of a belligerent, in the matter of the right of visit and search of allied merchant ships in the Marmara and the Aegean. This move hit the Greeks by preventing them from stopping up the illicit trade with the Kemalists. The Kemalists were not similarly affected, since they were in no position to impose a blockade on Greece. The allied interpretation of neutrality as obliging them to deny the Greeks the use of Constantinople as a naval base was a further blow.[20]

Finally, before the Greeks could launch their great summer attack the Allies made one further attempt at intervention. Throughout these months, the exiguous allied garrison at Constantinople, under General 'Tim' Harington, successor to Milne, continued to control the old Turkish capital (still the seat of the Sultan and his now wholly ineffective regime) and to police the straits. Harington had at his disposal no more than token forces, a symbol of British commitment (as were the British ships in the Bosphorus) but quite insufficient to resist a serious attack. In May British concern over the situation in the Near East brought Harington to London to submit his views. At a Cabinet meeting on 31 May he described the deteriorating situation, and raised the spectre of the Greeks being driven back on Smyrna, the allied positions at Constantinople left uncovered and vulnerable.[21] Harington claimed that the retention of a small force at Constantinople without hope of reinforcements was militarily unsound. In reply, Curzon argued that withdrawal would be 'far-reaching and calamitous, involving the sacrifice of all the results of the Allied victory over Turkey'. Churchill pointed out the danger of withdrawal on the British position in Mesopotamia and Palestine, except as part of a comprehensive peace settlement. The Cabinet decided to set up a special Cabinet Committee on the Future of Constantinople.

At three meetings, on 1, 2 and 9 June, this Committee tried to thrash out a policy for the Greco-Turkish affair.[22] The meetings were a triumph for Curzon's patient exposition of British policy. At the first meeting, he argued that withdrawal from Constantinople and surrender to Kemal would be an incalculable 'moral blow', making it impossible to carry out Britain's policy in Mesopotamia and Palestine:

We ought immediately to place ourselves in a war-like attitude against Mustapha Kemal; to make ourselves as unpleasant to him as possible, and to support the Greeks, on condition that they accepted our advice as to military command, organization and strategy, and our guidance as to policy.

This did not mean that Greek ambitions should be immoderately encouraged; but Britain should consider with her allies new terms of peace which the Turks could be induced to accept. The policy, in other words, was to bolster up the Greeks so as to be in a position to negotiate with Kemal from a position of strength. Even Edwin Montagu, the consistent champion of a lenient Turkish settlement, was led to agree that if the Ankara Government would not now acquiesce in the terms offered them at the London Conference in March, then Britain should assist the Greeks. But the policy of backing the Greek horse would fail if that horse was incapable of taking the jump. The state of the Greek army, its morale and effectiveness, must be assessed.

At the second meeting the Committee considered and rejected a set of typically radical proposals made by Winston Churchill in a letter to Lloyd George.[23] Churchill was determined to secure peace. He was appalled by the spectre of an enforced British evacuation of Constantinople in circumstances of humiliation for Britain. He now saw Muslim hostility to Great Britain spilling over from Turkey into Mosul and Palestine. His proposals were muddled but consisted essentially of demanding that the Greeks put themselves in Britain's hands, and promising them British moral and material support if they would make peace and evacuate Smyrna. But the Greeks wanted support in order to win victory, not to concede defeat. The Committee rightly decided that it would be useless to approach the Greeks with an offer of this sort.

At this second meeting, 'it was urged that a fresh attempt should be made to ascertain definitely whether Greece would be willing to place herself in our hands and, if so, whether she was worth supporting. If the results of these inquiries were unsatisfactory, it would be necessary to contemplate an evacuation [i.e. of the British garrison troops]'.

When the Committee met again a week later, Venizelos had visited London and talked with Curzon, Lloyd George and the C.I.G.S. He had told Curzon that the Greeks could not hold on in Asia Minor for more than six months without allied support. He told Wilson that the suggested changes made in the Greek army under British guidance would have to be radical, including the reinstatement of Paraskevopoulos and the replacement of most officers down to battalion commander level; if the army continued to be conducted as at present, 'within six months it would cease to exist'. Venizelos repeatedly insisted to Lloyd George that if Kemal refused to negotiate, 'the only alternative to the Allies of active support for Greece was a humiliating surrender to Mustapha Kemal involving not only their being driven out of Constantinople but eventually also from Mesopotamia, Syria and Palestine'.

This advice was not very helpful to the Committee. Venizelos insisted that in their own interests the allies should support the Greeks, yet his unfavourable report on the state of the army under Royalist command made it doubtful whether Britain would consider Greece worth backing. A report from Admiral Mark Kerr, the personal friend and constant defender of King Constantine, stated that the King hoped to win the Eski Shehir–Afyon Karahisar line in the forthcoming campaign, but doubted whether the Greeks had the staying power to hold on in Asia Minor.

The Committee also had before it a bulky dossier of reports on the Greek army, most of them unfavourable to the Greeks.[24] Harington's report of March 1921 referred to a 'general loss of efficiency' as a result of the return of Royalist officers. Sir Harry Lamb, the British Consul General at Smyrna, had reported on the poor discipline of new drafts that had landed in April and gone through to Ushak, loosing off shots at minarets and molesting Muslims in the streets. Stergiadis confirmed this to the British military representative in April:

Till a few months ago the population of the area under Greek control had been quiet and contented and the administration of the country had begun to show good results. With the arrival, however, of new officers and soldiers from Greece who were ignorant as to how to behave in Asia Minor ... trouble started and the Turkish population became incensed at various undesirable incidents which took place.*

Further reports pointed to Greek deficiencies in morale and in

---

* Stergiadis's account confirms Toynbee's impression of a deterioration throughout the Greek zone in the spring of 1921. The activities of marauding *chetté* bands (both Greek and Turkish) increased. Public order began to break down not only in the countryside but even in Smyrna itself, where all had been calm and well administered in 1920. Toynbee, *The Western Question*, pp. 157–8; also ch. vii, 'The War of Extermination', and above, p. 212. The reasons for this gradual breakdown of order were surely not simply the arrival of raw and undisciplined troops from Greece, but the unsettling effect of the renewal of military operations (March 1921), the strain placed on the Greek administration by the extension of the Greek zone of occupation, and the brutalizing effect of a prolonged occupation of hostile territory.

material resources, poor intelligence work and lack of communications equipment. Finally, there was an alarming telegram from G.H.Q. Constantinople to the War Office of 3 June, reporting on a plot by Kondylis and the National Defence in Constantinople to regain control of the Greek army for the Venizelist cause by a swift *coup de main*.[25]

According to the National Defence, the plan was for Colonel Kondylis to leave for Smyrna by ship with 1,000 men, General Ioannou for Bursa with 500; and another party for Ismid. All these parties were to arrive at their destinations on the same evening. The conspirators claimed that a picked force of 200 men in Bursa was ready to seize the higher Royalist officers when the signal was given.

In this way the National Defence would swiftly and bloodlessly take over the army. A provisional government with Stergiadis at its head would then be formed in Asia Minor. The Venizelist politician Pericles Argyropoulos would join this government from Constantinople, and also Admiral Koundouriotis 'on account of his well known personality'. Koundouriotis, with his impeccable Venizelist credentials as one of the governing 'triumvirate' of 1916, would have lent prestige to the *Amyna* in the eyes of the Powers. But it is probable that his name was here invoked without his knowledge. (In the case of Stergiadis this is not merely probable but certain.) The Admiral was at this time in Cannes, recuperating after his unpleasant experience at the hands of Royalist toughs in January.

British G.H.Q. reported: 'They say Kondilis [*sic*] has been informed by Venizelos that as Greece is being destroyed by present Government he can do what he likes in the matter of replacing it offering at same time to act if required as High Commissioner in London.' There were no immediate plans for a *coup d'état* in Athens. If the Royalist government remained in power, the National Defence contemplated a march on Athens of units from the army in Thrace. The Committee was anxious to launch its movement at once, but wanted the opinion of the British authorities first.

G.H.Q. commented that these proposals for taking over the army seemed 'sketchy', and suggested that if the War Office attached any importance to the plan, they should consult Venizelos. Nothing came of the scheme, which was temporarily shelved. But the episode shows to what lengths political passion had now led the Venizelist extremists.

The information on this dossier on the Greek army might have been expected to prejudice the Committee against the Greeks; but much of it was out of date, and it was not taken as final by Lloyd George, who called for a special report on the Greek army in the light of the changes since November 1920, from the military attaché in Athens.[26] The policy which emerged from the Cabinet Committee's three meetings was, in its broad lines, as follows.

The Allies would approach the Greek Government for authority to propose to the Turks a settlement based on the London Conference terms, modified in Turkey's favour. As to Smyrna, the Turks would be offered the maximum short of complete Turkish sovereignty and consistent with the safety of the Christian population – 'this might include the creation of an autonomous State under the protection of the Powers, protected by a force raised locally (if feasible), provision being made for the withdrawal of all Greek troops as soon as the Allied Powers declared the new force to be capable of carrying out its responsibilities'.

The Allies would give the Greeks an undertaking that, if the Turks refused these terms, they would support the Greeks through a naval blockade in the Black Sea; facilities for acquiring munitions and war material, including aeroplanes; relaxation of the financial blockade; and perhaps even permission to engage ex-servicemen as volunteers. Moreover, if the Turks rejected terms and the war continued, the terms over Smyrna would be once more open to revision if the Greeks won.

On 11 June Churchill wrote to Lloyd George to say that he had explained to Venizelos the conclusions of this Cabinet Committee, and that Venizelos had agreed. Churchill too had come to agree with the approach which had been mapped out, though he argued that the peace terms to be put to the Greeks and then to Kemal must include the evacuation of Smyrna by the Greek army. What appealed to Churchill was the prospect at last of a decisive policy and action in favour of either the Greeks or the Turks, depending on how they reacted to the allied mediation:

Half-measures and half-hearted support have been the bane of all the policy we have pursued, whether towards Russia or Turkey, since the Armistice, and they have conducted us to our present disastrous position.... I do not think there is any time to lose. If the Greeks go off on another half-cock offensive, the last card will have been played and lost and we shall neither have a Turkish peace nor a Greek army.[27]

Churchill defended himself against the charge of inconsistency on the grounds that his view of the aim – a just and stable peace with Turkey – had not changed, nor his disapproval of the policy of the Treaty of Sèvres. His support for the Cabinet Committee's approach was thus support for the only tactic left in these difficult circumstances which might serve to enforce peace on the two combatants. In fact Churchill was itching to knock the combatants' heads together and (rather in the manner of a child seeking to bend all alien objects and persons to his will) *make* them do what he had determined they should.

Only one nagging problem remained – whether the Greek horse really was reliable. A Greek defeat would produce a 'critical situation'. It was therefore understood that the policy set out above was conditional on the military reports on the Greek army, and might in any case have to be adjusted to meet the views of the French. Despite these qualifications, Lloyd George, Curzon and the Foreign Office had carried the day. The Gounarist policy of holding on to Greece's gains in Asia Minor by the sword suddenly seemed realizable.

The military reports turned out to be surprisingly favourable. Colonel Hoare Nairne, the British Military Attaché in Athens, arrived in Smyrna on 4 June. He found Stergiadis confident, but regretful that so many Venizelist officers had been sacked. Sariyannis too was confident, but 'anxious for the future' owing to the shipment of supplies to Kemal from the Bolsheviks by sea through Sinope, Samsun and Inebolu. In Sariyannis's view the ultimate fate of the Greek effort depended on whether this route were to be sealed off by blockade.[28]

After more than a week of inspection and discussion, Nairne sent in his conclusions.[29] The army was now 'a more efficient fighting machine than I have ever seen it'. Morale was good, the means of transport sufficient, the staff work properly coordinated. Nairne admitted that Papoulas was no more than a figurehead, but one who inspired confidence. He singled out the IV Bureau (Supplies) under the talented and energetic Colonel Spyridonos, for its good work.

On the controversial question of the numerous replacements

of senior officers, Nairne agreed with Colonel Pallis that on balance the army had benefited by the last eight months' changes in the command. The departure of Generals Nider and Tseroulis (7th Division) was a 'great loss'. Kontoulis, Nider's successor, was reliable, and Trikoupis (3rd Division) was 'a great asset'. Platis, on the other hand, commanding the 7th Division, was the 'weak horse', and Colonel Dimaras (5th Division) lacked experience. Fortunately, as Nairne wrote, the large majority of junior Venizelist officers had remained; 'Royalist officers were naturally not so good at handling their men in action as those who had fought in Macedonia.'

Nairne's report confirmed that Greek aviation and aerial reconnaissance was poor, and that more wireless sets were needed. He estimated the total strength of the Asia Minor army on 14 June at 169,000 men exclusive of sick, giving an actual fighting strength of 100,000 or more.* No one reading Hoare Nairne's report would have concluded that the Greek army was negligible and not worth backing. As Hoare Nairne wrote six months later: 'The Greek Army of Asia Minor, which now stood ready and eager to advance, was the most formidable force the nation had ever put into the field. Its morale was high. Judged by Balkan standards, its staff was capable, its discipline and organization good.'[30]

It only remained for Curzon to press British views on the French. On 16 June Lloyd George wrote from Criccieth a letter calculated to stiffen his resolution in the forthcoming meetings with Briand. It throws interesting light on Lloyd George's attitude even after the Cabinet Committee meetings. He reminded Curzon:

(1) that the Turk will not succumb to soft words ...†

(2) It is not safe to assume that British and French military opinion about the value of the morale of the Greek army can always be depended upon ...

(3) We must not put ourselves in the position of endeavouring to force the Greeks to do something which they are bound to refuse.... Constantine dare not retire.... He might make good. The failure of his offensive is by no means the end of Greek resistance.[31]

* This number of 169,000 would be increased by the newly formed 12th Division, and the 1912 class still to come from Greece, to about 200,000.

† A point about which Curzon needed no reminding; for this and other reasons the letter must have been like gall to the Foreign Secretary.

Lloyd George concluded that probably neither side could dislodge the other. If Constantine put up a good fight, Ankara might well cave in and make peace in return for a slackening of the financial controls and a British withdrawal from Constantinople and Ismid (but not from Gallipoli, from which Britain could control the Straits). The letter suggests that Lloyd George did not take the mediation proposal seriously, but hoped that even partial success of the Greek offensive would put Britain in a stronger position to negotiate a peace which would leave Britain in control of the Straits, and the Greeks firmly established in Asia Minor.

Curzon met Briand at the Quai d'Orsay on 18 and 19 June.[32] The discussions were on the whole successful. Briand agreed that the time had come for mediation, which might well be acceptable to both sides. The French (and later the Italians) accepted the broad lines of Curzon's proposals, though Briand was evasive over the question of support for the Greeks in case of Turkish refusal of terms. There was agreement over Smyrna and the necessity for the eventual withdrawal of Greek troops. The main difficulty arose over Thrace. Curzon argued for the Chatalja frontier and a small demilitarized zone, Briand for the ejection of the Greeks from Eastern Thrace and the creation of an international zone. When neither side would budge, it was agreed to reserve the question.

The Allies' message to the Greek Government offering mediation was delivered in Athens on 22 June.[33] Churchill wrote to Lloyd George and Curzon on 25 June, urging that if the Greeks refused the offer, as seemed probable, the British should make their policy effective:

I am sure the path of courage is the path of safety.... I think we should ask the French whether they will join with us in letting the Greeks know that unless they put themselves in our hands as we suggested, we shall definitely intervene to stop the war by blockading Smyrna to Greek ships. This threat is bound to be decisive.... As the counterpart to this, we should make it clear to the Greeks that if they do put themselves in our hands and Kemal is unreasonable we will give them effective support, including the full use of the naval blockade weapon against the Turks.... I may add that if the French decline to participate in the naval blockade, either of Greece or Turkey as the case may be, I should still be in favour of our going on alone.[34]

Venizelos sent a message via the Greek Legation in Paris, advising the Greek Government to accept the offer.[35] But the Allies had miscalculated the Greek will to fight as evidenced in the massive military build-up over the past two and a half months. Besides, the Greek offensive was due to begin in less than three weeks. A long and polite note was dispatched on 24 June, stating that for military reasons the offensive could not now be suspended, but that the Greek Government would be ready at all times to consider concrete proposals for a peace settlement.[36] Lloyd George's instinct, that the two sides must fight it out, had been right. On 10 July the Greeks advanced to meet the enemy.

King Constantine had embarked for Smyrna on 11 June, accompanied by the Chief of General Staff, Dousmanis, his Deputy, Xenophon Stratigos, and by Gounaris and Theotokis. The ministers' purpose in visiting the theatre of operations was illuminated by an amusing conversation between Gounaris and Dousmanis on board the *Lemnos*.[37] Gounaris first complained that Dousmanis had repeated in public that Gounaris had called Papoulas an illiterate and an ass. Dousmanis, in his obtusely irritating way, said that he had assumed that the remark, made at a ministerial meeting, could not have been meant to be secret. Gounaris then asked if Dousmanis knew why he and Theotokis were visiting Smyrna, and explained: 'We are coming because we wish there to be no rift between General Staff and the Asia Minor Command. The General Staff and the King will have no part in the direction of operations.' An unfriendly argument on this subject did not deflect Gounaris from his decision to use the King as a figurehead, with no power over the planning or direction of operations. This decision was not difficult to execute, for the King was by now a tired and sick man, without his old stubbornness and will. Dousmanis too, though never reluctant to press advice and memoranda on his colleagues and Papoulas, lacked effective power.[38] The operational plans of the Asia Minor Staff were approved at a meeting of both staffs in the King's house in Kordelio outside Smyrna.[39] Then, while the King remained in Kordelio, Papoulas left with his staff to direct the operations.

On 10 July, for the third time in one year, the Greek army moved forward to the attack.[40] The objective was once more the crucial railway line connecting Eski Shehir and Afyon Karahissar. The strategy was more sophisticated than for the March attack, when Northern and Southern Groups had advanced on Eski Shehir and Afyon Karahisar independently of one another. The main Greek concentration was now on the southern sector of the front. One column was sent eastwards to take Afyon Karahisar and then swing north towards Eski Shehir. A second column was sent north from Tulu Punar, the position where the Greeks had just held off the Turkish counter attack in April. This column and a third column moving south-east from Bursa were to converge on Kutahya, the key to the campaign, a town which lay near the Afyon–Eski Shehir railway line.

The tactic was successful. Kutahya fell on 17 July, and the Greek columns moved on north-eastwards to Eski Shehir. The Greeks hoped to encircle the bulk of the Turkish forces in the region of Kutahya (or, failing that, Eski Shehir) and destroy them. The Greek right wing was advancing towards a point east of Eski Shehir, to cut off the Turkish retreat. Ismet, commanding the Turkish forces in Eski Shehir, was relieved of the grim responsibility of ordering a retreat by Kemal himself, who came down by train from Ankara, studied the situation on the spot, and ordered a general retreat.[41] To cover the retreat, and to give time for the evacuation eastward of Turkish arms, equipment and rolling stock, the Turks fought harrying rearguard actions, and launched one full-scale counterattack on 21 July. It was repulsed, with heavy Turkish losses. Nevertheless, the Turks had escaped the net. When Greek forces entered Eski Shehir at last on 19 July, the town was empty of Turkish troops. Numerous guns and some thousands of prisoners fell into Greek hands during the campaign,[42] but the main Turkish army withdrew intact towards Ankara, beyond the immediate range of the Greek army. The Greeks hailed a great victory. Xenophon Stratigos, reckoning Turkish losses as at least one third of their entire strength, boasted of 'the end of the Kemalist army' and its imminent annihilation.[43] But, as Kemal had recognized in ordering retreat, the further the Greek forces were drawn from their bases, the more difficult and dangerous would be the attempt to annihilate the Turkish army.

In London, Lloyd George watched the Greeks' fortunes with eager interest. On 21 July he wrote to his War Minister, Sir L. Worthington Evans, a letter of the most mordant sarcasm:

I hear from Greek quarters that Eski Shehir has been captured and that the Turkish Army is in full retreat. Whichever way you look at the matter this is news of the first importance. The future of the East will very largely be determined by this struggle, and yet, as far as I can see, the War Office have not taken the slightest trouble to find out what has happened.... Even from the point of view of an interesting study of warfare under such conditions one would have thought it would have been worth the while of the General Staff to send someone there, either from Athens, or Constantinople, or from here. We all knew this attack was coming. The Staff have displayed the most amazing slovenliness in this matter. Their information about the respective strength and quality of the two Armies turned out to be hopelessly wrong when the facts were investigated, at the instance of the despised politicians. A few weeks ago they were trembling for the fate of Constantinople. We were told that this terrible Mustapha Kemal, with his invincible army, would be there in three weeks.

Have you no Department which is known as the 'Intelligence Department' in your Office? You might find out what it is doing. It appears in the Estimates at quite a substantial figure, but when it comes to information it is not visible.

Please look into this yourself.

Frances Stevenson, Lloyd George's secretary and mistress, noted his concern:

D. very interested in the Greek advance against the Turks. He has had a great fight in the Cabinet to back the Greeks (not in the field but morally) and he and Balfour are the only pro-Greeks there. All the others have done their best to obstruct and the WO have behaved abominably. However D. has got his way, but he is much afraid lest the Greek attack should be a failure, and he should be proved to have been wrong. He says his political reputation depends a great deal on what happens in Asia Minor, though I don't think people care a hang what happens there. But D. says that if the Greeks succeed the Treaty of Versailles is vindicated, and the Turkish rule is at an end. A new Greek Empire will be founded, friendly to Britain, and it will help all our interests in the East. He is perfectly convinced he is right over this, and is willing to stake everything on it.[44]

This was the critical moment, when the fortunes of both sides hung in the balance. Mustapha Kemal had staked his political existence on the unpopular policy of controlled withdrawal – a policy which required iron strength and confidence, to draw

Greek headquarters at a railway station, September 1921. Crown Prince George and General Papoulas in the centre.

Greek headquarters staff on the move, September 1921.

15 The destruction of Smyrna, showing refugees in boats, September 1922.

16 The Trial of the Six. The accused Ministers and soldiers sit in the front row: *from left to right* M. Goudas, G. Baltazzis, X. Stratigos, N. Stratos, N. Theotokis, P. Protopapadaki and General G. Hatzianestis. D. Gounaris is absent, sick with typhus fever.

the Greek army into not a trap but a wasteland where it would destroy itself. The Greeks felt that having gone so far they must make one more supreme effort for success. Ankara, the name which had been on all lips for two years and seemed by now to incorporate some of Kemal's own power, beckoned like a mirage; capture the city and the power would be dissolved.

Kemal himself laid down the Turkish tactics in a general directive:

After the army has been concentrated north and south of Eski-shehir, we must establish a large area between it and the enemy's forces, so that we shall be able to carry on our reconstitution, re-organization and reinforcement. For this purpose we should be able to retire even to the north of the Sakarya. If the enemy should pursue us without coming to a halt, he would be getting farther away from his base of operations.... Thus our army will be able to rally and meet the enemy under more favourable conditions.[45]

The disadvantage of this tactic was the effect on Turkish opinion of surrendering ground to the enemy. But Kemal succeeded in mastering his critics in the Assembly, and was appointed Commander-in-Chief with dictatorial powers for three months, in order to meet the crisis. With drastic energy he and his colleagues prepared to defend Ankara, drafting new classes and rushing supplies of arms and munitions from provincial depots to the Ankara front in convoys of ox-carts. The Turks had less than a month in which to prepare themselves.

The determining feature of the terrain was the river Sakarya, which flows eastward across the plateau, suddenly curves north and then turns back westwards, describing a great loop some fifty miles west of Ankara. This loop forms a natural barrier. The river banks are awkward and steep, and bridges were few, there being only two on the frontal section of the loop. East of the loop, the landscape rises before an invader in rocky, barren ridges and hills towards Ankara. It was here in these hills, east of the river, that the Turks dug in, on a front of some sixty miles. The front followed the hills east of the Sakarya from a point near Polatli southwards to where the Gök joins the Sakarya, and then swung at rightangles eastwards following the line of the Gök. It was good defensive ground.

For the Greeks the problem – whether to dig in and rest on their gains, or to advance towards Ankara in a last great effort to destroy the Turkish Nationalist army – was simply stated, but agonizingly difficult to resolve. Essentially it was the same problem that had faced the Greek Staff since 1919. The dangers of extending the lines of communication still further were obvious. The present front, giving the Greeks control of the essential strategic railway, was tactically the most favourable the Greeks could hope for. Yet because the Turkish army had escaped encirclement at Kutahya, nothing had been settled. For the Greeks to remain on the Afyon–Eski Shehir front would allow Kemal time to regroup his forces, to draft new recruits, and to negotiate settlements with the Powers which would enable him to concentrate all his forces on the western front. The temptation for the Greeks to make a new effort to achieve the 'knock-out blow' was almost irresistible.

The Greek political and military leaders met in Kutahya to decide on the next step. Gounaris had three questions for Papoulas: (1) whether the situation was such that the Greek army could now be considered secure in the occupied zone; (2) whether its position was so secure that the government could proceed to a gradual demobilization of the older classes of the reserves; (3) if the answer to these two questions was negative, what the next step should be.[46] The answers, of course, were negative, and this explains why the politicians were reluctant to halt the army on the Eski Shehir front. But Papoulas was nervous and uncertain.

At a Staff Conference on 26 July, Papoulas asked his advisers their views.[47] Sariyannis, Deputy Chief of Staff and Chief of III Bureau (Operations) was as usual the activist; he urged that the army should advance with the least possible delay, to take advantage of the enemy's disorganization and loss of morale. Lt-Col Spyridonos, the highly competent Chief of IV Bureau (Supply) argued that an immediate advance was ruled out by lack of ammunition, while a later advance, if pushed beyond the river Sakarya, would place such a strain on the lines of communication and means of transport (depleted after the recent campaign) as to risk a breakdown in supplies. To advance on Ankara was thus to risk a serious, perhaps decisive defeat. Pallis, well-educated and knowledgeable, but without the force to impose a view, hesitantly agreed with Sariyannis that the advance should take place.

It was decided as a compromise to advise the Government that the army, after some days for rest and refitting, could advance as far as the Sakarya: 'If the enemy resists within the loop of the Sakarya, the army will crush him and then, with a section consisting of one Division or even one Army Corps, occupy Angora for a certain period of time; then, after destroying the enemy's supplies there and the railway line, it will return to its starting place.' [48]

On the basis of this compromise III Bureau drew up a memo for the Government. The critical meeting took place on 28 July, attended by Papoulas and Pallis, Gounaris and Theotokis, the King, Dousmanis and Stratigos.[49] Neither Papoulas nor Pallis was a strong character. Whatever reservations they may have had about the projected advance were overborne by the desire of the politicians (Stratigos included) for decisive action. The War Council therefore decided that the army should resume the offensive and advance on Ankara. But the decision was based on the half-hearted memo of III Bureau, with its concessions to IV Bureau's doubts over transport and supplies. The crucial part of the memo ran as follows:

G.H.Q. has reached the conclusion that the army can advance as far as the eastern section of the Sakarya, i.e., the Beylik Keupru Kavak line.

If during this period it meets the enemy and defeats him, then the pursuit to Ankara by a section of the army will not present difficulties. If on the other hand the enemy retreats across the Sakarya, the army will advance or halt according to the circumstances at that time; i.e., if the circumstances are favourable (e.g. occupation of the railway line without its being destroyed, roads and automobiles in good condition etc.), [it will go forward], but otherwise it will return to Eski Shehir totally destroying the 100 km stretch of railway between Beylik Keupru and a point east of Eski Shehir.[50]

What a confusion of aims is here. Was the advance on Ankara to be the final knock-out blow, or simply a punitive raid? Apparently it was to be the former only if the Turks were good enough to stand and fight within the loop of the Sakarya, rather than retiring behind the river and digging in between the river and Ankara. The Staff, in deference to the doubts of Colonel Spyridonos's IV Bureau, excluded an all-out assault across the Sakarya unless every circumstance favoured it. Yet what, apart from the

knockout blow and the capture of Ankara, the moral centre of
Kemalism, could be the purpose of this great and costly advance
so deep into hostile territory? The destruction of 100 km of
railway track. This, despite the optimistic predictions of the
Staff, would not reduce Kemal to impotence.

The vagueness of the Staff's memo seems to have allowed
Papoulas and the politicians to expect different things of the
proposed operation. Papoulas allowed himself to be persuaded
into launching an attack in which he only half believed, and
whose object was imprecisely formulated, in the conviction that
if the army ran into difficulties it could simply retire with no
harm done. The politicians, on the other hand, took the conditional hopes of the Staff memo more seriously, and had high
hopes that the Kemalist army would be finally crushed. Theotokis
especially was exhilarated, and shortly before the advance began
remarked to the British military attaché that they would take tea
together in Ankara in three weeks' time.

There seems to have been little dispute at the War Council.
Pressure for energetic action came from Gounaris. Pallis explained the difficulties and expressed some doubts. Of those
whose reservations were the strongest, Papoulas and the King,
Papoulas allowed Pallis to speak for him, and the King apparently
offered no strong views. Dousmanis, though critical as always of
other military experts, approved of the advance in principle.
Stratigos was strongly in favour.

In his telegram to Athens reporting on the Council, Gounaris
set out the course of the discussion.

The enemy not having shown a disposition to negotiate and accept
peace, I asked the Army Command if it considers that annihilation
of the enemy allowing the above action [i.e. demobilization and a
unilateral settlement] is imminent. Army Command declared that
the enemy's army had suffered very important losses and is in a
state approaching dissolution, but that its state could not be termed
annihilation in the above sense.

To question what action if any can be taken to achieve desired
result all agreed that this can be achieved more or less fully but in
any case sufficiently by continuation of pursuit of enemy as far as
Ankara and the river Halys at furthest. This operation will require
20 to 40 days. There is probability that enemy will stand on Sivri
Hisar defensive line or further east but this side of Sakarya, in
which case his defeat and destruction is very probable. After this
continuation of operation was decided unanimously. . . .[51]

So the decision to advance was taken. Papoulas left for Eski Shehir. Gounaris and the King followed him soon after to review the troops and distribute medals. There followed a fortnight of intensive preparation – rest for the troops, concentration of supplies and ammunition, and above all the collection of every available means of transport, from camels to Fiat and Tyler lorries.

Papoulas claimed later that the King shared his doubts about the Ankara operation.[52] This could well be so. But the only authentic clue to Constantine's feelings – and one of the few personal relics of this complicated, tragic figure – is a letter written in Kutahya a few days after the Council of War.* The King wrote that his life in Smyrna had been 'by no means amusing', for Stergiadis had been so terrified that some harm might befall him that he had had to stay indoors almost the whole time.[53] Then came the trip to Kutahya by rail and then road 'terrible and almost as dusty as that from Milan to Salsomaggiore'.[54]

The country round is magnificent [wrote the King]. There is not a tree to be seen within a radius of several kilometres, but the cornfields

---

* Passas, pp. 115–16, cites an amusing account by the Metropolitan Bishop of Ephesus of a meeting with the King shortly after the Council: the Bishop found Constantine alone in his room at Kutahya.
' "It is true, Your Holiness," the King remarked with a light smile, resting his limpid eyes on me, "that the recent gratifying events have not left us time to think about the Church and its flock which has been considerably increased by the victories of our army. But now I am at your service..."
' "Your Majesty," I interrupted, "so long as the work of the army is uncompleted, it would be graceless on the part of the Church to complain, and especially now when others of her unfortunate children are to be liberated.... Or have you not decided, Your Majesty, on the expedition against Ankara?"
'These last words shook the King deeply.... He brought his fist down on the desk in front of him and answered with a voice like thunder, "I have decided nothing! I am not responsible! You can always ask those out there who actually govern!"
'And without adding another word he joined his hands behind his back and began to pace nervously up and down the room, whispering something from time to time through his teeth, in evident displeasure.'
The Bishop left hastily. Unfortunately this entertaining story does not show conclusively whether the King's displeasure was caused by the government's decision to order the advance on Ankara, or by his frustrating position as a powerless figurehead.

are splendid.... It is not too warm, but the nights are fresh, and at times, even cold....

The King shared the common Greek assumptions about the Turks, finding Turkish towns filthy and badly paved, with narrow winding streets:

It is extraordinary how little civilized the Turks are.... It is high time they disappeared once more and went back into the interior of Asia whence they came....

There are still some villages where dangerous fanaticism still reigns, and then the Turks go out by night and massacre, in the most atrocious manner, our men or the lorry drivers who happen to be isolated; they mutilate them or even skin them, which enrages our soldiers to such an extent as to give rise to disagreeable reprisals. The war is developing into wild fighting, and that is the reason why we have so few prisoners – they are all massacred on the spot....[55]

I hope that peace will not now be long in coming, for I confess that we are utterly weary of this war, but, I repeat it, *it was not my war*; it was a national war.... The other day at Eski-Cheir I held a review for the purpose of distributing decorations to the colours and the men.... This took place near the battlefield, with troops that had only just returned, and when I saw the 24 standards, tattered and riddled with bullets, lowered in front of me for the salute, I felt a big lump in my throat. I tremble with emotion as I write this.... Our losses are, thank God, bearable....

On 14 August, the Greek army emerged from its entrenched positions east of Eski Shehir and began the long march eastwards towards Ankara.[56] As in July, the Greek aim was to outflank the Turkish positions by rapid marching and not break themselves in a head-on assault. The Greeks advanced in three columns, each composed of three divisions of infantry. On the left, part of the 3rd Army Corps, marching up the Porsuk river which followed the course of the Eski Shehir–Ankara railway, was to make the frontal attack, seizing the Sakarya bridges in the 'loop' of the river. Meanwhile, the 1st and 2nd Army Corps, marching further south, were to take the Turkish left flank, swinging left to attack across the river Gök, a tributary of the Sakarya.

The Greeks marched hard for nine days before making contact with the enemy. On the far right, the 2nd Army Corps and the Cavalry Brigade, in carrying out the outflanking manoeuvre, were forced to swing southeast through the northern part of the great central Anatolian Salt Desert. The 5th, 13th and 9th Divisions marched doggedly across this waste land under a scorching August sun. At night there was coolness, even chill. The problems of supply were acute. Water had to be brought up to the marching divisions by truck. The clinging sand and choking dust penetrated axles and engines and caused breakdowns. The movements of the Greek columns could be detected from miles away by the plumes of dust hanging like ill omens in the sky above the marching troops.

In the desert vegetation and water scarcely existed. Only a few of the army's precious lorries could be assigned to water carrying. Fuel for cooking was unobtainable. The inhabitants of the scattered tiny settlements used dried dung. The soldiers, exhausted by the march on top of the previous hard campaign, kept the sacks in which bread was sent up from the field bakeries behind the advancing front, adding them to their bedding. The bread rotted in the supply centres. The advancing infantry had to rifle the poor Turkish villages for maize. They obtained meat from the flocks which were pastured on the fringe of the desert.

On 23 August, after nine days marching, the Greeks made contact with advanced Turkish positions south of the Gök river. The Turks had dug in under the supervision of Mustapha Kemal himself, who had made his headquarters at Polatli on the railway a few miles east of the Sakarya river. On 26 August, the Greeks attacked all along the line. Crossing the shallow Gök, the infantry fought its way step by step up onto the heights. The battle lasted for three weeks. Every ridge and hill top had to be stormed against strong entrenchments and withering fire. The fighting was fierce and desperate. Ridge by ridge the Greeks fought their way towards Ankara. By 2 September the commanding heights of Chal Dag were in Greek hands, and Turkish morale was depressed. All along the line the Greeks had fought themselves through the Turkish second line of defence.

This was the summit of the Greek achievement. The troops had now fought themselves to a standstill. For days during the battle neither ammunition nor food had reached the front, owing to successful harassment of the Greek lines of communications and raids behind the Greek lines by Turkish cavalry.[57] All the Greek troops were committed to the battle, while fresh Turkish drafts were still arriving throughout the campaign in response to the Nationalists' mobilization. For all these reasons, the impetus of the Greek attack was gone. For a few days there was a lull in the fighting, in which neither exhausted army could press an attack. Then the Turks, sensing that the Greek offensive spirit was broken, launched their counterattack, on 8–10 September.

The Greek line held, but the army had had enough fighting. On 11 September Papoulas gave the order to retire. That night I Army Corps evacuated Chal Dag, which had been taken at such cost, and a general retreat began. By 14 September the Greeks had retired unmolested across the Sakarya, taking with them their guns and equipment. Having suffered over 20,000 casualties and fought their heart out in the inhospitable hills of Anatolia, the troops retired to Eski Shehir and the positions they had left a month before. In the line of the retreating army nothing was left that could benefit the Turks. Railway bridges were blown up. Villages, abandoned by their inhabitants in the face of the advancing troops, were burnt.

This was the watershed in the Asia Minor policy of the Gounaris Government. The Greek army had shot its bolt. The retreat from the Sakarya marked the end of the Greek hopes of imposing a settlement on Turkey by force of arms, and the beginning of a new period in which the Government recognized that a face-saving settlement must come through the diplomacy of the Powers. It was to Curzon, rather than Lloyd George, that Gounaris was now forced to turn for help. Ironically, just when the Royalists were prepared to take heed of British views (as the Venizelist had always argued they should), the frail consensus over the 'national' policy for Asia Minor finally broke down.

The main reason was the impact of Venizelos's own views on his supporters in Greece. Venizelos's attitude had grown more pessimistic as time passed. By May 1921 he was predicting disaster due to Greece's diplomatic isolation, which he claimed could only be alleviated by the abdication of Constantine.[58] By June he was convinced that to undertake an offensive and therefore to reject the Powers' offer of mediation of 21 June was disastrous policy.

Venizelos gave reasons for this view in two letters to General Danglis. In the first, of 3 July, he at last completely dissociated himself from the Government's policy, writing that the refusal of the Government to accept the mediation of the Powers was its 'last crime against Greece'.

Venizelos argued that since the *basis* of the Asia Minor policy (the alliance with the Powers) had been destroyed, the Government should now seek a compromise, with the object of putting an end to the war and saving what could still be saved. Even the Liberals had not appreciated this, and were still under the illusion that the Government was carrying out a 'national' policy. He went on to argue, interestingly but implausibly, that the acceptance of his advice would still have saved the Treaty of Sèvres.

When I maintain that our Government has blundered criminally in not accepting the intervention of the Allied Powers, I do not consider that Turkey would have accepted a solution in accordance with the British point of view; but in the event of Turkey's refusal to accept such a solution, Great Britain would have appeared justified, in public opinion, in coming to our support in imposing the Treaty of Sèvres.... Now that the refusal has come from us, public opinion in England will not, under any circumstances, allow the Government to assist us.... Military victory such as will crush the enemy and force him to sign and execute the treaty we shall dictate, is absolutely out of the question.... To what other result can resumption of hostilities lead than to our complete economic and military exhaustion, which will place us in the position, after a few months, of having to beg for intervention under conditions incomparably harsher than those already offered? [59]

In his second letter to Danglis, written from Bagnères de Luchon on 26 August 1921 – during the advance on Ankara – Venizelos roundly condemned the offensive, which he claimed would not lead to victory since the Turks would be able to retire and escape the knock-out blow. Only the capture of Constantinople, wrote Venizelos, would be decisive, and that was forbidden by the Allies:

Certainly England, persuaded ... that a Great Greece would be a trustworthy ally of England in the Near East, and influenced much less than France by sentimental reasons, continues to desire the aggrandizement of Greece at the expense of Turkey. But England alone cannot impose her views. And the French reaction against us is sleepless.[60]

These two letters, which were published in the Greek press in September, raised a storm, and signalled the end of the united 'national' approach to the Asia Minor war. The final and open break in national unity came in the Assembly on 15 October 1921, when Gounaris, announcing his departure the next day with Baltazzis for Paris and London, sought a vote of confidence. The Liberals left the Chamber in a body, refusing to endorse the Government's handling of the national question. From this time on the schism extended to foreign as well as internal policy, and Venizelists began to impute treachery as well as incompetence to the government. Venizelos himself in his letter of 3 July to Danglis indicated the lines which criticism of the Government was more and more to take:

The fact is that the Government is continuing the war despite the isolation of Greece, because they want to harass the Greek people still further and lead them from failure to failure, to the point where the people themselves will seek with a great voice the end of the war at any cost, and consider those who give peace as benefactors; i.e. the events of 1915–16 are being repeated....[61]

These words were a clear indication that communications between government and Venizelists had irreparably broken down.

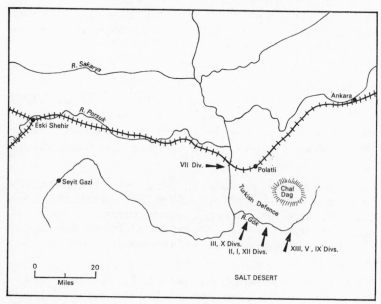

The Battle of the Sakarya River, August–September 1921

Something must be done quickly to remove us from
the nightmare of Asia Minor.

Prince Andrew to Metaxas, January 1922

I said it last week clearly to Mr Gounaris and Mr
Balto – what is the other one called? – Mr Baltazzis.
Personally I am a friend of Greece, but for the
reasons I have given you all my colleagues are
against me. And I cannot be of any use to you. It is
impossible, impossible.

Lloyd George to Patriarch Meletios

Let us go home and to hell with Asia Minor.

Greek soldiers, spring 1922

The military strategy of the Greeks having failed to yield victory,
both Government and opposition set themselves to reassess the
position. For the Government, empty of ideas, London glimmered
like a mirage on the horizon in an otherwise barren desert. Lloyd
George had helped to get them into trouble; perhaps he could
get them out of it again. Gounaris and his foreign minister Baltazzis set off for England in October.

As for the opposition, the parliamentary Liberal party had
withdrawn its support from the Government and the left wing
of the party, represented by Papanastasiou, Papandreou and
others, became ever more outspoken in its denunciations of the
regime and the Crown. Republicanism flourished. Meanwhile
the *Amyna*, or National Defence movement, extended its influence in Constantinople and Smyrna and prepared for action
to retrieve the situation in Asia Minor.

The Constantinople *Amyna* had originated in the upheaval
following the elections of November 1920.[1] It was formed by
Venizelists in Constantinople together with army officers who,
anticipating dismissal by the new regime, resigned or deserted
from the army. Their main aim, manifested in the approach to
Lloyd George before the London Conference, was to enlist the

active support of Venizelos and the British Government for a separatist movement on the lines of Venizelos's Salonika movement in 1916.

The Constantinople *Amyna* was divided into a military and a civilian group, which worked closely together. The military, consisting of some 150 to 250 officers, had no formal establishment. The best known among them were the tough Thessalian Kondylis, the brothers Zymbrakakis, and General Ioannou – all stalwart Venizelists tempered in the exhilarating revolutionary years in Salonika.

Besides these officers, the *haute bourgeoisie* of Constantinople and the Patriarchate were also strongly Venizelist in sentiment. It was doctors, lawyers and merchants of the prosperous Greek middle class who helped to lodge and subsidize the officers and formed a Committee of National Defence. And the Ecumenical Patriarchate worked on behalf of the Venizelist cause as the only salvation for the unredeemed Greeks of Asia Minor.

Venizelos was aware of the existence of the *Amyna* at an early stage. It was he who sent the three *Amyna* Greeks to see Lloyd George before the London Conference. He was briefed by old associates – Pericles Argyropoulos, the politician, who went to Paris to consult Venizelos at the end of December 1920, and Kondylis, who came from Constantinople. These two men set themselves up as the self-styled revolutionary leadership of the movement. Argyropoulos wrote later that Venizelos 'did not judge it expedient to put himself at the head of a revolutionary organization to overthrow Constantine', but that 'we activists had his blessing'.[2] Argyropoulos and Kondylis left for Constantinople to prepare for their Venizelist coup after the London Conference.

The revolution did not come off. Kondylis was the leading spirit behind the plan for a coup in the army before the offensive of summer 1921. This came to nothing. But the *Amyna* did not give up, and the political and military impasse of the autumn gave its efforts new point.

During the winter the *Amyna* spread, establishing committees in Smyrna itself and even in London.[3] The Smyrna Committee was formed some time around the end of October 1921 by six or seven energetic Smyrniots, including Dr A. Psaltof, the journalist S. Solomonidis and P. Evripaios of the Greek High Commission.[4] They kept in close touch with Constantinople; Argyropoulos himself at least once visited Smyrna secretly.[5] The founder-members of the Smyrna Committee, known as the *Mikrasiatiki Amyna*, were highminded Smyrniots of the middle class. Less actively Venizelist than the Constantinople *Amyna*,* they were united in believing that the Greek Government was prepared to 'betray' the Greek populations of Asia Minor and order an evacuation of the Greek army; and they agreed with Constantinople that, rather than submit to this, they should create an autonomous Greek zone and defend it with a volunteer army.

While the *Amyna* gathered strength, Gounaris and Baltazzis were pursuing their sad journey round the capitals of western Europe. In Paris, they had two interviews with Briand, who found them 'intractable', and urged the necessity of a rapid peace settlement.[6] Gounaris and Baltazzis in their turn were depressed by the negative French reaction to their démarche over the right of search over French ships carrying supplies for the Kemalists – a continuing source of dispute between the Greeks, French and Italians from now on.[7] Briand told them that despite the hostility of French public opinion to Constantine, he understood the reasons for the recall of the King in November 1920.† Apart from vague expressions of sympathy, the Paris talks produced nothing for the Greeks.

From Paris the two Greeks crossed to England, where Curzon awaited them with a new plan for allied mediation in his pocket. Curzon had been sniped at by his colleagues for his ineffectiveness as a peacemaker. Montagu complained that the F.O.'s attitude prevented it from exercising any influence at Ankara. Churchill, in his anxiety to *make* both sides accept a peace settlement, recommended that the Royal Navy blockade their chief

---

* According to Rodas (*Greece in Asia Minor*, p. 262), the Smyrna Committee decided in January 1921 to invite Venizelos to represent them abroad, but Stergiadis forbade them to send the telegram of invitation. There is no evidence, however, that the Smyrna Committee was ever interested in overthrowing the regime in Old Greece; whereas as late as 8/21 August 1922, Kondylis in Constantinople was speaking of organizing for a *coup d'état* (Venizelos Papers, 317; Kondylis to Venizelos, 8/21 August 1922).

† Briand told Hardinge, the British Ambassador, that he did not approve Venizelos's idea that the first step towards a peace settlement must be Constantine's abdication; Frangulis, *La Grèce*, ii, p. 311; *D.B.F.P.*, xvii, no. 417. Hardinge's account of this interview confirms Gounaris's description of Briand's attitude in his defence at the Trial of the Six.

ports if necessary. Stung by these criticisms, Curzon had circulated a long justification of British policy.[8] '*Te Deums* have been sung at Athens,' he wrote, 'and public rejoicings have taken place at Angora. We are reminded of the battle of Jutland, which was simultaneously celebrated as a triumph in London and Berlin.'

Curzon argued that the military situation was probably now a stalemate,[9] with time tending to favour the Turks. Secret information showed that just before the Greek retreat the Turks had run very short of ammunition and guns, lorries and petrol.

We know, however, that they are receiving ammunition in coasting boats from Batum, and General Harington admits a leakage from Constantinople, apparently from stores under French control, which the Greek warships can only partially stop in the Black Sea.... It is also clear from secret sources that the French are negotiating for the direct supply of ammunition to the Kemalists.

All this suggested that the Turks' position was improving. However, British intelligence suggested that although the Russians had helped Kemal with arms and ammunition, the Kemalists were still suspicious of Bolshevik agents and designs. Thus in Curzon's view the Turkish Nationalists might now be more ready to treat; but their terms would still entail the evacuation of Smyrna by the Greeks. As for the Greeks, their growing financial crisis, the necessity of calling yet another class (that of 1922) to the colours, and the general depression caused by the Sakarya reverse, all suggested that they would accept mediation. The procedure Curzon recommended was first preliminary talks with the Greeks; then an allied conference to produce peace terms and to break the Anglo-French deadlock over Thrace which had threatened to wreck the proposed mediation in June; and finally the issue of invitations to both Greeks and Turks to attend and receive the Allies' proposals for peace.

Just after Curzon circulated this memorandum, and before the Greek Ministers called on him, the situation in Anatolia had swung against the Greeks. For months the French had been on the lookout for a settlement with Nationalist Turkey which would relieve them from the strain of holding onto Cilicia. The understanding reached in March in the corridors of the London Conference had never come into effect, being repudiated by the

Turkish National Assembly. But since then Henri Franklin Bouillon, a talkative and insinuating Turcophil French deputy, had been first unofficially and then as plenipotentiary seeking for an opening to resume negotiations. He finally reached an agreement on behalf of the French Government with the Turkish Nationalists in Ankara on 20 October.[10] This 'Frankin Bouillon Agreement' threw Curzon into paroxysms of fury. Long and bitter letters proceeded from Whitehall to the Quai d'Orsay setting out in how many ways this Franco-Turkish understanding was a breach of allied solidarity, a betrayal of the cardinal principle that none of the Allies should make a separate peace with any enemy state, and a setback to Curzon's efforts at peacemaking. But the damage was done, the French had succeeded in cutting their losses in Cilicia, and eventually Curzon resumed the thankless task of trying to set up an interallied peace conference.

For the Greeks, this agreement was bad news. Morally, it confirmed their isolation. Materially, it weighted the balance against them by relieving Kemal of his preoccupation with the Cilician theatre, leaving him free to concentrate against the Greeks on the western front. And it won for the Turks quantities of war materials which the French left behind on leaving Cilicia. Formally, the agreement put an end to the state of war between the two parties, and provided for an exchange of prisoners of war and the evacuation of Cilicia by the French. Apart from the Greeks themselves, only the Italians in the south west of Anatolia and the Allied garrison in the straits zone now remained as a threat to Turkish independence. The Italian presence was by now no more than nominal, and came to an end in 1922 when the Italian occupation was quietly wound up.

Gounaris and Baltazzis visited Curzon at the Foreign Office on 27 October. Curzon told them that if the Greek Government wanted peace, and would put Greece's interests in the hands of the Allies, Britain would argue in the coming negotiations for the same regime in the Smyrna zone as had been proposed in June, and for no change in the regime for Thrace, except, perhaps, a slight modification in the Chatalja frontier.[11]

It would have been madness to reject this suggestion, for Greece could not now hope for better terms. The proposed regime for Smyrna did entail the withdrawal of the Greek army – but in an orderly fashion, after the establishment of a mixed gendarmerie

under allied supervision, and masked by the 'guarantees' which
the Allies would exact on behalf of the Christian populations.
Moreover, Curzon was undertaking to defend the Greek claim to
eastern Thrace against the French, because a Greek Thrace was
a guarantee of the freedom of the Straits. Gounaris and Baltazzis
told Curzon on 2 November that the Greek Government accepted
the allied mediation.[12]

Gounaris had now transferred the burden of seeking a settlement from his own to Lord Curzon's shoulders. It was one of the
chief accusations of the Venizelists against Gounaris and his
colleagues that they had betrayed Greece's sovereignty and vital
interests by giving the allies *carte blanche* to negotiate a settlement for the Near East.[13] The accusation was unfair. In putting
their case in the hands of the Allies, the Greeks did not bind
themselves unconditionally in advance to accept the results of
mediation whatever they might be; and it was precisely in order
to secure better terms than Greece could hope to secure on her
own that Gounaris accepted Curzon's proposals. Now that the
Greek army had shot its bolt in Asia Minor, it was to the advantage of Greece that her relations with Turkey be regulated as
part of a general Near Eastern peace settlement. Only if allied
rivalries made such a settlement impossible would the Greek
Government be obliged to force a settlement with Turkey on its
own, either by evacuation, renewal of the war, or direct negotiations. The fairer accusation against Gounaris (and this too was
made by his Venizelist opponents) is not that he accepted mediation now, but that he had rejected it earlier.

The economic burden of the war was becoming intolerable.
Travelling through the Greek countryside in the late summer,
Toynbee found that even in conversation with a stranger, the
people 'spoke less of the supposed victory than of its cost – of the
young men absent for years at the war and of the remorseless
rise in prices'.[14] The Greeks were in desperate need of financial aid
if their army was to remain on a war footing in Asia Minor.
There was in particular a need for foreign exchange. The
drachma exchange rate had been falling since mid-1920, and
prices were rising steadily.[15] Rising prices in Greece had sapped
the Government's domestic support, and some striking success
was needed to revive its waning fortunes. Gounaris asked the
British Government for a loan.

The British attitude to the financial question was a test of the strength of British support for Greece. A loan floated on the British market would have been evidence of British confidence in Greece and willingness to back Lloyd George's policy. The reaction to Gounaris's request revealed serious doubts in the Foreign Office about Lloyd George's premise that the Greek horse was worth backing. But if the Greeks could not be kept going at least until Curzon's projected Near East Conference took place, the British would have no 'trump cards' with which to impose 'reasonable' peace terms on Ankara, thus protecting their interests in the Straits zone and further east in Mosul. The Foreign Office therefore sought a means of giving a fillip to the Greek negotiations for a loan without violating the allied financial blockade of December 1920.[16] But Curzon refused to take any positive action for fear of offending the French.[17]

When it seemed that the Greeks were to get nothing, the intervention of Lloyd George suddenly revived their hopes. Ignoring the delicate diplomatic questions involved, he told Sir Robert Horne, the Chancellor, to stop shilly-shallying and concede an agreement with the Greeks. Horne wrote to Gounaris on 22 December enclosing for Gounaris's signature an agreement which in itself won nothing for the Greeks but merely removed some of the obstacles to the raising of a loan on the open market.[18]

Under the Gounaris-Horne agreement, the British Government consented to Greece's assigning her revenues as securities for a loan of up to £15 million, to be contracted in Great Britain. In return for this concession,* Greece waived all claim to the unused balance of the credits of £12 million opened by Britain for Greece and blocked by the December 1920 financial blockade. Thus the Greeks renounced £6·5 million unused and frozen credits in return for the *possibility* of raising a loan on the British capital market. The agreement removed an unjust burden from the shoulders of the Greeks, but did no more. In a gloss on it, Curzon wrote that the agreement did not constitute 'raising of financial blockade', nor imply that the Government was prepared to give financial assistance to Greece.[19] The Greeks might or might not

---

* The advances to Greece under her 1918 agreement with the Allies had not been repaid by Greece; and until they were, according to the 1918 agreement, Greece could not assign her revenues without the consent of France, Britain and the U.S.

succeed in raising a loan on the open market. At least they were now free to try.

Armed with the Horne agreement, Gounaris applied to Armstrongs Bank to arrange a loan. The negotiations broke down, owing partly to the Greeks' evasiveness and delay in producing an account of Greece's financial position, but also to the reluctance of British capitalists to negotiate seriously in the absence of forthright official backing for the loan by the British Government.[20] The failure to obtain a loan brought Gounaris a long step nearer to the point at which the Greeks must face evacuation. By the time the question of a loan was briefly revived, in February 1922, this point had been reached.

The Greek army in Asia Minor had endured much and now that victory was seen to be unattainable the strain was telling. A disturbing analysis of the situation was given in a private (and therefore uninhibited) letter from Prince Andrew to his close friend Metaxas. Andrew had handed over the command of the II Army Corps on 1 October, during the retreat from the Sakarya, and was now in Smyrna, taking part in a 'Council of Lieutenant Generals'. He was well placed to know the minds of the Staff, who considered a Turkish offensive likely in the early spring:

Systematic defence of the front we now hold is very difficult, if not impossible, on account of its terrible length and the insufficiency of the forces. We are very likely therefore to be forced to retreat, whether of our own initiative or under pressure from the enemy. You would think that under such conditions there would have been some study already and the beginning of preparation of a second, more restricted line, which could be held with the resources at our disposal. Nothing of the sort has happened; there is no second line, not even a plan for one! The state of the army does not inspire much confidence in me. Its offensive spirit is exhausted, and if it remains for the time being peacefully in the line, it does so in the belief that we shall soon have peace. But if the negotiations drag on too long or Gounaris returns without having achieved anything, and the war goes on, then what? I do not think that the army will be in a state to face a serious action by the enemy; but failure at one point of the front will inevitably drag down the rest in its wake, and then where will it end? At one stroke we shall lose the whole issue, or rather all our sacrifices – and the optimism of Messrs Gounaris and Phontas will be worth nothing to us![21]

Prince Andrew was one of the first, apart from Metaxas himself. to speak these harsh truths.* He continued:

Something must be done quickly to remove us from the nightmare of Asia Minor. I don't know what, but we must stop bluffing and face the situation as it really is. Because finally which is better? – to fall into the sea or to escape before we are ducked? I am afraid I shall be labelled a defeatist for saying this, or too influenced by my temperament. But I assure you that this is not so. I cannot see however that with the continuation of the war we are saving the existence and substance of Greece. On the contrary I see the opposite, and so clearly that even at the risk of misunderstanding I am writing to you to put my thoughts to you. They would talk differently if the war was in Greece, and the feelings of the public would be different then. What do we gain by a catastrophe or even by a defeat here? Why chase shadows here instead of chasing the reality in Epirus and Thrace?

I have heard something else. The standing of the high command is seriously weakened among the troops – as you know, I myself lost all confidence in it long ago.... What *Le Temps* wrote about the Crown Prince's visit to the front was true to this extent, that at Afyon almost the whole of the 4th Division (Dimaras) received him with wild shouts for demobilization, so that Kontoulis was forced to intervene and make a speech from the platform. Any idea of some sort of an uprising on the part of the army with a view to remaining here – there is some sort of work going on to this end – contrary to the orders of the Government can in my view be absolutely ruled out. When the troops learned that they were being demobilized and that the officers were preventing them from going away, they would tie us up, if not kill us, with perfect right on their side!

Prince Andrew's closing words, bitter and perhaps unworthy, were written under the stress of political passion and out of the exhaustion of a long war fought far from home on behalf of men who were called compatriots and brothers but whose manners and traditions were often foreign. The ideals of May 1919, of a

---

* He also described his long talk with Stergiadis, who was 'convinced that the army cannot give more than it has given up till now.... He does not know how things will develop, but the idea of evacuation of Asia Minor does not frighten him.' Stergiadis assured Prince Andrew categorically that he would not on any terms involve himself in Greek politics, since 'he, Stergiadis, and parliamentarianism were two irreconcilable poles'.

noble struggle to redeem Greek territories and peoples, had crumbled away.

The people here are generally disgusting [wrote the Prince]. A swollen Venizelism prevails.... It would really be worth handing over Smyrna to Kemal so as to kick all these worthless characters who behave like this after we have poured out such terrible blood here; blood of Old Greece, because the boys of the best families here are serving in Smyrna and the rear lines, and heaven help us if some unit formed entirely of Asia Minor Greeks were to come face to face with the enemy....

My God, when shall I get away from this hell here?

Andrew was not alone in these views. 'We have nothing to hope for from the so-called Greeks here,' wrote Stergiadis's representative at Ushak to the High Commission.[22] This was a not uncommon reflection of the tensions between occupiers and indigenous Greeks.

The most serious problem now was to maintain the morale of the army. The officer corps was discontented. Apart from the disputes of Venizelists, Royalists and neutrals, all had in common an angry contempt for the War Ministry and those they regarded as idlers in Athens, and in Smyrna. General Kontoulis voiced this resentment in a letter to Papoulas in October, citing as an example the fact that of twenty-eight recent promotions to major general, only eight had served in the recent campaign in Asia Minor.[23] It was felt that the War Ministry was lavishing promotion and easy desk jobs on those with the right political views, and leaving the fighting officers at the front unrewarded. The effect of this unfairness was to encourage officers to seek transfer to the home front.

Many officers, having succeeded in getting leave in Old Greece, simply failed to return to the front, fixing matters as best they could with the authorities at home. The ordinary soldiers were not affected to the same extent by political divisions, but were still more anxious to get back home to their families and homes. Draft evasion and desertion, problems throughout the war, reached proportions so serious that the War Ministry was forced to offer periodic amnesties to those who came forward to serve.

In a largely agricultural society like Greece, where harvest and seedtime played a predominant role in men's lives, it was difficult for the authorities to enforce the draft. In the mount Pelion area near Volos in the early summer of 1921 the defaulters formed themselves into an organized division several hundred strong, haunting the southern slopes of the mountain, burning charcoal which they supplied to the villagers in return for food, and requisitioning meat from the shepherds.[24] They had the sympathy of the local population and were able to defy the gendarmerie. Elsewhere in Thessaly, and throughout Greece, public order had deteriorated as draft evaders took to brigandage as their only way of making a living. In Asia Minor the problem was the same. Large numbers of deserters swelled the existing *chetté* bands or turned to brigandage on their own account.

To these problems were added those of stagnation and boredom, unpleasant food, and delays in pay, owing to the exhausted state of the Treasury. A steady stream of complaints went from G.H.Q. in Asia Minor to the War Ministry in Athens on these two latter issues. Worst of all was the insidious, will-sapping question which was now asked more and more insistently – what are we fighting for here in Asia Minor now that victory is seen to be impossible?

In December 1921 an election took place for the vacant seat of the Ecumenical Patriarchate in Constantinople. The Ecumenical Patriarch was first among equals of the Orthodox Bishops, and spiritual leader of the Greek Community outside the Greek Kingdom. The election was therefore of great importance, and keenly and unscrupulously disputed between Venizelists and their opponents. In the end, after an election of dubious legality, the winner was Meletios Metaxakis, a Cretan in origin, Venizelist in politics, liberal and progressive in Church affairs.[25]

Meletios had been Archbishop of Athens before the change of regime in November 1920.[26] After his dismissal by the Royalists, he went to the United States to uphold the Venizelist cause among the Greek communities there, which were as bitterly divided as the Greeks in Europe.[27] He continued to regard himself as Metropolitan of Athens, and did not recognize the restored Royalist Synod. He was supported in his stand by a majority of the bishops outside Old Greece.

Meletius regarded his election as a political victory and as a prelude to the return of Venizelos himself to the political scene. On his way from America to take up his new appointment, he met and conferred with Lloyd George in London. The interview caused a scandal when it was eventually published in Greece.

Lloyd George had spoken freely of his frustration at the present turn of events in Asia Minor:

> The post-November regime has destroyed all the sympathies which the Greeks had won before. The general situation now is such as to prevent Greece's friends from being of use to your country. Because of the Restoration of the monarchy those who sympathized with the Turks have now become much more powerful.... I said all this recently quite clearly to Mr Gounaris.... With the present regime in power it is impossible, absolutely impossible, for you to remain in Asia Minor. I said this clearly and definitely to Mr Gounaris.[28]

The Patriarch observed that the Gounarists were deceiving the Greek people, allowing them to believe that while France was against them, England was not. Lloyd George demurred:

> No, we are all of the same mind as regards the Restoration. England supports Greece's just claims, but is against the regime. I said it last week clearly to Mr Gounaris and Mr Balto – what is the other one called? – Mr Baltazzis. Personally I am a friend of Greece, but for the reasons I have given you all my colleagues are against me. And I cannot be of any use to you. It is impossible, impossible.

From London Meletios proceeded to Constantinople, where Kondylis, Argyropoulos and their friends found him a willing and prestigious ally. The moral force of the Patriarchate could now be exerted on behalf of the salvation of the Greek community of Asia Minor through Venizelism. At about the time of Meletios's arrival the *Amyna* addressed itself to the essential task of enlisting Stergiadis and Papoulas in their plan for a separatist movement, or at least reconciling them to it.

Stergiadis's initial reactions were not encouraging.[29] He was in a difficult position. To ban the movement altogether would have offended an influential section of the Greek community in Smyrna. But active support of the *Amyna* was out of the question. An autonomous Asia Minor would be deprived of the financial support of the Greek Government; the army would be split apart. Temperamentally Stergiadis disliked initiatives which escaped his own control. But there was a further and clinching reason for his refusal to support the *Amyna*: by early 1922 he had become convinced that the Greek zone in Asia Minor could not be held. Stergiadis made no secret of his opinion.

If Stergiadis rejected the idea of leading a separatist movement, he equally continued to reject the idea of imposing his views by breaking into Athenian politics.* He told Lindley in February 1922 that 'the present government must liquidate the war, and it was the duty of patriotic Greeks to help them'.[30] To a man with these views, the *Amyna* movement was an irritation, irrelevant to the problem how to end the war and effect an evacuation of Asia Minor. Because of Stergiadis's dictatorial powers in the Smyrna zone and immense prestige with the Greek Government, his attitude spelt death to the *Amyna's* chances of success.

General Papoulas was their second hope. In late December 1921, Dr Siotis, a prominent member of the Constantinople *Amyna* who later served as minister in the revolutionary Government of Gonatas, visited him in Smyrna to sound him out.[31] Papoulas said that he could not act without government approval, but left no doubt that he was interested. Before matters could be taken further, events in Europe lent point to these consultations by leading Gounaris to face the possibility of evacuation of Asia Minor.

Gounaris and Baltazzis had left London for Rome, returning from there to Cannes, at Lloyd George's suggestion, for the Conference dealing with Reparations and the Anglo-French Guarantee.† Lloyd George and Curzon met them on 12 January.[32] Lloyd

* But there was continuing speculation that he might change his mind. Lindley, the British Ambassador, wrote to Curzon on 10 February: 'He is universally respected both for his political and financial honesty, and public opinion is more and more turning towards him in this critical time ... He did not touch on the possibility of his forming a government, but I have since learned that he contemplates it seriously – after but not before – he has carried out the evacuation of Smyrna.... His programme is that of a statesman and a patriot, but there is no doubt that he will meet with serious difficulties.... How long his collaborators will stomach his despotic methods and violent temper is another matter; still more, perhaps, how long his compatriots will bear with his superiority to themselves. The examples of Aristides and Venizelos are not encouraging.' FO 421/302, no. 21.

† On the question of the Guarantee, see Cmd 2169, 1924; also *D.B.F.P.*, xvi, no. 634, n. 2, no. 768. In an important memo of 30 May 1921, written in response to the proposals of the Sec. of State for War on the evacuation of Constantinople, Crowe had argued that Constantinople was so important that even failing effective Greek cooperation in its defence, Britain should perhaps still try to defend the Straits by buying French support for her Near Eastern policy in return for a guarantee of security against a German attack on the Rhine frontier; *D.B.F.P.*, xvii, no. 201. Curzon used this memo as his brief in the Cabinet meeting of 31 May.

George was uncharacteristically firm with the Greeks. He told them that Britain had now done all that was in her power. 'We had made a settlement of the Eastern Question a condition of our Treaty of Guarantee with France and this settlement was the best that we could hope to have.' The settlement involved withdrawal from Smyrna, and a modification of the Thracian frontier in Turkey's favour. If they withdrew from Smyrna, steps would be taken over the Christian minorities. If not, they would have to fight it out on their own.

For once Lloyd George was fully and wholeheartedly backing up his Foreign Secretary. He urged the Greeks to put themselves in Curzon's hands in the forthcoming negotiations, and Gounaris agreed to do so. The British attempt to make the Near Eastern settlement and the Treaty of Guarantee dependent on each other was a stratagem which, though it offered hopes of a final settlement more favourable to Greece than could otherwise be achieved, would complicate negotiations and mean further delay. Meanwhile the Greek army was bleeding to a slow death on the uplands of Anatolia.

All circumstances seemed to conspire to delay a settlement. It was at this same conference at Cannes that Briand was tempted on to the golf course by Lloyd George, incurred the displeasure of President Millerand, and fell from power, to be succeeded by Raymond Poincaré. Poincaré, who took the Ministry of Foreign Affairs for himself, was equally unsympathetic to British and Greeks, determined not to be rushed into unwise decisions, contemptuous of Lloyd George's slapdash conference circuit.[33] Poincaré was not loved by British statesmen. Lloyd George thought him 'poor stuff'. Someone once said that possibly he had many sterling qualities. 'Well,' said Balfour, 'he has no business to look like that, then.'[34]

Poincaré formed his ministry on 15 January, and the very next day Curzon, on his way from Cannes, visited him at the Quai d'Orsay. 'The whole peace of the East was trembling in the balance,' said Curzon, urging speed in arranging a Conference.[35] Poincaré insisted on a cool and methodical approach, based on an exchange of written views.

A preliminary foreign ministers' meeting had been fixed for 1 February, but was delayed by a petulant exchange of notes between the Foreign Office and the Quai d'Orsay.[36] Then the Bonomi Ministry fell in Italy, and it was not until 26 February that a new Government was formed. In the end, after these successive delays, the foreign ministers did not meet in Paris until 22 March – five months after Curzon had persuaded the Greeks to put their fortunes into the Allies' hands! The delay, due mainly to the important differences of opinion between France and Britain, which were camouflaged in bickering over procedural minutiae, and reflected in Poincaré's maddening and purposeful deliberation, was too much for the Greeks. By late January, Gounaris had brought into the open the hitherto unmentionable word – evacuation. The failure of British diplomacy had forced Greece to consider unilateral action.

On 23 January Papoulas was informed that the Powers' delays had led the government into an intolerable situation, and asked for his views on the military position, to serve Gounaris in framing a final appeal to Great Britain.[37] He replied that the morale of the men was good, but that G.H.Q. required reinforcements in men, money and materials. If these could not be provided, then evacuation was necessary. G.H.Q. rejected the idea of concentration within a front west of that presently occupied, as militarily unsound and bad for morale.[38]

Using Papoulas's data, Gounaris in London drew up a long letter for Curzon. It was a last appeal for help, and a threat that if no help were forthcoming, Greece would have to take unilateral action, evacuating Asia Minor and leaving Great Britain to settle her own affairs with Kemal.[39] The implicit message was clear – either Britain must step in and provide material, not merely moral, support, or risk seeing the whole of her Near Eastern policy collapse in flame and ruin with the withdrawal of the Greek army from Anatolia.

In response to the desperate appeal the Foreign Office once more took up the question of a loan for Greece;[40] but again to no effect. Curzon telegraphed for Lindley's views on the theory that a Greek evacuation and concentration in Thrace might be a good thing: 'I am not quite certain that it would not be better to get Greece out of Asia Minor before she is beaten and before she gets a loan (if she does) than for us to incur the odium of the loan and her the ignominy of defeat.' Lindley commented in reply that although most responsible Greeks would be glad to evacuate Asia Minor, he did not believe the present Government would have the nerve to do so without adequate guarantees for the safety of the Christian populations. Hence the Greek threat to evacuate was probably bluff.

Bluff or not, Gounaris pulled out every stop in order to put pressure on the British Government. On 27 February he wrote to Lloyd George asking for a final interview before he left for Athens. The interview was not granted. The next day he tele-graphed to Athens to prepare his colleagues for failure over the loan and the request for war material: G.H.Q. should be told of the situation so as to take 'measures preliminary to withdrawal' if these were militarily necessary.[41]

On 6 March Curzon replied to Gounaris's letter.[42] He expressed the hope that the military situation in Anatolia was not so critical as Gounaris had suggested. The letter contained no grain of hope of financial or other aid to come. Curzon simply renewed his opinion that the only solution to the impasse was to be found in diplomacy. Regretting the postponement of the allied Foreign Ministers' meeting, he nevertheless recommended the Greeks to continue to entrust their fate to the hands of the Allies.

Greece was thus advised by Great Britain to hold on. The reason for this advice is quite clear. Britain desired that Greek evacuation, which was not accepted as inevitable, should take place in an orderly way and as part of a general Near Eastern settlement. A panicky, unilateral decision to evacuate before the beginning of the spring campaigning season might set the dominoes tumbling one after the other at Constantinople, the Straits, Thrace, Mesopotamia and throughout the Near East. Curzon explained to Lindley that 'our idea is if possible to arrange for immediate evacuation of Anatolia by arrangement with Angora. Mr Gounaris will doubtless so interpret my note but meanwhile you should not breathe a word of this but adopt attitude of complete reserve.'[43] The docile Greeks put on one side their thoughts of evacuation, and accepted Curzon's advice.

It was in this context, when the liquidation of the war had for the first time become a real issue, that Papoulas's contacts with the *Amyna* were renewed. Siotis returned to Smyrna in early February, bringing from the Constantinople Committee a long memorandum for Papoulas to read.[44] The memo stated that the evacuation of the Greek army and the autonomy of Asia Minor under a Christian governor (the Great Powers' solution to the Greco-Turkish impasse) would be a disaster for the Christian populations:

From this terrible catastrophe only a patriotic revolutionary movement ... can save us. And this movement, Generalissimo, only one Greek can bring about – yourself. Your Excellency commands the confidence of both the Royalist and Venizelist parties in the army.... Above all we look to the support of England, the only power with an interest in preserving the Greek army in Asia Minor.* We are in a position to know that the English ... have always heard your name with favour.

The *Amyna* proposed that Venizelos should represent the new 'Mikrasiatic State' in London and Paris. It suggested a six-point programme of action, a vision to dazzle Papoulas's eyes:

1. A mass meeting in Smyrna at which Papoulas would be given a vote of confidence and invested with the powers to proceed with the establishment of the 'Ionian' state.

2. Formation by Papoulas of a government of his choice.

3. Announcement to the army of the formation of a government, and the invitation to the army to swear an appropriate oath, should this be deemed necessary.

4. Announcement to the Greek Government of the formation of the new regime and the reasons which led to it.

5. Announcement to the Powers and a request for their support.

6. An invitation to the Greek communities of Europe, America, Egypt, Romania, etc., to support the new state 'with their money and their blood'.

* The *Amyna*'s confidence in British support was 'based on indications from Englishmen of undoubted prestige', such as General Harington's Chief of Staff, whom the *Amyna* reported as having told them, 'Act and show your determination to hold Asia Minor and you will have England's support' (Passas, *The Agony of a Nation*, p. 183). What can have been at most a friendly remark by a Philhellene was here interpreted as a reliable indication of government policy. Although British liaison officers with the Greek army got on well with them on the whole, the climate of opinion in the British army was pro-Turkish; see the letter of Field Marshal Sir Henry Wilson to General Harington, 14 December 1921: 'We will never do any good until we clear out of Constantinople altogether, and we will certainly never do any good until we make friends with the Turks. But when I asked Montagu ... whether he had made any progress in educating L G in that direction his reply was "absolutely none", and he added that "you [Tim] are taboo because L G thinks you are pro-Turk". You are running in good company because you have galloping alongside of you not only the CIGS but every officer of the British army!' (Harington, *Tim Harington Looks Back*, p. 87). A. A. Pallis informs me that Harington, in private conversation with him at this time, expressed his disapproval of Kondylis's aims and methods.

The *Amyna*'s estimates of the support in men and money which the new state could expect were fanciful. In fact the ingredients of this remarkable document were flattery and unreal hopes. The *Amyna* unconvincingly protested political neutrality: 'Neither King Constantine nor Eleftherios Venizelos has ever influenced our personal feelings, or inspired this or that political line.' [45] The Venizelist orientation of the movement was as evident as its revolutionary nature. The *Amyna*'s true feelings about the Gounaris government and King Constantine were suppressed in deference to Papoulas, and in the hope that competent Royalist and 'neutral' officers would not be deterred from joining the movement.

Papoulas's response to the attempted seduction was characteristic. He kept his virtue intact, but gave his suitors enough encouragement to keep them knocking at his door. Papoulas kept his options open by insisting to the *Amyna* that he would have to keep the government informed of their negotiations.[46] For this purpose he sent Siotis and Colonel Sariyannis of his Staff to Athens. Siotis's attempt to interest the Government in the movement failed. The Government decisively refused to endorse any form of 'unofficial organization', and invited all Greeks who wished to contribute to the struggle either to enlist or to contribute money.[47] Thus ended the first round of contacts between Papoulas and the *Amyna*.

At last, on 22 March, the foreign ministers of the three Powers, Curzon, Poincaré and Schanzer of Italy, met in Paris.[48] Their conversations were tough but at last moderately realistic. The long argument over Thrace ended in compromise.[49] The French wanted to keep Greeks and Turks away from each other's throats by making the Enos–Midia line the frontier, and creating an international buffer state in eastern Thrace. Curzon, whose first interest was control of the Straits, argued for the Midia–Rodosto line, which would leave the Greeks masters of the Dardanelles. A compromise frontier was agreed which would leave the Greeks in Gallipoli but exclude them from Rodosto.

Poincaré had stated at the outset that France would not accept any settlement without the evacuation of the Greek army. The problem was how to achieve this. The Conference addressed itself seriously to the practical problems involved in a Greek withdrawal, and a group of military experts, including Foch,

Weygand, Gouraud and Harington, worked out a scheme for the evacuation of the Greek army based on recommendations of the allied generals in Constantinople.[50]

On 26 March the Conference produced a long exposé, for the press and the Greek and Turkish Governments, of its proposals for a settlement.[51] The Allies had already sent their recommendation of an armistice to the two belligerents. It had been accepted at once by the Greeks, but not yet by the Turks.* The procedure now was for the belligerents to announce their acceptance of both armistice and the Allies' terms in principle; the Allies would then convoke a final Peace Conference to work out the details; and it would not be until both sides had accepted the preliminaries of peace that the Greek army would begin to evacuate Asia Minor.

The outline settlement drafted in Paris was more practicable than any previous proposal. It recognized the reality of Turkish Nationalist sovereignty in Anatolia. But the settlement could not, except theoretically, guarantee the safety of the Christian populations under Turkish rule; that would depend on the temper of the Turks after the Greek withdrawal. It was this aspect of the settlement which caused the Powers' proposals to fall like chill rain in Greece. For the armistice was proposed 'with the avowed intention of assuring the peaceful evacuation of Asia Minor by the Greek forces'.† Evacuation was thus at last brought within the area of public debate, and with it, the danger to the Greek population of Asia Minor.

Gounaris and Baltazzis told Lindley on 29 March that 'a regular panic would ensue as soon as proposals were known. Every Greek who had means would leave. They would be followed by general exodus of frenzied inhabitants who would achieve destruction of Greece.' They emphasized that the proposed guarantees for the Christians were insufficient. The mobilization of Asia Minor Greeks (including Ottoman citizens) gave

* The armistice terms proposed are summarized in Stratigos, *Greece in Asia Minor*, p. 324; they provided that the belligerents should remain in their present positions, without reinforcement or transfer of forces; the armistice would be for three months, automatically renewable until the belligerents accepted the peace preliminaries; allied commissions would supervise the observance of the terms. The Greeks accepted subject to a few very minor reservations.

† The phrase is part of the Allies' public communiqué of 26 March, and reflects the French position.

the government a special responsibility: 'How could these people be left to be massacred as rebels?' [52] *

The reaction of the press to the allied proposals was almost uniformly unfavourable. The Venizelists walked out of the foreign policy debate in the Chamber on 1 April, leaving the Gounarists to win a hollow vote of confidence by 163 to 52 votes. The effect of the Allies' peace proposals was to sap the confidence of nationalist Greeks in the Government's handling of the Asia Minor question and to boost the *Amyna* movement.

The Greek Government had accepted the armistice proposal, but refused for reasons of internal politics to bind themselves to the Allies' unpopular peace terms before the Nationalist Turks had even agreed to an armistice.[53] The Turks spared them the necessity of doing so by accepting an armistice only if the Greek army were to begin the evacuation immediately on the signature of the armistice agreement.[54]

This novel demand was made on the grounds that the Greeks might take advantage of an armistice to launch a new attack. It was enough to ruin Curzon's patient labours of the last six months and to renew the weary round of dispute. The Greek army was Britain's guarantee of a satisfactory peace with the Kemalists, and it was essential that it should remain on Turkish soil until such a peace had been agreed. Lloyd George had consistently argued in this spirit.† The General Staff now commented on the Turks' demands that they must 'on no account be granted'. If they were, the Turks would reach the Peace Conference with the Anatolian question already settled, and could thus move on to Constantinople and Thrace. If the Greeks too concentrated in Thrace, the allied force in Constantinople would be caught in a dangerous pincer.[55]

The Turkish refusal of an armistice without a simultaneous Greek evacuation of Asia Minor wrecked the Powers' last serious

---

* The Greeks' reported words nicely illustrate the two preoccupations of the Government; the first (which Royalist historians claim was dominant) concern for the Asia Minor Greeks; the second (which Venizelists emphasize) fear of the anarchy and revolution which might come with an influx of refugees. The second preoccupation played a larger role than the Gounarists cared to admit.

† He told Gounaris in October 1921, 'Above all, the Greek Army must remain in its present positions and repel the attacks of the enemy until the Conference takes place; for if it withdraws, any negotiations will be superfluous'; Frangulis, ii, p. 330.

attempt at mediation. Though negotiations dragged on, no new initiative was taken. A sort of lethargy enveloped the proceedings. In the exchange of notes which continued throughout the summer, the French supported the Turkish suggestion of preliminary talks at Ismid with no preconditions as to the final peace terms, while Curzon continued to urge a phased approach (armistice – acceptance of peace terms in principle – conference to settle preliminaries of peace – evacuation of Greek army – final Peace Treaty) like that which the Turks had just rejected.[56] By late August the Great Powers had only recently succeeded in agreeing on Venice as the locale for preliminary talks at which the Paris proposals of March, or something like them, would be put to the belligerents once more.[57] But by then developments on the ground in Anatolia had overtaken the diplomatic exchanges.

Venizelos's policy continued to be that no compromise was possible over Greece's claims recognized in the Treaty of Sèvres. And he still believed that it was only the dynastic issue which prevented the Allies from upholding those claims. In October 1921 he had tried to get the British to tell Gounaris that Constantine must go.[58] By early 1922 however Venizelos was in America, where he had gone on holiday with new wife, Elena Schilizzi, one of the London community of Greeks, who had done great services to Venizelism and Venizelos with her ample wealth.

The Powers' proposals of March and their chilling effect on the Greeks lent new energy to the activities of the *Amyna*, who at last, in March, succeeded in getting Venizelos to give his advice. From all sides he was assailed by friends with appeals for intervention. The Patriarch kept calling on him not to desert the unredeemed Greeks. Politis, Repoulis and Benakis, the liberal cotton millionaire from Egypt, all urged him to return to Europe.[59] Finally Meletios sent a dramatic telegram: General Papoulas at the head of the united national army was preparing to put himself at the disposition of the Greeks of Asia Minor, who would constitute themselves an independent state and continue the war without regard to the attitude of the Greek government: 'General Papoulas compte en vous comme représentant diplomatique. Convaincu caractère purement nationale mouvement vous prie de ne pas nous priver de votre précieux appui.'[60] This telegram was forwarded to Venizelos by Benakis in Paris with the comment that his friends in Paris thought the movement stood little chance of success. In falsely assigning the initiative for the movement to Papoulas Meletios hoped no doubt to emphasize its 'purely national' character and the extensive backing within the army.

At last Venizelos was persuaded to speak. From Mexico he answered his friends' appeals in a long and interesting letter to Benakis.[61] Being so far from the scene of action, he completely misinterpreted Papoulas's involvement:

From the initiative which General Papoulas seems to be taking in this matter, I infer that the movement which is being prepared is being succoured or rather activated from Athens. If this suspicion is correct, then it is clear that those in Athens, caring for nothing except the salvation of Constantine, have planned this movement so as to gain time, diverting the attention of public opinion in Greece towards it and postponing the crisis which will break out as soon as the army in Asia Minor returns to Greece after the shipwreck of the national dreams.

Such an action by those in Athens is doubly criminal. First because it will expose the action of the Greeks in Asia Minor, which they have undertaken so as to save their lives, to complete failure, by ... arousing the Powers against the movement. Second, because it will prevent Greece from gathering herself together urgently, as she must do, if the prolongation of the present bloodletting – especially economic bloodletting – is not to lead her to death.

Venizelos emphasized that being so remote from affairs, he would 'never venture to advise the Greeks of Asia Minor to undertake their own defence by force of arms, knowing how colossal is the enterprise and how small the hopes of success'. On the other hand he would not actually dissuade them:

It is so certain that a return of Turkish administration to the Smyrna area would mean the complete destruction and uprooting of the Greek and Armenian populations at least, that in so far as those who are immediately concerned are conscious of this danger and determined to resist it with weapons in hand, I cannot dissuade them from this decision. But in this case I feel it my duty to advise them what they should avoid doing if they are not to increase the great dangers which now threaten them....

The first condition of success is that the movement should give the impression of being not Greek or broadly national in character, but simply humanitarian. Greeks, Armenians and whatever other non-Turkish nationals may wish to cooperate, will rise up and

declare that, in the consciousness that a return to Turkish administration means their complete destruction, they are taking up arms
to resist this. They will declare at the same time that in the desire
to facilitate the work of the Allies and the U.S.A. they do not object
to the preservation of the Sultan's sovereignty, on condition that it
be absolutely nominal, giving no right of involvement in the internal
affairs of the new state. They will declare further that they are
ready to accept any other settlement of their political future which
the Allies and the U.S.A. may approve, provided this settlement
excludes the danger of a return to Turkish administration.

Venizelos recommended that the formation of a provisional
government, and the appeal to the Greek army to assist the
struggle, should be put off until the moment when Old Greece
recalled the Greek functionaries and the army. In this way the
new state would not have to undertake the economic burden of
supporting a heavy military-administrative complex until the
last possible moment. On the economic front, he suggested that
the new government should found its own State Bank, issuing
its own currency notes, and lay hands on the income of the
Ottoman Public Debt and the Régie.* The danger of the first
measure was inflation of the second alienation of powerful allied
interests.

There will also be a need for ruthless economies in the army and
the whole administration. After some time, if the interest of world
opinion and especially America is moved, one can aim at economic
aid from outside not only by contributions but perhaps also by a
loan. And it is precisely so that interest abroad may be aroused
successfully that I emphasize that the movement must not have a
purely Greek character. The participation of the Armenians will
give it great moral force, especially in America. The establishment
of the new state should also be presented as aiming not only to
save the non-Turkish populations already established within it, but
also to provide asylum for the Greeks and Armenians who are being
slaughtered every day by the Turks outside the limits of the new
state.

Finally Venizelos turned to the question of political leadership:

* In a later draft telegram, Venizelos asked Benakis to delete this
passage concerning finance before communicating his views to Meletios;
Venizelos Papers, 268, draft telegram corrected in Venizelos's hand, 29
March 1922.

For the direction of such a colossal task a man with strong shoulders and firm hands is required. For this reason it must at all costs be ensured that it be entrusted to Stergiadis, who should remain as High Commissioner for the present and direct the Representative Assembly with his advice until the moment when the Greek authorities are withdrawn and he will undertake the leadership of the movement as head of the Government. No one can replace Stergiadis, and if he refuses the venture can be considered utterly lost. He alone can both appreciate and deal with the varied and complex diplomatic issues, and also impose complete and absolute security for all the inhabitants, and especially the Turks, within the new state, which is an essential condition for the movement's prospects of success. Such protection of the Turkish population does not exclude working for an exchange of the Turkish populations within the state for the remaining Greek and Armenian populations in Turkey.

This important letter is the only surviving record of Venizelos's detailed and considered views on the *Amyna* movement. Various drafts found in his papers dating from this time give further glimpses of his mind at work. In a long draft of a telegram which was probably sent to Benakis, Venizelos suggested that the Assembly should invite the officers, N.C.O.s and men in Asia Minor to help form a provisional army for the new state. The movement's chances of success would, in Venizelos's view, be increased if a great number, a third or even a half, refused to volunteer, since the participation of the whole army would compromise the movement by giving the impression that it was inspired from Athens. Those who did not wish to stay should be assured a free return to Athens with all honours.[62]

As to the question whether Venizelos would undertake to be diplomatic representative of the separatist movement in Europe, his pen hovered between alternative responses reflecting differing degrees of commitment to the *Amyna*. It was a terrible choice to have to make. Acceptance meant embarking once more on a revolution of uncertain success. Refusal looked like rejection of his friends. It is uncertain whether Venizelos finally committed himself.[63]

Venizelos showed realism in insisting that if the movement was to have any hope of success Stergiadis must be involved. Despite this cautionary note his letter was taken as an encouragement to the *Amyna* to proceed with their plans. The 'colossal difficulties' of which he spoke were economic and military. The war in Asia Minor was costing the Greek treasury more than dr. 8 millions a day.[64] However 'ruthless' the economies practised by the new state, it was inconceivable that it could sustain the burden without prolonged and generous allied support; and Venizelos had no evidence that this would be forthcoming. As for the military aspects of the question, there were evident dangers to the Greek position in Asia Minor during the transitional period in which officers and men were departing for their homes in Old Greece, and *Amyna* officers from Constantinople were reestablishing themselves in the army. Defended by an army of at most 50,000 men, deprived of the economic support of Old Greece, dependent for supplies on far-distant Allies whose attitude was unknown, the new Ionian state could hardly have survived.

It was clear to the Government from their earlier discussions with Siotis and Sariyannis that Papoulas was deeply involved with the *Amyna*, and in early March he was summoned to Athens to explain the position. In late January Papoulas had recommended evacuation if his demands in men and equipment could not be met. He now told the Cabinet that after the sacrifices of the Greek state in Asia Minor, the Greek zone must not be abandoned: 'But if the government is forced, on account of the present impasse, to abandon and evacuate Asia Minor, then I beg to be allowed to proclaim the autonomy of Asia Minor, and otherwise to be replaced.'[65] This romantic proposal from the Commander in Chief came just after the Powers' latest proposals from Paris. Papoulas's concrete recommendations tended to show that the Greek position in Asia Minor was untenable. But because of the 'moral factors',[66] Papoulas himself would not accept this.

Papoulas believed that the Government must allow the separatist movement to go forward without withdrawing all of its financial and military support; thus the movement would be all gain and no loss for the Greek cause. That he could have hoped for this is an indication of a political naiveté which the *Amyna* had exploited. The *Amyna* movement was born out of the belief that Constantinism and Constantine damaged the Greek cause in Asia Minor, which could only be saved by a separatist movement completely dissociated from his name. Flattered by the appeal to his vanity, Papoulas used the movement to promote reconciliation. But neither he nor any other mediator could reconcile the incompatible views of Venizelos and Meletios, on the one hand, and the Government on the other.

The Government's views on the movement were finally disclosed when Gounaris and Theotokis met Papoulas and Siotis for a long discussion on 31 March. Gounaris demolished the *Amyna*'s diplomatic, economic and strategic pretensions. He argued that without the support of Old Greece, an Ionian state would have no hope of survival. A proclamation of autonomy, with an invitation to the army to remain and fight as volunteers, would simply result in the dissolution of the army, already exhausted and tried almost beyond endurance.[67] Gounaris stated that the only solution was for the army to be withdrawn under cover of a general peace settlement including guarantees for the minorities.

The decisive factor in the *Amyna*'s scheme was the military, and on this Gounaris was unquestionably right. In public the *Amyna* put the most optimistic gloss on the numbers of men they could command. Meletios in his message to Venizelos had referred to General Papoulas at the head of the *united army*. This was nonsense. *Amyna* sources had estimated that 45,000 troops could be raised. But this army existed only on paper. According to calculations by Apostolopoulos, of the Liberal Party Bureau, based on interviews with the *Amyna*'s representatives in April, less than 40,000 could be raised, on the most optimistic forecast.[68] And of these, almost half would be raw recruits. 'This army,' wrote Apostolopoulos wryly, 'would be able to maintain order in the Smyrna area *only in the event that Europe would protect this territory from every* Kemalist attack, because the army in question would be incapable of acting even as a defensive force.'

In any case, there was no question of men from Old Greece staying on in Asia Minor as volunteers. In support of this pessimistic conclusion Apostolopoulos enclosed an interesting letter from a Venizelist officer who described the situation at the front and the recent outbreak of desertions in the 27th and 30th Regiments:

First of all, the morale of our men is pitiable. Just imagine, they heard with enthusiasm the report that Asia Minor was to be evacuated.... 'Let us go home and to hell with Asia Minor.' ... I fear that with a battle lasting a few days we would run the risk of dissolution....

A few days ago when the question of evacuation of Asia Minor was disclosed, we were told to speak to the men and sound them out on how they would accept a possible decision of the Army Command to defend Asia Minor in the event of evacuation being ordered. We knew what the result would be in advance, as you will realize. Even those soldiers with the most self-respect say, 'Fine, I'm sorry for Asia Minor, but above all I'm interested in getting home.'

The anonymous correspondent reported that Venizelist newspapers were eagerly sought at the front. There was no longer any confidence in the Government: 'Gounaris is insulted foully night and day.' The neutralist officers, now thoroughly disenchanted with the new regime, had swung back towards Venizelos. The picture is of an army near breaking point.

Papoulas returned to Smyrna with the Government's assurance that it would continue the struggle and not abandon Asia Minor. He found awaiting him a letter from Argyropoulos and Kondylis which described the *Amyna*'s negotiations with Venizelos and tried to stir Papoulas to action with encouraging reports of British support.[69]

The British attitude to the movement was in fact one of frigid reserve. Curzon had instructed Lindley to make it clear to the Greeks that such a movement would be viewed by Britain with the greatest disappointment and could only have disastrous results.[70] Baltazzis assured Lindley on 1 April that 'government had nothing to do with movement and disapproved it'.[71] Three weeks later Lindley discussed the question with Stergiadis:

Monsieur Stergiadis informed me today that he had come to Athens to discuss the question of local resistance after evacuation of Asia Minor. He had as I knew always opposed it and could positively affirm that there had been no distribution of arms to population and would be none if he could prevent it. Unfortunately, certain Greeks gave out that movement was encouraged by influential persons abroad and he appealed to me to help dispel idea that there was one official and another unofficial policy regarding this question.[72]

Lindley guessed that Stergiadis was referring to Venizelist Greeks in London when he spoke of 'influential persons abroad'. It seems probable that the reference was actually to Lloyd George. As a result of this conversation it was decided that Harold Nicolson should tell Sir John Stavridi and his friends that 'they cannot be allowed to work in London against the policy of H.M.G. and equally against the policy of the Greek government'. Nicolson conveyed this warning; and Stavridi telephoned in his presence to General Phrantzis, a representative of the National Defence, telling him to inform the Patriarch and Papoulas that in no circumstances would H.M.G. countenance the movement.

Papoulos would not move. In an angry reply, he complained to the *Amyna* that his attitude had been completely misrepresented, that they had sought his cooperation, and not the other way round, and that he had always insisted that the government must be kept informed of the negotiations.[73] He claimed that the request for Venizelos's diplomatic support, which he had never authorized, was an attempt to exploit for party political purposes the patriotic sentiments of honest men such as himself.

Papoulas had now realized the *Amyna*'s true political orientation. Their conception of a 'spontaneous' movement of the Greeks of Asia Minor, represented by Venizelos abroad, and utterly dissociated from the Constantinist regime in Greece, and Papoulas's conception (never wholly clarified, even in his own mind – probably the unthought-out reaction of a simple, brave, vain man to the prospects of national disaster) of a patriotic movement endorsed by the government, and unconnected with Venizelos, could not now be reconciled.

Even now, the *Amyna* did not give up the attempt to persuade Papoulas. Argyropoulos left Constantinople for Smyrna on 15 April, taking with him a scheme for a separatist movement which followed in every detail Venizelos's recommendations, even to the condition that Stergiadis must be persuaded to accept the leadership.[74] His mission failed.[75] Papoulas would not commit himself wholeheartedly to the *Amyna*, ignoring the consequences for his relations with the Greek Government. Thus at the same time as the ineffective diplomacy of the Powers reduced the Government to impotence, Papoulas's stand and Stergiadis's hostility condemned the *Amyna* to confusion and despair.[76]

The *Amyna* was now a spent force. Resigning its hopes of an Ionian state, it concentrated on negotiating with Papoulas for the return to the army of some of the Venizelist officers in Constantinople.[77] Despite Papoulas's willingness to accept them back, these negotiations too had broken down by 25 May when Papoulas resigned and the hopes of the Constantinople *Amyna* were finally extinguished. Meanwhile, Stergiadis, with *carte blanche* from the Government to deal with the *Amyna* as he saw fit, kept the Smyrna Committee in impotence, determined that nothing should impede the Government's efforts to negotiate an evacuation, or threaten his own control of the Greek zone.[78] His harassment of the *Amyna* finally cost him the friendship of Venizelos himself.

12 | A Maze with no Exit

It is certain that all of us here and in Smyrna and
in Athens are struggling in the dark and hitting out
at friends and enemies without any definite aim
any more, since we are desperately divided even in
our conception of the general interest of the
country.

The Ecumenical Patriarch Meletios to Venizelos,
April 1922

Greece must go through the wilderness, she must
live on manna picked up from the stones, she must
struggle through the stern trial of the present time.
If she did so, she would win the Promised Land.

Lloyd George to Venizelos, May 1922

The failure of the Paris talks of March to bear fruit marked the
beginning of the end for the Greeks. Throughout the summer
the Government seemed nerveless and devoid of ideas, reliant on
Lord Curzon to get Greece out of the present mess. In June
Stergiadis urged that the Powers make some decision over Asia
Minor and enforce it. In July Baltazzis asked Britain to 'tell
Greece what she was expected to do and what support she would
obtain in doing it'.[1]

The Greeks were trapped in a maze with no exit. Their object
was to liquidate the war, even by evacuation if that were necessary. The Paris talks had brought the question of evacuation into
the open, thus raising a political storm against the Government
inspired by the Greeks of the *Amyna* and disgruntled politicians
such as Stratos. This storm made it still more difficult for
demoralized Government to contemplate evacuation as a unilateral action to put an end to the war.[2] For internal political
reasons therefore, evacuation must be camouflaged by an interallied settlement with 'guarantees' for the minorities. From this
circle there seemed to be no escape.

The Government had given up hope of a loan from England.
They now acted courageously to raise the resources necessary to

maintain the army in Anatolia. On 3 April Protopapadakis introduced his famous Forced Loan Bill, by which all paper currency in circulation was literally cut in half. One half of each note remained in circulation, worth half the value of the original note; the other half became a bond, redeemable eventually by the state. In this way the Government raised about 1,500,000 million drachmas for the maintenance of the army on a war footing.[3] But even this large injection of funds could not last long at the present rates of expenditure. Protopapadakis told Lindley in May, 'almost with tears in his eyes', that this windfall was just sufficient to effect the demobilization of the Greek army, for which purpose it should be used.[4] Though the loan was received stoically by the people, it did nothing to increase the popularity of the Government in the country.[5]

The balance of political forces in the country was such that however unpopular the Government became, there was little possibility of change by constitutional means. Owing to the composition of the Chamber, any government must come from the anti-Venizelist bloc, consisting of the Gounarists and the much smaller following of Nikolaos Stratos. Stratos, who had flirted with the Venizelists and with the Asia Minor *Amyna*, and opposed Gounaris throughout the winter with all the wiles of frustrated ambition, could not hope to achieve power except at the head of an anti-Venizelist coalition. The possibilities of manoeuvre were further restricted by the fact that the current chamber was a Constituent Assembly, of which the King's powers of dissolution were constitutionally limited.

The Gounaris Government fell on 12 May, after surviving a vote of confidence by the inadequate margin of one vote. A Venizelist journalist described the scene after Gounaris's resignation:

Some of us Liberal journalists and politicians had met in Danglis's house. ... None of us doubted that immediately after the resigning Prime Minister, the King would summon Danglis, since he was leader of the strongest opposition party, amounting to 105 deputies. ... The politicians discussed the question whether Danglis should accept if the King invited him to form a Government. All were agreed that he should accept. But the hours passed, Kalogeropoulos was called to the palace – leader of a small group in the Chamber – and no word came for Danglis, when in the early afternoon we were told to our amazement that the King had

entrusted the formation of the new Government to Stratos who num-
bered only about thirty friends in the Chamber.[6]

Stratos appeared before the Chamber on 17 May, and although
the Venizelists voted for him, lost a vote of confidence by 154
to 170 votes. The way was now open for a Coalition Government,
which was duly formed on 21 May. The Gounarists held eight
ministries, the Stratists five. Protopapadakis became prime
minister, Gounaris, Baltazzis and Theotokis retained the port-
folios of Justice, Foreign Affairs and War, and Stratos took on
the Ministry of the Interior. This, after a great deal of fuss, was
the mixture much as before.

The incident thus brought to a close [wrote the British Ambas-
sador] can best be described as farcical. It is part of the parliamentary byplay necessary to form a government comprising elements
outside the personal following of M. Gounaris. M. Stratos, who has
30 followers, was determined not to take part in such a government
until he had enjoyed the personal satisfaction of being Prime
Minister: and he admitted to my Rumanian colleague that he was
also determined to have a good look at the political dossiers in the
Ministry of Foreign Affairs... I cannot help thinking he must have
discovered some rather interesting material since he has succeeded
in securing more seats than was expected in the new Cabinet.[7]

The crisis simply served to swell the numbers of the Cabinet
from eleven to fourteen.

Four days after the formation of Protopapadakis's ill-fated
ministry, General Papoulas at last resigned, to the relief of
Stergiadis and the Government, and the despair of Patriarch
Meletios and the National Defence. The Patriarch's conception
of himself as spiritual and political leader of the unredeemed
Greeks brought him inevitably into conflict with Stergiadis, the
representative of a Greek Government which Meletios rejected
and despised. The unfortunate Papoulas, torn this way and that
by conflicting feelings of revolutionary compassion and of loyalty
as Commander in Chief to his political masters, bore the brunt
of Stergiadis's contempt for the political naiveté of the separatists.
Athens and Greek Constantinople were in a state of undeclared
hostilities. Meletios had opened his heart to Venizelos a month
before Papoulas's resignation:

Among the many difficult problems which we face is the general attitude of Mr Stergiadis. Towards the Patriarchate he maintains a more hostile stance than even Gounaris. While he proclaims that the state cannot prolong the occupation in Asia, he expels with insults the Metropolitans sent by us to tend the people. His recent stay in Athens left the impression that no one has been working more warmly on behalf of the regime....

It is certain that all of us here and in Smyrna and in Athens are struggling in the dark and hitting out at friends and enemies without any definite aim any more, since we are desperately divided even in our conception of the general interest of the country. This is why we all await the rays of your genius ... if you see the continuation of the struggle in Asia as unpatriotic, like Mr Stergiadis, tell us to order the stance of the Patriarchate accordingly. But if Mr Stergiadis is in error, we beg you not to be slow in reminding him of his duty towards all those who suffer the thunderbolts of the Constantinian group in the belief that they are serving the country.[8]

As a political figure and a representative of Venizelism Meletios was bound to arouse the hostility of Stergiadis, who could tolerate no threat to his supremacy within his sphere. Meletios's very election had been a political act, the subject of bitter struggles between opposing political factions within the Orthodox Church, and unrecognized by the Greek Government. This is why Stergiadis, as representative of the Government, would not recognize Meletios's tame bishops. But in any case Stergiadis would have regarded such men as troublemakers and a threat to order; he had never approved of political priests, or indeed priests at all.

Though Stergiadis was master in his own zone, capable of keeping even the clergy in order, he could not touch Meletios. Constantinople was an autonomous world. But by striking at those the Patriarch wished to use, such as Papoulas, he was able to maintain his sphere of influence inviolate. The day before Papoulas's resignation was made public, Meletios sent Kondylis with another letter to Venizelos:

I continue to wait for a few words from you.... We need encouragement especially since Stergiadis decided to turn his iron fist against the people of Asia Minor.... The crushing of Papoulas is the work of Stergiadis, who used as evidence your telegrams and letter which I communicated to him in confidence, thinking I was addressing the Stergiadis I knew. Unfortunately I was too slow in assessing previous events which should have convinced me that Stergiadis is the most fanatical instrument of the Constantinian regime, and not the liberal suffering for the safety of Asia Minor.

No nomarch or governor-general has exceeded Stergiadis in his measures against the higher clergy who recognize the Patriarch.

Now both here and in Smyrna there is indignation not against Gounaris any more but against Stergiadis, who struggles to choke every voice of protest against the return of the Asia Minor Christians to the Turkey of Kemal.[9]

Meletios complained that the Government in Athens was doing all it could to make his position difficult, to the extent of recognizing a rival Synod in Constantinople. But this was hardly surprising; for Meletios himself rejected suggestions from Athens that he should recognize Constantine. He claimed that those priests who were within the Greek King's worldly jurisdiction had an obligation to honour him as their king; but that the Ecumenical Patriarch was free of all such obligation and determined his attitude to the regime in Greece according to his conception of the good or harm his relations with Constantine would have on the fortunes of the unredeemed nation.

Venizelos was now back home in Europe. He went to see Lloyd George in the House of Commons on 30 May 1922.[10] The conversation is extraordinarily interesting in the light it throws on the thinking of the two men – the unwavering consistency with which Lloyd George held to his belief in a resurgent Greece in Asia, and Venizelos to the hope that the situation could be saved if the French would modify their attitude.

Venizelos began by saying that the Kemalists would not accept any sort of terms. He had told Poincaré recently that he would be obliged to accept any conditions which the Turks cared to impose if he did not make some stand against them now. 'They might come and demand mosques in London, Paris and Rome with cupolas higher than St Paul's, Notre Dame and St Peter's.' A Greek evacuation of Smyrna would end in 'complete humiliation for the Allies all along the line'. When once France realized this and saw that whatever Kemal got, he would demand more, she might change her policy and indicate that she would support Greece if Constantine were to abdicate. 'If he abdicated it might be possible to expel the Turks from Constantinople and to come to a really satisfactory settlement in Asia Minor.'

Venizelos's argument was a variation on the well-known 'thin end of the wedge'; he had even told Poincaré that the French position in Syria depended on the Greek position in Smyrna.

Lloyd George responded with an emotional justification of his Greek policy:

He had always been in favour of the Greeks, the Italians and the French taking over the regeneration of the coast lands of Asia Minor. He had told the Italians at Genoa that they had made a fatal mistake in not working with Mr Venizelos in 1919. Sonnino was right in his policy, but he was too greedy. The Italians needed an outlet for their surplus population and they could find it easily in the rich lands of Southern Asia Minor.... They would be bound to come back to that policy in time. Meanwhile Greece must stick to her policy. He would never shake hands with a Greek again who went back upon his country's aims in Smyrna. If he were out of office, he would speak freely upon this point. In office he could not do so, but he felt most strongly that this was the testing time of the Greek nation, and that if they persevered now their future was assured. Great Britain would go back to her original ideas about Asia Minor in due course.... Greece must go through the wilderness, she must live on manna picked up from the stones, she must struggle through the stern trial of the present time. If she did so, she would win the Promised Land.... The tide was turning, and the Greeks must keep their hearts up until Constantine disappears from the scene and opinion throughout the west came round them [*sic*] as it certainly would do.... A quick settlement would be a bad settlement for Greece. They must be patient and stick it out.

This is perhaps the clearest statement of Lloyd George's policy after the November 1920 elections. That policy was, without committing himself to the offer of material support, to encourage the Greeks to keep going, in the hope that circumstances would eventually arise where a favourable settlement could be made. In the summer of 1921 it was Lloyd George's hope that the victories of the Greek army might create such circumstances. In May 1922 it was simply a question of holding on in the hope that something would turn up. Lloyd George's positive disavowal of a quick settlement was no service to the Greek army and Government.

Venizelos made one effort during the summer to moderate Stergiadis's hostility to the *Amyna*, by asking two of his supporters, G. Exindaris and D. Lambrakis, to visit the High Commissioner on his behalf. Exindaris's description of the meetings shows the strain under which the High Commissioner was suffering because of his unpopular stand on the question of evacuation.[11] The first meeting was amicable. Stergiadis agreed that a meeting with his old friend Venizelos was desirable. Three days later Exindaris met him again :

I found before me a different man in the grip of a total nervous paroxysm. What had happened? He had received in the meantime a pile of letters, some anonymous, others signed, and some actually from Crete; in some of them he was severely attacked for his attitude, in others the honesty of his character was doubted, and in others he was insulted in the most foul way. Such letters must have been sent to him in Smyrna too, but it appears that his private secretary and Gounarakis agreed to conceal them from him. At the same time he had been informed – and this seemed to me to have hurt him especially – that you too share the views of his critics and have expressed yourself very harshly about him. In general he had realized that the confidence and respect of the liberals for him had been succeeded by animosity and mistrust. All this had created in him a stormy psychological state.... He thought that rarely had a man been in his difficult position, and that in the execution of what he considered to be his duty he had spent his spiritual powers to the point of exhaustion and shown mental endurance beyond the usual human limits. And instead of recognition of the exceptional difficulties of his work ... he suddenly discovers a general outcry against him. ... I felt real pity. After all this the question of meeting you took or seemed to take a different form in his mind. 'I shall seem,' he said, 'to be going to defend myself. And I will not do that even if they are going to kill me. If Christ himself said to me: Light me one candle and you can go to heaven, I would answer: Leave me alone, you and your heaven.' These were almost literally his phrases.

The meeting with Venizelos therefore did not take place. At this late stage, it could hardly have led to useful results. It is little wonder that Stergiadis's nerves were wearing thin in the summer of 1922. The savagery of the attacks on him was due not only to his arbitrary and dictatorial methods, and violent temper, but also to the fact that he recognized that Greece's enterprise in Asia Minor was condemned to failure and put all his force into the ending of it. It was years before the breach with Venizelos was healed.

In his letter of resignation,[12] Papoulas reminded the Government that there were two lieutenant generals who could succeed him – Dousmanis and Hatzianestis. The Government's stormy relationship with Dousmanis was continued by an offer to him – soon withdrawn – to become Chief of General Staff again. General

George Hatzianestis, then in command of the Greek army in Thrace, was invited to become Commander in Chief of the Asia Minor army, and accepted. At his own insistence he continued also to hold the Thracian command.

This was the man of whom Lloyd George later wrote that he was now a 'mental case ... labouring under the delusion that his legs were made of sugar and that they were so brittle that if he stood up they might break'.[13] A better witness, the British Military Attaché in Athens, wrote of Hatzianestis shortly after his appointment to the Asia Minor command as

an unemployed officer who never talked politics to me and who was obviously intensely devoted to King Constantine. He was said to be Anglophobe, but I always found him wellbred, cultured and courteous, and he spoke to me often of the time fifteen years or more ago, when he was attached for a time to a battery of artillery at Woolwich. He had eccentricities of manner and was almost universally said to be mad. In his appearance he is like a well-trimmed and well-dressed Don Quixote. As far as his military qualities are concerned, I had to form my judgement from what I was told from time to time by a number of officers of every age and grade and of varied political colour who had served with him. It was on their unanimous reports that I gave you an opinion as to his unfitness for command, which I now recognize was probably exaggerated. He has always been highly-strung and excitable, and has worried those under him by an exaggerated sense of discipline, which sometimes reached absurdity. He was greatly attached to his wife, and for some time after her death a few years ago he really was mad, but I think there is no doubt that he has recovered much of his balance. For the rest, he is an educated soldier, and with Dousmanis, Jean Metaxas and Tricoupis, was one of the first officers selected when the Greeks began to form a General Staff before the Balkan Wars.[14]

This is perhaps as near as we can come to the mystery of Hatzianestis's character. He was not certifiably insane at the time of his appointment, but was widely *thought* to be unbalanced, which was almost as bad.[15] In his insistence on trivial matters of discipline, he betrayed a lack of proportion which was dangerous when dealing with an experienced but exhausted army.[16] There were fighting generals – notably Trikoupis, commanding the I Army Corps – who were experienced, familiar with the situation in Asia Minor, and widely respected throughout the army. Hatzianestis's appointment was an extraordinarily unwise one.

Hatzianestis arrived in Smyrna on 5 June, determined to sweep through the army like a new broom. The old Staff of Pallis and Sariyannis was replaced by General Valettas and Colonel Passaris. After only three days in Smyrna, Hatzianestis set out on an extended and exhaustive tour of inspection of the front. The British Military Attaché, who toured the front only a few days behind General Hatzianestis, reported a general feeling of relief at finding him much more reasonable than had been expected. 'Every officer in Asia Minor whom I asked about him and who had known him in the past said that, apart from his absurdities, he was a "good soldier". . . .' [17] But Hatzianestis and Colonel Hoare Nairne were deceived as to the real condition and morale of the troops. Hatzianestis concluded from his tour that a Turkish offensive would be repulsed without difficulty. Colonel Hoare Nairne reported after a month's tour of the Greek zone that within certain limits morale was as good as ever. [18] Reliable officers such as Trikoupis were sure that better organization, recreation and firmer discipline had reduced political dissension among the troops. The men were well in hand and capable of repelling a Turkish attack. But this was the limit of their spirit. There could not be a new Greek offensive. And Hoare Nairne found a general consciousness among officers that withdrawal from Asia Minor or at least a shortening of the front would soon be unavoidable:

Several senior Greek officers spoke anxiously of the internal and financial situation in Greece, and of the urgent need of an early settlement of the Asia Minor situation. They have no doubt as to the security of their present line in the face of Kemal's present forces and resources; but they recognize that it has been only by an enormous effort that Greece has kept her army supplied during this year, and has even succeeded in giving the troops their arrears of pay. They know that the end of both supplies and money is now in sight. . . . They recognize that in these circumstances a withdrawal to a line nearer their base, if not the actual evacuation of Asia Minor, may soon be necessary; but they are convinced that a withdrawal without a real settlement would mean death or ruin to the Christian inhabitants and probably to thousands of Circassians and Turks who have befriended the Greeks.

What then did the Greeks intend to do? Withdraw that year? If so, how much time was left to them? The answer depended on the state of the roads and the weather. Although both Eski Shehir and Afyon Karahisar were supplied by railway, the line down from Afyon to Alashehir was a single track running on steep gradients, and insufficient to cope with the entire southern group of the Greek army in a forced evacuation. It would be necessary therefore to use road as well as rail. But in September the autumn rains would break, and the roads would become impossible for heavy transport. It followed that if an evacuation was to take place before the onset of another winter, the movement of stores and heavy transport could not be delayed beyond the middle of August. The Greeks did not have much time left for decision.

For the time being, there were no indications of an imminent retirement. Work was continuing on the front line trenches, and not on the rearward lines:

> The impression I gained was that the Greeks mean to hold on to their present general line until circumstances absolutely force them to draw back, and that in the meantime they are going to continue to work on the improvement of their position as earnestly as if it were to be permanent. Whether the Government and the army commander will judge the last limit to be reached in August, I cannot say; but after that month, without a settlement or some financial relief, the retention of the Greek army in its present position will become a gambler's risk.

Colonel Hoare Nairne's report is a useful account of the Greek army on the eve of disaster, tinged with a sad and absorbing irony. He overestimated the moral effects of the sympathy felt by the Greek soldiers for the Christians of Asia Minor. Relations were often bad between the indigenous Greeks and the soldiers from mainland Greece; but officers talking to a foreigner would tend to play up the compassionate and patriotic aspects of the Greek endeavour. He underestimated the moral discouragement of fighting in a cause which, in their hearts, most Greeks now knew was lost.

There is general agreement that over the winter of 1921–22 the morale of the Greek army had sunk low. The very efforts of officers to improve the recreational facilities at the front and to get the men working, were symptoms of a lack of action and a waiting on political events which tried the nerves. To the moral discomforts of separation from home and families, to isolation and political dissension, were added the material evils of indifferent food, defective clothing and equipment, and overdue pay. Hatzianestis's arrival had no more than a superficial impact on the deteriorating situation. He was successful in extracting long overdue money from the exchequer for his troops, and in rooting out the *embusqués* and idlers from Smyrna and sending them to the front; but these efforts were more than cancelled out by his tactical and disciplinary eccentricities.

It was in any case too late. Faction and discontent now seethed just below the surface. The communists had profited from three years of war to make inroads on the sympathies of the men. From time to time Bolshevik leaflets had been dropped by the Turks behind the Greek lines exhorting the Greeks in stilted Greek to go home and leave their Turkish comrades in peace.[19] These had little effect. But a few energetic organizers from the party in Old Greece were able to set up a network of sympathizers throughout the southern group of the army who were ready to encourage defeatist tendencies; for the communists had consistently opposed this colonialist war. They were particularly well established in the communications centres – in telegraph stations and on the railway lines. In these positions they were able to disseminate communist brochures and the party newspaper *Rizospastis* to all parts of the front, and to assist the human traffic in deserters making their way back to Old Greece.[20] The communists could not themselves engineer a collapse of the front or a breakdown in morale. But they could take every opportunity to encourage the men to ask the question, 'Why are we here and who are we fighting for?' (The Marxist answer to this was British imperialism and in particular the British interest in Middle Eastern oil.)

The men's complaints were genuine and not dreamed up by agitators. By the summer of 1922 the Greek army was like an apple eaten out inside by insects or disease, superficially whole and apparently firm, but ready to disintegrate at the first sharp blow. Not even the enemy knew how near it had come to dissolution.

Indeed, the war had now gone on so long, the front was so extended, that in some sectors a sort of unsigned armistice prevailed. Eleftherios Stavridis, who was busy building up a network of communist cells throughout the army, found such a situation in his unit of the Southern Army Group on the river Meander:

The opposing armies had their outposts on either bank of the river. We held the north bank, the Kemalists the south. The river was only about 50 metres wide in many places, and only knee deep in the summer. Often Greeks and Turks washed their clothes together or washed their feet in the river and talked. Often Kemal-ist Turkish private soldiers brought eggs, cheese and fruit to our men and asked for cigarettes. At that time the State doled out to the army such revolting tobacco that the men did not use up their share (half a packet a day) but called them 'suicide cigarettes'! Once this form of barter with the 'enemy Turks' started, the men collected their full share in order to exchange them for eggs, cheese, honey, fruit.

Often the Turks brought whole wild boar, killed by them in the vast forest of Denizli, where there were plenty of them. They did not eat them because of the prohibition in the Koran.... The con-versations were almost always the same: 'When will this war end? We've had enough of it, we and you. You won't be able to beat us in the end, nor will we be able to beat you! That is evident from the facts. And so we have both suffered, both sides, for years now!' [21]

In mid-July rumours began to fly that the Greeks were about to launch some sort of attempt on Constantinople. This possibil-ity had been aired from time to time in Greece in the last two years, sometimes sufficiently loudly for the British to issue warn-ings that no such attempt would be tolerated. But now troop movement in Thrace gave the rumours substance.[22] At first the British refused to believe it: neither Harington, nor Hoare Nairne, nor Lindley, could credit that the Greeks would take so desperate a step.

In considering with Hatzianestis the possibility of an attempt on Constantinople, the Government had made it clear that if the attempt would weaken the Asia Minor front it must be aban-doned. As a result of his tour of the Asia Minor front Hatzianes-tis concluded that reinforcements for the Thracian army could be detached from Asia Minor without significantly weakening the front. It was this conclusion which led the Government to decide to go ahead with the plan.

Hatzianestis moved three infantry regiments and two battal-ions from Asia Minor to Thrace. How much their removal affected Greek defensive capacity in Anatolia it is impossible to say. What can be said is that the removal of these troops from the vital front to a theatre of secondary importance where no im-mediate threat was posed to the Greek position was an act of desperation on the part of the Government.

Although there was no official indication that the Greeks in-tended to move on the city, these troop movements and transfers of petrol to Dedeagatch were not concealed. By 29 July the indications were sufficiently alarming for Britain to concoct an official warning to the Greeks that any violation of the neutral zone of Constantinople and the Straits would be resisted by allied forces. This came too late. The Greek Government had already announced their intention to act. Baltazzis handed a long note to the allied representatives announcing that only the occupation of Constantinople by Greece could now bring about the conclusion of peace.[23]

The Allies suddenly found themselves with a crisis on their hands. It was evident in Athens from Baltazzis's attitude that the Greeks' motive was to force the Powers to reach a decision and impose a peace settlement. He assured Bentinck, the British Chargé d'Affaires, that Greek troops would not enter the neutral zone without allied consent.[24] But the bluff was sufficiently realistic to alarm General Harington, who toured the Thracian frontier on 29 July. Large numbers of Greek troops were now massed on the frontier.

Harington's attitude was a simple one. The Allies were declared neutrals in the Turco-Greek war, and the zone of the Straits was a neutral zone. Encroachment on the zone must therefore be resisted, from whatever quarter it came. Harington told the French General Charpy that he would send a British brigade to support the French troops on the Thracian frontier against any Greek attempt to cross the line. He added, with foresight, that he counted on the support of a French brigade in the event of a Nationalist advance into the neutral zone from the Anatolian side.[25]

On 30 July the allied High Commissioners, generals and admirals in Constantinople sat down to a council of war. The French proposed to use this rash move on the part of the Greeks as a means of exerting further pressure. The French High Commissioner recommended exacting stringent guarantees against the possibility of any further Greek mischief.[26] The Greek troops recently sent to Thrace must be withdrawn, the Greek military and naval missions in Constantinople suppressed. The French later suggested in Churchillian style an allied blockade of the principle Greek ports, or ports occupied by the Greeks.

The British attitude was milder. Balfour's sensible view was that no ostentatious precautions should be taken against a danger unlikely to materialize.[27] The British therefore did their best to damp down the excitement, so as to avert a frontier incident which might spark off a disastrous explosion. Nevertheless, if the Greeks had crossed into the zone, Britain would have joined the French in sanctions against them.

Greek and allied troops now faced each other on either side of the frontier, as Turkish and allied troops were to do at Chanak four months later; and on 1 August the Greeks actively reconnoitred the allied lines. It was a dangerous moment. But the Greeks stayed their hands. The allied representatives in Athens handed in a note formally stating that any Greek advance into the neutral zone would be repelled by force.[28] Before this categorical warning, the Greeks capitulated, and no more was heard of the move on Constantinople.

The manoeuvre had been ineptly carried out. What had the Greeks hoped to gain by it? Baltazzis claimed that since the Allies' declaration of neutrality in the Greco-Turkish war, what had originally been a means of *pressure* on the Turks – the occupation of Constantinople by allied forces – had turned into a means of *protecting* the capital city of one belligerent against the other. It was in the Greek view unfair that Greece as a belligerent should be prevented from bringing the war to a successful conclusion by the quickest and most painless means, the occupation of Constantinople. Such reasoning, so far as it went, was perfectly valid. The Allies had adopted the entirely illogical position of declaring themselves neutral in a war in which they did not recognize belligerent rights to the belligerents (this was the French and Italian position over the Greek right of visit and search of ships suspected of carrying contraband for the Kemalists).[29] But to expect the Allies to appreciate this point of view when an allegedly vital interest such as the integrity of Constantinople was at stake was optimism gone mad. Balfour himself, friend of Greece as he was, called the project insane.

Nevertheless, the Greek Government persuaded itself that Great Britain, even if obliged to make hostile noises out of allied solidarity, would accept a *fait accompli*. There were rumours in Athens that a 'leading British statesman' had let it be understood that Britain would be pleased if the Greeks went ahead and forced the issue.[30] For those in the Cabinet who had these hopes, the attempt presented itself as the last means – a desperate attempt – of extracting Greece from the war.

The Greeks' bluff was called because they miscalculated the

importance set by Great Britain on allied solidarity and the defence of the *status quo* in the Straits zone. That the Greeks should
actually defy the Allies' ban, and march on Constantinople, was
inconceivable. This is not to say that the Greeks could not
physically have occupied the City; there was very little to stop
them. But in the long run they were at the mercy of the British
fleet, which could close the Straits, blockade Piraeus, and take
other measures necessary to bring them to heel. The Greeks'
inhibitions in any case were psychological. The basis of Greek
policy was cooperation with Britain. With British support,
Greece could defy France and Italy. Against the will of the three
united Allies she was powerless to act. It was the British coolness
therefore which exposed the desperate situation of the Greeks.

The Greek move on Constantinople was combined with a
démarche of Stergiadis designed to relieve the Greek Government of some responsibility for Asia Minor, and to prepare the
way for withdrawal of the army. On 28 June, on one of his visits
to Athens, Stergiadis had discussed with Lindley the increasingly
worrying situation in Asia Minor.[31] Stergiadis approved of the new
Commander in Chief, but strongly opposed his plan to shorten
the front, on several grounds, and particularly because the Greek
administration would have to cope with many thousands of
refugees from the evacuated area. In Stergiadis's view, 'Greece
could neither evacuate nor continue the war alone'; the Powers
must decide what was to be done, and enforce their decision.

In a second talk, Stergiadis recommended that the Powers
should set up an autonomous zone under the sovereignty of the
Sultan – a zone large enough to be self-supporting, with gendarmerie and administration formed out of the local elements.[32]
Drafts of Asia Minor Greeks, together with 50,000 of the Greek
army, would defend the zone against Kemal during the transitional period. Stergiadis was emphatic that the Powers should
act now, while there was still time.

At first sight this suggestion looks like the *Amyna*'s impracticable scheme for an autonomous Ionia. But Stergiadis's autonomous zone was to be, not a breakaway creation of one political
faction, but the creation of the Powers themselves, backed by
their prestige and influence. Moreover, Stergiadis had in mind
not a narrowly Greek (or even a Christian) régime but a multiracial administration. With that freedom from the nationalist
assumptions of his compatriots that seemed to them chillingly

inhuman, he wished to give the Muslims a greater share in the government of the region.

The Greek Cabinet approved Stergiadis's plans, authorizing him to reorganize the occupied zone with greater authority for the local elements. Baltazzis told Lindley that the purpose of the reorganization was to enable the Christian population to survive a Greek evacuation;[33] an explanation which smacks of euphemism for the disengagement of Greek responsibility for the zone.

Stergiadis returned to Smyrna on 14 July. On 31 July, two days after Baltazzis announced the attempt on Constantinople to the Powers, he issued a 'declaration' for the Greek zone,[34] which spoke of the 'work of liberation' being continued by the 'liberating people itself' (a hint that the Christians could no longer rely on the Greek Government to protect them), and promised a reorganization of the system of government.

Stergiadis convoked a mass meeting in front of Government House on the morning of 31 July. Government employees were obliged to attend, and shops were closed by order. After the declarations of the Greek Government and the High Commissioner had been read out, delegates of the local communities made perfunctory expressions of satisfaction. Addressing them in reply, Stergiadis tried to evoke a local patriotism that would cut across religious differences. In an attempt to win the support of the Muslims, he emphasized that the Sultan continued to be Caliph under the allied peace settlement, and would retain intact all his prestige throughout the Islamic world.[35]

Sir Harry Lamb, the British Consul General in Smyrna, saw in the declaration a deliberate abdication of responsibility by the Greek Government.[36] Bentinck, on the other hand, from Athens, urged that the move be viewed with sympathy as a half-way stage to whatever autonomous regime the allies might in the end impose on the area: 'It will be a distinct advantage to the latter to have a framework, constructed by a man of the experience and capacity of M. Stergiadis, upon which to build.'[37]

Any chance that the scheme might be taken seriously was scotched by the indifference of the public within the zone and by the attitude of the Powers, who expressed their formal reservations to Greece on 15 August, on the grounds that any permanent regime in Asia Minor must depend on the eventual treaty settlement between the Allies and Turkey.[38] No more was heard of the scheme.

The declaration of 'autonomy' of 31 July and the threat to Constantinople formed a two-pronged attempt, born out of desperation at the allies' procrastination, to force an issue to the Asia Minor war. The Greeks would advance with allied or at least British permission, to occupy Constantinople. The occupation of the city would be a victory carrying enough prestige to camouflage the liquidation of the war in Asia Minor and evacuation of the Greek army, with its attendant risks to the Christian populations. It would also be a gage in the hands of the Greeks for their negotiations with the Turks and the Allies. Meanwhile in Smyrna a new autonomous regime would spring up, less abhorrent to the Turks once the provocation of the presence of the Greek army on Turkish soil disappeared. Even if neither of these hopes was realized, at least the Greek initiative would spur the Allies into hastening their search for a settlement.

The Greeks hoped for British support for both parts of the scheme. But the whole logic of Curzon's attempts to negotiate a peace settlement since the time of the London Conference made it inevitable that Britain refuse to recognize a unilateral attempt to force the issue and anticipate interallied decisions. For the Greeks to hope otherwise was inept.

It was now that Lloyd George made his final gesture. Lindley, the British Minister to Athens, had gone on early leave to London to impress on the Government the desperate situation of the Greeks. He told Balfour and Lloyd George that Greece would inevitably collapse in the autumn unless she received both moral *and material* help from Great Britain.[39] Lloyd George's response was his famous Commons speech of 4 August, which was intended (in Lindley's view) to take the place of that material assistance postulated as a necessary condition of continued Greek resistance:

I forget who it was who said that we were not fair as between the parties. I am not sure that we are. What has happened? Here is a war between Greece and Turkey. We are defending the capital of one of the parties against the other. ... If we were not there, there is absolutely no doubt that the Greeks would occupy that capital in a very few hours, and that would produce a decision. There is only one way now in which the Greeks can have a decision, and that is by marching through almost impenetrable defiles for hundreds of miles into the country. I do not know of any army that would have gone as far as the Greeks have. It was a very daring and a very dangerous military enterprise.... There are even suggestions, not altogether, perhaps, without foundation, that the Kemalist forces are being re-equipped from Europe. The Greeks, under other conditions, would have been entitled to blockade the coast of Asia Minor.... Peace the Kemalists will not accept, because they say we will not give them satisfactory armistice terms: but we are not allowing the Greeks to wage the war with their full strength. We cannot allow that sort of thing to go on indefinitely, in the hope that the Kemalists entertain, that they will at last exhaust this little country, whose men have been under arms for ten or twelve years, with one war after another, and which has not indefinite resources.[40]

The speech with its fine sentiments of sympathy aroused great enthusiasm in Greece. There was a demonstration in front of the British Legation. Stratos and Baltazzis called to express their pleasure. Extracts from the speech were circulated to the army in an order of the day.[41] But the speech was bluff, intended to keep up the Greeks' morale so that they would hold their positions until the time came for negotiations. It held out vague hopes, but made no promises of aid. It was Lloyd George's final intervention, eccentric (in that it virtually repudiated his Government's action in keeping the Greeks out of Constantinople) but consistent with his policy of encouraging Greece without committing Britain. The effect of the speech was to hasten the climax in Asia Minor, for the Turks, anxious lest the speech might foreshadow practical measures of assistance for Greece, pushed on at feverish pace with their plans for an offensive.

13 | Catastrophe

August came. There was not now time to carry out a plan of evacuation before the rains broke in September. The prospect of another long winter in the trenches and on the cold, windswept uplands of Anatolia began to loom up before the Greeks.

The Greek army was still strung out over the long, sickleshaped front which it had occupied with only minor variations since July 1921. Starting at Kios on the Sea of Marmara, the front followed a line south-eastwards, cutting the Eski Shehir–Ankara railway, then turning south to Afyon Karahisar. From Afyon the front ran westwards down the right bank of the Meander river to the Aegean Sea. The key points in this 400 mile front were the railway junctions of Eski Shehir and Afyon Karahisar. The northern sector, running from the Marmara past Eski Shehir to a point east of Kutahya, was held by III Army Corps under General Soumilas. The southern sector, including the dangerously exposed salient at Afyon Karahisar itself, was held by I and II Army Corps, under Generals Trikoupis and Digenis. Previously these had formed one command, the Southern Army Group. But Hatzianestis had unwisely abolished this system and set up the two Corps as independent commands responsible to himself in Smyrna. Only in cases of urgency, where contact with G.H.Q. was impossible, was Trikoupis to take overall command of the sector. This new system made no sense. For in the event of a Turkish offensive the outcome of battle would depend on the rapidity of the Greek redeployment of forces and reinforcement

---

* 'Homewards!'

of hard-pressed sectors of the front; and this required unity of command in the sector.

Trikoupis's headquarters were at Afyon, near the point of the salient held by the Greek 12th, 4th and 1st Divisions. It was a critical point in the Greek line of defence. Afyon itself and the railway were dangerously close to the front line.

The opposing forces in this southern sector of the front were approximately equal. The Greeks mustered eight Divisions, of which four formed Trikoupis's I Corps centred on Afyon, and four in Digenis's II Corps held the central sector running north from Afyon up the railway line towards Eski Shehir. The Turkish 'army of the Western Front', commanded by Ismet Pasha, the cautious and persistent hero of the battles of Inonu, was of about the same strength. The Turks were now adequately equipped with Skoda and Krupp artillery, and with their squadron of French aeroplanes held command of the air. In their cavalry, simply mounted on rapid and surefooted Anatolian hill ponies, they had a weapon which was flexible and penetrating.

The Greek front was too long. Its length meant that there was disturbingly little in reserve. Most disturbingly, the 2nd Division was strung out over more than seventy miles from near Tulu Punar to Ortanza on the Meander river. For Saraphs, serving in a remote outpost of the 31st Infantry Regiment, it was an eight-hour journey by mule to the seat of the Regiment at Boulanta, without passing a single outpost on the way.

Of the twelve Greek Divisions, ten were deployed in the front line. The Greek communications system did not favour rapid deployment. Although the Greeks had occupied this front for a year the main and subsidiary roads remained inadequate. This was not all. With G.H.Q. in Smyrna, some hundreds of miles away from the front, the timelag between the telegraphing of reports from the front and the receipt of G.H.Q.'s orders was a matter of hours not minutes. Greek signals communications were in any case unreliable. There was only one wireless set per Army Corps. And telegraphic and telephone communications were liable to interruption from bombardment and the incursions of Turkish *chettés* or regular cavalry. The main telegraph line running from Afyon parallel with the railway line to G.H.Q. in Smyrna was particularly important and vulnerable.

Despite these hazards, the Greeks had no alternative strategy but to stand and fight. When Hatzianestis arrived in Asia Minor, he had been amazed that no second line seemed to exist, and had told Spyridonos to make a study of the various possible defensible fronts.[1] These studies were set in hand too late. When the Turkish offensive interrupted them, the Greeks still sat on their old lines, with no fully prepared fallback positions.

Finally, there were Greek deficiencies in morale and material, notably a shortage of ammunition, of which the Turks had obtained ample supplies from the French armies when they left Cilicia. Despite all these problems, the Greeks could reflect that they had withstood with ease every Turkish offensive to date in the Anatolian campaign, and that the history of the past eight years showed how difficult it was for attacking troops to break through well entrenched defensive positions in modern warfare. Such was the situation when in early August reports from Turkish deserters suggested that a disquieting Turkish build-up was taking place in the Afyon Karahisar sector of the front line.

In early August 1922 the bulk of the now formidable Turkish forces was concentrated against the southern sector of the Greek front. Fourteen infantry divisions and four cavalry divisions were concentrated opposite the Afyon Karahisar salient, four of them, and one cavalry division, in the line, the rest in reserve near Tsai on the Afyon–Konya railway.

The II Turkish Army, under General Sevki Pasha held the central sector of the front stretching from Afyon some forty miles northwards. The I Army, under the ambitious Nureddin Pasha, held the front south of Afyon and had three divisions in reserve down the Afyon–Konya railway line. Further down the line, at Ak Shehir, was the headquarters of Ismet; still further was the V Cavalry Corps at Ilgin.

Kemal had decided in the early summer on a massive Turkish offensive. He later described the developments of his plans in the great speech he delivered in 1927 to the Turkish Assembly: how in the early stages he had told only Fevzi, the Chief of General Staff, Kiazim, the Minister of National Defence, and Ismet:

We considered the right solution to be to concentrate our main forces south of the enemy's right wing, which was in the Afyon Karahisar area between Akar Tsai and Tulu Punar. The enemy's most important and most vulnerable position was there. If we attacked from this flank there was the chance of a swift and decisive result.[2]

In great secrecy the Turkish plan of attack was developed by Ismet and Fevzi Pashas. It was in essence simple. The II Army, reduced to skeletal form, would hold the Greek troops on the central front between Eski Shehir and Afyon Karahisar. It would try to cut the communications between Eski Shehir and Afyon, thus isolating the southern army group. Meanwhile, the I Army, reinforced with divisions from elsewhere, would launch the Turks' main thrust along the southern flank of the Greek line south of Afyon Karahisar. The main offensive would be supported by cavalry attacks on the Greek communications.

Kemal left Ankara on the evening of 23 July for Ak Shehir, where the Headquarters of the western front had been established. There he and Fevzi decided to set things moving so as to be ready by mid-August.

On the pretext of attending a football match [said Kemal in the dry narrative of his speech] we summoned the Army, and some Corps commanders to Ak Shehir. The night of 28–29 July I exchanged views with them on the attack and after a further consultation with the Chief of Staff and the Commander of the Western Front, we arranged the details of the attack. Kiazim Pasha, the Minister of National Defence ... also came to Ak Shehir on the afternoon of 1 August. We arranged the measures to be taken by the Ministry to complete the army's preparations. When I had ordered these preparations to be carried out and the attack to be pushed on rapidly I returned to Ankara.[3]

In Ankara Kemal informed his Cabinet of the plans for an offensive. On 13 August Fevzi left Ankara for the front. Kemal's own departure a few days later was shrouded in the utmost secrecy. Plans for systematic deception of the outside world were put into operation. The papers announced that he had given tea to his mother. In fact he had left Ankara by night and driven by car across the salt desert for the front.

At Ak Shehir Kemal gave the go-ahead for the orders of battle and conferred with his commanders. For some time troops had been secretly brought down from other parts of the front to the Afyon sector. Now these troops moved into their new positions under cover of darkness, resting by day in the villages or under the camouflage of trees. In an attempt to deceive the Greeks, road repairs were simulated in various parts of the front zone besides being carried out where they were needed. On 24 August Kemal moved his quarters near to the front. All was now ready.

In the hour before dawn on 26th August, the Gazi [Kemal] rode slowly up the dark rounded hill of Koje Tepe, from which he was to direct the battle. . . . He was silent and evidently wrapped in thought. Continually he looked eastwards towards the horizon, where presently a slight red glow announced the rising of the sun above the Anatolian plateau. Then with a thunderous roar the artillery barrage began.[4]

The Turkish guns pounded at the Greek positions along the ridges and flanks of Akar Dag. From his lookout point on Koja Tepe, Kemal with Fevzi and Ismet looked northwards at the line of hilltops, each strongly fortified, which the Turkish infantry were to take by assault. Then under a pall of smoke from the artillery, the Turkish infantry went into battle.

It was a shattering and bloody assault. The Turks had achieved by their stealthy formations over the past days a massive local superiority. Now they stormed uphill, tough Anatolian foot soldiers, in the face of deadly Greek fire all along a twenty-five-mile front from Sinan Pasha to the railway east of Afyon. The first points of the front to crumble were Kamelar in the sector of the 4th Division, lost after a fierce struggle, and Tilki Kiri Bel, abandoned without resistance by the 1st Company of the 49th Regiment, 1st Division at 8 a.m. The 49th was a Regiment plagued by disciplinary troubles, and well known to be unreliable. It was unfortunate that it held this key section of the front. Two communist sergeants were said to have given the slogan for flight and encouraged the men to abandon their positions as soon as the attack began.[5]

All along the front the battle raged all day. Except by the 49th, ground was not given easily. The names of hills and defensive positions toll like bells for the Greek army in Asia Minor – the 'Wooded Hilltop' in the 5th Division sector; Hasan Bel; 'Black Rock' and 'Saw-toothed Rock' in the Kaletzik sector. Each left its heaps of broken dead bodies on its flanks as witness to a Turkish breakthrough, a Greek counterattack. By the evening of 26 August, the situation was not yet lost. Tilki Kiri Bel had been retaken by the 1st Division, reinforced by the 7th. Near by, the Turks had not succeeded in breaking through at Hasan Bel, and the commander of the 57th Division, Resat, committed suicide to expiate his failure to capture this point as swiftly as he had promised Kemal.

But the position was very serious. During the day the Turkish cavalry had threaded through the Greek lines between Sinan Pasha and Elvan Pasha, across rough and inaccessible country which the Greeks considered impregnable and left only tenuously guarded. Pushing through this gap, a small detachment of cavalry descended on the railway station at Koutsoukioi, and cut the telephone and telegraph communications between Afyon and Tulu Punar, on which the Greek I Corps depended. While the Turkish cavalry was making trouble behind the Greek lines, Trikoupis and the I Corps became aware that reinforcements were moving into the Turkish lines and that they could not resist a sustained attack of the same weight as they had experienced that day.

During the evening there arrived the first of a series of orders from G.H.Q. in Smyrna which successively reflected less and less of the reality of the situation on the ground. I Corps was ordered to counterattack and recapture the lost positions. II Corps was to attack towards Tsai. III Corps in the north was to collect four infantry regiments and send them to the aid of the southern group. But such a movement would require days, and the situation demanded flexible and rapid response. Trikoupis had asked II Corps to send down the 9th Division to Afyon as reinforcement. In view of G.H.Q.'s order, Digenis now declined to send the division, but sent only the 26th Infantry Regiment, which together with Plastiras's 5/42 Regiment of Evzones of the 13th Division was thrown into the line in support of the battered 4th Division. The 7th Division of II Corps had been taken out of its positions in reserve north-west of Afyon and thrown in to support the 1st Division. With these inadequate reactions to the Turkish assault, the situation had just been held through 26 August.

Early in the morning of the 27th the assault began again, concentrating most powerfully on the 4th Division. After a hard struggle the Turks overran the Saw-toothed Rock and the defensive positions at Kamelar. At about midday, as the Turks drove through the opening gap in the Kaletzik sector of the front, and threatened to push on northwards, isolating Afyon and the eastwards sections of the 4th Division and the 12th Division, Trikoupis took the difficult decision to abandon his positions and retire to a new line west of Afyon Karahisar. Under heavy pressure, and covered by the 26th and 5/42 Evzones, I Corps retreated, sweeping along with it a crowd of Armenians and Greeks, uprooted humanity which knew it could not stay. II Corps also retired, whole and intact, to take up its new positions on the left of Trikoupis's I Corps. Throughout, Digenis's troops had been wasted.

It was noon on 27 August when the Greek first line of defence was abandoned. Exhaustion was already setting in, and ammunition was running low. Communications were unreliable; apart from the interruption to I Corps's telegraphic communications on 26 August, at about midday on 27th the Corps lost wireless contact with G.H.Q. and with some of its own divisions. In these circumstances the best decision would probably have been to order and execute a rapid and comprehensive retreat of the entire southern group of the army onto the next fortified line of defence, that of Touklou Tepe-Tulu Punar some thirty miles west of Afyon. This was a defensible line lying athwart the railway. Retreat still further on to Ushak might also have enabled the southern group to reassemble, reestablish communications with Smyrna and take a grip on the situation. But such bold decisions were impossible. A fighting retreat, under pressure, was inherent in the Greek organization and structure of command.

When Trikoupis and the first batch of his retreating troops reached Bair-Giol he received, via II Army Corps, the latest order from Smyrna. The 9th Division was at last put under his direct command, and he was ordered to hold his positions on Akar Dag while the II Army Corps launched a counterattack towards Tsai. It was evident that the G.H.Q.'s picture of the situation was so distorted and so far from reflecting the confusion of the battle that the commanders in the field would have to rely on their own judgement.

The Greeks now suffered a blow which made it impossible for them to re-form on a new defensive line and hold the Turkish offensive. The 1st and 7th Divisions under General Frangou had been fighting hard all day to hold their positions on Akar Dag. Frangou had not received Trikoupis's order to retreat. In the afternoon, however, recognizing that the position was untenable he gave the order to retire and take up new positions on the heights of Bal Mahmout. The retreat took place in considerable confusion.

In the course of the general retreat the main body of the I Army Corps, under Trikoupis, and the subsidiary body consisting of Frangou's 1st and 7th Divisions lost contact with each other.

The most exposed line of the retreat was followed by the 4th Division under Dimaras, which had been based on the town of Afyon at the point of the salient. The 26th Infantry Regiment under Lt.-Col. Kaliagakis, and Plastiras's detachment of the 13th Division successfully held the heights due west of Afyon while the 4th Division retired more or less intact north-westwards up the railway line. As night fell these two rearguard groups themselves retired, taking up new positions protecting the southern flank of the division. Kaliagakis's men established themselves on the heights at Inas. Plastiras's group, finding their appointed position already occupied by another regiment (which soon vacated it) pressed on westwards towards Bal Mahmout, leaving an important gap in the defences of the retiring army. This was a mistake, and – for Plastiras was a notedly courageous figure – a significant one. For it marked the beginning of a process whereby field officers, losing confidence not only in G.H.Q. but also in their Corps and Divisional commanders, began to take matters into their own hands, feeling that their ultimate responsibility lay to their men and themselves and not to an inefficient and remote authority.

While the retreat was in full swing General Trikoupis had telegraphed to G.H.Q. in Smyrna his latest report on the situation, and recommended that I and II Corps should now be brought under a single command and retire to the Tulu Punar line. Late on 27 August he gave the necessary orders to I Corps to start the retreat to Tulu Punar at dawn, the southern flank being protected by the 1st and 7th Divisions on the heights of Bal Mahmout. This order never reached these two divisions, and from this point on no communication was possible between Trikoupis and Frangou. The Turks had succeeded in driving a wedge into the Greek southern army at a vital point. Frangou and his two divisions, hugging the railway, trekked westwards towards Smyrna and Old Greece, while the main body of I Corps under Trikoupis was pushed deeper and deeper into the Anatolian hills, trying desperately and with ever remoter chances of success to break out and fight their way through to join their comrades.

27 August was crowned by one final irony – yet another order from G.H.Q. to the effect that Trikoupis should recapture the lost positions, and only in absolute necessity retire to the line Resil Tepe–Akar Dag. II Corps was once again to counterattack.

It was too late. Akar Dag was now lost, and the Greek army irreversibly in retreat.

As dawn broke on 28 August, the weather still holding fair, the Greeks pushed their weary bodies into motion again. They had been fighting and marching now for forty-eight hours. Already the cohesion of their formations was to a large extent destroyed. Instead of an army, they were scattered groups of soldiers, some frightened and anxious to run, others held together by dynamic commanders or a sense of necessity in this hostile environment. Worse was soon to come.

Marching down the railway line in the early morning, aiming for Koutsoukioi, the 4th Division was suddenly attacked by enemy infantry and cavalry at a point north of Bal Mahmout. Afterwards, Plastiras was blamed for having left open the gap through which the attacking Turkish troops were able to pass. The 4th Division was thrown into confusion and split in two. The 8th and 11th Infantry Regiments left the road and became enmeshed in the defiles and gullies of Resil Tepe. The rest of the Division, under its commander Dimaras, proceeded towards Oloutzak.

Trikoupis was utterly isolated from the outside world. He had lost his wireless, and was far from the telegraph lines. From the sound of distant gunfire, and from his own military instinct, Trikoupis could guess that his 'lost' divisions under Frangou were retiring onto Tulu Punar. The only hope for I Corps was to slip out westwards before a Turkish pincer movement could close on them, or to break out fighting and rejoin Frangou's group at Tulu Punar, reestablishing a defensive line there which could be supplied up the railway from Smyrna. Thus Trikoupis set his men on the march again on 29 August.

As they started westward, the 12th, 5th and 9th Divisions ran into severe Turkish fire. The bulk of the Turkish offensive forces were concentrated on Trikoupis's group, leaving Frangou to proceed relatively undisturbed to Tulu Punar. All that afternoon Trikoupis's men fought their way westwards between Tsat Kouyiou and the Pursak springs. Trikoupis hoped for the intervention of Frangou's divisions. When no help came, realizing that the direct way through to Tulu Punar was blocked, he ordered his troops to try to get through to Tulu by a skirting movement northwards and then westwards of the 12th and 5th

Divisions, while the 9th and 13th held the southern flank. Though 9th Division fought its way to within five miles of Tulu Punar, a position from which the Frangou group was tantalizingly close, it could not close the gap in the face of the Turkish firepower.

After nightfall on 29 August Trikoupis gave orders for another attempt to break through, not knowing that Tulu Punar had now been vacated by Frangou and was in enemy hands. The 5th, 12th and 13th Divisions, covered by the 4th and 9th, were to press on to Salkioi and thence down the main road to the town.

On 28 August, the Frangou group, together with various semi-independent detachments, including Plastiras's 5/42 Evzones, pressed on westwards down the line of the railway, losing all contact with Trikoupis's group, until in the early hours of 29 August they reached Tulu Punar. Here was a possible point of renewed resistance. The town was strongly fortified, and well supplied from Smyrna via Ushak.

As Trikoupis's 9th Division fought its way towards Tulu Punar from the north east, their desperate battle on the flanks of Resil Tepe became visible to the Greeks in Tulu Punar. Plastiras from his look-out point on the hill Hasan Tepe on the very left of the line saw what was happening and reported. Frangou ordered an immediate supporting attack by the 7th Division. But before the attack could be launched, the 1/38 Regiment of Evzones holding the strongpoint of Touklou Tepe on the right of the Greek line were routed by a Turkish attack and fled westwards sweeping away with them the 4th Infantry Regiment. The whole right wing of the Frangou group was put in danger. Action in support of Trikoupis was abandoned. Instead, Frangou ordered the evacuation of Tulu Punar and a resumption of the retreat. Perhaps the last real chance of resistance was gone. No better defensive position was likely to present itself. Frangou's group trekked west towards Ushak, Alashehir, Smyrna and the sea.

Under cover of darkness and in weary disorder the Trikoupis group marched to Salkioi. Passing through the village in the early morning of 30 August the 12th Division pushed on down the public road towards Tulu Punar. At about 7 o'clock the heavy Turkish artillery opened up from the heights of Arsanlar over-looking the road. As the 12th Division prepared to break through this artillery fire, Turkish columns reached Salkioi from the east.

The remainder of the Trikoupis group, shambling and hungry, escaped from Salkioi on the road westwards up a valley to the little village of Ali Vera.

Trikoupis now accepted that the road to Tulu Punar was blocked, and ordered a general retreat through Ali Vera to Banaz. By now his group had lost all contact with the main east–west arteries and was deep in the heart of the hill country. The Banaz road was a narrow, rough track leading across the northern flanks of the mountain Murad Dag. Along with the troops went a crowd of refugees and irregulars, who slowed the progress of the retreat.

As the Greek divisions entered the little plain below Ali Vera, they came under fire from Turkish troops on the wooded heights above the plain to the north. Soon the Greeks were under attack from south and east as well. A trap was closing. Only the road westward remained open.

Throughout the afternoon of 30 August the Greek divisions in the Ali Vera valley endured the withering fire of the Turkish artillery as they waited for nightfall to escape to the west, hoping that the Turks would not have time to close the gap. As night fell, the road was still open. The Greeks began to move out of the valley. The main body escaped, and marched through the night towards Banaz. A large group, with the 4th Division Commander Dimaras, lost their way and blundered from one side to the other of the valley without finding the exit, surrendering on the morning of 1 September to the Turks.

All through 31 August the main group of survivors stumbled on as far as the village of Oyoutzouk before snatching a little rest. Here once more the party lost a splinter group. The greater part of the 9th Division under Colonel Gardikas pushed on westwards, and eventually struck the main Gediz–Ushak road, where they made contact with the 5th Division. The two Divisions, a disorganized mass some 25,000 strong, met the main Frangou group on 1 September.

Only some 5,000 utterly weary men now remained of the I and II Army Corps under Trikoupis. Rounding the northern flank of Murad Dag they wheeled south towards Ushak, and yet another hope of contact with fellow Greek troops, supplies, and communications with Smyrna. The men had been fighting and marching in difficult country under pressure for almost a week, with only short and dangerous rests. Their only food was fruit and vegetables snatched from the roadside. For four days they had had no contact with the outside world.

At about noon on 2 September, as the column approached Ushak, they realized with despair that the town had fallen to the Turks. Trikoupis decided to get his men off the road where they could take up defensive positions and rest until nightfall, before trying to retire on to a new line south of Ushak. The column took up positions on Hill 1155, south of Karatza Hisar.

During the afternoon the column's observers reported the approach of Turkish cavalry, and, further away, a large force of Turkish infantry. The Greek positions soon came under fire. Trikoupis ordered Colonel Kaibalis, commanding the 13th Division, to take the necessary measures. But soon the Colonel came back to his commander with the report that the reserve company whom he had ordered into the front line of defence had refused to move, shouting that they had not enough rounds of ammunition left and that it was a useless sacrifice of lives.

Suddenly, nearby, a bugle was heard sounding the Cease Fire – as if it were the knell of Greece's presence in Asia Minor – and some of those holding the defensive line to the south abandoned their positions. The enemy was now only 600 metres away.

The ordinary soldier had had enough. Trikoupis, a career officer imbued with the nationalist pride of the Greek army of the Balkan wars, hurried up to the offending bugler and ordered him to sound the Open Fire. It was too late. Neither this sound, nor arguments, appeals to honour, threats, had effect. Commanders of other units came in with the news that the contagion had spread. When 31st Division artillery, at Trikoupis's orders, prepared for action, the men in the vicinity surrounded the gunners and threatened to kill them if they provoked the Turks further by opening fire.

In such a fearful situation [wrote Trikoupis later] with a heavy heart I ordered the destruction of the artillery and machine guns, and this took place. Then I was given signed declarations by the nearby officers about the attitude of the men ... and finally, when I saw that the Turkish lancers had almost reached our lines, and that the men would be slaughtered without resistance, I agreed to the raising of the white flag.[6]

With Trikoupis and his men taken prisoner, and the Turks pressing close behind, the retreat of most of the surviving divisions became a rout. The men were past caring for military discipline or even self-defence. Many threw away their rifles for the sake of unencumbered speed of movement. In their panic fear the troops burned and ravaged what lay in their path.

On 1 September Frangou's scattered bodies of men were retreating from Kapaklar through Ushak, which was evacuated in the morning. Colonel Stylianos Gonatas, commanding the 2nd Division which brought up the rear of the retreat, saw the last trains leaving the town at 11 o'clock, and an 'endless line of vehicles moving parallel with the railway on the metalled road which runs alongside the railway line'. Those which would not start were burned.

Major Panagakos, a staff officer sent up the line from G.H.Q. for liaison duties, sent back a series of reports on the dissolution of the army. On 1 September, 'I came on the 5th Division and men of various other divisions at the 12th kilometre of the Ushak-Gediz road. They were all mixed up in one column. There followed the 9th Division and men of various units and formations. The state of the men in general exceptionally poor.' Later that day he reported, 'The few units which now make up the skeleton of the army are dissolving one after the other. Throughout the whole valley a rabble is moving westwards with no thought in mind but to get to Smyrna. Hunger will complete the catastrophe.'[7]

For the rearguard under Gonatas, the pattern was forced marches by night, lit by moonlight, and defensive stands by day. In every town and village could be seen the signs of panic and dissolution and breakdown of morale. The men hoped to find food, trains to carry the wounded down the line to Smyrna, at the very least a telephone line to link them with the Staff in Smyrna. All they found was smouldering or flaming ruins of houses and railway stations.

General Frangou, trying to create order out of the chaos of a retreating army, borrowed most of the 2nd Division staff from Gonatas, leaving him with only one officer. Gonatas himself reported to G.H.Q. that the army lacked the staff and the communications to restore the situation:

There are no more heavy artillery and Skodas. Only four batteries of field artillery are still working. The men do not seem prepared to undertake new struggles but desire the situation to be brought to an end somehow. The continuous leakage of men to Smyrna, which you are aware of, is reducing day by day the strength and morale of those who remain.[8]

So passed 2 September. After an all night march the remnants of the army, pursued by the Turkish 1st Army, reached the line east of Alashehir on which Frangou had been ordered to make a stand. The positions were not held. On 4 September Alashehir too was abandoned. As Gonatas and his men passed through, the town was burning from one end to the other. The mad frenzy of destruction and plunder had seized the people. From time to time great explosions from the stores of ammunition lit up the sky. The communist leader Stavridis, in the 31st Infantry Regiment under Mavroskotis, passed through the town by the burning railway station: 'Many corpses, which smelled horrible in the fire and smoke. Who was to care what corpses they were? We passed through hurried, stooping, like ghosts, amid the smoke.'[9]

On 5 September the retreat continued from Alashehir west to Salihli:

A long, endless column [wrote Gonatas]. All the divisions are moving virtually on the same road, on the railway track and on either side of it, and they need a foreguard, rearguard and flank detachments to guard the flanks, because *chettés* and enemy cavalry are in a position to surprise the columns and sow panic, to break up the baggage trains and take them prisoner. The feet of most of the men are swollen from the long march. The sick and those with bad feet fall by the side of the roads and ask the rest to take them. But no one pays any attention, it is each man for himself now. Many go to sleep and then when they wake up follow whichever unit is passing. When we go past we wake them up and shout to them that there are no more detachments behind us and that if they stay there they will be taken prisoner, that is if they are not killed. The column moved very slowly.... To the other hardships was added lack of food. If there had not been grapes on the vines at that period, the army could not have been kept going.[10]

Salihli too was burning as the Greek rearguard marched through. Here Turkish cavalry under Fahreddin caught up with the Greeks. They had ridden hard for 50 kilometres, ditching their saddles and spare baggage in order to make speed. Their arrival inspired panic in the milling Greeks in Salihli, many of whom fled to the mountains. Plastiras's detachment drove away the Turkish troops and reopened the road to Smyrna. As the

Greek columns trekked on towards Menemen, burning the railway bridges as they went, Fahreddin and his troops saw flames light up the sky above Manisa.

The mass of retreating troops reached Kassaba in the evening of 6 September, the rearguard defended by the 2nd Division, the Cavalry Division and the few other detachments which retained their discipline. The next day the retreat continued undisturbed by the enemy to Nymphaion. The troops had now reached the line which had long been recognized as the last defence of Smyrna. The city itself was only some 25 kilometres away. But on the afternoon of 8 September the order came through that the retreat should continue throughout the night and that the thought of defence of Smyrna should be abandoned. The army was to retire on the metalled road from Nymphaion, and on approaching Smyrna to swing round the town on the southward side and enter the peninsula which led to Chesme opposite the island of Chios. Thus on 9 September the frightened inhabitants of Smyrna saw the main Greek columns, their only protection against the Turks, bypass the city and trudge towards the sea and their homes in Old Greece.

During the early trials of the Southern Army Group, the III Army Corps to the north, holding the front from the Sea of Marmara to Eski Shehir, had remained unscathed. The Turkish reinforcement of the southern sector had left the northern sector thinly manned and incapable of breaking through III Corps's defences. From 26 August until 2 September the Corps held its positions. Only the 'Independent Division' under Nikolaos Theotokis, a cousin of the War Minister, had been detached from the Seyit Gazi sector on the right of the III Corps front to go to the aid of Trikoupis and the Southern Group. On 2 September, when Trikoupis was taken prisoner and Frangou's divisions had almost reached Ushak, it was at last recognized that III Corps must retire.

The line of retreat for the Corps lay north-westward through Bursa to the Sea of Marmara, where Greek command of the sea would allow evacuation from Mudania and Panderma to Eastern Thrace. As the Greeks withdrew the Christian populations too began to crowd towards the coast. Under pressure from the Turks, the retreat proceeded in order but for the 11th Division under Colonel Kladas. A gap opened up between this division and its neighbour the 10th. Unwisely taking a slow and difficult route through the mountains to Mudania, the 11th became isolated and enmeshed in the hills, lost its cohesion under Turkish pressure, and surrendered to the Turks.

The rest of the III Corps, continuing its march westwards to Panderma, successfully embarked, holding off the incursions of Turkish troops, and by 19 September the last Greek fighting troops had left the soil of Asia Minor. There remained only the dead and the many thousands of prisoners.

The Independent Division, under Colonel Theotokis, marching south from Seyit Gazi on 28 August to the relief of Trikoupis, reached Kutahya to find it already taken by the Turks. The swiftness of the dissolution of the southern front meant that aid to them was too late. Very soon the Division was ordered by G.H.Q. to fend for itself. The I and II Corps were in full retreat towards Philadelphia. The Independent Division itself was almost surrounded by Turkish forces. But it succeeded in fighting its way out through a gap at Gediz and from there through Simav and Bergama to Dikeli on the coast. There the Division helped to evacuate the Greek and Armenian refugees who had crowded down to the beach before itself embarking, with its equipment intact, for eastern Thrace. Of all the Greek formations in Asia Minor, the Independent Division best preserved its cohesion and discipline during its lonely march to the sea.

On 28 August in Smyrna a brief communiqué had announced the evacuation of Afyon Karahisar. Rumours of disaster sped from mouth to mouth. Anxious visitors to the G.H.Q. were met with worried faces of staff officers who themselves could not assess the extent of the catastrophe. Hatzianestis remained in Smyrna; at this stage to set off for the front would be useless. Stergiadis visited him to discover the true situation, and then telegraphed to Athens that in view of the critical situation of the army the War Minister should come to Smyrna immediately. On 1 September Theotokis and Stratos arrived on the *Aigion* and consulted at length with Hatzianestis and his staff. No encouraging statement was issued. The two ministers sailed back to Piraeus.

On 1 September Stergiadis dispatched a circular telegram to all his provincial representatives instructing them to collect their archives and papers together and prepare in absolute secrecy to leave their posts and retire to Smyrna. The representative at Kios, the little port on the Marmara in an area where brutalities of Turks against Greeks and Greeks against Turks had been commonplace, replied that the Greek population was panic-stricken and requested instructions. The gist of the High Commission's reply was that the provincial representatives must encourage the Greek populations to stay in their homes.[11] And throughout the days which followed, the High Commission, reflecting the temperament of Stergiadis, attended coldly and a trifle inhumanly to the winding-up of its own business and the evacuation of its archives. The unfolding human tragedy seems to have been of such dimensions as to overwhelm the Greek bureaucracy.

The tension steadily increased in the city of Smyrna. Those trains which rolled into the railway stations from up country brought wounded soldiers with grim accounts of the crumbling of the Greek front, and frightened refugees clutching what they had been able to carry with them. From villages and towns in the hinterland the Greeks began to crowd the roads down to Smyrna, knowing in their bones that the Greek occupation was at an end.

Knowing that the Turks were coming, each prepared as best he could. The Powers sent ships to protect their own. Admiral Sir Osmond de Beauvoir Brock, in the *Iron Duke*, presided as it were from the harbour, supported by the *George V, Cardiff* and *Tumult*. French, Italian and American ships were also there. The Asia Minor National Defence League, in a despairing gesture, started to issue rifles to the citizenry, hoping still to join with sound sections of the retreating army in defending the city and its surroundings. It was too late. The army would not stop for any cause.

The Metropolitan Chrysostom, anxious for the fate of his flock, sent a despairing message from himself and his Armenian colleague to the Archbishop of Canterbury appealing to him to use his influence with the British Cabinet to help keep Kemal out of the city. The Rev. Charles Dobson, the British chaplain entrusted with this message, took it to Admiral Brock, who was blandly complacent, saying that he did not expect a disorderly occupation by the Turks, but would give protection to those who needed it if disorder ensued. The Metropolitan was unimpressed by these assurances.[12]

The British, French, Italian and U.S. consuls visited Hatzi-

anestis to ask what measures he could take to prevent violence
and disorder on the part of the demoralized Greek troops during
their retreat. Hatzianestis had not lost his coolness. He talked of
a well-disciplined regiment from Thrace which he was expecting
at any moment, and which he would throw out as a screen to
prevent straggling bands from entering the city. Skarlatos's
Adrianople Division arrived by ship on 5 September. To the
surprise of the Smyrniots, many of the men did not disembark,
and those that did were useless to stem the tide of anarchy. The
contagion of defeatism and broken morale had crossed the
water and infected these troops from Thrace with the spirit of
mutiny.

Hatzianestis had failed. On 4 September the Greek Government appointed General Trikoupis to command the Greek army
in Asia Minor. The appointment was a good one, had it been
made in time. But Trikoupis was in the hands of the Turks: it
was said that he learned of his appointment from Kemal himself; the story whether true or not was at any rate *ben trovato*.
When the news of Trikoupis's capture came through from the
front the Government appointed General George Polymenakos
to the command. He took over the job as the southern army were
falling back onto the narrow Erythrai peninsula with but one
thought – to evacuate Asia Minor and return home.

As the black news, distorted by rumour, continued to arrive
from the interior, the trickle of refugees had swelled to a steady
stream, confirming by their arrival the knowledge of all that this
was the end of the Greek presence in Asia Minor. The refugees
came by their thousands into Smyrna and all the coastal towns.
They slept in the churches, in schools, in the American charitable
foundations, mission schools and Y.M.C.A., and in the street.
Caiques, loaded with the refugees and their belongings, plied
between the Turkish coasts and the Greek islands. George
Horton, the American Consul, noticed a curious feature of the
scene – the number of sick and disabled brought to light by the
panic. Many of the refugees were carrying sick upon their
shoulders.[13]

Officers packed off their families to the islands. The clerks of
the National Bank bought their tickets for Piraeus and the Bank
closed its doors. Under Stergiadis's supervision, section by section
of the High Commission was neatly wound up and evacuated.
The Greek state in Asia Minor was being dismantled. The front

seemed to be forgotten. The air was rancorous with defeatism and despair.

A British eye-witness described the refugee trains as 'a wonderful sight: passengers standing all along the footplates and others swarming on the roof. In the carriages the passengers were so crowded that dead bodies were passed out at stations on their way to Smyrna.' [14] After the refugees came those parts of the army which did not bypass the city:

Then the defeated, dusty, ragged Greek soldiers began to arrive, looking straight ahead, like men walking in their sleep. . . . In a never ending stream they poured through the town toward the point on the coast to which the Greek fleet had withdrawn. Silently as ghosts they went, looking neither to the right nor the left. From time to time some soldier, his strength entirely spent, collapsed on the sidewalk, or by a door. . . . And now at last we heard that the Turks were moving on the town. [15]

The Metropolitan Archbishop Chrysostom had been busy comforting and helping to feed and shelter his flock, seeking aid from the allied representatives, writing to those such as the Ecumenical Patriarch who might help. Now on 7 September he wrote to Venizelos, his last letter, heavy with the sense of the impending destruction of a part of the living tissue of Hellenism:

Dear friend and brother, Eleftherios Venizelos,
The great moment for a great gesture by you has come. Hellenism in Asia Minor, the Greek state and the entire Greek Nation are descending now to a Hell from which no power will be able to raise them up and save them.

For this unimaginable catastrophe it is of course your political and personal enemies who bear the blame; but you too bear a great weight of responsibility for two of your actions.

First because you sent to Asia Minor as High Commissioner an utterly deranged egotist. Secondly because before you had completed your work and put the crown and seal on the unimaginably fine and magnificent creation you had built up, the establishment of the foundations of the most glorious Byzantine Empire, you had the unfortunate and guilty inspiration to order elections on the very eve of your entry to Constantinople and the occupation of it by the Greek army in the implementation of the Treaty of Sèvres – now alas for ever destroyed.

But what is done is done!

There is still time though, if not to save the Treaty of Sèvres, at least to save the whole Greek Nation from destruction through the

loss not only of Asia Minor but also of Thrace and perhaps even
Macedonia. ... I have judged it necessary above all out of the flames
of catastrophe in which the Greek people of Asia Minor are suffering
– and it is a real question whether when Your Excellency reads this
letter of mine we shall still be alive, destined as we are – who knows –
for sacrifice and martyrdom by the inscrutable decrees of divine
providence – to direct this last appeal to you. ...

If in order to save Greece you judged it your duty to initiate the
revolutionary movement of Salonika, do not hesitate now to initiate
a hundred such movements in order to save the whole of Hellenism
everywhere and especially that of Asia Minor and Thrace, which
nourishes such a religious adoration for you. ...

It is not necessary for this Hellenism and these territories with
Constantinople to be united with Greece, because that dream has
been removed from us for at least a hundred years, but hasten to
raise your powerful voice so that these territories may be made an
autonomous Eastern Christian state, even under the sovereignty of
the Sultan, with your noble self as High Commissioner.[16]

Throughout 7 September the milling people on the front
continued to press for a place on the boats which sailed for
Chios and Mitylene. Army headquarters was still issuing passes
to soldiers and their families to sail on requisitioned boats; but
the system of allocation was breaking down. Throughout the
night in the darkness of the streets (the foreign company which
operated the street lights had cut off the supply of light after a
brush with Stergiadis) the sound of oxcarts and soldiers trudging
through the outskirts could be heard.

8 September dawned, and the Greeks crowded down to the
quay once more, as on 15 May 1919 when the Greek army
had first set foot in Asia Minor. All hoped for a ticket on
one of the remaining boats to leave Smyrna. All knew that the
Turks would soon reach the town. As the day passed the Smyrniot
Greeks saw themselves deserted by one after another of the
Greeks from across the water. The Cavalry Division under
General Kallinski rode through, still smart and seemingly untouched by the ravages of war, riding along the front before
swinging westward to Chesme, and witnesses noticed that, like
all the Greek troops, they were staring straight ahead with dead
eyes. General Polymenakos, his first loyalty to the defeated army,
moved himself and his staff from the barracks on shore onto a
Greek warship so as to be ready to move down the peninsula to
Chesme where the bulk of the Greek army was now concentrated.

The higher Greek officials embarked on the *Naxos* with their passes personally signed by Stergiadis. Despite the High Commissioner's orders, some others, including some sick and wounded, succeeded in getting a berth on the *Naxos* thanks to the humane intervention of a naval officer. Only the Samian porter of the High Commission, appropriately named Dimos (as it were Everyman), remained at his post, presiding over the empty, resounding corridors, the doors swinging on their hinges, the darkened halls. One other man remained hidden on shore – the High Commissioner himself.

Throughout the day the great crowd remained on the waterfront, swayed by rumours and alarms that the Turks were coming, watching the stragglers passing through Smyrna. The barracks and military hospitals were now empty. The *Naxos* sailed away, bearing the archives of the Greek occupation and the Athenian civil servants who had served as district commissioners and bureaucrats in Smyrna. By the late afternoon only the Greek and foreign warships and a few foreign merchant ships remained in the harbour, as a comfort to the Christian population. Then as the evening set in the Greek ships raised anchor, and steamed out of the harbour, saluted by the foreign warships. From the French battleships *Ernest Renan* and *Waldeck Rousseau* could be heard across the water the strains of the Greek national anthem, Dionysius Solomos's hymn to freedom. As the *Elli* left Smyrna harbour, the last link with the Greek state was severed. The Greek fleet steamed to Chesme to evacuate the Greek army.

Stergiadis remained as the embodiment of the Greek state in Asia Minor. He had been seen some days before stopping his car at a florist's to buy flowers for a lady. Thereafter he had remained in his house, suffering from the strain of a popular hostility which was now almost palpable. At about 7 in the evening of Friday 8 September a launch chugged across the harbour from the *Iron Duke* and put in at the quay. The door of Stergiadis's house opened, and the High Commissioner himself in his dark suit and gold rimmed spectacles emerged, stick in hand, and hurried across to the launch. A few steps and he was in the boat and smoothly crossing the harbour to the British battleship. The Harmost of Ionia had left his domain and with him the Greek state ceased to exist in Asia Minor. He was never again to set foot on Greek or Turkish soil. Transferred the next day to a Romanian ship, he sailed via Constantinople to Romania, and from there made his way to France, where he lived out his life.

With the departure of the Greek civil and military authorities, the Christians of Smyrna were left to their own resources and the good offices of the Powers. The latter had landed parties of marines to take the place of the departed Greek gendarmes and to protect their own nationals and protégés, their consulates and other properties. The consulates had done what they could for the Levantines who carried passports entitling them to protection. Others had to fend for themselves.

George Horton, the American Consul, called together the leading United States citizens to discuss what could be done. A Provisional Relief Committee was formed on the spot and money collected. The big American companies lent lorries and transport. Stocks of flour were bought, and soon the Committee was feeding the refugees. At Horton's insistence two American destroyers were sent to Smyrna.

On 9 September, everyone knew that the Turks would soon be there. Bertram Thesiger, the Captain of the *George V*, landed early in the morning and went up to the gas works on the outskirts of town near the railway station to see that all was well with the guard of British marines which had been placed there. At the gas works he received an urgent message from the manager of the railway to go and see if he could put a stop to the looting of the railway stores. Walking over to the stores, Thesiger saw in the distance a crowd of Greeks, some armed, looting. Suddenly there was a general scream, a rush of feet, shots were fired, and the cry went up, 'The Turks are coming!' The looters fled. And then there were the Turks, some 400 cavalry, with swords drawn, riding into town.

Thesiger courageously interposed himself between the Turkish cavalry and the retiring Greeks. The Turkish colonel asked him in French who he was. Haltingly, Thesiger explained that the Greek troops had evacuated the town, and that the British force had been landed solely in order to keep order. He suggested that if the Turks went quietly along the front instead of through the back streets, there would be no trouble. A shot rang out and a man near Thesiger fell dead. It seemed as if a Turkish horseman had asked a man for money, and being refused had shot him. Thesiger asked the colonel to leave a patrol to guard the railway stores. This was done. The cavalry then rode on into town, and Thesiger returned to the *Iron Duke* to report.[17]

Witnesses agree on the proper demeanour and the relative order of the Turks' entry into Smyrna at 11 o'clock on 9 September. The British chaplain was on his way to the British Consulate when he first saw them. There was suddenly a lot of screaming, and a woman threw herself on her knees shrieking for protection. The next moment a squad of mounted rifles swept round the corner at an easy gallop. Some held sabres: most carried rifles at the ready across the crupper. They pulled their horses aside to avoid riding down the woman. Amid the trampling of hooves, the shouts and screams, the occasional shots, Dobson still felt a relief that some proper authority had come to take charge. George Horton, coming to the door of his office when he heard the screams, watched the cavalry ride by – 'sturdy looking fellows passing by in perfect order. They appeared to be well-fed and fresh.'[18]

On the evening of the 9th, the looting and killing began, at first sporadically. Shots were heard during the night. The next morning, a Sunday, Dobson went out from the Orthodox Church of St John, which like all the other churches was crammed with terror-stricken refugees in insanitary conditions, and under the protection of a Union Jack toured the streets with a Greek priest. They found many corpses, including five near the Aydin railway station.

The symbols of order existed. Turkish police patrols toured the city. But it soon became clear that the discipline was superficial and confined to the main streets, while in the back streets, Turkish civilians and later Turkish troops were taking their revenge for three years of humiliation by the Greeks.

The story of these days is confused. But there is agreement that one of the causes of the breakdown in order was the imperishable hatred between Armenian and Turk.

On entering the town the Turkish commander had been furnished with lists of Greeks and Armenians compromised by their activities during the Greek occupation. These men were rounded up, court martialled and shot. According to one witness, it was in pursuing Armenians who were said to have registered with the Asia Minor Defence League that Turkish regular soldiers entered the Armenian quarter and, accompanied by irregulars pursuing plunder or private vengeance, gave it over to looting and violence with the bayonet and the knife.[19] The shops in the Armenian quarter were stripped bare. Carts and donkeys loaded with cloths and stuffs trundled out of the quarter. Later, cartloads of corpses were seen by the Americans taking the same route.

The Greeks were cowed; they knew their day was gone. The Armenians were less submissive. They were not prepared to surrender their arms. They resisted arrest and violation, and they even threw bombs. This was to invite a terrible penalty. By the night of the 10th the slaughter of Armenians had become systematic, and involved the Turkish regular army. There were horrible incidents of carnage. Armenians who were gathered in their churches were rounded up and marched away to their death.

The foreign communities naturally suffered less. But there were incidents even here. Colonel Murphy, a retired officer of the Anglo-Indian Medical Service, was stunned by a party of regular Turkish troops in his house in Burnabat and then stood up and shot while attempting to protect his servants from violation. He died during the night at the English nursing home. A Dutch merchant, Oscar de Jongh, and his wife, were shot dead.

Eventually order broke down entirely and something like massacre ensued, as batches of Armenians were rounded up, taken to the Konak and murdered. What made these scenes the more frightful was the impotence – in the case of officials, impotence as a matter of policy – of the foreigners. British marines stood by, deliberately idle, while Turkish troops goaded and chased their Armenian victims into the sea, then coolly shot them as they swam for safety. The consulates did what they could to preserve the inviolability of their soil, but without entire success. The troops were clearly under strict instructions not to interfere with the course of events but to confine themselves to the protection of their nationals' lives and properties.

All this time the refugees had been crowding the quay, cramming the boats and naval lighters. Perhaps some 1,000 to 2,000 in all had lost their lives. But the worst was still to come.

The Archbishop Chrysostom had been tireless in looking after the crowds of frightened refugees in the cathedral church and in using all his powers of persuasion – to little effect – on the foreign representatives to provide some protection for the Christians. Early on the 9th a Turkish policeman called at the Cathedral of St Photeini and asked Chrysostom to accompany him. It was about this time that Nureddin Pasha, the commander of the

Turkish 1st Army and well known to the Greeks from his previous service as nomarch of Smyrna as a ruthless and ambitious officer, arrived to take command in the town. The Greeks in the cathedral became uneasy, but around 5 o'clock the Archbishop returned. He had been taken to the police station to sign a proclamation that the Christians should remain in their homes and surrender all weapons to the Turkish authorities.

That evening a car drove up to the cathedral and the same policeman with two soldiers asked the Archbishop to go with them again. This time Chrysostom, with three elders of the Greek community, was taken to Nureddin Pasha in Government House. Nureddin received the Archbishop in his office, where a few days earlier Hatzianestis had had his headquarters. What passed between the two men will never be precisely known. Legend soon encrusted the encounter and subsequent events. It is probable that Nureddin reproached Chrysostom with his active encouragement of the nationalist Greek cause, and support for the Asia Minor Defence League, calling these treason in view of Chrysostom's Turkish nationality.

The French patrol in the square outside saw Chrysostom leave the building. Nureddin appeared on the balcony, and called to the crowd that Chrysostom was theirs to judge and deal with. The square was crowded with some hundreds of Muslims. They seized the Archbishop and manhandled him to the shop of Ismael, a Levantine barber. Here Chrysostom was dressed in a white barber's coat. The crowd began to strike and revile him. Knives were drawn, and the mob closed in. Before he died, the Archbishop was horribly mutilated. One source relates that a Turcocretan for whom Chrysostom had once done a favour mercifully put an end to his agony with four shots.

On Wednesday 13 September, in the early afternoon, fire broke out in the Armenian quarter, near the American Intercollegiate Institute. It was probably lit, as it was certainly fed, by the Turks.*

* Some suggest that the Armenians themselves in their desperation lit the fire, or that it was kindled accidentally. But what evidence there is points to the Turks. After the destruction of Smyrna, the Rev. Charles Dobson, living in the Malta Lazaretto as a refugee, compared notes with his fellow refugees and found general agreement on Turkish responsibility. See Dobson's evidence in Oeconomos, *The Tragedy of the Christian Near East.*

The American Miss Minnie Mills, dean of the Institute, watched Turks going from house to house with petrol cans, and fire bursting out of the houses immediately afterwards. In a few hours the foreign quarters of the town were in flames. The direction of the wind was such that the Turkish quarter remained unscathed.

As the fire began to spread, refugees and inhabitants crowded down onto the quay. As night fell thousands on thousands were congregated and packed all along the broad promenade between the fine spacious waterfront houses and the seawall. When walls and masonry became intensely hot from the fire nearby, the wooden timbers and frameworks of the Smyrna houses would suddenly catch inside the plaster, and the masonry would crumble away. Thus the fire spread and swept down towards the quay, pushing the people before it.

The time was now come to evacuate the burning city. Horton had collected his colony of about 300 American citizens with their families in the Théâtre de Smyrne on the quay. The cruiser *Simpson* was in the harbour waiting to take them off. A detachment of blue-jackets guarded the theatre. As clouds of smoke began to fill the consulate, and the crowd on the quay increased until its density threatened to leave no way through for the foreign colony, the decision was taken to leave. The Americans boarded ship.

Sir Harry Lamb's British colony too, much larger than the American, had to leave. British guards were landed and placed at each of the piers from which embarkation took place to check the lists of British subjects and not let others through.

Bertram Thesiger, on the *George V*, described the fire as it appeared from the sea:

About 1 a.m. the fire broke through these front houses almost simultaneously. It was a terrifying thing to see even from the distance. There was the most awful scream one could ever imagine. I believe many people were shoved into the sea, simply by the crowds nearest the houses trying to get further away from the fire. ... Many did undoubtedly jump into the sea, from sheer panic. Actually the people on the front were not in danger, had they only known it. The houses burnt out so quickly, and I believe I am right in saying that no person on the front was actually badly burnt. If only they could have stayed still. ...

The C. in C. made a signal to send boats to save as many people as we could. I went in with our boats and made for the place where the fire seemed worst. It was certainly a horrible scene; mothers with their babies, the fire going on over their heads, and many of the bundles of clothes also on fire, and the people all screaming.[20]

Thesiger's boat was rushed and started to capsize. He managed to decant the extra passengers on to a cutter. The boats, loaded down with refugees, left the quay. 'The few hundreds we took off were a mere fleabite compared with the total number.'

The fire raged throughout the night. The ubiquitous journalist, Ward Price of the *Daily Mail*, filed a dramatic dispatch:

What I see as I stand on the deck of the *Iron Duke* is an unbroken wall of fire, two miles long, in which twenty distinct volcanoes of raging flames are throwing up jagged, writhing tongues to a height of a hundred feet. Against this curtain of fire, which blocks out the sky, are silhouetted the towers of the Greek churches, the domes of the mosques, and the flat square roofs of the houses.

All Smyrna's warehouses, business buildings, and European residences, with others behind them, burned like furious torches.

From this intensely glowing mass of yellow, orange and crimson fire pour up thick clotted coils of oily black smoke that hide the moon at its zenith.

The sea glows a deep copper-red, and, worst of all, from the densely packed mob of many thousands of refugees huddled on the narrow quay, between the advancing fiery death behind and the deep water in front, comes continuously such frantic screaming of sheer terror as can be heard miles away.

Added to this there is the frequent roar and crash of exploding ammunition stores, accompanied by the rattle of burning cartridges, which sounds like an intense infantry action.

Picture a constant projection into a red-hot sky of gigantic incandescent balloons, burning oil spots in the Aegean, the air filled with nauseous smell, while parching clouds, cinders and sparks drift across us – and you can have but a glimmering of the scene of appalling and majestic destruction which we are watching.[21]

The Armenian, Greek and 'Frankish' or European quarters were almost entirely destroyed. Only the Jewish and Turkish quarters remained. Among the well-known landmarks of the old city which ceased to exist were the Armenian, French and Greek cathedral churches, the Splendid, Palace and Smyrna Palace Hotels, the French, British, American, Danish and Dutch Consulates, the Sporting and Smyrna Clubs, the Smyrna Theatre, and the fine shops of Frankish Street. With a horrific appropriateness, the fire expressed in symbolic terms the rooting out and destruction of Greek and Armenian Smyrna. Hellenic Smyrna was dead. Christian Smyrna, too, one of the great ancient Christian foundations of Asia Minor, was dead. The phoenix to rise from these ashes was a Turkish Izmir purged of two thousand and more years of history.

For about a week the retreat of the Greek army into the Erythrai peninsula had continued, as stragglers made their way westwards and the troops concentrated in Chesme to await evacuation by the Greek fleet. On 14 September Polymenakos issued detailed orders for the evacuation. A detachment of 1,200 still disciplined men of the 1st Infantry Regiment under Lt.-Col. Odysseus Maroulis, with two batteries of mountain artillery, held the peninsula as the southern group embarked. Finally, at 9 p.m. on the 15th, Maroulis's men, covered by fire from the Greek fleet, marched down to Chesme and themselves embarked. Maroulis himself was last to embark in the small hours of the 16th. Thus the Greek army and fleet sailed away from Asia Minor. There was little pressure on the rearguard. The Turks' attention was now concentrated on Smyrna, the straits and Thrace.

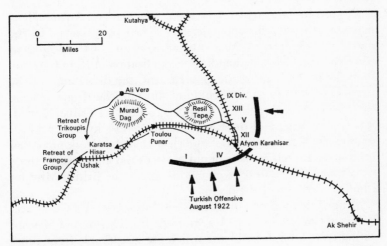

The Turkish Offensive of August 1922

The political and military Constantinist clique
must be neutralized.

Manifesto of the Revolutionary Committee,
17 October 1922

The remains of the Southern Army Group had been taken off by
ship to the islands of Chios and Mitylene, where the more
dynamic of the middle ranking officers took charge. Colonels
Plastiras and Gonatas, both distinguished soldiers, the former of
long-standing Venizelist loyalties, the latter hitherto an un-
political figure, emerged as leaders and spokesmen for the revolutionary and antidynastic tendencies of the younger officers,
who required action to purge the shame of their defeat. With
Captain Phokas of the battleship *Lemnos*, they formed a Revolutionary Committee. Most of the army was in a state of dissolution; it was a moment when a small, determined band of men
could thrust themselves to power.

The revolution reached Athens on 26 September. An aeroplane
flew over the city dropping leaflets signed by Gonatas, in the
name of the officers of the army and navy and of the peoples of
Mitylene and Chios, demanding the abdication of King Constantine, the resignation of the Government, the dissolution of the
Chamber, and the strengthening of the Thracian front. During
the course of the day Prince Nicholas requested a British man-of-
war for the King and the Royal Family, whose lives he claimed
were in danger. When it became clear that the Greek navy had
mutinied – for telegrams sent out to Greek warships, except those
at Constantinople, were receiving no reply – the British Minister
Lindley wired for a British ship.

Meanwhile the *Lemnos* with its revolutionary crew was steam-
ing from Chios across the Aegean to Attica. The journey was not
without the farcical incidents which are inseparable from times
of crisis. The rivalries of the would-be leaders of the revolution
found expression in undignified disputes about whose signature
should be appended to their proclamations. Commander Petro-
poulakis, who commanded the revolutionary fleet, took this

question of precedence so seriously and argued with such neurotic vehemence that he was forcibly confined to his cabin as suffering from a nervous breakdown. During the evening the fleet arrived off Lavrion, site of the ancient silver mines which were the source of ancient Athens's wealth and degradation, near the promontory of Sounion. At 7.30 the Revolutionary Committee led by Gonatas and Plastiras dispatched an ultimatum to the Government in Athens, giving them until 10 p.m. to accept the terms of the revolutionary proclamation. The first of these terms was the removal of the King. Metaxas described the situation in Athens that evening:

> With Souliotis by car to the palace. The King and the Crown Prince. The demands of the revolutionaries. I recommend the King to abdicate quickly to avert further damage to his House. If they form a Government of Venizelists, to abdicate at once. We discuss further the last two years and the politics behind the scenes of the Asia Minor war.[1]

Metaxas returned home very late. Meanwhile the Government had resigned without putting up any struggle; its last act was to send General Papoulas down to Lavrion to assess the strength of the revolution and if possible to negotiate with them. In the early hours Metaxas was called from his bed again:

> The King alone without Ministers, without civil servants, without friends. Telegraphic ultimatum about resignation arrives from the revolutionaries.* We recommend that he should do so quickly. ... Papoulas comes back. The revolutionaries are implacable on the question of the King. Papoulas confirms that the revolutionaries will allow the King freedom to choose where to live within or outside Greece.† The King decides to abdicate. He instructs me to compose the letter and proclamation of abdication. I am very moved. I stay near the King all day.[2]

Thus King and Government bowed to superior force and will. Only the firebrand General Constantinopoulous caused well-justified alarm by continuing his preparations for resistance throughout the morning before giving up. Around midday the King's proclamation of abdication was published, and it was clear that the Revolution had succeeded: 'At 3 in the afternoon the

---

* This was a new ultimatum, giving the King until 5 a.m. to abdicate.
† Gonatas denies this in his *Memoirs*, p. 238. If the revolutionary leaders did say what Papoulas claims, they very soon changed their minds.

new King is sworn in. Then Constantine says farewell to me. I weep. I stayed near him until the last moment. But that does not satisfy me entirely against the feeling that somehow I contributed to his fall.'[3]

Another visitor to Lavrion was Apostolopoulos of the Liberal Party Bureau, one of Venizelos's more observant and mordant informants. He and a colleague were sent by Alexander Karapanos to convey a three-pointed liberal view to the revolutionaries: the abdication of the King, the avoidance of bloodshed, and the appointment of Venizelos as diplomatic representative abroad. Apostolopoulos reported his first impression of the revolution:

I communicated in Lavrion with high and low ranking officers, and asked them various questions, and I came to the conclusion that the revolutionary army landed in Attica without really knowing what it had come to do, and that the revolution is the work of the officers and not the men.

The men are tired out in body and mind, and indifferent about everything, including Constantine. ... The officers on the contrary, some anti-Constantine men of the *Amyna*, others Constantinians until the other day, are at one on the national necessity which has made imperative the departure of King Constantine. This coincidence of views of officers of different origins, and further their very professional interests as officers of a state which risks further diminishment, were the two causes of the revolution. ...

On the morning of the 27th when I was returning from Lavrion I met sections of the army marching towards Athens, and when I informed them that Constantine had abdicated and the revolution had succeeded, I sought in vain for the enthusiasm with which the revolutionary army of 1917 had received similar news.[4]

The main body of troops, 12,000 strong, marched into Athens on the morning of the 28th. 'They looked very tired and worn,' wrote Lindley, 'But I was struck by their organized appearance – officers in the right places, pack animals properly loaded, horses in fair trim and distances kept. They were in no sense a rabble.'[5]

The revolutionary triumvirate of Gonatas, Plastiras, and Captain Phokas assumed authority in Athens, and the work of the revolution began. Gounaris, Theotokis, Protopapadakis, Stratos and Goudas were arrested at once. It was expected that they would be tried by drumhead court martial and shot without ceremony. Lindley, disturbed by the vindictive spirit of the Venizelists, invited Gonatas and Plastiras to meet him and the French Minister.

The meeting took place at 5 p.m. The Colonels confirmed that their intention was to deal summarily with those they considered responsible for the national disaster, and then to declare a general amnesty. Lindley and his French colleague de Marcilly argued vigorously that the ex-ministers should be tried in a civil court after a regular government had been installed. Gonatas and Plastiras were evidently nervous of the reaction of their extreme supporters, but promised to do what the Ministers requested.

Lindley asked what the Committee intended to do about forming a Government; and 'it became clear ... that Colonel Gonatas was well satisfied with the present state of affairs and that he considered himself quite fitted to continue to direct the state.'[6] Lindley recommended them to stick to the army and to leave the business of government to professional politicians. Both colonels laughed heartily at this observation, and suggested that since the whole idea of the revolution was to be friendly to the Entente, it would solve a number of problems if the two ministers were to suggest the members of a government themselves. Gonatas then recited a list of names and asked whether there were any objections to them. And thus a puppet government was formed. The veteran Alexander Zaimis was the natural choice as Prime Minister, but he was abroad. Until his return from Vienna, the job was undertaken by the pleasant Mr Krokidas, whose indiscretions during his short term of office were so great that the Foreign Ministry's censor refused to allow interviews with him to be sent abroad.

Meanwhile the new King, the young George II, had sworn the oath. Within a few days of his accession, four prominent Venizelists had signed a republican manifesto. A number of the revolutionary officers too were for abolishing the monarchy once and for all. The King's chances looked none too good.

The announcements of the Revolutionary Committee confirmed that the persons arrested as responsible for the disaster would remain in detention until the new national assembly decided how they were to be tried. This was an important concession to justice and impartiality. It was unfortunately soon to be reversed. The Committee confirmed too that its first task was the reorganization of the army so as to preserve Greek Thrace.

One of the revolution's first acts was to send a telegram to
Venizelos in Paris asking him to represent them abroad with the
Entente powers. He accepted the request. Venizelos had sympathy for the aims of the revolution, and accepted its necessity
as a short-term measure. But he recognized the total inexperience
of the revolutionaries and the danger this posed. At this time of
national disaster, what was required in Venizelos's view was
patient reconstruction and recovery based on cooperation with
Britain and France. Thus he took up the task of talking to
ministers in Paris and London, preparing a position for Greece
in the peace conference which the allies had arranged to take
place at Lausanne.

Meanwhile, without fuss, the ex-king slipped away. On the
afternoon of 30 September Metaxas went up to Tatoi to say
goodbye:

> I tell him he will not return to his throne but will live happily as
> a private citizen. He accepts all this. He simply wants to live in his
> own home. The queen is very dignified. The King says he has always
> had confidence in me and still has. A moving farewell. . . . So ended
> the reign of Constantine.[7]

The ex-king embarked quietly at Oropus that evening, and left
Greece for the second time as an exile. He died at Palermo the
following year.

From Smyrna, Panderma, Mudania and other vacated towns,
the Turkish troops had marched on with little pause towards
Constantinople and the neutral zone of the straits, still held by
General Harington and his little band of allied troops. It was
their task to keep the Greeks out of Constantinople, the Turks
out of Europe, and to protect the west's 'vital interest' in the freedom of the straits. Kemal was warned not to violate the zone. The
British Cabinet agreed on firm action including the use of force
if necessary to prevent the Turks crossing into Europe. A small
and resolute band consisting of Lloyd George, Balfour, Austen
Chamberlain, Birkenhead, Churchill and Worthington Evans
determined that the moment had come to make a stand.
Churchill issued a bellicose communiqué announcing the
Government's willingness to respond with force to Turkish aggression. It had been decided to ask for the help of the Dominion
governments in defending the freedom of the straits. Owing to a

muddle, Churchill's communiqué was carried in the press, and read by the Dominions, before this appeal had been delivered. Not surprisingly, their reaction was chilly.

These gestures by the British were too much for the French. After all his efforts to bring the Turks to terms, Poincaré was not prepared to go to war with Turkey in defence of an interest which he believed could be better protected through a commonsense mixture of appeasement and strong talking. The French troops were therefore ordered to withdraw their support from Harington. The Italians too decided to remain neutral. The British were left nervously facing the Turkish troops across the barbed wire at the little town of Chanakkale on the Straits, hoping that Kemal would not decide to advance.

In this critical situation, Lord Curzon went to Paris to mend fences with the French. After a painful session in which he was subjected to a series of humiliating insults, it was agreed that Harington and his French colleagues should negotiate with Kemal a limit to the Turks' advance as a preliminary to a peace conference at which the question of Thrace would be open to negotiation. It looked as if the crisis could be averted by diplomacy. But Kemal's troops suddenly advanced on Chanakkale and confronted the British troops across the dividing line.

The curious scenes that ensued were described by an eye-witness:*

The next day the Turkish infantry closed right up to our wire, and all had wire-cutters. They were eventually prevailed to retire 100 yards. That day a very excited Turkish officer came up and said that he was in great trouble as their General was coming to inspect their lines and they had no wire up. Could we possibly lend them some? We said, certainly, if they returned it as soon as the General left. They gave the required promise, and started to put up the wire, without much success. After a short time they came to us again and said could we possibly be so good as to put the wire up for them, as they thought our wire entanglement so good. This we accordingly did.[8]

Not all was comic. There was a real risk of war. But somehow through ten days of crisis and muddle peace was maintained. Harington crossed to Asia and met Ismet at Mudania. The Turks demanded to be allowed to cross into Europe and occupy Eastern

* Bertram Thesiger, Captain of H.M.S. *George V*, which had arrived from Smyrna via Malta to strengthen the defences of the neutral zone.

Thrace at once. The French General Charpy was inclined to agree, but Harington's instructions would not permit it. The wheels of the negotiations were oiled by the ubiquitous Turcophil Franklin Bouillon, known as Boiling Frankie to the British and thoroughly disliked by Lloyd George among many others. Ismet presented an ultimatum: the Turks would attack Chanakkale on 6 October if their demands were not met.

Once more Curzon crossed the Channel to confront Poincaré. By his firm exposure of the British determination to defend the straits with or without French support he won French agreement to a formula whereby the Greeks would withdraw west of the Maritsa river, out of Eastern Thrace, which would be occupied by the allies pending its final assignment to Turkey. Curzon returned to London to the congratulations of the Cabinet.

The armistice agreement reflecting these terms was signed at Mudania by Harington, Charpy, Ismet and Mazarakis on 11 October. In theory the solution was a compromise. In practice the Turks (and the French) won what they wanted, and the Greeks consented to the loss of Eastern Thrace. By their tough and risky stand the British simply gained a few weeks' breathing space before negotiating with the Turks at Lausanne. The country did not appreciate this display of brinkmanship. On Thursday 19 October at a famous meeting in the Carlton Club Bonar Law took the Conservative party out of the wartime coalition government. Lloyd George at once resigned, never to hold office again. The Greeks and the Turks had done for him at last.

A great exodus of Christians had taken place from Anatolia. Ships of many nations put into the ports of Asia Minor to take off the refugee cargoes. Of the able-bodied men, it was only the fortunate who made their escape. The rest, those between the ages of 18 and 45, were rounded up by the Turks in Smyrna and, having been formally declared prisoner by a decree of the Turkish state, were sent into the interior to join labour battalions. For many this spelled death. The women and children were separated from their husbands, crowded onto the ships, and shipped to Piraeus or Salonika. They arrived, as all observers noticed, deprived of will power. It took months in the improvised refugee camps, living under canvas in the precinct of the temple of Zeus in Athens and in the other camps, nourished by

volunteer helpers with soup and bread and blankets, before the
will to make their way returned.

In all some 1,500,000 refugees came to Greece in the aftermath
of the disaster. They came from Smyrna and the other coastal
towns of the western littoral, whose beaches were crowded
with despairing humanity. This was the first wave. Soon there
was added a new torrent of refugees from Eastern Thrace, where
the shadow of the disaster in Asia Minor fell over the Greek
communities.

After the armistice at Mudania, all over Thrace, a primitive,
communal instinct of panic fear told the Greeks that it was time
to leave at once. From the hinterland they trekked down the mud
roads, towards the sea. As early as 17 October, a week after the
armistice, whole villages could be seen without a Christian in
them. Such was the panic that men threw their treasured possessions off their wagons in order to preserve their supply of food.
Pregnant women tramped alongside the oxen in the mud rather
than weigh down the carts. Tiny children toddled by the carts
until they dropped in weariness.

At Silivri, a little port which served some twenty villages, the
refugees sat around their bundles of goods on the beach patiently
waiting for their turn to embark. Three steamers stood offshore
loading up. When the ships were fully loaded, the crowd on the
beach was still swelling with new arrivals. They waited with an
awful resignation, through the night. Further along the coast,
the substantial port of Rodosto was congested with ships taking
off the Greek troops who had garrisoned Eastern Thrace. Here
was the comparative order of a military operation. But it was
the exodus by land which truly took the breath away of those
who witnessed it :

The picture from Lule Burgas beggars description. All the way
northward the road is cumbered with a vast amount of transport,
which is continually being increased by arrivals along the tracks to
the east and west of whole processions from the villages coming
together with a few menfolk under arms to protect the convoy from
bandits and raiders. Unutterable misery is written on every face,
and pain at leaving their homes and farmland steads is apparent
everywhere. But fear of the Turks' approach overwhelms all sense
of personal loss and the terrified people press forward regardless of
fatigue. . . .

It was curious to note that in that long trail signs of bivouacs were few until past Lule Burgas, signifying that the refugees thought it unsafe to stop until they had put many miles beween themselves and Constantinople. Then I saw their columns outspanned, families sleeping beside the wagons and the oxen, which were too tired to feed, and a weary Greek standing sentinel. Further northward, at Baba Eski, the mud tracks ended, and the ox teams were able to make better progress on the rudely metalled road....

From within twenty kilometres of Adrianople the roads presented the amazing spectacle of an absolutely continuous line of refugees, sometimes with wagons two abreast, and all except the aged and infants walking, mostly in bare feet. At places of hopeless congestion – points where the manoeuvring of beasts on uneven ground slowed up this column of agonized humans, numbers pulled out to rest and formed camps as big as those occupied by a brigade of British artillery. The hapless people drank and washed in the dirty streams....

This stream of refugees, I am told, has been moving for three days as it was today. One authority estimates that at least 100,000 refugees have already passed through Adrianople, and to judge from what I saw on the road the stream must continue for another week.[9]

So the Greeks abandoned homes and fields in Eastern Thrace.

Another witness was the young American reporter, Ernest Hemingway, who had crossed Europe to be in at the end of the Greek adventure:

In a never-ending, staggering march the Christian population of Eastern Thrace is jamming the roads towards Macedonia. The main column crossing the Maritza River at Adrianople is twenty miles long. Twenty miles of carts drawn by cows, bullocks and muddy-flanked water buffalo, with exhausted, staggering men, women and children, blankets over their heads, walking blindly along in the rain beside their wordly goods.

The main stream is being swelled from all the back country. They don't know where they are going. They left their farms, villages and ripe, brown fields and joined the main stream of refugees when they heard the Turk was coming. Now they can only keep their places in the ghastly procession while mud-splashed Greek cavalry herd them along like cow-punchers driving steers.

It is a silent procession. Nobody even grunts. It is all they can do to keep moving.[10]

The ancient city of Adrianople was a depressing transit camp, the station a mud-hole crowded with soldiers and with the flotsam and jetsam of a retreating army and a migrating people.

The nightmare scene was lit by kerosene flares. Troops were piling up and there were no trains left to evacuate them. The rain fell and fell, turning the muddy torrent of the Maritza into a brick-red flood a quarter of a mile wide.

With the wretched, numbed Greeks went their animals. Chickens dangled, tied by the legs to the ox-carts. Pigs were strapped to the carts alongside piles of bedding and furniture. In among the procession weaved Greek army mules loaded with stacks of rifles, some camels grunting under their loads, the occasional battered Greek staff car. Hemingway watched the 'eternal procession of humanity' crawl along the great stone road that runs from Adrianople across the valley of the Maritza to Karagatch and then into Western Thrace and Macedonia:

There are 250,000 Christian refugees to be evacuated from Eastern Thrace alone.... Nearly half a million refugees are in Macedonia now. How they are to be fed nobody knows, but in the next month all the Christian world will hear the cry: 'Come over into Macedonia and help us!'

In Athens, Lindley and his colleagues (except de Marcilly, who was now forced by the instructions of the French Government to keep silence) were working for the lives of the accused ministers. The chances of success were never great. The Greeks were almost unanimous in wanting condign punishment, but those whom Lindley met tried to shuffle off the blame on to other shoulders. Politis, foreign minister in the puppet government, claimed that the Revolutionary Committee could not afford to be moderate because of their 'wild men'. The manifesto issued by the Committee on 17 October probably represented the temporary feelings of the majority of officers.

The Revolution cannot rest content with the resignation of Constantine.... Because the political and military Constantinist clique must be neutralized. The Revolution proclaims unity, but unity would be immoral if it signified the forgetting or putting aside of responsibilities and the confusion of innocent and guilty. The exemplary punishment of the enemies of the country is therefore necessary.

On 19 October, the Revolution set up a Commission of Enquiry into the responsibilities for the Asia Minor disaster, presided over by General Pangalos. A ruthless staff officer whose ambition and social background rather than any liberalism had inclined him to the Venizelist cause, he had been in eclipse over the past two years after serving as Chief of Staff to General Paraskevopoulos. As soon as word reached Athens of the revolution in Chios, he had been one of the first to prepare the ground in Athens for a transfer of power to the revolutionaries. But Plastiras and Gonatas had treated him with some coolness. His appointment now was a sign that the hardliners of the revolution were coming to the surface, that the leaders felt the need to placate their extremists, and that the early talk of reconciliation was unlikely to be realized.

On 23 October it was announced in the press that the Ministers would be tried by a special Court Martial. The promise extracted from Gonatas and Plastiras was not to be kept. Lindley therefore visited Politis and warned him of the effect such a trial would have abroad. Politis defended the proposed court martial. When he heard that Prince Andrew and Baltazzis had now been arrested, Lindley intervened again. This time Politis adopted a quite different tone, promising that he would do everything in his power to have the trial postponed, and would resign rather than consent to judicial executions. Diplomatic pressure seemed to be having some effect.

On 10 November Lindley sent Politis a stern official warning. On the same day he was instructed by Lord Curzon to go further and obtain written assurances that no executions would take place. He hastened to read the telegram containing these instructions to Politis, who asked him not to follow them, since if he tackled the Revolutionary Committee now about written assurances and the Committee refused to give them, the Government would be forced to resign; and there was more chance of moderation from the Government than from the Committee. Zaimis gave the same advice. Nevertheless, on 14 November Lindley threatened (obscurely and irrelevantly) that the Protecting Powers would enforce 'the observance of the Greek Constitution of which the two governments are the guarantors' if assurances were not received that the death penalty would not be inflicted.

Two days later Politis made a suggestion that seemed to offer new hope. Would the British Government guarantee that the ex-ministers, if not sentenced to death, would not return to Greece for a certain period of time? Lindley said it was out of the question for the British Government to bind themselves in this way over the future actions of the ministers. Then what if they were to give their word to Lindley, as the representative of the British Government, that they would not return? Lindley promised to report this suggestion to London, but doubted whether it would be entertained. It was; but Lord Curzon's approval arrived too late to be of use.

Meanwhile the implacable General Pangalos had completed his preliminary examination, and presented his findings, which also formed the act of accusation against the accused, to the Court Martial. The document contained a formidable list of alleged offences.[11] In brief, the ministers Gounaris, Protopapa-dakis, Baltazzis, Stratos and Theotokis, together with Xenophon Stratigos and Michael Goudas, and General Hatzianestis, were accused of high treason:

in having voluntarily and by design permitted the incursion of foreign troops, of the Turkish National Army, into the territory of the kingdom, viz. in the region of Asia Minor occupied by Greece, adjudged to her by the Treaty of Sèvres, and in having delivered to the enemy towns, fortresses, a great part of the army and matériel of war of great value, etc.

Though wrapped up in impressive legal terminology the charges can now be seen to have been a necessary cover for an attempt to do two things: purge the national shame incurred by the army in its defeat in Asia Minor; and cow and destroy the royalist anti-Venizelist faction by means of the political assassination of its leaders. The charges could not stand up because no act of deliberate treason was involved. The ex-ministers were being tried for inefficiency, failure, panic, corruption, for the anti-Venizelist excesses of their supporters, and for their political views.

Ironically, the main charge, of surrendering Greek territory, was itself legally unsound, since the territory in question was juridically not Greek.[12] In the detailed charges which followed the ministers were accused of having led Greece to the catastrophe by ignoring the Allies' warning notes about the consequences of the return of King Constantine; of having failed to annexe Northern Epirus and the Dodecanese; of placing inexperienced officers in positions of command and of throwing out the capable and experienced Venizelist officers; of failing to advise King Constantine to abdicate despite the well-known attitude of the Allies towards Greece so long as the King remained on the throne; of ordering the offensive of March 1921 before the partial mobilization in course was complete and thus bringing about Greece's first defeat in the campaign; of ordering the Ankara offensive of summer 1921 contrary to the views of the Commander in Chief, General Papoulas. The accused were further charged with wasting the nation's moneys in indemnities to their political supporters at a time when the army needed equipment and food; of betraying Greece's interests by giving the Allies *carte blanche* in the negotiations during the winter of 1921; of appointing Hatzianestis who was 'well known to everyone including yourselves as an unbalanced element'; of giving the enemy the opportunity to launch his attack through removing troops from Asia Minor to Thrace in order to make their infantile attempt on Constantinople; and of tolerating the formation of a 'secret government' consisting of Prince Nicholas, George Streit, Dousmanis and others, which by 'assassinations, threats and aggression against unarmed citizens, inspired terror in order to preserve their power'. There were other lesser charges. They well reflected the muddle, the inefficiency, the political passion of the last two years, but they did not constitute treason.

On 13 November the Court Martial began to sit in the parliament building, where there was ample room for spectators. The Court consisted of ten officers under General Othonaios as President. They were handpicked for their sympathy with the aims of the revolution, though not all were overt Venizelists. The accused men, Gounaris, Stratos, Protopapadakis, Baltazzis, Hatzianestis, Goudas and Stratigos, sat in a decorous row, their Homburg hats laid on the table before them. For a fortnight, through the mouths of political and military witnesses, and of the accused themselves, the grim tale of political, military and diplomatic muddle and failure was retold.

As always in Greek trials, the preliminaries of the Trial of the Six were taken up with plausible arguments from the defence that the court was incompetent to try the issue – irrelevant to a military court which cared only for revolutionary law. A major who lost his temper and shouted at Gounaris during these disputes was swiftly sentenced to a fortnight in goal for contempt of court. Then the real trial began. Politicians and soldiers were brought into the witness box: General Papoulas, Colonels Passaris and Spyridonos, Major Skylakakis, George Rallis, son of the old politician Dimitrios Rallis who had been the first Prime

Minister of the post-November regime, and the Venizelist politician Rentis for the prosecution; Generals Trilivas, Valettas, Pallis (Papoulas's Chief of Staff), Hexadaktylos (an experienced staff officer in Athens), and the moderate centre politicians Zavitsianos and Demertzis for the defence.

One after the other they told their stories. A wonderfully varied and vivid picture was built up of the actions of the accused over the past three years. The evidence was allowed to range freely over every aspect of the Asia Minor campaign and the political actions of the accused; since the political substance of royalist Gounarism was at stake this was inevitable. But at no time did the witnesses seriously attempt to approach the charge of deliberate high treason. Those politicians that did consider the matter, such as Rallis, Demertzis and Zavitsianos, brushed aside the suggestion of evil intent.

Half way through the trial Gounaris went down with severe typhus fever. He had attended the first few sessions and made a good showing in cross examination. His absence made the proceedings even more hollow than before. The principle that the accused must be allowed to present his defence and face his accusers was violated. The protests of the other accused men and their counsel were brushed aside, and the court ruled that the trial must proceed; that 'essential justice' (a term invented by the revolution to bridge the gap between the law and their own inclinations) would be satisfied by the continuation of the trial on the basis of Gounaris's deposition to the preliminary enquiry. The accused were therefore called on to make their speeches of defence. Hatzianestis spoke first, followed by the ministers. When it came to the turn of Gounaris, after all the rest had spoken, a clerk of the court read out the long pencilled manuscript which Gounaris had written out in the Averoff prison for Pangalos's Commission of Enquiry. It was his last political document.[13]

In the meantime, while the slow-moving drama was played out in the court room, there had been developments outside. The British Minister Lindley had kept up his steady pressure on the regime. On 24 November, as the Trial of the Six was drawing to a close, and no sign had been given that the revolution were prepared to exercise clemency, he warned Politis that if the British view was not accepted within two days, he would have to leave Greece and diplomatic relations between the two countries would be severed.

The Krokidas Cabinet met that afternoon. Politis, who had suffered the brunt of Lindley's interventions and knew they carried the full weight of Lord Curzon's authority, threw in the towel. He was, we know from other evidence, all for severity to the accused; but he was not himself prepared to take the responsibility of it as a member of the Government. His attitude angered Lindley. The nerve of the Krokidas Government now broke, and they resigned. The Revolutionary Committee met that night and decided to take matters formally into their own hands.

Events now moved rapidly and ineluctably towards a climax. The revolutionary leaders were in touch with Venizelos who had arrived in Lausanne to represent Greece at the peace conference. So was Curzon, who became convinced from his talks with Venizelos and from Lindley's dispatches that the Revolution really intended to execute their political opponents. Curzon took this threat so seriously that he not only begged Venizelos to do what he could to avert the executions but also sent Commander Gerald Talbot, who had preserved close contacts with Venizelos, out to Greece to intervene with the Revolutionary Committee.

While Talbot was on his way to Greece, the Trial of the Six was in its closing stages. The revolutionary leaders pressed on with the trial as rapidly as possible. It is probable that they had decided to have done before the arrival of Talbot, of which they had been warned. At all events, the Tribunal sat on Sunday 26 November, as the ministers made their defence. On Monday the new revolutionary Cabinet swore the oath before the young and isolated George II. Gonatas became Prime Minister, Pangalos War Minister, and the young Venizelist Rentis Minister for Foreign Affairs. Plastiras remained outside the Government as Leader of the Revolution. During the afternoon Lindley made a last attempt to dissuade the leaders from their intentions. Strong words were exchanged. At midnight that night the Court Martial rose to consider its verdict.

At 6.30 on Tuesday 28 November the President of the Court Martial, General Othonaios, entered the court room in the old parliament building and announced that the Court was in session again. At this hour in the morning there were few present in the hall. There was a furtive air about the proceedings deriving from the haste with which the revolution was driving towards a conclusion to the affair, and the anxiety to avoid publicity. During the night the accused had been transported by truck to the

Averoff prison, not far from the place where at Goudi the military league had carried out its revolution in 1910, and where military executions were carried out. They were not present to hear the verdict.

In a low voice Othonaios read the verdict. The judgement was long. All eight of the accused were found guilty of high treason. Gounaris, Stratos, Protopapadakis, Baltazzis, Theotokis and Hatzianestis were sentenced to death, Stratigos and Goudas to life imprisonment.* Hatzianestis, Stratigos and Goudas were also condemned to military degradation. All the condemned were heavily fined. Having read the verdict and the penalties, Othonaios hurriedly left the room.

While the accused ministers were speculating on their fate in the small room near the court, and then in the Averoff prison, Gounaris was in bed in a clinic in Asklipiou Street, following the proceedings with as lively an interest as he could muster. At 2 in the morning two large trucks drew up in front of the clinic and disgorged troops. At about the time the verdict was being read in the court, a police officer entered the clinic and demanded that Gounaris get up and come to the Averoff prison. Gounaris was helped to get up and dress. He then asked for paper and pen and wrote a brief will. He was helped down to the street and into the ambulance that was waiting. In the Averoff prison courtyard, a light chill rain was falling. Gounaris waited shivering in the yard.

The prisoners' relatives waited outside the prison. New detachments of troops kept arriving. Andreas Stratos, son of the condemned politician, was allowed in and told the prisoners of the verdicts against them. Meanwhile Lindley, hearing the news, succeeded in raising Rentis (but not Plastiras) on the telephone and insisted that the relatives of the condemned men should be admitted to them. Shortly afterwards this was done.

At about 9 o'clock Colonel Grigoriadis, one of the officers of the court martial, arrived to read the judgement to the condemned men. He was persuaded to allow the sick Gounaris to go indoors. Gounaris entered the prison and greeted his colleagues before the Colonel entered and read out the long judgement. There followed a few minutes to make farewells to wives, children and relatives. The six then took the last sacrament from a priest who had been brought into the prison for this purpose. At about 10.30 they were told to say goodbye to their relatives and come.

* They were released after a few years.

Outside the prison there were lorries waiting. The solemn procession drove down the Alexandras Avenue and out to Goudi, where the military ground below Mount Hymettus was surrounded by troops. A little circle of troops, a few journalists and other bystanders who had been allowed through, stood in the middle of the plain as the lorries drew up.

The diplomatist Frangulis, though not an eye witness, was a friend and political associate of the condemned men and doubtless discussed the events in detail with those who were. He described the scene:

At 11.05 the lorries bringing the condemned men appeared. A hundred soldiers advanced. Orders were shouted. The first lorry stopped and the door opened. Mr Stratos was the first to jump out and helped Mr Gounaris to get down, giving him his right arm. Since no one helped them, Mr Stratos, looking to see where he could take Mr Gounaris, said to him, 'Where are we going?' Mr Gounaris said, 'To the other world,' and took a few steps. He was very cold, and turned up his collar and put his hands in his pockets.

The second lorry arrived. General Hatzianestis got down, and looked quickly and closely at the soldiers. These were in a square commanded by an officer who took a piece of paper from the clerk's hands and read out the last phrases of the judgement. Then he asked the condemned men if they had anything to say. All answered no. Mr Gounaris was seen to lean his head on his right shoulder and shrugged.

General Hatzianestis was to be degraded, and was read the part of the judgement concerning his degradation. At the moment when they approached him to remove his military insignia, he tore off his epaulettes himself, not wishing anyone to lay hands on him.

Little hollows had been dug for the bodies to fall into. An officer, with drawn sword, told the condemned men to follow him and showed each one his place naming them one after the other. Mr Theotokis was on the far right; and every 12 metres, from right to left, were Baltazzis, Stratos, Gounaris, Protopapadakis, and General Hatzianestis. Mr Stratos took his place only after having helped Mr Gounaris to take his.

Before each of them, at 15 paces distance, there were five soldiers. ... The impassivity of the condemned men was absolute. Mr Gounaris stared attentively at the firing squad; Mr Baltazzis put on his monocle after having wiped it with his handkerchief; General Hatzianestis stood to attention. None of the six agreed to have his eyes bandaged.[14]

Britain had frequently threatened to sever diplomatic relations with Greece if the six were executed. Lord Curzon was informed of the verdict on them in Lausanne. He approached Venizelos during a tea break in the negotiations and – in Venizelos's words, 'deeply moved' – read out the signal announcing the death penalty and underlined the horrible impression this would make:

Although as you know [reported Venizelos] I am careful to avoid intervening in the internal affairs of the country, nevertheless I regard it as my duty to affirm that the impression created will indeed be as Lord Curzon presented it and to draw your attention to the fact that my position here will become extremely difficult.[15]

This lukewarm massage arrived too late to have any effect.

Lindley learned of the executions at 2 p.m. on 28 November, and left Athens by train that evening, seen off by the heads of all foreign missions. It was his view that Venizelos could have prevented the executions had he wished; but until it was too late he had deliberately refused his advice:

The Venizelists were inspired by fears for their own personal safety in the future, by the belief that the death of the heads of all the old parties would make a certainty of the election and by the belief that exemplary punishment was necessary for the political education of the country. The corps of officers desired, naturally, to revenge themselves on those whom they considered responsible for their military defeat, and thus to wipe out the memory of their own disgraceful conduct in the field. Many of them had also become obsessed with the idea that, unless exemplary punishment were dealt out to ... 'les grands coupables', it would be impossible to deal adequately with such smaller fry as deserters and insurbordinates.[16]

One more of the *grands coupables* remained. Prince Andrew, who had commanded the Second Army Corps in the campaign of summer 1921, had been arrested and put on trial for refusing to execute an order during the Sakarya battle. Papoulas and Sariyannis were brought on to give their evidence. Whether or not Andrew had been guilty of insubordination, it was an absurd charge to bring fifteen months after the event, given that he had not been relieved of his command at the time (though his Chief of Staff had been sacked). The Court Martial found the Prince guilty of disobedience and sentenced him to degradation and banishment.

This time there had been negotiations behind the scenes. Commander Gerald Talbot had arrived at the British Legation at 12 noon on Tuesday the 28th on his errand of mercy, half an hour after the execution of the Six. He immediately went into a series of long and secret interviews with Plastiras and the members of the Greek Cabinet. Plastiras eventually promised that if the sentence on Andrew was death it would be commuted to perpetual banishment, and that Talbot could take him away in a British warship. H.M.S. *Calypso* steamed into Phaleron on Sunday morning. In the early afternoon Prince Andrew, Princess Alice, Talbot and Pangalos arrived, and the royal couple went on board. Talbot and Pangalos returned to Athens for a final interview with the politicians – Plastiras, Pangalos, Gonatas and Rentis – at which they promised that there would be no more executions, with the possible exceptions of the journalists Vlachos and Kampanis, Papoulas himself, and General Constantinopoulos and his assistant.[17] In the event all these escaped untouched.

The invitation to Venizelos to represent Greece's interests in Western Europe inevitably involved him in politics again. He continued to insist that he had no intention of involving himself in *internal* Greek politics.[18] Nevertheless his advice was sought and he felt bound to give it.

With extraordinary resilience of mind Venizelos was able to accept the disaster and make a new start, building bridges with the western Allies in order to gain their help. One of the first problems to be tackled was the settlement of the refugees. Venizelos did not, as did many in Greece, cry for the moon, for the return of the refugees to their Asian homelands. While Plastiras and Pangalos were thinking still in terms of war with Turkey over Eastern Thrace, Venizelos had at once accepted and adjusted to the fact of the disaster and was prepared to salvage what he could through an exchange of populations between Greece and Turkey.[19]

The main burden of Venizelos's advice to his friends was that the revolution must make way for a political democracy. He was well aware that the Revolution had left the Greeks cold and indifferent to what they regarded as a new essay in faction. Venizelos knew Plastiras and Pangalos well. The grossly ambitious Pangalos wrote to him at the end of October, under the letter-heading 'Committee of Enquiry into the Guilty of the National

Catastrophe' – an interesting example of the Revolution's prejudice in the literal sense. He found the revolutionary leaders too
soft:

> The Revolution at first wished to achieve the famous bridging of
> the gap through decency and restraint. Since I disagreed I withdrew
> completely. ... Very soon the leaders were persuaded that they had
> been wrong. The revolution began to degenerate and the remaining
> kernels of the Constantinian infection began boldly to lift up their
> heads. Then they sought my co-operation and I was persuaded to
> undertake the work of the Commission of Enquiry. ... The tepid
> nature of the revolution resulted in concentrating around me almost
> all the revolutionary officers, which imposes on me the obligation to
> involve myself more actively in its future direction. ... I have decided
> to pursue the formation of a dictatorial government.[20]

Venizelos's reply was swift and terrible. He realized that not
only was the revolution in danger of turning into a permanent
dictatorship but also that Plastiras and Pangalos could not
accustom themselves to the fact that the war with Turkey was
lost and the refugees were a fact to be lived with. Both men were
itching to take on the Turks again in Thrace and advance to the
Straits. Venizelos regarded such a scheme as diplomatically insane. Greece's first priority after so great a national disaster must
be to re-establish a reputation for responsibility and obtain the
support of the western powers. Otherwise how could she cope
with the burden of the refugees, and the slow process of national
recovery? He would have been content to take on the Turks in
Europe alongside the western Allies, but not without their support.

> In such a case only madmen would think of Greece continuing
> the war alone against Turkey, with the probable consequence of our
> finding ourselves driven back this side of the Haliakmon in three
> months. Besides, England and France are disposed to support our
> interests sincerely and I hope – apart from the danger to the
> Dodecanese – that the peace will not impose new sacrifices on us.[21]

The military situation therefore, Venizelos argued, did not call
for a dictatorial government; and such a government would have
disastrous political and economic results:

> One of my best friends wrote to me that he and many others were
> thinking of establishing a Republic through a *coup d'état*,[22] since
> they had no hopes of the people agreeing to it by their vote. My

answer is that democrats of this sort, who deny the very basis of democracy, respect for the lawfully expressed will of the people, should be shut up as quickly as possible in the lunatic asylum.

I must tell you sincerely [Venizelos ended] that your letter and that of Skoulas in the same vein fill me with melancholy and inspire an almost total despair. It seems that for reasons I do not understand we are condemned to utter disappearance as a state. On the one hand almost half the Greeks led the country to calamity simply in order to gratify their obstinacy and their passions. On the other the remainder, suffering from some brainstorm, are seeking the cure in the use of medicines which will finish off the patient altogether.

A day later Venizelos amplified these thoughts in a friendlier but none the less firm letter to Colonel Plastiras, who had written that only revolutionary regimes and not parliamentary government could produce impartial and worthy men. He tried to move Plastiras, who lacked the cancerous ambitions of Pangalos, with an impassioned defence of democracy which has lost nothing of its force in the intervening years in Greece:

All the forms of government have many and great deficiencies. And it follows that even democracy has great deficiencies, and in the term democracy we must include royal as well as republican democracy. But all reasonable men have long ago recognized that democracy has less drawbacks than monarchy and oligarchy. ... Democracy bring to the political surface and thus to power the most capable men, provided only that they have a temperament apt for struggle. We have the proof of this even in Greece, where the political leaders revealed by our royal democracy, Trikoupis, Theodore Zaimis, Deliyannis, Theotokis, Rallis were undoubtedly the best of their period for the government of Greece. Gounaris was revealed and imposed much more by the King trampling on the constitution than by the popular vote. The elections of 1 November were certainly a colossal error of the people. But what people has not made colossal errors in its history? [23]

This advice may have helped slightly to steady Plastiras. At any rate the colonel wrote a long letter of self-justification, claiming (in words which have a familiar ring) by 'dictatorial regime' to have meant not a permanent regime, but 'a regime necessary for the circumstances, whose length would be the shorter the sooner the reasons which imposed it disappeared'.[24]

Plastiras's chief justification of the revolution was the complete dissolution of army and state. The army had been 'ready to leave the way open through Thrace and Macedonia to Athens.

... Deserters and fugitives in thousands flooded the country.' Besides this there were the refugees. Only a revolutionary government could have faced such a situation. The Government had decreed the death penalty for desertion; as a result, thousands of deserters were now coming to re-enlist. The army had been re-created and was now capable, given the right conditions, of successful action in Thrace.

As for the future, Plastiras was hopeful. Although ideally the revolutionary period should last for some two or three years, the regime lacked the necessary charismatic leader to give it direction for such a period; the country should therefore return as soon as possible to normal political life through the holding of elections, even though the state organism would still be rotten. Meanwhile Plastiras had undertaken a propaganda campaign of 'popular enlightenment', sending out teachers, priests and speakers into the provinces to preach the message of the revolution. Reservist Leagues were being formed, imbued with revolutionary ideals, to succeed the moribund Royalist Political Clubs. It was in these new leagues that the Colonel pinned his confident hope of a majority for the revolutionary candidates at the general elections.

The gulf between the revolution and Venizelos was illustrated again when the two soldiers wrote to him in December. Pangalos wrote that 'within a week we shall be able to shut the Turks for ever into Asia'.[25] Plastiras tried to convince Venizelos that war might be salutary, and could prove necessary, even without allied support;[26] if a reasonable Greco-Turkish agreement proved impossible to find at Lausanne Greece should advance to the Bosporus with or without allied permission. Plastiras believed the Greek army could reach the Straits with two army corps in ten days:

> You must bear in mind, Mr President, that if the return of the refugees to their homes is not achieved, there cannot be peace in Greece and I say with conviction that within a few years we will dissolve as a state. ... Therefore on no account must we agree to sign an exchange of populations.

These were arguments that Venizelos won. When it came to the point the wild men of the revolution, like schoolboys with a headmaster in their relationship with Venizelos, did not translate words into action. To resist the combined pressures and counsels of the allied Powers – with whom they wished to re-establish cordial relations – and their mentor Venizelos, was psychologically too difficult a step so soon after the shattering defeat in Asia Minor. (Rational calculation might well have led the Greeks to stand firm in Eastern Thrace in October and refuse to evacuate the territory; but having missed their opportunity at Mudania, it was now too late for warmongering.) Inexorably and reluctantly the Government was led towards an exchange of populations with Turkey and a new and sensible relationship based on a respect for the new situation.

The execution of the Six and the banishment of King Constantine – to be followed into exile just over a year later by his son King George II – brought to an end the unhappiest phase in the history of the modern Greek state. It was unhappy not least because the waste of lives and spirit in Asia Minor was to a large extent self-imposed. Among the Anatolian Greeks and the ordinary Greek soldiers in the army the loss and waste was incalculable. On a more trivial scale, the execution of the Six cast its gloomy shadow for the next generation over Greek political life which had before been free from such barbarities.

A new era was beginning for Greece, in which, to compensate for these losses of blood and treasure, there were to be gains: new blood and talent imported with the refugees, a new realism and the ability to view the near eastern world more clearly than through the distorting prism of the Great Idea. This era was ushered in by the Treaty of Lausanne, which after long and tortuous negotiations, which often threatened to break down (and once did so), was agreed in July 1923. At Lausanne Ismet Inonu and Venizelos found an accommodation and laid the basis for a lasting settlement.

In its territorial provisions the treaty mainly ratified the existing state of affairs as decided in war. The Greco-Turkish frontier was confirmed as the River Maritsa, and Turkish sovereignty thus recognized over Eastern Thrace as well as Istanbul and the straits zone. The islands of Imbros and Tenedos off the mouth of the Dardanelles were restored to Turkey. The Dodecanese and Kastellorizo remained with Italy (now under Mussolini) which refused to surrender them. It was not until after the Second World War that Greece won them at last. Lemnos, Samothrace, Chios, Samos, Mitylene and Ikaria were confirmed in Greek sovereignty, and the latter four islands, off the Aegean coast, were demilitarized.

The freedom of the Straits was guaranteed by an International Straits Commission – a solution satisfactory to Great Britain, acceptable to Turkey, and unwelcome to the Russians, to whom the freedom of the straits meant freedom for foreign warships to enter the Black Sea.

The most radical provisions agreed at Lausanne concerned the minorities. A convention signed by Greece and Turkey on 30 January 1923 solved the problems they posed in a novel way. Article I stated:

As from the 1st May, 1923, there shall take place a compulsory exchange of Turkish nationals of the Greek Orthodox religion established in Turkish territory, and of Greek nationals of the Muslim religion established in Greek territory.

These persons shall not return to live in Turkey or Greece respectively without the authorization of the Turkish Government or of the Greek Government respectively.[27]

The important word was 'compulsory'. Only the Greek inhabitants of Constantinople and the Muslim of Western Thrace were excluded from the provision. No one wished to take credit for initiating the idea of a compulsory exchange, so repugnant to liberal principles. But the measure solved the age old problem of the minorities at a stroke though at the cost of much suffering and dislocation of families and lives.

So far as the Greeks were concerned the convention largely formalized an existing state of affairs, since the populations of Eastern Thrace and Asia Minor had already been forced to leave their homes. Others, and the Muslims in Greece, were obliged to leave flourishing family homesteads because of the high politics of their governments. There were heart-rending scenes in Crete and elsewhere as families were uprooted and took ship – families who had been integrated many generations before in all but religion into the country they were leaving, and were alien in language and custom to the country they were going to. By the end of 1924 the grim migration was almost complete. The million and more Christian refugees had already changed the face of the big towns and the texture of the social and political life of Greece.

The names from Greek Asia Minor survived in the shanty towns of Athens and Salonika. The dream of Ionia remained with the refugees as a perpetual nostalgia. But several forms of life had died in 1922 in the fires of Smyrna and the panic trek to the coast – the lives of the bourgeois Greek merchants of Smyrna and the interior, of the peasant farmers of the coastal strip, of the Turkish-speaking Karamanli Christians from the interior of Anatolia. All these were consigned to the folk memory of the refugees and the collecting, recording instinct of the Greeks.

Biographical Notes

The following notes give biographical information which is not available elsewhere about a number of the protagonists in this book.

ARGYROPOULOS, PERICLES (b. Athens 1881) Nomarch of Larissa, 1910, and of Salonika, 1912. A leader of the Venizelist Salonika movement, 1916. Governor General of Macedonia 1917–18. With Kondylis A. inspired the Venizelist National Defence (*Amyna*) movement in Constantinople, 1921–2. Later in life he moved towards the extreme left.

BALTAZZIS, GEORGIOS (1866–1922) Born Smyrna, studied there at the Evangelic School and at Athens University. 1902, elected deputy. 1908, Foreign Minister in Theotokis Govt. 1915, Minister in Gounaris Govt. 1921–2, Foreign Minister. Found guilty at Trial of the Six and executed, Nov. 1922. Of the six, he least deserved this fate.

BENAKIS, EMMANUEL (1843–1929) A millionaire who made his money in the Egyptian cotton trade; one of the wealthy, cosmopolitan patrons of Venizelism (cf. the Embireikos family). 1910, elected deputy for Attico-Boeotia; Minister of Agriculture, Trade and Industry in Venizelos's first government. 1914, mayor of Athens. 1920, B. retired to France, returning in 1924.

BOUSIOS, GEORGIOS (1875–1929) Of an old family from Grevena, B. was prominent in the Macedonian struggle. Elected to the Ottoman parliament after the Young Turk revolution. After Balkan Wars, active in the N. Epirus struggle. At the elections of May/June 1915, B. and Ion Dragoumis formed an independent group in Macedonia to represent the special interests of the New Territories; eight deputies were elected. Aug. 1922, Minister in Triantaphyllakos Govt.

BUXTON, NOEL (1869–1948) Travels in the Balkans in the late nineteenth century awoke a lifelong interest in the politics of the region. 1903, B. with Bryce founded the Balkan Committee, to promote Balkan unity and liberation from Ottoman rule. With his brother C. R. Buxton, B. undertook an unofficial mission to the Balkans early in the war, at the suggestion of Lloyd George and Churchill, to secure Bulgarian cooperation. B. joined Labour Party, 1919. Created Baron Noel-Buxton, 1930.

DANGLIS, PANAGIOTIS (1853–1924) Artillery officer and instructor, trained in France. 1904–9, member of the newly formed 'Staff College' (*Soma Genikon Epitelon*). Introduced the Schneider-Danglis gun (rapid-firing mountain artillery) into Greece. Service in Balkan Wars. 1915, elected deputy for Ioannina; War Minister in Venizelos Govt. 1916, D. was one of the triumvirate who established the Provisional Govt. in Salonika. 1918, Commander in Chief of the Greek army, resigning at the end of the year. Nov. 1920, leader of the Liberal parliamentary party after Venizelos's departure into exile. A good-hearted man and a voice of moderation in the Venizelist party.

DIOMEDIS, ALEXANDROS (1875–1956) Deputy for Spetsai, 1910. Finance Minister in Venizelist Govt., 1911. A distinguished Liberal Minister and financier, who became Director of the National Bank and first Governor of the Bank of Greece.

DRAGOUMIS, ION (1878–1920) Son of Stephanos D. Ion, served in the consular service in Macedonia, Thrace, Bulgaria, Constantinople, Alexandria, etc., and in the Foreign Ministry at Athens, between 1902 and 1914. Volunteer in army in 1897 and in the Balkan Wars. Greek Minister in Petrograd, 1914–15. Entered parliament as deputy for Florina and Kastoria, Sept. 1915. Exiled to Corsica as a leading anti-Venizelist ideologist, June 1917; returned Nov. 1919, and joined the United Opposition in 1920. Murdered 13 Aug. 1920. The leading theorist of the modern Greek identity of his generation.

DOUSMANIS, VICTOR (1862–1949) A staff officer who in 1904 joined the newly formed 'Staff College'. 1905–09, as head of the personnel section in the War Ministry under the Theotokis Govt., D. played an important part in the Theotokan programme of military reorganization, training and planning. Chief of Staff during Balkan Wars and after, and again under the Gounaris Govt. in 1921. An arrogant, dictatorial figure, on close terms with King Constantine.

GOUNARIS, DIMITRIOS (1867–1922) After a brilliant performance in the law faculty of Athens University, and studies in Germany, France and England, G. practised law in Patras, for which he was elected deputy in Nov./Dec. 1902. A radical intellectual, influenced by Bismarckian social legislation, he became the leading spirit in the so-called 'Japanese Group' formed under Stephanos Dragoumis in 1906 in opposition to G. Theotokis's Govt. The group collapsed when G. joined the Theotokan Govt. in 1908 as Finance Minister. G. himself was soon forced to resign, his radical intentions frustrated by the entrenched interests of the Theotokan party stalwarts. A brilliant parliamentarian, progressive in his view of society but conservative in his attitude to extra-constitutional sources of change and free himself from the taint of the 'old parties' (*palaiokommatismos*), he was the natural leader of the opposition to Venizelos and the new Liberal Party. Prime Minister after Venizelos's resignation, 1915. Exiled to Corsica, 1917. Prime Minister, 1921–2. Executed Nov. 1922 after Trial of the Six. Founder of the Popular Party (*Laiko Komma*). A superb rhetorician. His undoubted gifts were sadly wasted in sterile opposition or, when in power, in the attempt to master circumstances that were too much for him.

HATZIANESTIS, GEORGIOS (1863–1922) Artillery officer, studied at Evelpides, and in France, Britain and Germany. 1904–9, General Staff Corps. 1912–13, Chief of Staff of 6th Division. 1917–20, retired at own request; recalled Nov. 1920, and promoted General. April 1922, commander of Thrace army. May 1922, commander of Asia Minor and Thrace armies. Nov. 1922, executed for high treason after the Trial of the Six. Eccentric, energetic, an absurdly strict disciplinarian, H. was an extraordinary appointment as Commander-in-Chief.

KALOGEROPOULOS, NIKOLAOS (1852–1927) Elected deputy for Chalkis, 1885; supporter of Trikoupis and then G. Theotokis. Minister of Justice, 1903; Finance and Interior, 1905–8. Briefly Prime Minister, 1916, and again, 1920–21. An undistinguished figure.

KONDYLIS, GEORGIOS (1878–1936) Joined the infantry as volunteer, 1896, rising from the ranks. 1904–8, guerrilla leader in Macedonia, then 'teacher' in Thrace. Served in Balkan Wars in 5th Infantry Regt. Prominent in the Venizelist revolution of 1916, after which promoted Major. Served on the Macedonian front in 1917, in Russia in 1918–19; Col. in Asia Minor 1919–20. Nov. 1920–Sept. 1922, promoted anti-Royalist movement of National Defence (*Amyna*) in Constantinople. Thereafter prominent in Greek politics, moving from an extreme Venizelist and Republican position to an anti-Venizelist and Royalist position in the 1930s.

KOUNDOURIOTIS, PAVLOS (1855–1935) Admiral, responsible for Greek victory over the Turkish fleet in the Balkan wars. Member of the governing Triumvirate (Venizelos-Danglis-K.) at Salonika, 1916–17. Regent, Oct.–Nov. 1920. First President of the Greek Republic, 1924.

METAXAKIS, MELETIOS (1871–1935) Cretan prelate, leader of the Venizelist faction in the Orthodox Church. In church affairs, M. promoted the ecumenical movement, showing a great interest in Anglicanism. After holding the See of Kitium in Cyprus, M. succeeded the deposed Theoklitos as Metropolitan of Athens, was himself deposed in turn when the Royalists returned to power in Nov. 1920, and went to the U.S.A. Elected Ecumenical Patriarch Meletios IV of Constantinople, 1921. In Constantinople M. became a leader of the Venizelist National Defence (*Amyna*) movement. After the Smyrna disaster M. argued unsuccessfully that the Ecumenical See should be moved from Constantinople to Salonika or Mount Athos. Persuaded to abdicate his throne, Nov. 1923. See Harry J. Psomiades *The Eastern Question: the Last Phase*, Salonika, 1968, pp. 87–96.

METAXAS, IOANNIS (1871–1941) After studies at the Berlin Military Academy, M. with Dousmanis played a distinguished part in the Theotokan reorganization of the army and in the staff work for the Balkan Wars. His resignation on 17 Feb./2 March 1915 as Acting Chief of General Staff over Venizelos's Gallipoli plans helped to provoke the crisis which led to Venizelos's resignation, and confirmed M.'s status as a 'political' Colonel. Exile in Corsica, 1917. Retired as General after the Nov. 1920 elections, and refused to be enticed back during the Asia Minor campaign as C.G.S. or C. in C. M. entered the political world overtly in 1923. Dictator, 1936 until his death. With Venizelos he dominated the first forty years of the century. No adequate biography exists.

MICHALAKOPOULOS, ANDREAS (1875–1938) A lawyer from Patras. Elected deputy for Patras on Venizelist ticket, 1910. Minister of National Economy, 1911. Minister of Agriculture 1917–18, 1920. Prime Minister, 1924–5.

PANGALOS, THEODOROS (1878–1932) Military studies at Evelpides and in Paris. 1909, active in the Military League of Goudi. 1916, joined the Salonika movement. 1917, Chief of Personnel Dept. at the War Ministry. 1918–20, Chief of Staff to Paraskevopoulos's G.H.Q. Macedonia and Asia Minor. An ambitious and ruthless political general, P. returned to politics with the Plastiras revolution of 1922, engineered the Trial of the Six, and became Dictator 1925–6.

PAPANASTASIOU, ALEXANDROS (1876–1936) Studied political economy and philosophy in Berlin; on his return to Athens founded the Sociological Society. Champion of land reform in Thessaly. Elected deputy, 1910, and joined the Liberal Party with his radical followers. 1917–20, Minister of Communications and other posts. 1922, P. jailed after issuing 'Republican Manifesto'. Leaves Liberal Party to found the Republican Union (*Dimokratiki Enosis*). In 1924, as Prime Minister, P. proclaims the Republic. The intellectual leader of the liberal-republican wing in Greek politics.

PAPANDREOU, GEORGIOS (1883–1968) Liberal politician. Nomarch of Lesvos, 1915. Governor-General of Lesvos, Chios and the Aegean islands, 1916–20. A long and active political career culminated in the prime ministership, 1944, and (as leader of the Centre Union) 1963–5. A master of rhetoric.

PAPOULAS, ANASTASIOS (?1857–1935) Promoted from the ranks.

1904, secret government mission to Macedonia. 1912–13, Col. i/c 10th Infantry Regt. in Epirus and Macedonia. 1917, tried for treason and imprisoned in Crete; Nov. 1920, released, promoted Lieut.-Gen., C. in C. Greek army in Asia Minor. Resigned May 1922. Nov. 1922, key witness at the Trial of the Six. Thereafter switched sympathy from the anti-Venizelist to the Venizelist cause; 24 April 1935, executed for alleged involvement in the attempted Venizelist *coup d'état*; a courageous, vain, gullible figure.

PARASKEVOPOULOS, LEONIDAS (1860–1936). Studied at the Evangelic School, Smyrna, then at Evelpides Military Academy and in Switzerland and France. A long military career culminated in the command of the Venizelist Army of National Defence after P. joined the Salonika movement in 1916. C. in C. Greek army, 1918, and allied armies in Macedonia, 1919. Nov. 1920, resigned and retired to Paris. A bluff, nationalist soldier.

PLASTIRAS, NIKOLAOS (?1883–1953) Professional soldier turned politician. After service in the Balkan Wars and N. Epirus, P. joined the Venizelist Salonika movement in 1916, winning rapid promotion for distinguished service in Macedonia and Russia. As Colonel and Regimental Commander in Asia Minor, P. remained in the army at the front after Nov. 1920 despite his known Venizelist loyalties. Leader of the revolution of Sept. 1922, P. pursued thereafter an active political career until his death.

POLITIS, NIKOLAOS (1872–1942) A distinguished international lawyer from Corfu. 1898–1914, Professor of International Law at Aix, Poitiers and Paris. In 1914, at the invitation of the Venizelist Govt., P. returned to Greece to take up a leading post in the Foreign Ministry. Joined the Venizelist Salonika movement, 1916. Minister of Foreign Affairs until Nov. 1920.

PROTOPAPADAKIS, PETROS (1860–1922) Studied engineering in Paris; then Professor of Engineering at Evelpides, and active in work on the Corinth canal (1890–92), Kavalla–Dedeagach railway, etc. 1902, elected deputy for Paros-Naxos (later for the Cyclades). A faithful political follower of Gounaris, P. was first a Theotokan, then a member of the Japanese Group, then a Gounarist. 1915, Minister of Finance. 1921–2, Minister of Finance in Gounaris Govt. May 1922, Prime Minister of Royalist Coalition Govt. Nov. 1922, executed after the Trial of the Six. A competent Minister.

RALLIS, DIMITRIOS (1844–1921) Born in Athens of an established political family. Deputy for Attica from 1872 until his death. 1875–84, member of Ch. Tricoupis's party, twice minister. 1888, formed his own 'Third Party'. Around the end of the century R. joined forces with Deliyannis, whose mantle he assumed after Deliyannis was murdered. A man of violent temper, much respected in his old age. Prime Minister Nov. 1920–Feb. 1921.

REPOULIS, EMMANUEL (1863–1924) A journalist, elected deputy in 1899. Returned for Argolidocorinth in 1906, R. left the Theotokan party and joined S. Dragoumis's radical Japanese Group in opposition. On the dissolution of the group, R. remained independent until Venizelos's arrival from Crete, when he joined the Liberals, becoming Minister of the Interior, Oct. 1910. 1913, Governor General of Macedonia. As Minister of the Interior and Deputy Prime Minister in Venizelos's 1917–20 Ministry, R. incurred much of the odium for the excesses of the regime. He left no mark on history.

SARRAIL, MAURICE (1856–1929) C. in C. allied armies in Salonika, 1915–17. An arrogant and dictatorial warlord, he made himself hated by anti-Venizelists for his repressive espousal of the Venizelist cause, and infuriated even the Venizelists by his insensitivity to Greek susceptibilities. Career and political leanings are discussed in A. Palmer, *The Gardeners of Salonika*, Deutsch, 1965.

SOPHOULIS, THEMISTOCLES (1860–1949) An archaeologist from Samos. In 1912, S. as revolutionary leader proclaimed the *enosis* of Samos with Greece in the Balkan Wars. 1914, Governor General of Macedonia. 1915, elected deputy for Samos. Joined Venizelist Salonika movement, 1916, becoming Minister of the Interior. 1917–20, President of the revived Chamber (i.e. Speaker of the House). Leader of the Liberal Party after Venizelos's death, and more than once Prime Minister.

STAVRIDI, SIR JOHN (1867–1948) Reuter correspondent, London solicitor, friend of Lloyd George. Consul General of Greece, 1903–16, 1917–20. Knighted in 1919 for 'valuable public services rendered during the war', e.g. for acting as intermediary between Lloyd George and Venizelos and undertaking a mission to Greece in 1915 to negotiate and gather facts on behalf of the British Govt. His diary and papers provide valuable evidence for the war years.

STERGIADIS, ARISTEIDIS (1861–1950) B. Heraklion in Crete of a family from Salonika. Law studies in Paris. Active in Cretan revolutionary politics before *enosis*. A legal adviser to the Venizelist Govt. in 1913, especially in questions of Muslim law. 1917–20, Governor General of Epirus. 1919–22, High Commissioner in Smyrna. After the Smyrna disaster S. retired to the south of France. A capable, dictatorial proconsul, S. left tantalizingly little evidence of his views and actions. He wrote a memoir which has not survived.

STRATIGOS, XENOPHON (1869–1927) Studied at Evelpides and Berlin Military Academy. 1904, joined the newly formed 'Staff College'. On the staff of G.H.Q. in the Balkan Wars. Nov. 1920 elected deputy for Corfu. Recalled to the army as General, S. served the

Gounaris Govt. as Deputy Chief of General Staff. 1922, Minister of Communications. Sentenced to life imprisonment at the Trial of the Six, but later freed under amnesty and retired to Switzerland.

STRATOS, NIKOLAOS (1872–1922) A lawyer, elected deputy as an independent in 1902. S. joined Venizelos on his arrival on the political scene. President of the 1911 Revisionary Assembly, then Minister of Marine. Nov. 1913, resigned after disagreement with Venizelos over alleged corrupt practices. 1916, S. formed his own party, the *Ethnikon Syntiritikon Komma* (National Conservative Party). Minister of the Interior in the 1922 Coalition Govt. Executed after Trial of the Six, Nov. 1922. A shrewd, ambitious politician, moderate at heart but driven by ambition and resentment of Venizelos to waste his talents in opposition.

STREIT, GEORGIOS (1868–1948) A learned jurist, university professor and academician. Ambassador to Vienna, 1910–13. Minister for Foreign Affairs, 1914, S. soon resigned over a dispute with Venizelos. King Constantine's closest friend and adviser.

THEOTOKIS, GEORGIOS (1844–1916) A distinguished Corfiot politician, follower of Ch. Trikoupis and inheritor of the Trikoupis mantle; Prime Minister frequently in the first decade of this century, and leader of the 'Theotokan Party'.

THEOTOKIS, NIKOLAOS (1878–1922) Son of G. Theotokis; Corfiot diplomat and politician. Ambassador in Berlin at the outbreak of the Great War, T. retired to Switzerland on the severance of relations with Germany. Nov. 1920, elected deputy for Corfu. War Minister, 1921–2. Found guilty in the Trial of the Six and executed, Nov. 1922.

VENIZELOS, ELEUTHERIOS K. (1864–1936) A Cretan of bourgeois nationalist background. Entered Cretan politics in 1889. Leader of the revolutionary movement for *enosis* with Greece, through which and through his opposition to Prince George, High Commissioner of Crete, he won a national reputation. From the moment when he arrived in Athens in 1910 at the invitation of the Military League of Goudi revolutionaries, he dominated Greek political life until his death in exile in 1936. Founder and leader of the Greek Liberal party from which derive the modern parties of the Centre. Friend of Lloyd George, admirer of British parliamentary institutions. A man of overwhelming charm and eloquence, and violent, almost neurotic, changes of mood. The character of the 'private' man, if such existed, is still an enigma. There is no modern biography. The best account remains Doros Alastos, *Venizelos*, Lund Humphries, 1942.

Notes and References

1. THE GREAT IDEA (pp. 3–19)

1. Markezinis, *Political History of Modern Greece*, i, p. 208. On the concept of the *Megali Idea* see Zakythinos, *Political History of Modern Greece*, 2nd edn, ch. 3, 'National and political life of the modern Greeks'.

2. Alexandris, *Political Memoirs*, p. 16.

3. The conversations are described in detail in Sir John Stavridi's diary for 1912–15, to be found in the Stavridi Papers. Stavridi was present throughout the talks.

4. *Livre Blanc Grec*, Paris 1918, no. 2.

2. THE BACKGROUND IN ANATOLIA (pp. 24–5)

1. Campbell and Sherrard, *Modern Greece*, pp. 21–3; the chief exponent of such views was George Gemistos Pletho, who recommended to the Emperor Manuel II the reconstruction of a national 'Hellenic' state in the Peloponnese and a return to the religious and philosophical tradition of the ancient Greeks.

2. See, e.g., N. Politis, *Selections from the Songs of the Greek People* (*Eklogai apo ta Tragoudia tou Ellinikou Laou*) 4th edn, Athens 1958, pp. 12–13.

3. Toynbee, *The Western Question in Greece and Turkey*, pp. 122–3, citing Finlay's *History of Greece* and G. Sakkaris, *History of Kydonies*, Athens 1920. *Kydonies* is the purist Greek version of the name, introduced by the classicizers; it means the same as the common Turkish name *Ayvalik*, 'Quince Trees'.

4. This and the following examples from A. Philippson, *Reisen und Forschungen in Kleinasien*, Gotha 1910–15, cited in *Le Caractère grec de l'Asie Mineure*, Paris 1919, pp. 79–93. The latter is a propagandist work citing the testimony of authors favourable to the Greek cause. Dr Philippson, Professor of Geography at Bonn University, was an authority on whom Venizelos relied heavily in his statement of Greek claims at the Peace Conference. However good Philippson may have been as a geographer, he was utterly *parti pris* on behalf of the Greeks and against the Turks, writing for instance that the

Turk would always depend on the Greeks; 'il a vécu, il vit, il vivra toujours d'eux et par eux'; op. cit., p. 83.

5. Toynbee, p. 123.

6. Foreign Office, *Peace Handbooks*, x, no. 59, *Anatolia*, p. 50. This handbook, produced by the historical section of the Foreign Office for the benefit of the British Delegation to the Peace Conference, contains an excellent brief account of the economic and human geography of Anatolia.

7. ibid., p. 53.

8. See Toynbee, pp. 122-3, and *Peace Handbooks*, x, no. 59 *passim*.

9. On the Karamanli Christians, see R. Clogg, 'The publication and distribution of Karamanli Texts by the British and Foreign Bible Society before 1850', *Journal of Ecclesiastical History*, xix, nos. 1 and 2, 1968; despite the intimidating title, this article is of general interest for the Karamanlides and the literature on the subject.

10. W. M. Leake, *Researches in Greece*, London 1814, p. 87, cited by Clogg, op. cit., p. 66.

11. British and Foreign Bible Society, 13th Report, 1817, p. 23, cited by Clogg, p. 58.

12. For instance, in Afyon Karahisar, Kula, Alashehir, Konya, Isparta, Burdur, Denizli and Mihalich, all of which were visited by the Rev. J. Brewer in 1834 in the course of a tour in which he distributed Bible Society editions in Greek characters; Clogg, p. 188.

13. Gaston Deschamps, lecture on Hellenism in Asiatic Turkey published in *Le Caractère grec de l'Asie Mineure*, Paris, 1919; see pp. 40-1. Deschamps was given a common and lurid account of the origins of the Karamanli phenomenon; 'On a coupé la langue à toute une génération d'hommes et de femmes, afin que les uns et les autres désapprissent leur langue maternelle.' Pinkerton of the Bible Society was told the same story, which symbolizes the powerful national sentiment of the Karamanli despite their ignorance of the Greek language; see Clogg, p. 60.

14. Toynbee, p. 125.

15. Murray's Handbook, *Turkey in Asia* (? 1870 edn.), p. 18.

16. ibid., p. 17.

17. *Peace Handbooks*, x, no. 59, p. 196, gives figures for 1910-11; *Hellenism in Asia Minor* (pamphlet issued by London Committee of Unredeemed Greeks, 1919), which gives an interesting account of Smyrna's trade with France, especially Marseilles, from the seventeenth century on, estimates that trade passing through Smyrna exceeded that of Constantinople by about 1887.

18. *Peace Handbooks*, x, no. 59, pp. 107-8.

19. A. A. Pallis, 'Racial migrations in the Balkans during the years 1912-1924', *Geographical Journal*, lxvi, no. 4, Oct. 1925; an excellent survey.

20. See Toynbee's discussion of *chetté* bands, and definitions of the term, in *The Western Question*, pp. 278–80.

21. Toynbee, p. 140, basing his description on the account of the Bergama Greeks themselves.

22. Félix Sartiaux, article in *The New Europe*, xiv, no. 175, 19 Feb. 1920.

23. Report of M. Manciet, one of the French eye-witnesses, quoted in Horton, *The Blight of Asia*, pp. 47–8. Horton was U.S. Consul in Smyrna at the time of the Greek occupation, and sympathized with the Greek cause.

24. Pentzopoulos, *The Balkan Exchange of Minorities and its Impact upon Greece*, p. 56.

25. Toynbee, pp. 143–4.

3. GREAT WAR AND NATIONAL SCHISM

1. F.O. Papers, series 371, vol. 2242; Grey to Elliot, 23 Jan. 1915.

2. Compton Mackenzie, *First Athenian Memories*, London 1931, pp. 320–1.

3. These arguments and variations on them are deployed in the two works which best convey the day-to-day reactions of anti-Venizelists in the early months of the war: Streit, *Diary* (3 vols; see esp. ii, A) and Metaxas, *Diary*, ii.

4. The clearest statement of this position is in Venizelos's third memo to the King, of 17 Feb./2 March 1915; text in Markezinis, *Political History of Modern Greece*, iii, pp. 376–8.

5. The development and crystallization of these conditions can be followed in Streit, *Diary*, i and ii, A and B.

6. Frangulis, *La Grèce, son statut internationale, son histoire diplomatique*, 2nd edn, i, p. 184. D. Rallis condemned this at once as *marchandage*.

7. Frangulis, i, pp. 186–7; Streit, ii, A, pp. 29–31.

8. Details in my doctoral thesis, p. 59.

9. Metaxas, *Diary*, ii, p. 338; entry of 17 Aug. 1914.

10. ibid., ii, p. 348; 3 Sept. 1914.

11. ibid., ii, pp. 366–7; 21 Sept. 1914.

12. ibid., ii, p. 340; 26 Aug. 1914.

13. See Politis's description of Streit's memorandum of 26 March 1915, with its careful calculations of the probable effects of every possible combination in the Balkans, as 'the budget of a provincial grocery store' in his speech to the Chamber on 26 August 1917; *The Vindication of Greek National Policy*, p. 52.

14. See Metaxas, ii, entries for 4, 5, 13, 14, 15, 30, 31 August 1914 (all dates Old Style).

15. Streit, ii, A, p. 64.

16. ibid., ii, A, pp. 49–50, entry for 6/19 Mar. 1915.

17. F.O. 371, vol. 2241, Elliot to Grey, 7 Jan. 1915.

18. Stavridi Papers, 1915; confidential 'Notes on the Balkan States', January, 1915, parts i and ii, by N. and C. R. Buxton. 'If the transfer of Kavalla (at the end of the war) should be decided on, it should be done in conjunction with a promise of Smyrna ...' (part i, p. 4). The Buxtons saw such a policy as 'the true solution of the problem of Balkan unity'.

19. Stavridi Papers, 1915; Stavridi to Venizelos, 22 Jan. 1915.

20. F.O. 371, vol. 2242, Buchanan (Petrograd) to Grey, 22 Jan. 1915.

21. Stavridi Papers, 1915, Stavridi to Venizelos, 22 Jan. 1915.

22. Text in Markezinis, iii, pp. 372–4.

23. Suspicion of Bulgaria dominated the minds of the Staff and the Royal Family; see the letters from Prince Nicholas (Constantine's brother) to Crawfurd Price, written in 1915 and sent on by Price to Lloyd George; Ll. G. Papers, File D 20/2/26.

24. Text in Streit, ii, A, pp. 181–2.

25. Metaxas, ii, p. 385.

26. ibid., ii, pp. 386–90. See also Pallis, *Greece's Anatolian Adventure – and After*, pp. 20–28, for a discussion of Metaxas's views at this time.

27. Compare Toynbee's discussion of the historical background to attempted invasions and occupations of Asia Minor in *The Western Question*, pp. 220–24.

28. Toynbee, pp. 214–15.

29. Metaxas, *Diary*, ii, pp. 391–2. Metaxas wrote his notes on the interview on 19 Jan./1 Feb. 1915.

30. Text in Markezinis, iii, pp. 374–6; memo of 30 Jan. 1915.

31. Texts of the acrimonious exchanges between Venizelos and Gounaris in Markezinis, iii, pp. 378–80.

32. Driault and Lhéritier, *Histoire diplomatique de la Grèce de 1821 à nos jours*, v, p. 191; see also Ll. G. Papers, C 25/11/1.

33. Driault and Lhéritier, v. p. 194.

34. Ll. G. Papers, C 25/11/1; full text also in Streit, *Diary*, ii, B, pp. 155–7.

35. Text of the Treaty of Alliance of 1 June 1913, *Greek White Book*, ii, 1920, no. 2; text of Military Convention ibid., no. 4. The treaty and the extent of Greece's obligations under it have been endlessly discussed. For two opposing viewpoints, see Sakellaropoulos, *The Shadow of the West*, 2nd edn, pp. 419–24, and Ventiris, *Greece 1910–1920*, pp. 391–407.

36. Letter of 3 May 1931 to George Ventiris; Ventiris, ii, appendix 4, p. 418.

37. The article, complaining of the violations of Greek sovereignty, is in *Politiki Epitheorisis*, 1917, p. 705.

38. Malainos, *History of Foreign Interventions*, v, pp. 5–6, citing the relevant decrees.

39. ibid., v, p. 7.

40. ibid., v, pp. 7, 9.

41. Malainos (v, p. 10) calculates that 7,332 public servants (including professors and mayors) were dismissed from the civilian ministries. A great number of these were teachers (3,149 from the Ministry of Education and Cults). See Markezinis, iv, p. 231, who rightly warns that these figures should be treated with caution. Frangulis, i, p. 572, gives figures sufficiently similar to suggest that Malainos has based his estimate on Frangulis and other secondary sources rather than on the *Govt. Gazette* as he half implies. Venizelos, *Journal of Debates*, 1920, pp. 775–6, naturally sets the figures much lower. For a convincing estimate we must await a complete study of the schism years based on *Govt. Gazette* and the archives of the ministries concerned. Malainos estimates dismissals in the army as 3,000 officers and War Ministry personnel; also 3,000 gendarmes.

42. On the nature of Greek political parties, see Campbell and Sherrard, *Modern Greece*, pp. 390–404; Legg, *Politics in Modern Greece*, pp. 125–62.

43. Sophoulis, President of the Chamber, at the session of 23 Nov. 1918 celebrating the allied victory, called Venizelos 'worthy of Greece, worthy of the Great Fatherland, worthy of the national gratitude of Hellenism'; Markezinis, iv, p. 258.

4. THE PARIS PEACE CONFERENCE

1. Howard, *The Partition of Turkey*, 1966 edn, pp. 208–9. French text of the armistice in Frangulis, ii, pp. 14–16.

2. D. Kitsikis, *Propagande et pressions en politique internationale, la Grèce et ses Revendications à la Conférence de la Paix*, Paris, 1963, p. 181.

3. Ll. G. Papers, F 55/1/11; covering letter only in Lloyd George, *The Truth about Peace Treaties*, ii, pp. 1228–31.

4. Nicolson, *Curzon: the Last Phase*, pp. 76–7.

5. Eastern Committee 42nd meeting, 9 Dec. 1918, CAB 27/24.

6. Text in J. C. Hurewitz, *Diplomacy in the Near and Middle East*, Princeton, 1956, ii, p. 19.

7. Nicolson, *Peacemaking 1919*, p. 221.

8. ibid., p. 205.

9. Seymour, *Letters from the Paris Peace Conference*, p. 56.

10. Ll. G. Papers, F 55/3/2; Elliot to Hardinge, 9 April 1917.

11. Cmd 671, 1920; see Article 9.

12. Text of Anglo-French-Italian agreement of 18 Aug., usually referred to as the Agreement of St Jean de Maurienne, in *D.B.F.P.*, iv, pp. 640–41. For the conversations at St Jean de Maurienne in April, ibid., pp. 638–9, and Lloyd George, *Peace Treaties*, ii, pp. 773f. The Agreement of 18 August was prefaced by the words 'Sous réserve de l'assentiment russe', words which later provided Lloyd George with a convenient escape clause. *F.R.U.S. 1919*, v, pp. 484, 720.

13. Seton-Watson, *Italy from Liberalism to Fascism*, p. 464, n. 3.

14. *D.D.I.*, 6th series, i, no. 393, pp. 195–200; memo of 28 Nov. 1918 on the postwar colonization programme by the Chief of the Army General Staff.

15. Ll. G. Papers, F 56/2/16; Rodd (British Ambassador in Rome) to Balfour, private letter of 19 Dec. 1918, reporting on the effect of Venizelos's talks on Nitti and the Italian Cabinet. Rodd concluded that there was a good chance of the Italians conceding the Dodecanese (except for Rhodes) and Northern Epirus. *D.D.I.*, 6th Series, i, p. 423; Bonin Longare (Italian Ambassador in Paris) to Sonnino, 6 Jan. 1919.

16. *D.B.F.P.*, iv, no. 573, n. 3, pp. 848–51.

17. Memo and covering letter of 2 Nov. 1918 in Ll. G. Papers, F 55/1/11.

18. Pentzopoulos, *The Balkan Exchange of Minorities and its Impact upon Greece*, pp. 55–6.

19. *Greece before the Peace Congress*, London, 1918. For Venizelos's statements before the Council of Ten see *F.R.U.S., 1919*, iii, pp. 856–75.

20. Report of Commander Talbot, R.N.V.R., on Greek Negotiations at the Peace Conference, F.O. 421/298, no. 6. Commander Talbot was attached to the Greek delegation as liaison officer and established close relations with Venizelos.

21. Venizelos before the Council of Ten, 3 Feb. 1919; *F.R.U.S. 1919*, iii, p. 861.

22. ibid., pp. 872–3. The Greeks of Pontus continued to press their claim. See *The Pontus Question*, memo submitted to the Peace Conference on 10 March 1920 by the Pontus Delegation led by Chrysanthus, Metropolitan of Trebizond; Venizelos Papers 315 and 316 *passim* for appeals from various committees of Pontus Greeks to Venizelos in 1920 and 1922.

23. Nicolson, *Peacemaking 1919*, pp. 208–9.

24. Venizelos to Repoulis, 4 Feb. 1919; text in *Tachydromos*, no. 793, 21 June 1969. *Tachydromos* nos. 788–802 (2 May–22 Aug. 1969) contains a series of letters from Venizelos in Paris to Repoulis in Athens, an extract from Venizelos's diary for May 1919, and a narrative of the events surrounding the Smyrna landing by G. Roussos. These original materials come from the archive, at present restricted, of D. Lambrakis.

25. *F.R.U.S. 1919*, iii, p. 875.

26. Nicolson, *Peacemaking 1919*, pp. 105–6. Nicolson was attached to the Greek Committee as expert technical adviser and drafted the final report.

27. Frangulis, ii, pp. 48–9. For the development of the Thracian question, see Venizelos to Repoulis, 9 Aug. 1919, in *Tachydromos*, nos. 795–6 of 4 and 11 July 1969.

28. Nicolson, *Peacemaking 1919*, pp. 236–7.

29. Venizelos to Repoulis, 27 Feb. 1919, in *Tachydromos*, no. 792, 13 June 1969; F.O. 421/298 no. 6 (Talbot's report on Greek negotiations at the Peace Conference).

30. Nicolson, *Peacemaking 1919*, pp. 255–6.

31. Mantoux, *Les Délibérations du Conseil des Quatre*, i, pp. 455–6.

32. Nicolson, *Peacemaking 1919*, p. 264.

33. Mantoux, i, p. 486.

34. Callwell, *Field-Marshal Sir Henry Wilson: his life and diaries*, ii, p. 188.

35. Mantoux, i, p. 499.

36. Venizelos, Diary, *Tachydromos*, no. 788, 16 May 1969 (cf. n. 40 below).

37. Callwell, ii, p. 190.

38. ibid., loc. cit.

39. Venizelos, Diary, pp. 10–11.

40. The diary, an unvarnished account of the events of 6–19 May 1919, is published in *Tachydromos*, nos. 788–91, 16 May–6 June 1969. Venizelos describes its inception, thus: 'After the dinner I decided to write down all this, which is of such vital significance for the future of the nation, and if possible to continue to keep a diary until the end of the crisis. A good decision, even if taken rather late. But will I keep it? I doubt it. Already I have spent more than an hour in writing this, and I am afraid I may have ruined my sleep in doing so, in which case I shall be incapable of much, or rather of good, work tomorrow.'

41. Mantoux, i, no. 66; Venizelos, Diary, p. 14.

42. Mantoux, ii, no. 75, p. 49. Clemenceau was later to insist, against Venizelos and Lloyd George, that the Greek occupation had always had a provisional character.

43. Mantoux, ii, no. 76, p. 51.

44. Nicolson, *Peacemaking 1919*, p. 280; Nicolson suspected that the child was himself.

45. By Nicolson, *Curzon: the Last Phase*, p. 93.

46. Mantoux, ii, no. 77.

47. Nicolson, *Peacemaking 1919*, pp. 272–3.

48. ibid., p. 274.

49. ibid., p. 276.

50. ibid., p. 277.

51. Churchill, *The World Crisis: the Aftermath*, p. 366.

52. Nicolson, *Curzon: the Last Phase*, pp. 79–80.

53. Venizelos, Diary, pp. 9–10.

54. Churchill, p. 367.

55. This justification of the Lloyd George policy was well put by Nicolson in a minute of 20 Dec. 1920; *D.B.F.P.*, xii, no. 488.

56. Venizelos, Diary, pp. 10–11, for Constantinople; Mantoux, ii, p. 59, meeting of 13 May 1919, for Cyprus.

5. THE OCCUPATION OF SMYRNA

1. Rodas, *Greece in Asia Minor*, ch. 1.

2. Archive of the Greek High Commission in Smyrna (hereafter cited as High Commission (H.C.) Papers), File 4; Report of 11/24 April 1919.

3. For Venizelos's proclamations to the army and to the people of Smyrna, see Greek General Staff, *The Asia Minor Expedition*, i, *The Greek Army in Smyrna, May 1919–May 1920*, appendixes 2 and 3.

4. For these and other incidents, see Toynbee, pp. 270–73, 390–405; Report of the Interallied Commission of Enquiry, *D.B.F.P.*, 1st ser., ii, no. 17, app. A.; F.O. 406/41, Balfour to Curzon, 18 June 1919, enclosing reports of these incidents and atrocities by neutral observers including U.S. naval officers, an eye witness from the Swedish Consulate in Smyrna, and the Secretary of the American Y.M.C.A.; Ll. G. Papers, F 206/4/5, Memorandum respecting the Greek Occupation of Smyrna, 26 Aug. 1919, drawn up for the War Cabinet on Curzon's instructions, giving a summary of Greek and Turkish excesses at Smyrna, Aydin, etc.

5. Report of the Interallied Commission of Enquiry, p. 241; Toynbee, *The Western Question*, pp. 272, 392–4.

6. F.O. 406/41, no. 56; evidence of the Captain of U.S.S. *Manley*.

7. *Tachydromos*, no. 795, 4 July 1969, Venizelos to Repoulis, 29 May 1919.

8. The Greek censorship was set up in parallel with, and as a check on, the interallied censorship, owing to friction between the latter and the Greek High Commission; *D.B.F.P.*, ii, no. 20, apps. B and C. There were no less than eight Greek, seven Turkish, four Armenian and two Jewish newspapers in Smyrna as well as numerous periodicals. After the dismissal of Skepheris for the reason given above, the censorship was entrusted to Michael Rodas, who describes the Smyrniot press and the operations of the censorship fully in *Greece in Asia Minor*, pp. 116–18, 141–2, and *passim*.

9. See his views on the recruitment and training of gendarmerie and civil servants in *Tachydromos*, no. 793, 21 June 1919, Venizelos

to Repoulis, 4 Feb. 1919.

10. Rodas, p. 173; Markezinis, *Political History of Modern Greece*, iv, app., pp. 58–60, citing the unpublished memoirs of G. Athanasiadis Novas.

11. Rodas, p. 126.

12. Markezinis, iv, app., p. 59.

13. Zavitsianos, *Recollections . . .*, ii, p. 146.

14. Metaxas, *Diary*, ii, p. 356; 10 Sept. 1914.

15. Pallis, *Greeks Abroad*, p. 155.

16. Rodas, pp. 173–4.

17. Law 2251 of 14 July 1920 'concerning the foundation and operation of the Greek University in Smyrna', in *Govt. Gazette*, 1920 A, ii, p. 1347.

18. Toynbee, pp. 163–7. The whole chapter is of cardinal importance.

19. Horton, *The Blight of Asia*, p. 80.

20. Saraphis, *Memoirs*, i, pp. 182, 187; Saraphis's book, written in demotic Greek, gives a quite different picture of the occupation from the more stilted accounts of generals and politicians.

21. *D.B.F.P.*, ii, no. 20, app. B.

22. Paraskevopoulos, *Memoirs*, pp. 229–30.

23. ibid., p. 245. Paraskevopoulos was partly to blame, since he had chosen Miliotis for the post on grounds of seniority, knowing him to be unsuitable owing to his 'exaggerated good nature and great trust in those who surrounded him'.

24. On Pangalos's activities see Mazarakis, pp. 255, 283; Danglis, *Memoirs*, ii, pp. 253–6.

25. Paraskevopoulos, pp. 249–51.

26. Repoulis to Venizelos, Diomedis (Acting Foreign Minister) to Politis, both of 1/14 July 1919; texts in Markezinis, iv, app, pp. 58–61, from the archive of A. Diomedis.

27. e.g. Mazarakis, who was serving in Asia Minor at the time, and advised Diomedis to replace Stergiadis with Lambros Koromilas or A. Michalakopoulos; Mazarakis, *Memoirs*, pp. 266–7.

28. Markezinis, iv, app., pp. 62–4; Venizelos to Diomedis, 18/31 July 1919.

29. Toynbee, pp. 201–4.

30. Horton, pp. 85–7.

31. Toynbee, p. 169, citing an estimate of their numbers of between 200,000 and 325,000 by the Ottoman Ministry of Refugees in spring 1921.

32. Toynbee, p. 167. Toynbee cites cases he came across of Greek gendarmes in Turkish rural districts who made no effort to learn Turkish; as he says, there was something more in this than laziness, since the Greeks are good linguists when the occasion demands it.

6. TURKEY ALIVE

1. Rawlinson, *Adventures in the Near East 1918–22*, p. 180.
2. *D.B.F.P.*, iv, no. 433, n. 5.
3. ibid., iv, no. 433, Webb to Sir R. Graham, 28 June 1919.
4. ibid., no. 467; Calthorpe to Curzon, 27 July 1919.
5. ibid., no. 506; Webb to Curzon, 7 Sept. 1919.
6. ibid., loc. cit.
7. ibid., no. 500; de Robeck to Curzon, 18 Nov. 1919.
8. loc. cit.
9. ibid., no. 506.
10. *D.B.F.P.*, i, p. 84; 12 July 1919.
11. *D.B.F.P.*, i, p. 106.
12. ibid., no. 12.
13. Text of 'Venizelos–Tittoni Agreement' of 29 July 1919 in Frangulis, *La Grèce...*, ii, pp. 93–8; see also ibid., pp. 100–101.
14. *D.B.F.P.*, i, pp. 130, 152; 18 July 1919.
15. ibid., i, p. 330; 5 Aug. 1919.
16. ibid., p. 879.
17. ibid., loc. cit.
18. *D.B.F.P.*, ii, p. 349.
19. ibid., p. 263.
20. French text of the report and Mazarakis's minority report in *D.B.F.P.*, ii, no. 17, app. A, pp. 237–58. English text in *F.R.U.S. 1919*, ix, pp. 44–73.
21. *F.R.U.S. 1919*, ix, 71.
22. ibid., ix, p. 72.
23. *D.B.F.P.*, ii, no. 17, p. 229.
24. ibid., ii, pp. 295–6.
25. ibid., p. 352; letter of 15 Nov. 1919.
26. *D.B.F.P.*, ii, pp. 352–3; Venizelos to Clemenceau, 15 Nov. 1919.
27. Ll. G. Papers, F 92/12/6; Clemenceau to Venizelos, 18 Nov. 1919.
28. Ll. G. Papers, F 92/12/6; Venizelos to Crowe, 20 Nov. 1919.
29. Ll. G. Papers, F 92/12/6; Crowe to Curzon, 26 Nov. 1919.
30. Ll. G. Papers, F 92/12/4; conversation between Lloyd George and Venizelos at Clairefontaine Manor, Normandy, 5 Sept. 1919; Venizelos to Repoulis, 19 Sept. 1919, in *Tachydromos*, no. 796 of 11 July 1969.
31. Ll. G. Papers, F 55/1/26.
32. Callwell, *Sir Henry Wilson*, ii, p. 213.
33. *D.B.F.P.*, iv, nos. 631–3; 22–23 Dec. 1919.
34. ibid., no. 646 of 4 Jan. 1920.
35. Nicolson, *Curzon: the Last Phase*, pp. 100–102.
36. *D.B.F.P.*, ii, no. 55; 11 Dec. 1919.
37. *D.B.F.P.*, vii, p. 54.

38. ibid., p. 186; 21 Feb. 1920. Millerand, once the decision had been taken, said that he had changed his mind on account of the promises which he found had been made to Greece, and treated Venizelos very cordially thereafter; ibid., nos. 25 and 26, pp. 230, 239.

39. *D.B.F.P.*, vii, nos. 36–8, of 28 February; see also on the Marash affair, Kinross, *Ataturk*, pp. 203–4; Paillarès, *Le Kémalisme devant les Alliés*, pp. 107–16.

40. *D.B.F.P.*, vii, nos. 38, 50, 55.

41. Kinross, *Ataturk*, pp. 205–9.

42. *D.B.F.P.*, vii, pp. 452–4; 10 March 1920.

43. See the dispatches of Admiral de Robeck, British High Commissioner in Constantinople, from August 1919 onwards, in *D.B.F.P.*, iv, nos. 486, 513, 543, 597; and especially xiii, no. 17 of 9 March 1920.

44. Notes of a conversation held at the War Office, 19 March 1920; Ll. G. Papers, F 199/9.

45. Callwell, *Sir Henry Wilson*, ii, p. 230.

46. Letter of 19 March 1920, in Stratigos, *Greece in Asia Minor*, pp. 88–9.

47. *D.B.F.P.*, xiii, no. 17, de Robeck to Curzon, 9 March 1920.

48. The General Staff were consistently sceptical about Greece's ambitions in Asia Minor for military reasons; they also tended to disapprove of Lloyd George's policy on political grounds, having none of the British Liberals' distaste for the Turks. See *D.B.F.P.*, xiii, no. 23; General Staff memo of 15 March 1920 on the situation in Turkey; Ll. G. Papers, F 206/4/19, General Staff comments of 7 April 1920 on the Foch report; Churchill, *The World Crisis: the Aftermath*, pp. 371–2, citing General Staff memo of Dec. 1919.

49. Ll. G. Papers, F 12/3/24; Curzon to Lloyd George, 9 April, 1920.

50. *D.B.F.P.*, viii, pp. 1–252.

51. *D.B.F.P.*, iv, no. 635.

52. Venizelos to Foreign Ministry, 15 June 1920; Stratigos, pp. 111–12.

53. loc. cit.

54. See Curzon's letter to Venizelos of 24 February 1920, warning that any unauthorized advance might prejudice Greece's claims, *D.B.F.P.*, xiii, no. 7.

55. *D.B.F.P.*, viii, no. 26 (Proceedings of the Second Conference of Hythe).

56. ibid., no. 33, p. 349 (Proceedings of the First Conference of Boulogne).

57. Stratigos, *Greece in Asia Minor*, pp. 116–17. This telegram of course referred to private discussion with Lloyd George and the Supreme Council assented to no such arrangement for the partition of Turkey.

58. Greek General Staff, *The Asia Minor Expedition*, ii; Toynbee,

The Western Question in Greece and Turkey, pp. 228-9.

59. Greek General Staff, ii, app. 19.

60. *D.B.F.P.*, viii, no. 47, p. 444.

61. Callwell, *Sir Henry Wilson*, ii, pp. 248-9, 252; conversations of 4 and 10 July.

62. Greek General Staff, ii, app. 25.

63. See War Office memo of 13 August 1920 on 'Stores available for the Greek and Polish Armies' in Ll. G. Papers, F 9/2/39.

64. Greek General Staff history, *Operations in Thrace (1919-23)*, Athens 1969, pp. 45-62; Paraskevopoulos, *Memoirs*, pp. 328-36; Mazarakis (who commanded the Smyrna Division), *Memoirs*, pp. 272-6. For reactions in Athens, *D.B.F.P.*, xiii, no. 108.

65. Treaty Series no. 11 (1920). Treaty of peace with Turkey, signed at Sèvres, 10 Aug. 1920, Cmd. 964.

66. Text in Frangulis, ii, pp. 109-11. As in the Venizelos–Tittoni Agreement, Italy agreed to cede to Greece the Dodecanese except for Rhodes, the fate of which was made to depend on that of Cyprus. This agreement was to come into force on the same day as the Treaty of Sèvres; it therefore remained a dead letter and the Dodecanese remained Italian.

67. Poincaré, *Histoire politique: chroniques de quinzaine*, i, p. 264: 'La ville de Sèvres a maintenant, elle aussi, son fleuron dans la couronne de la paix. Le traité turc a été signé, à la manufacture nationale, au milieu des biscuits et des flambés. C'est lui-même un objet fragile, peut-être un vase brisé. N'y touchez pas.'

68. Treaty Series no. 12 (1920). *Tripartite Agreement between the British Empire, France and Italy respecting Anatolia...*, Cmd. 963.

69. Treaty Series no. 13 (1920). *Treaty between the Principal Allied and Associated Powers and Greece...*, Cmd 960. Western (Bulgarian) Thrace had been ceded by Bulgaria to the Allied Powers by the Treaty of Neuilly of 1919, and was now ceded by them to Greece. Eastern (Turkish) Thrace was ceded by Turkey to Greece under the Treaty of Sèvres.

70. Rodas, *Greece in Asia Minor*, pp. 179-80, describes the ceremony. Greek powers and functions were defined in Law 2493, *Govt. Gazette*, ser. A, i, 10 September 1920. Stergiadis, as High Commissioner, was given Cabinet rank, and virtually absolute powers within the zone.

71. F.O. 406/44, no. 183.

72. *D.B.F.P.*, no. 102; de Robeck to Curzon, 28 July 1920.

73. Greek General Staff, *The Asia Minor Expedition*, ii, app. 27.

74. *D.B.F.P.*, xiii, no. 152; Venizelos sent a similar 'urgent and secret' telegram to Henry Wilson on the same day (Stavridi Papers, 1920) but significantly not to the Foreign Office.

75. *D.B.F.P.*, xiii, no. 152.

76. Wilson's questions in Stavridi Papers, 1920, Caclamanos to Venizelos, 5 Oct. 1920. Venizelos's reply in Stavridi Papers, 1920, Venizelos to Caclamanos, 12 Oct. 1920.

77. Stavridi Papers, 1920; Venizelos to Greek Legation in London, 16 Oct. 1920, transmitting message for Lloyd George.

78. Toynbee, *The Western Question*, p. 227.

7. THE MONKEY'S BITE

1. Markezinis, *Political History of Modern Greece*, iv, p. 310.

2. ibid., pp. 319–20.

3. *Govt. Gazette*, ser. A, i, 11/24 Sept. 1920.

4. See, e.g. Venizelos Papers, 267; Venizelos to Alexander, 15 June 1917.

5. Ll. G. Papers, F 55/3/5; Granville to Hardinge, 19 May 1918.

6. Ll. G. Papers, F 55/3/4; Granville to Hardinge, 3 Nov. 1917.

7. There is an interesting analysis of the attitude of the Venizelists, and others, to the marriage, in Ll. G. Papers, F 94/3/41; Irene Noel Baker to J. Allen Baker, M.P., 6 April 1918, concluding that Venizelos, while 'personally in favour of the marriage ... is sincerely convinced that it will be extremely unpopular ... and proposes indefinite postponement'; whereas his Ministers are against the marriage altogether.

8. Ll. G. Papers, F 55/3/5; Granville to Hardinge, 19 May 1918.

9. Ll. G. Papers, F 55/3/6; Granville to Hardinge, 27 Dec. 1918.

10. Zalokostas, *Alexander*, p. 128.

11. Venizelos Papers, 267; Venizelos to Alexander, 6 June 1920; Markezinis, iv, p. 315.

12. Ll. G. Papers, F 55/3/8; Granville to ? (unnamed), 3 Dec. 1919.

13. Venizelos Papers, 315; Aspasia Manos to Venizelos, 16 March 1920.

14. Markezinis, iv, p. 315.

15. In his letter of 19 May 1918; Ll. G. Papers F 55/3/5.

16. Zalokostas, pp. 188f, contains a full account of the incident. Zalokostas was a friend of the King. Scurrilous accounts were circulated, e.g. Saraphis, *Memoirs*, p. 200: 'They said he wanted to see if he could breed from his wolfhound and the female monkey he held, and the male monkey bit him in jealousy.'

17. *D.B.F.P.*, xii, 497; Russell (chargé d'affaires) to Curzon 25 Oct. 1920: 'in the event of King Alexander's death, which is now regarded as inevitable, Prince Paul will be declared king and invited to assume the crown ... subject to conditions ensuring the formal abdication of ex-king.'

18. In the latter stages of the war, Venizelos had ruled out the possibility of establishing a republic in deference to British, Russian and Italian views; Ventiris, *Greece 1910–1920*, ii, p. 417.

19. *D.B.F.P.*, vii, pp. 377–8.

20. *D.B.F.P.*, xii, no. 335, p. 405.

21. Venizelos Papers, 315; Politis to Venizelos, 14–27 Feb. 1920.

22. *Govt. Gazette*, 1920, ser. A, i, Law 2485 of 7 Sept. concerning parliamentary elections in Thrace; Law 2492 of 10 Sept. concerning the annexation of Thrace, Imbros and Tenedos. The Peace Treaty had *not* yet been ratified, so these laws were of doubtful validity.

23. *Govt. Gazette*, 1920, ser. A, i, Law 2484 of 10 Sept.

24. e.g. Mazarakis, *Memoirs*, p. 283 (a 'terrible mistake'); Zavitsianos, ii, p. 84.

25. Vakas, *Venizelos as War Leader*, p. 428; Vakas was one of the officers involved, and regrets in his book that the plan came to nothing.

26. For such accusations, see the debate in parliament of 1/14 Feb. 1921 in Ethnikos Kiryx, *Speeches of the Greek Parliament 1909–56*, Athens 1958, 2nd period, vi, p. 51.

27. Malainos, *The Asia Minor Disaster*, pp. 77–8, citing the unpublished notes of General K. Mazarakis, the divisional commander in question.

28. Mazarakis, *Memoirs*, p. 283.

29. Spyridonos, *War and Freedom*, p. 104.

30. Danglis, *Memoirs*, ii, pp. 377–8; for a good example of the 'radical' Venizelist see Papanastasiou, *Studies, Speeches, Articles*, pp. 282–6.

31. Venizelos Papers, 267; undated autograph notes.

32. Long extracts from Venizelos's speeches in the electoral campaign, in particular his final speech at a rally in Athens on 28 Oct., are printed in Markezinis, iv, app., pp. 41–7.

33. Markezinis, iv, p. 316, with list of members.

34. Calogeropoulos and Stratos, *Notes on the Greek Question addressed to the President Woodrow Wilson*, p. 6.

35. I. Dragoumis, *Mémoire sur les affaires de Grèce adressé à la Conférence de la Paix à Paris*, p. 3. Dragoumis remarks that Greek claims, 'loin d'être basées sur des visées impérialistes, ne représentent que le minimum auquel la Grèce, en toute justice et selon le principe des nationalités, aurait droit.' I. Dragoumis, 'Second Memorandum on the Greek Question addressed to the Paris Peace Conference', in *Community Nation and State*, ed. P. Dragoumis, Athens, 1923.

36. Dragoumis, 'Second Memorandum...' pp. 31–2, accusing the two Powers of 'des velléités d'établir un protectorat sur la Grèce'; Calogeropoulos and Stratos, p. 56.

37. Stratigos, *Greece in Asia Minor*, pp. 114–15.

38. Kampanis, *Dimitrios Gounaris and the Greek Crisis of 1918–1922*, p. 292.

39. *Kathimerini*, 18/31 Oct. 1920.

40. ibid., 19 Oct./1 Nov. 1920.

41. Markezinis, iv, app., pp. 39–40.

42. ibid., app., p. 36.

43. Text in Kampanis, pp. 293–8.

44. Pallis, *Greeks Abroad*, pp. 176–7.

45. *D.B.F.P.*, xii, no. 437; Granville to Curzon, 19 Nov. 1920.

46. ibid., no. 428.

47. Daphnis, *The Greek Political Parties 1821–1961*, pp. 131–2.

48. Korisis, *Die politischen Parteien Griechenlands*, p. 76. The system of voting by ballots, not paper slips, was annulled in the revised constitution of 1911, but remained in practice until the elections of Nov. 1920, the last time on which it was used.

49. Lloyd George, *The Truth about the Peace Treaties*, ii, p. 1346.

50. Alastos, *Venizelos*, p. 206.

51. Zavitsianos, ii, p. 100.

52. Metaxas, *Diary*, ii, p. 506.

53. Triantaphyllou, *Asia Minor Disaster*, p. 152.

54. Phessopoulos, *The Disputes of Our Officers and the Dissolution of our Army in Asia Minor*, pp. 22f.

55. Campbell and Sherrard, *Modern Greece*, p. 267, commenting on the fall of Karamanlis's E.R.E. Government from power in 1963.

56. Zavitsianos, ii, p. 83; for similar views, see Ventiris, ii, pp. 362–3; Triantaphyllou, pp. 110–12.

57. Ventiris, ii, pp. 418–19; Venizelos's letter was written long after the event, in April 1931.

58. Ventiris, ii, p. 420.

59. ibid., p. 419.

60. Alexandris, *Political Memoirs*, pp. 63–6. The Romanian royal family's interest, apart from the solidarity of ruling houses, was in Prince George as a prospective husband for Princess Elizabeth of Romania.

61. Alexandris, loc. cit.; Venizelos Papers, 314; B. Dendramis (Consul General in Berne) to Venizelos, 3/16 Sept. 1919, reporting a conversation with Theotokis.

62. Zavitsianos, ii, p. 49; Venizelos Papers, 315; Politis to Venizelos 16/29 Sept. 1920, reporting a conversation with Embireikos, who argued in favour of Prince George. On the contribution of the Embireikos family to Venizelism, see Kitsikis, *Propagande et pressions en politique internationale*, pp. 312–13, 393.

63. Venizelos to Foreign Ministry, 2/15 June 1920, cited in Stratigos, pp. 111–12.

64. Paraskevopoulos, p. 368, writes that he was not consulted in this question. It was however true that there would have been pressure from below against an accommodation with Constantine, from politicians, officers, civil servants and businessmen who had profited by Venizelism and had a personal interest in excluding their royalist competitors from public life or commercial opportunities.

65. 'Vasilikon Ktinos': Ktinos is stronger than the English 'brute'

66. Markezinis, iv, p. 314.

8. THE NEW REGIME: CONSTANTINE RETURNS

1. Markezinis, *Political History of Modern Greece*, iv, pp. 322–3, cites a description of the events by Ioannis Koundouriotis, the Regent's brother, published in *Estia*, 30 Aug. 1935; Zavitsianos, *Recollections*, ii, p. 90.

2. *Govt. Gazette*, i, 4/17 November 1920. Markezinis, iv, app., pp. 48–9.

3. E. Chivers Davies, 'Election week in Athens', *Balkan Review*, iv, no. 5, Dec. 1920, pp. 342–3.

4. *D.B.F.P.*, xii, nos. 432, 433.

5. *D.B.F.P.*, xii, no. 434, Derby to Curzon, 18 Nov. 1920 reporting the views of Leygues, the new President of the Council; ibid., no. 438, conversation between Crowe and Paul Cambon, 19 Nov. 1920.

6. General Staff (War Office) appreciation of the military situation in Russia, Caucasia and Turkey, 19 Nov. 1920; Ll. G. Papers, F. 92/13/3.

7. For Soviet-Kemalist relations, see Kapur, *Soviet Russia and Asia*, pp. 90–114.

8. Memorandum by the Secretary of State for War, 23 Nov. 1920; Ll. G. Papers, F 92/13/4; see also Roskill, *Hankey, Man of Secrets*, ii, pp. 199–200.

9. *D.B.F.P.*, xii, no. 438; minute by Curzon on report of conversation between Crowe and Cambon of 19 Nov. 1920.

10. In the Eastern Committee of the Cabinet on 9 Dec. 1918.

11. *D.B.F.P.*, xii, no. 439.

12. ibid., no. 440, Curzon to Lindsay (Paris), 22 Nov. 1920.

13. ibid., no. 448, Russell to Curzon, 24 Nov. 1920.

14. ibid., no. 451; Keogh (Consul at Nice) to Curzon, 25 Nov. 1920, transmitting Stavridi's telegram.

15. Minutes of the Conference in *D.B.F.P.*, viii, ch. 14.

16. *D.B.F.P.*, viii, p. 816.

17. Text of Curzon's note in *D.B.F.P.*, viii, pp. 837–40.

18. *D.B.F.P.*, xii, no. 456, Granville to Curzon, 1 Dec. 1920.

19. *D.B.F.P.*, viii, p. 839.

20. *D.B.F.P.*, xii, no. 457.

21. Frangulis, *La Grèce* . . . , 2nd edn, ii, p. 175. Granville had communicated the warning by 5 Dec.; *D.B.F.P.*, xii, no. 436.

22. See e.g. Rentis, *Greek Foreign Policy after 1 November*, pp. 31–46, 62–6 and *passim*; and Venizelist witnesses in the Trial of the Six.

23. Rentis, p. 39.

24. Text of February 1918 Convention in *Govt. Gazette*, i, 4 April 1918; see Diomedis, *The Greek Economy before and after 1 November 1920*, pp. 7–12.

25. In his memo of 20 November; *D.B.F.P.*, xii, no. 439.

26. ibid., no. 451, Granville to Curzon, 4 Dec. 1920.

27. ibid., nos. 486–7, 489–91 for this and the Admiral Kelly incident.

28. ibid., no. 487, Granville to Curzon, 20 Dec. 1920.

29. ibid., no. 489, Curzon to Granville, 21 Dec. 1920.

30. ibid., no. 488.

31. In minutes on Nicolson's memo of 20 Dec.

32. Churchill, *The World Crisis: the Aftermath*, p. 377.

33. *Govt. Gazette*, 1920, iii, entries for 9/22 and 14/27 Nov. The information about dismissals and appointments in the subsequent paragraphs comes from *Govt. Gazette*, iii, and can be found under the date cited; hence I am not citing references for each statement (but note that dates in the text are New Style, and must be translated into Old Style to find date as in *Govt. Gazette*).

34. Resignations include: 6/19 November, Ministry of Finance, Director General of Accounts and General Economic Inspector; 8/21 November, Ministry of Justice, Secretary General; 9/22 November, Ministry of Communications, Secretary General; 16/29 November, Ministry of Relief, Secretary General.

35. For the work of these three, who were in the forefront of the educational reform movement of these years, see G. K. Gatos, unpublished memorandum of Delmouzos to E. Venizelos (*Anekdoto Ypomnima tou Delmouzou pros ton El. Venizelo*), in *Epoches*, July 1965. On the whole, the Venizelist Liberal Party contained, in its left wing, the demoticist, reforming elements, and the anti-Venizelists stood for a conservative attitude to education and language; but there were exceptions such as the demoticist Ion Dragoumis.

36. Royal Decree of 8/21 Nov. 1920; see also Malainos, *History of Foreign Interventions*, vi, pp. 11–12.

37. Legislative Decree of 4/17 Dec. on the 'reinstatement of the dismissed permanent functionaries'.

38. L.D. of 4/17 Dec. on the 'reinstatement of the dismissed . . . professors of the National and Capodistrian University'; L.D. of 21 Dec./3 Jan. on the 'reinstatement of the dismissed professors of the National Metsovo Polytechnic'.

39. Royal Decree of 8/21 Nov. on the 'provision of an amnesty'.

40. On 13/26 Nov., eighty-one sentences were quashed, and fifteen reduced by Royal Decree: *Govt. Gazette*, 1920, iii, no. 255.

41. *Govt. Gazette*, 1920, iii, lists appointments and dismissals.

42. The law was known as the *dekaminon* ('ten month law').

43. *Govt. Gazette*, 1920, i, no. 287; Legislative Decree of 15/28 Dec. on the 'restoration of officers to their order of seniority'.

44. Rodas, *Greece in Asia Minor*, pp. 188–90.

45. Rodas, pp. 188–9, describes how a Royalist committee demanded that Stergiadis sack the Chiefs of Police and Press Bureau; he naturally refused.

46. Greek General Staff, *The Asia Minor Expedition*, ii, pp. 265–8. This, the official history, states flatly that 'after the failure of the Venizelos Government was officially made known, General Paraskevopoulos decided to transfer the 8th Cretan Regiment ... from Salihli to Smyrna ... with a view to active intervention on behalf of Eleftherios Venizelos' (p. 266); a not implausible statement, but one that is not conclusively proved by the evidence of the history, which shows only that Royalist officers *believed* that a Venizelist coup was imminent.

47. *D.B.F.P.*, xiii, no. 178; Rumbold to Curzon, 21 Nov. 1920, transmitting report of E. C. Hole, Acting Vice-Consul in Smyrna.

48. ibid., no. 179; Rumbold to Curzon, 22 Nov. 1920, transmitting report by Hole.

49. See, e.g. Malainos, *History of Foreign Interventions*, vi, p. 21; Mazarakis, *Memoirs*, p. 291.

50. I. Passas, *The Agony of a Nation*, Athens 1925, p. 171; the quotation is from Papoulas's report to the War Minister of 15/28 Dec. 1921.

51. Estimates of their numbers vary from 60 (Spyridonos, *War and Freedom*, p. 108), to 140 permanent officers and 200 reservists (Malainos, *History of Foreign Interventions*, vi, p. 22).

52. *Govt. Gazette*, 1920, iii, no. 257 of 16/29 Nov. 1920; Nider submitted his resignation, but was persuaded to delay it. He told the British Vice-Consul that his retirement was enforced by the conviction that his personal friendship with Venizelos would deprive him of the new Government's confidence; *D.B.F.P.*, xiii, no. 185. He was finally relieved very suddenly shortly before the March operations; Rodas, p. 207. It was odd, to say the least, that the Government and G.H.Q. should thus break up the successful First Army Corps so shortly before offensive operations, when Nider had shown that he was prepared (for a time at least) to carry on as Corps Commander.

53. Saraphis, *Memoirs*, pp. 205–6.

54. Such a study, which would be interesting, would have to be based on the *Govt. Gazette* (appointments, dismissals, etc.) and on

the archives of the War Ministry. According to Spyros B. Markezinis, in a letter to me, part of the General Staff archives has been destroyed, so that there would be gaps even in a study based on these sources. The General Staff history of the Asia Minor campaign (Greek General Staff, *The Expedition to Asia Minor*) contains information only on the higher posts, viz. Corps, Division and Regimental commanders and staffs and Battalion commanders, and General, Corps and Divisional Staff officers.

55. This is Saraphis's own estimate; *Memoirs*, p. 207.

56. For this charge, see Lloyd George, *The Truth about the Peace Treaties*, ii, p.1347: a superbly derisive account of the Royalists' handling of the army. For the anti-Venizelist point of view, see Malainos, *History of Foreign Interventions*, vi, pp. 17–23; Prince Andrew, *Towards Disaster*, prologue.

57. Spyridonos, generally the most reasonable of those who took part in the campaign, writes that the return of the *apotaktoi* 'caused a certain lessening in the fighting spirit of the army especially in the operations up till May 1921, after which the experience gained by the *apotaktoi* improved the situation'; *War and Freedom*, p. 107. See also Mazarakis, pp. 290–1.

9. THE LONDON CONFERENCE

1. F.O. 421/300, nos. 92, 97; 421/301, no. 44; Sessions of Parliament of 5/18, 6/19, 10/23 May.

2. Pallis, *Greeks Abroad*, pp. 177–8.

3. F.O. 421/300, nos. 82, 98, 119; 421/301, nos. 44, 51, 74.

4. *D.B.F.P.*, xv, no. 4, p. 36. The decision to convoke a conference was taken in Paris on 25 Jan.

5. *Trial of the Six*, pp. 241–3; Venizelos communicated his own record of the conversations with Kerr on 26 January and with Lloyd George on 29 January to D. Rallis, the prime minister, via P. Metaxas, Greek Chargé d'Affaires at Paris. The letter was the subject of lengthy discussion in the Trial of the Six. See Lloyd George papers, F 90/1/36, for Kerr's record of his conversation.

6. In Greek, *symptyxis* ('shortening of the front').

7. Stavridi Papers, 1920; Venizelos to Stavridi, 29 Dec. 1920.

8. Ll. G. Papers, F 90/1/34; the note is marked 'secret'.

9. Ll. G. Papers, F 90/1/34.

10. See Lloyd George's remarks to Venizelos on 30 May 1922: 'The tide was turning and the Greeks must keep their heart up until Constantine disappeared from the scene and opinion throughout the west came round them [*sic*] as it certainly would do...'; Ll. G. Papers, F 86/2/3.

11. *D.B.F.P.*, xii, no. 453, p. 530, n. 4.

12. Ll. G. Papers, F 90/1/34.

13. e.g., Anglelomatis, *The Chronicle of a Great Tragedy*; Passas, *The Agony of a Nation*; and witnesses in the Trial of the Six.

14. Ll. G. Papers, F 55/2/1; Stavridi to Philip Kerr, 17 Jan. 1921.

15. Proceedings of the Conference (the Third Conference of London), in *D.B.F.P.*, xv, ch. 2, pp. 125–425; also Frangulis, ii, pp. 182–229.

16. *D.B.F.P.*, xv, pp. 34–5.

17. ibid., xvii, no. 38; memo of 12 Feb.

18. ibid., xv, no. 13, pp. 125–6; 18 Feb. 1921.

19. ibid., no. 15, app. 2, p. 135; memo on the Greek Army in Asia Minor handed to the British and French by the Greek delegation on Monday 21 Feb. 1921.

20. Ll. G. Papers, F 55/2/3; A. Rizo Rangavis (Greek Minister in London) to Philip Kerr, 22 Feb. 1921, enclosing, on Kalogeropoulos's instructions, confidential memo on the Greek army in Asia Minor 'for the personal use of the Prime Minister'. The quotations in the text are from the memo, not the letter. Rizo Rangavis sent Kerr a second memo for Lloyd George on 25 Feb. with annexe giving detailed figures of Greek effectiveness, arms, ammunition, lorries, etc. This second memo gives an optimistic picture of Greek morale and readiness for an offensive towards Eski Shehir and Afyon Karahisar; Ll. G. Papers F 55/2/4.

21. Metaxas, *Diary*, iii, p. 87. Gounaris made the remark on 11 April 1921.

22. *D.B.F.P.*, xv, p. 150.

23. ibid., no. 17.

24. ibid., no. 22, 24 Feb. 1921. Curzon's draft proposal embodying the decision of the Conference is on p. 193. The idea was initiated at this session of the Conference by Briand, but was already in the air before this date. See the note from Montagu to Lloyd George of 21 Feb. in Ll. G. Papers, F 206/4/27.

25. *D.B.F.P.*, xv, no. 24, app., pp. 202–3.

26. ibid., no. 32, p. 266.

27. Stratigos, *Greece in Asia Minor*, pp. 172–3; Kalogeropoulos to Minister of Foreign Affairs, Athens, 1 Mar. 1921.

28. e.g. by Stratigos, p. 174.

29. *D.B.F.P.*, xvii, no. 66, n. 1, p. 85. The Italian Ambassador asked Crowe on 22 March if there was any truth in the statement that the Greek Government had been told that 'a forward movement on the part of the Greeks at this moment had the fullest sympathy of the British Government'. Crowe said no. Curzon minuted, 'I am afraid that, with the memory of certain intercepts in my mind, I could not have given the emphatic assurance of Sir E. Crowe.' See also Roskill, *Hankey, Man of Secrets*, ii, p. 223.

30. According to Hankey, it was only at Curzon's insistence that

Lloyd George spoke thus to the Turks, in his parting interview with Tewfik Bey; Roskill, ii, p. 223.

31. Stratigos, *Greece in Asia Minor*, pp. 187–8.
32. ibid.
33. *D.B.F.P.*, xv, no. 32, pp. 268–9; the meeting was attended by Lloyd George, Kalogeropoulos, Rizo Rangavis, Hankey and Kerr.
34. *D.B.F.P.*, xv, no. 33; meeting of 4 March.
35. ibid., no. 32, p. 268.
36. ibid., no. 48, pp. 346–7.
37. Roskill, *Hankey, Man of Secrets*, ii, p. 222.
38. Stevenson, *Lloyd George, a Diary*, p. 241.
39. *D.B.F.P.*, xv, no. 52, text of proposals at pp. 370–1.
40. ibid., no. 54, p. 382.
41. ibid., no. 52, p. 370.
42. ibid., no. 69, p. 449, 18 Mar. 1921.
43. ibid., p. 451.

10. SUMMER OFFENSIVE

1. See on the March campaign Greek General Staff, *The Asia Minor Expedition*, iii, pp. 151–321; Toynbee, *The Western Question in Greece and Turkey*, pp. 233–5, 246–54.
2. Toynbee, who observed this phase of the campaign, attributes the Greek failure to poor staffwork and overconfidence: 'Expecting to meet nothing but *chettés* and to disperse them as easily as before, they did not regroup their forces, but simply sent forward on each front the divisions that had been in winter quarters there. The three northern divisions were thus thrown without reserves against fortified positions at forty to fifty miles' distance from their base at Brusa and with no communications but roads never intended for motor transport' (Toynbee, op. cit., p. 234).
3. ibid., p. 247.
4. ibid., p. 252.
5. F.O. 421/302, no. 47.
6. Metaxas, *Diary*, iii, pp. 71–7.
7. ibid., iii, pp. 77–101; entry for 11 April 1921.
8. ibid., iii, p. 82.
9. ibid., iii, p. 83.
10. Passas, *The Agony of a Nation*, pp. 67–8.
11. *D.B.F.P.*, xvii, no. 97; Granville to Curzon, 7 April 1921, citing Theotokis's estimate of 40,000, but stating that this estimate is probably optimistic. The official history estimates that these three classes, with the two reservist classes called up in April, and certain others mobilized for the home front, yielded 'about 58,000 men'; Greek General Staff, *The Asia Minor Expedition*, iv, p. 23.

12. For these preparations, see Stratigos, pp. 206–10; Greek General Staff, iv, pp. 22–35

13. *D.B.F.P.*, xvii, no. 233.

14. F.O. 421/302, no. 47.

15. Toynbee, p. 273.

16. Cmd 1478 (1921).

17. Cmd 1478 (1921).

18. Report of the Interallied Commission in Cmd 1478 (1921); Red Cross enquiry in M. Gehri, 'Mission d'enquête en Anatolie (12–22 mai 1921)', *Revue Internationale de la Croix Rouge*, no. 31, 1921.

19. Ll. G. Papers, F 13/2/18, Vansittart to Kerr, 26 April 1921; *D.B.F.P.*, xvii, nos. 100, 130, 135.

20. *D.B.F.P.*, xvii, nos. 128, 159.

21. CAB 44 (21), of 31 May 1921; there is an extract in Ll. G. Papers, F 206/5.

22. Proceedings of the three meetings of the Cabinet Committee on the Future of Constantinople in Ll. G. Papers, F 206/5; see also Walder, *The Chanak Affair*, pp. 138–49. Members were Lloyd George, Curzon, Churchill, Montagu, Mond (Health), Worthington-Evans (War); H. A. L. Fisher attended the second meeting. Besides these politicians, Sir Henry Wilson attended all three meetings, Sir Edward Grigg the first two, and Hankey and Harington the first only.

23. Text in Walder, pp. 142–4. See also Sir M. Hankey's recommendations in a memo of 2 June for Lloyd George, in Ll. G. Papers, F 25/1/36. These, which Hankey said had crystallized out of the recent discussions, were close to the line finally agreed.

24. They are summarized in Walder, pp. 146–8.

25. Ll. G. Papers, F 206/5.

26. For the military attaché's report, see *D.B.F.P.*, xvii, nos. 233, 239, 240, 242.

27. Churchill, *The World Crisis: the Aftermath*, pp. 395–6.

28. *D.B.F.P.*, xvii, no. 213; Lamb to Curzon, 7 June 1921. Sariyannis had expressed similar views in even stronger terms in May; Ll. G. Papers, F 206/5, Dossier of Reports on the Greek Army considered by the Cabinet on 9 June 1921.

29. *D.B.F.P.*, xvii, nos. 233, 239, 240, 242 of 16–18 June.

30. F.O. 421/302, no. 47; Lindley to Curzon, enclosing Hoare Nairne's military chapter for 1921.

31. Ll. G. Papers, F 13/2/32; Lloyd George to Curzon, 16 June 1921.

32. *D.B.F.P.*, xv, nos. 88, 89.

33. Text in *D.B.F.P.*, xvii, no. 88, app. 2.

34. Churchill, *The World Crisis: the Aftermath*, pp. 396–7.

35. Text in Vakas, *Venizelos as War Leader*, p. 439, undated.

36. Frangulis, *La Grèce . . .*, 2nd edn, ii, pp. 284–5.

37. Dousmanis, *Memoirs*, pp. 260–61.

38. Dousmanis, *The Internal Aspect of the Asia Minor Entangle-ment, passim,* esp. pp. 52–68, 81–90. The book contains the texts of the memoranda with which Dousmanis bombarded King and government throughout this period. Dousmanis's object was to per-suade the government to put real power into the hands of the King (and *a fortiori* of Dousmanis himself). His book is marred by its arrogance and petulant tone of self-justification.

39. Passas, pp. 85–6; Dousmanis, *The Internal Aspect,* pp. 53–4.

40. Description of the campaign in Greek General Staff, iv; Spyri-donos, *War and Freedom,* pp. 140–55.

41. Kinross, *Ataturk,* pp. 268–9.

42. Greek gains are incompletely listed in Brig. Gen. X. Stratigos, *General Summary of the Military Operations in Asia Minor from 7 to 21 July 1921,* Greek War Ministry, 1921.

43. Stratigos, loc. cit.

44. Stevenson, *Lloyd George, a Diary,* p. 230.

45. Kinross, p. 271.

46. Spyridonos, pp. 158–9.

47. ibid., loc. cit.

48. ibid., p. 159.

49. Passas, pp. 113–15; Spyridonos, p. 161; Stratigos, *Greece in Asia Minor,* pp. 243–7; Dousmanis, *The Internal Aspect,* p. 81.

50. Text in Passas, p. 114.

51. Text in Stratigos, *Greece in Asia Minor,* pp. 245–6.

52. Spyridonos, p. 161.

53. Constantine, *A King's Private Letters* (Nash & Grayson, un-dated); letters to Princess Paola of Saxe-Weimar; letter of 18 June 1921.

54. Constantine, op. cit., letter of 9 August.

55. For this aspect of the war, see Toynbee, *The Western Question,* vii, 'The War of Extermination'. Constantine, his brother Prince Andrew, and S. Saraphis are among the very few Greeks who men-tion it.

56. Description of the campaign in Greek General Staff, *The Asia Minor Expedition,* v; Spyridonos, pp. 164–90.

57. The Turkish cavalry was a constant menace to the Greeks' security, capturing pack animals and lorries in its daring raids. On 27 September, cavalry actually attacked Greek G.H.Q. at Uzumbey. The Crown Prince, who was present, displayed a cool nerve; Spyri-donos, pp. 175–6.

58. Danglis, *Memoirs,* ii, p. 396; Venizelos (Monte Carlo) to Danglis, 20 May/2 June 1921.

59. Text in Danglis, p. 409. An incomplete English translation is given in Alastos, *Venizelos,* pp. 210–12.

60. Danglis, pp. 410–11. The letters were published at Kavaphakis's

suggestion in *Eleftheros Typos*, 19 and 20 Sept. 1921, without the name of the recipient being revealed. They were discussed in cabinet, after which Gounaris issued a statement replying to them; which in turn provoked a Venizelist press campaign against the Government's policies by A. Kavaphakis, S. Simos, A. Diomedis, K. Zavitsianos, D. Lambrakis, K. Rentis and others.

61. Danglis, *Memoirs*, p. 409.

11. WINTER DISENCHANTMENT

1. *D.B.F.P.*, xii, no. 472.

2. Argyropoulos, File 9, p. 3.

3. On the Smyrna Committee, see Rodas, *Greece in Asia Minor*, p. 265; on the London and other foreign Committees, Venizelos Papers, letters to E. Venizelos, 1921–22, *passim*; Argyropoulos, File 9, pp. 23–4.

4. Rodas, p. 265.

5. Venizelos Papers, 316; N. Apostolopoulos to Venizelos, 17 May 1922.

6. *D.B.F.P.*, xvii, no. 417; Hardinge to Curzon, 21 Oct. 1921.

7. Frangulis, *La Grèce*, 2nd edn, ii, p. 310. On the question of allied neutrality and Greek rights of visit and search, see Frangulis, ii, pp. 328–35, 354–8, 389; *D.B.F.P.*, xvii, pp. 376–8, 385, 409, 463, 497.

8. *D.B.F.P.*, xvii, no. 405; memo by Curzon on 'Intervention between Greece and Turkey', 7 Oct. 1921.

9. Cf. Toynbee, *The Western Question*, pp. 238–9; 'Stalemate had been reached and further offensive operations by either party were foredoomed to failure.'

10. Frangulis, ii, pp. 294–7; *D.B.F.P.*, xvii, no. 502 (text of agreement with analysis).

11. *D.B.F.P.*, xvii, no. 425; see also Frangulis, ii, pp. 312–13.

12. ibid., no. 431; Frangulis, ii, pp. 314–15.

13. *Trial of the Six, passim*; in particular item 10 of the indictment; Frangulis, ii, p. 476.

14. Toynbee, pp. 243–4.

15. For the economic situation in general, see Diomedis, *The Greek Economy before and after 1 November 1920*, and Andréadès, *Les Effets économiques et sociaux de la guerre en Grèce*; also F.O. 286/750, *passim*.

16. *D.B.F.P.*, xvii, no. 469; minutes by Nicolson, Crowe and Curzon on Vansittart's record of a talk with Baltazzis on 2 Dec.

17. *D.B.F.P.*, xvii, nos. 478, 485.

18. Frangulis, ii, p. 321; see also *D.B.F.P.*, xvii, no. 493.

19. *D.B.F.P.*, xvii, no. 499; Curzon to Bentinck, 2 January 1922.

20. *D.B.F.P.*, xvii, no. 549, n. 3, for Nicolson's comments on the

loan, and an interesting letter from Sir G. Armstrong of Armstrong's Bank to Viscount Long, 22 Jan. 1922.

21. Metaxas, *Diary*, iii, app. 13; Andrew to Metaxas, 1 Jan. 1922.

22. High Commission Papers, File 30; letter of 15/28 Oct. 1921.

23. Passas, pp. 162–3; Kontoulis to Papoulas, 15/28 Oct. 1921. See also General Polymenakos's letter of 2 Nov. in Passas, *The Agony of a Nation*, pp. 163–4, and the whole section, pp. 160–73, for the problems of morale and Papoulas's reports to the War Ministry.

24. F.O. 286/756; W. L. C. Knight, Vice Consul at Volos, to Granville, 17/31 May.

25. Venizelos Papers, 267; Venizelos to Stavridi, 16 Dec. 1921, for Venizelos's enlistment of Lloyd George's support for Meletios.

26. For an account of Meletios's stewardship as Metropolitan of Athens, see Papadopoulos, *Meletius of Athens and the Holy League*.

For an extreme Royalist view of Meletios, see Karolidou, *Accusation before the Holy Synod*. This document is interesting for the light it throws on the views of the extreme conservatives of the academic world at the time of the *dichasmos*. It combines pedantic erudition on points of orthodox dogma with a personal spite and abuse reminiscent of the propaganda diatribes of the ancient world, such as those of Octavius Caesar and Mark Antony. According to Karolidis, Metaxakis was born in Crete of an unknown family. His brother was a sheep-thief. Having schemed his way to the top, Meletios squandered the moneys of the ecclesiastical chest on luxury furnishings, banquets, etc., made trips to Europe and the United States 'purely for pleasure', adopting Frankish dress and clipping his beard while he was abroad, extorted contributions for marriages, baptisms, etc., cheated the customs over an imported motor car, absconded with some Patriarchal robes, and tampered with the church's traditional music. More seriously, Karolidis condemns Meletios's interest in the ecumenical movement, accusing him of being soft on Anglicanism, and claiming that his views lead to 'anti-Christian atheism'. The document also contains an account of Meletios's attitude to King Constantine and the Royalist Bishops, and of his 'uncanonical and illegal' establishment as Metropolitan of Athens.

27. Venizelos Papers, 316; Meletios (Greek Orthodox See in America) to Venizelos, 8/21 July 1921.

28. *Eleftheros Typos*, 2 Feb. 1922.

29. Rodas, p. 265; Angelomatis, *Chronicle of a Great Tragedy*, p. 130.

30. F.O. 421/302, no. 34; Lindley to Curzon, 24 Feb. 1922.

31. Passas, p. 174; Stratigos, pp. 337–8; Papoulas's evidence in *Trial of the Six*, pp. 64–6.

32. *D.B.F.P.*, xvii, no. 504.

33. His views on the Greeks and the Near Eastern question emerge forcefully in his *Histoire politique: chroniques de quinzaine*, 4 vols., Paris 1920–22.

34. Stevenson, *Lloyd George, a Diary*, p. 242.

35. *D.B.F.P.*, xvii, no. 508; conversation between Poincaré and Curzon, 16 Jan. 1922.

36. *D.B.F.P.*, xvii, nos. 509, 511, 514–19.

37. Passas, p. 151; Theotokis to Papoulas, 5 Feb. 1922.

38. Passas, pp. 151–2; Papoulas to Theotokis, 8 Feb. 1922.

39. Gounaris to Curzon, 15 Feb. 1922; English text in Ll. G. Papers F 199/9/3, French text in Frangulis, ii, pp. 350–52.

40. See *D.B.F.P.*, xvii, nos. 529, 536. For further evidence of the British difficulty in finding a policy, ibid., nos. 515–16, 519, 524, 526.

41. ibid., no. 544.

42. English text in ibid., no. 549; French text in Frangulis, ii, pp. 352–3.

43. *D.B.F.P.*, xvii, no. 548; Curzon to Lindley, 6 March 1922.

44. Text in Passas, pp. 177–84.

45. Passas, p. 179.

46. See the *Amyna*'s letter to Papoulas of 1 March; Passas, pp. 187–9.

47. Passas, p. 187; Theotokis to Papoulas, 3 March 1922.

48. *D.B.F.P.*, xvii, ch. 4; Conversations in Paris, 22–26 March 1922.

49. ibid., nos. 564, 565.

50. ibid., no. 560, n. 11.

51. French text, Frangulis, ii, pp. 360–65; English, Cmd 1641, 1922; *D.B.F.P.*, xvii, no. 568, annexe 1 contains Curzon's final draft.

52. *D.B.F.P.*, xvii, no. 575; Lindley to Curzon, 29 March 1922.

53. Frangulis, ii, p. 372; *D.B.F.P.*, xvii, nos. 600, 654.

54. ibid., no. 583; Rumbold to Curzon, 5 April 1922, enclosing condensed version of Yussuf Kemal Bey's reply to the Allies' proposals; see also no. 603 for Yussuf Kemal's later note of 22 April, and French texts in Frangulis, ii, p. 378. Curzon approved the French reply to Ankara that the Allies would advance the date of the Greek evacuation to 'as soon as the body of the peace conditions have been accepted' (*D.B.F.P.*, xvii, no. 594, Curzon to Rumbold, 12 April); but further than this he would not go, nor did the Turks accept the conditions.

55. *D.B.F.P.*, xvii, no. 583, n. 5.

56. The full course of this depressing correspondence between April and August 1922 can be traced in *D.B.F.P.*, xvii, nos. 583, 594, 603, 607, 609, 615, 619, 627, 630, 632, 638, 639, 645, 646, 656, 659, 676, 680, 699, 728, 730, 733, 737, 742, 743.

57. ibid., nos. 742–3.

58. F.O. 286/757; memo by Sir Eyre Crowe of talk with Venizelos, 13 Oct. 1921.

59. Venizelos Papers, 316; Benakis 'et amis' to V. (in Havana), 7 Feb. 1922, and *passim*.

60. Text in Venizelos Papers, 268.

61. Venizelos Papers, 268; autograph draft letter, Venizelos to Benakis, 19 Mar. 1922.

62. Venizelos Papers, 268; this draft is in a dossier marked *Simeioseis* (notes), which contains various jottings and a bundle of telegrams and drafts concerning the *Amyna*. The draft, which is not in Venizelos's hand, is undated, and the recipient unnamed.

63. In the first draft of the telegram cited, Venizelos toyed with 'dans ces conditions générales je croirais devoir, si étais invité, accepter représentation diplomatique', and the much weaker 'je pourrais envisager possibilité accepter'. The final draft in English reverts to 'under these conditions I should consider it my duty'. But it is uncertain in what form the telegram was sent.

64. F.O. 286/750; Bentinck to Curzon, 30 Dec. 1921.

65. Passas, p. 191.

66. Passas, p. 193; the quotation is from Papoulas's memo to Theotokis of 16/29 March.

67. Passas, pp. 194-6, citing Gounaris's statement verbatim; Stratigos, pp. 354-5.

68. Venizelos Papers, 316; Apostolopoulos to Venizelos, 10 May 1922.

69. Text in Passas, p. 198; Argyropoulos and Kondylis to Papoulas, 18/31 March 1922.

70. *D.B.F.P.*, xvii, no. 578.

71. ibid., no. 580.

72. ibid., no. 601.

73. Passas, p. 199; Papoulas to 'the Patriarchate', undated.

74. Passas, pp. 201-2, citing Papoulas's account. Papoulas wrote in ignorance that the scheme was Venizelos's; it was to the advantage of the *Amyna* to present it as their own.

75. Papoulas and Argyropoulos give differing accounts of the reasons; Passas, pp. 201-2; Argyropoulos, File 9, pp. 14-16.

76. The despair is mirrored in Meletios's eloquent letter to Venizelos of 8 May 1922; Venizelos Papers, 316.

77. Passas, pp. 202-7, 211.

78. Passas, pp. 197, 235-6. Besides conducting intermittent warfare on the clergy in the zone who recognized and supported Meletios, he had A. Lambrou, one of the leaders of the Smyrna Committee, arrested and banished to Naxos. He also played a part in bringing about the removal of Papoulas.

12. A MAZE WITH NO EXIT

1. *D.B.F.P.*, xvii, no. 678; Lindley to Balfour, 7 July 1922.

2. This is repeatedly emphasized in dispatches and telegrams from the British Minister in Athens to the Foreign Office, e.g. *D.B.F.P.*, xvii, nos. 536, 575 and 576 of 19 Feb., 29 and 30 Mar. 1922.

3. On the Loan, see Andréadès, *Les Effets économiques et sociaux de la guerre en Grèce*, pp. 59–60.

4. *D.B.F.P.*, xvii, no. 636; Lindley to Curzon, 20 May 1922.

5. F.O. 421/302, no. 48; Lindley to Curzon, 8 April 1922, stating that the loan had not created panic or revolution, as opponents had predicted, but that 'the Public have accepted the law very philosophically.... M. Gounaris was always confident that the law would not prove unpopular, and maintained that the Greek peasant was sufficiently intelligent to appreciate the damage done to his savings by an unlimited issue of paper, and would prefer a forced loan.... The skill with which M. Protopapadakis, the Minister of Finance, piloted the measure through the Chamber has also added much to the prestige of the Government.' Lindley, who had himself expected 'an immense issue of new paper', gives the Government credit for courage.

6. G. Vrachinos, cited in Danglis, p. 433.

7. F.O. 421/302, nos. 83, 89; Lindley to Curzon, 18, 25 May 1922.

8. Venizelos Papers, 316; Meletios to Venizelos, 25 April 1922.

9. Venizelos Papers, 316; Meletios to Venizelos, 24 May 1922.

10. Ll. G. Papers, F 86/2/3: 'Notes of a Conversation held in the Prime Minister's room, House of Commons, 30 May 1922'. The minute is marked 'Very Secret'. Present were Lloyd George, Venizelos and Sir Edward Grigg.

11. Venizelos Papers, 317; Exindaris to Venizelos, 16/29 Aug. 1922.

12. Passas, *The Agony of a Nation*, p. 251.

13. Lloyd George, *The Truth about the Peace Treaties*, ii, p. 1348.

14. F.O. 424/254, no. 67, enclosure; Col. Hoare Nairne to Lindley, 13 July 1922.

15. According to Theodore Stephanides, in conversation with the author, the men called Hatzianestis 'glass-legs' (*gyalopodi*). His reputation as an eccentric dated largely from an incident in 1915 at Drama, when a number of troops under his command mutinied.

16. Passas, p. 257; Phessopoulos, *The Disputes of our Officers*, pp. 51–2. Hatzianestis described himself at the Trial of the Six, with pride, as one who suffered from inflexibility of the backbone (metaphorically); i.e. he was pig-headed.

17. F.O. 424/254, no. 67, enclosure; Hoare Nairne to Lindley, 13 July 1922.

18. loc. cit. Hoare Nairne found that the troops' clothing was satis-

factory. The food was sufficient, but monotonous – macaroni appeared on the menu every day. Arms were well cared for. The health and spirits were excellent, the relations between officers and men good. More training was being carried out by troops in local reserve for the front line than ever before; and for the first time during the war he saw the men enjoying organized amusements, including football and amateur dramatics.

19. Mr Theodore Stephanides kindly gave me a good example of these.

20. Stavridis, *Behind the Scenes of the K.K.E.*, pp. 56–67.

21. ibid., pp. 79–80.

22. *D.B.F.P.*, xvii, no. 54; Harington to War Office, 17 July, reporting that the French have evidence of troop movements, and doubting whether they mean anything.

23. French texts in Frangulis, ii, pp. 391–3.

24. F.O. 424/254, no. 90; Bentinck to Balfour, 29 July 1922.

25. F.O. 424/254, no. 54; Harington to War Office, 17 July 1922.

26. F.O. 424/254, no. 100; Rumbold to Balfour, 30 July 1922; see also *D.B.F.P.*, xvii, nos. 717, 724.

27. *D.B.F.P.*, xvii, no. 718.

28. F.O. 424/254, no. 106; French note in Frangulis, ii, p. 393.

29. Frangulis, ii, pp. 328–35, 354–8, 389; and *D.B.F.P.*, xvii, *passim*.

30. Report of S. de Bilinski in F.O. 424/254, no. 148. Frangulis defends the Greek Government's actions on these lines, writing that on 31 July the Greek Chargé d'Affaires in London telegraphed that 'the British Cabinet Minister about whom I have telegraphed to you before continues to recommend that we display firmness and resolution'; Frangulis, ii, p. 393. I have found no documentary evidence to suggest that the Greeks were at any time encouraged to look towards Constantinople, and much evidence to the contrary (e.g. warnings on the subject issued by Granville in 1921, on Curzon's instructions).

31. F.O. 424/254, no. 20; Lindley to Balfour, 30 June 1922.

32. F.O. 424/254, no. 18; Lindley to Balfour, 8 July 1922.

33. F.O. 424/254, no. 40; Lindley to Balfour, 14 July 1922.

34. Frangulis, ii, p. 388.

35. F.O. 286/790; Lamb to Bentinck, 1 August 1922.

36. ibid.; Lamb to Bentinck, 31 July 1922.

37. F.O. 424/254; Lindley to Balfour, 14 July 1922.

38. F.O. 286/790; Note Verbale of 15 August 1922. A new treaty settlement was required because the Treaty of Sèvres was of course still unratified.

39. Lindley's annual report for 1922, cited in *D.B.F.P.*, xvii, no. 727, n. 5.

40. *Parliamentary Debates*, H.C. v, 157, cols. 1997–2006; 4 Aug. 1922.
41. *D.B.F.P.*, xvii, no. 727; Bentinck to Balfour, 7 Aug. 1922.

13. CATASTROPHE

1. Spyridonos, *War and Freedom*, p. 212.
2. *Discours du Ghazi Moustafa Kemal*, Oct. 1927, Leipzig 1929, p. 528.
3. ibid.
4. Kinross, *Ataturk*, p. 311.
5. Stavridis, *Behind the Scenes of the K.K.E.*, pp. 81–2. Stavridis was told over his own communist telephone network of the crumbling of the 4th Division front and the action of the two sergeants. He thereupon hit on the slogan '*Sta spitia sas*' (Home, let's go home) and instructed his communist contacts to meet up in Smyrna.
6. Trikoupis, *The Command of Large Units in War*, p. 368.
7. Greek General Staff, *The Asia Minor Campaign*, vii, p. 283 and app. 21.
8. Gonatas, *Memoirs*, p. 207.
9. Stavridis, p. 87.
10. Gonatas, p. 209.
11. Angelomatis, *Chronicle of a Great Tragedy*, pp. 175–6.
12. Dobson's account in Oeconomos, *The Tragedy of the Christian Near East*.
13. Horton, *The Blight of Asia*, p. 118.
14. Admiral Sir Bertram Thesiger, *Naval Memories*, privately printed.
15. Horton, pp. 119–20.
16. Venizelos Papers, 317; Chrysostom to Venizelos, 7 Sept. 1922.
17. Thesiger, *Naval Memories*.
18. Horton, p. 126.
19. Mr Wallance, quoted in Oeconomos.
20. Thesiger, *Naval Memories*.
21. Ward Price, *Daily Mail*, 16 Sept. 1922, quoted in Oeconomos, pp. 9–10.

14. REVOLUTION: TRIAL OF THE SIX

1. Metaxas, *Diary*, iii, entry for 13/26 Sept. 1922.
2. ibid., for 14/27 Sept. 1922.
3. loc. cit.
4. Venizelos Papers, 317; Apostolopoulos to Venizelos, 3 Oct. 1922
5. F.O. 421/303, no. 52; Lindley to Curzon, 1 Oct. 1922. Lindley's dispatches are the basis of much of this section.
6. ibid., loc. cit.

7. Metaxas, *Diary*, iii, entry for 17/30 Sept. 1922.

8. Thesiger, *Naval Memories*.

9. *Daily Telegraph*, 23 Oct. 1922; quoted in Oeconomos, *The Tragedy of the Christian Near East*.

10. *Toronto Daily Star*, 22 Oct. 1922, 'A Silent, Ghastly Procession', reprinted in Hemingway, *By-Line*, ed. W. White, London, 1968.

11. Text in Frangulis, *La Grèce*, ii, pp. 473–7.

12. The Treaty of Sèvres had not been ratified by any signatory; in any case, even the Treaty of Sèvres did not purport to annex Smyrna definitively to Greece.

13. Annotated text in Mostras, *The Asia Minor Venture*.

14. Frangulis, ii, pp. 565–6. (This section is largely based on Frangulis's account.)

15. Frangulis, ii, p. 567.

16. F.O. 421/303 no. 108; Lindley to Curzon, 8 Dec. 1922.

17. F.O. 421/303, nos. 100, 103.

18. Venizelos Papers, 268; Venizelos to Mourellos, 25 Oct. 1922 and *passim*.

19. Venizelos Papers, 268; Venizelos to Fridtjof Nansen, 17 Oct. 1922. Nansen, the explorer, had been working in Constantinople on refugee relief and was at once involved in the problem of the Greek refugees.

20. Venizelos Papers, 318; Pangalos to Venizelos, 30 Oct. 1922.

21. Venizelos Papers, 268; Venizelos to Pangalos, 20 Nov. 1922.

22. See Venizelos's letter to Politis of 3 Nov. in Venizelos Papers, 268.

23. Venizelos Papers, 268; Venizelos to Plastiras, 21 Nov. 1922.

24. Venizelos Papers, 319; Plastiras to Venizelos, 13 Dec. 1922.

25. ibid.; Pangalos to Venizelos, 16 Dec. 1922.

26. ibid.; Plastiras to Venizelos, 30 Dec. 1922.

27. Psomiades, *The Eastern Question: the last phase*, p. 120.

Bibliography

Titles of Greek books are cited in English translation, with the transliterated Greek in brackets.

Those who want further bibliographical material will find it in the books of Triantaphyllou, Kitsikis, Toynbee, Driault, Pentzopoulos and Psomiades, all of which appear below in the section 'Books and Articles'; and in my doctoral thesis, 'The Greek occupation of Western Asia Minor, 1919–22, and the National Schism' (Bodleian Library, Oxford), where I have added short notes on the sources listed. An asterisk indicates books which contain important primary materials.

ABBREVIATIONS

D.B.F.P. *Documents Relating to British Foreign Policy*
D.D.I. *I Documenti Diplomatici Italiani*
F.R.U.S. 1919 *Papers Relating to the Foreign Relations of the United States, The Paris Peace Conference 1919*

UNPUBLISHED DOCUMENTS AND MANUSCRIPT SOURCES

Athens
Papers of Eleftherios Venizelos (cited as Venizelos Papers): in the Venizelos Room of the Benaki Museum in Athens.

Papers of the Greek High Commission in Smyrna (cited as H.C. Papers). These papers, which were brought out of Smyrna when the Greeks evacuated, are housed in the National Archives in the Academy of Athens. The papers give the impression of being incomplete, and there is very little written by Stergiadis himself.

Argyropoulos Memoirs. The typescript memoirs of Pericles Argyropoulos, in the possession of Mme Marie Argyropoulou.

London
Papers of Sir John Stavridi (cited as Stavridi Papers). These papers have been given by Sir John Stavridi's son, V. J. G. Stavridi, to St Antony's College, Oxford. There is a valuable diary covering the

period 10 November 1912 to 6 November 1915. The papers are useful mainly for the period 1912–23.

Lloyd George Papers, in the Beaverbrook Library (cited as Ll. G. Papers).

Public Record Office, Foreign Office Archives (cited as F.O.).
1. Confidential Print. Material on Greece, 1919–22, in Further Correspondence, S.–E. Europe, Series 421, vols. 297–303 (F.O. 421/297–303). Turkey, 1922, in F.O. 424/254, 255. Eastern Affairs, in F.O. 406/41–50.
2. Greece, Embassy and Consular Archives. Series 286, vols. 750–835. 1921–2; especially those on the I.F.C. and on Greek Territorial Expansion, F.O. 286/750, 756–8, 790.

PUBLISHED OFFICIAL DOCUMENTS

Greece Before the Peace Congress, no place or date of publication. Venizelos's official statement of Greek claims, written by him personally in 1918 for presentation to the Peace Conference.

Documents on British Foreign Policy 1919–1939. First Series, London 1947f. All citations in the text are from the First Series, cited as *D.B.F.P.* without series number.

Papers Relating to the Foreign Relations of the United States, The Paris Peace Conference 1919, 13 vols., Washington 1942–7. Cited as *F.R.U.S. 1919*.

I Documenti Diplomatici Italiani, Sixth Series, 1918–22, Rome 19??. Cited as *D.D.I.*

Frangulis, A. F., *La Grèce, son statut international, son histoire diplomatique*, 2nd edition, 2 vols, Paris undated.

Mantoux, Paul, *Les Délibérations du Conseil des Quatre*, 2 vols., Paris 1955.

BOOKS AND ARTICLES

* An asterisk indicates works containing important primary materials.
ALASTOS, DOROS. *Venizelos*, London 1942.
ALEXANDRIS, A. *Political Memoirs (Politikai Anamniseis)*, Patras 1947.
ANDRÉADÈS, A. and others. *Les Effets économiques et sociaux de la guerre en Grèce*, Paris 1928.
ANDREW, PRINCE. *Towards Disaster*, London 1930.
ANGELOMATIS, CH. E. *Chronicle of a Great Tragedy (Chronikon Megalis Tragodias)*, Athens undated.
ATHANATOS, K. *The National Movement of Chios and Mitylene (To Ethnikon Kinima Chiou kai Mitylinis)*, Athens 1923.

BEAVERBROOK, LORD. *The Decline and Fall of Lloyd George*, London 1963.

CALLWELL, MAJOR-GEN. SIR C. E. *Field-Marshal Sir Henry Wilson: his life and diaries*, 2 vols., London 1927.

* CALOGEROPOULOS, N. and STRATOS, N. *Notes on the Greek Question addressed to the President Woodrow Wilson*, Geneva 1920.

CAMPBELL, JOHN and SHERRARD, PHILIP. *Modern Greece*, London 1968.

* CHURCHILL, W. S. *The World Crisis: the Aftermath*, London 1929.

CLOGG, RICHARD. 'The publication and distribution of Karamanli Texts by the British and Foreign Bible Society before 1850', *The Journal of Ecclesiastical History*, xix, nos. 1 and 2, 1968.

CONSTANTINE, KING. *A King's Private Letters*, Nash and Grayson undated.

DAKIN, DOUGLAS. *The Greek Struggle in Macedonia 1897–1913*, Salonika 1966.

* DANGLIS, P. G. *Memoirs, Documents, Correspondence (Anamniseis, Engrapha, Allilographia)*, ed. X. Lefkoparidis, 2 vols., Athens 1965.

DAPHNIS, G. *The Greek Political Parties 1821–1961 (Ta Ellinika Politika Kommata 1821–1961)*, Athens 1961 (Galaxia edn.).

DAWKINS, R. M. *Modern Greek in Asia Minor*, Cambridge 1916.

DIETERICH, KARL. *Hellenism in Asia Minor*, New York 1918 (a translation of Dieterich's work in German of 1915, published by the American-Hellenic Society).

DIOMEDIS, A. N. *The Greek Economy before and after 1 November 1920 (Ta Ikonomika tis Ellados pro kai meta tis 1 Noemvriou 1920)*, Athens 1922.

DOUSMANIS, V. *Memoirs (Apomnimonevmata)*, Athens undated.

* DOUSMANIS, V. *The Internal Aspect of the Asia Minor Entanglement (I Esoteriki Opsis tis Mikrasiatikis Emplokis)*, Athens 1928.

* DRAGOUMIS, ION. *Mémoire sur les affaires de la Grèce adressé à la Conférence de la Paix à Paris*, Ajaccio 1919.

* DRAGOUMIS, ION. 'Second Memorandum on the Greek Question addressed to the Paris Peace Conference', in P. Dragoumis, ed. *Community, Nation and State 1907–1919 (Koinotis Ethnos kai Kratos 1907–1919)*, Athens 1923.

* DRAGOUMIS, ION. *My Hellenism and the Hellenes (O Ellinismos mou kai i Ellines)* and *Greek Civilisation (Ellinikos Politismos)*, ed. P. Dragoumis, Athens 1927.

DRIAULT, E. and LHÉRITIER, M. *Histoire diplomatique de la Grèce de 1821 à nos jours*, vol. v (1908–23), Paris 1926.

EDIB, HALIDÉ. *The Turkish Ordeal*, London 1928.

* ETHNIKOS KIRYX. *The Speeches of the Greek Parliament 1909–*

1956 (*Ai Agorefseis tou Ellinikou Koinovouliou 1909–1956*), 2nd period, vol. vi, Athens 1958.

EVANS, L. *U.S. Policy and the Partition of Turkey 1914–1924*, Baltimore 1965.

FOREIGN OFFICE HISTORICAL SECTION. *Anatolia* (*Peace Handbooks*, vol. x, no. 59), London 1920.

*FRANGULIS, A. F. *La Grèce, son statut international, son histoire diplomatique*, 2nd edition, 2 vols, Paris undated, a new edition of Frangulis's *La Grèce et la crise mondiale* (Paris 1926).

GONATAS, S. *Memoirs* (*Apomnimonevmata*), Athens 1958.

*GREEK GENERAL STAFF (Genikon Epiteleion Stratou). *The Asia Minor Expedition 1919–1922* (*I Ekstrateia eis tin Mikran Asian 1919–1922*), 7 vols., Athens 1957f.

HANKEY, LORD. *The Supreme Control at the Paris Peace Conference 1919*, London 1963.

HARINGTON, GEN. SIR CHARLES. *Tim Harington Looks Back*, London 1940.

HORTON, GEORGE. *The Blight of Asia*, Indianapolis 1926.

HORTON, GEORGE. *Recollections Grave and Gay*, Indianapolis 1927.

HOWARD, H. N. *The Partition of Turkey: 1913–1923*, New York 1966 (reprint of 1931 edition).

KAMPANIS, A. *Dimitrios Gounaris and the Greek Crisis of 1918–1922* (*O Dimitrios Gounaris kai I Elliniki Krisis ton Eton 1918–1922*), Athens 1946.

KAPSIS, G. P. *Lost Homelands* (*Chamenes Patrides*), 2nd edition, Athens undated.

KAPUR, HARISH. *Soviet Russia and Asia 1917–1927*, Geneva, Institute of Graduate Studies, 1966.

KINROSS, LORD. *Ataturk: the Rebirth of a Nation*, London 1964.

KITSIKIS, D. *Propagande et pressions en politique internationale: la Grèce et ses revendications à la Conférence de la Paix*, Paris 1963.

*KORDATOS, G. K. *History of Modern Greece* (*Istoria tis Neoteris Ellados*) (vol. v, 1900–24), Athens 1958.

KORISIS, H. *Die Politischen Parteien Griechenlands*, Nürnberg 1966.

*LLOYD GEORGE, DAVID. *The Truth about the Peace Treaties*, vol. ii, London 1938.

MACCAS, LÉON. *L'Hellénisme de l'Asie Mineure*, Paris 1919.

MALAINOS, E. I. *History of Foreign Interventions* (*Istoria ton Xenikon Epemvaseon*), 6 vols., Athens 1955–63.

MALAINOS, M. I. *The Asia Minor Disaster* (*I Mikrasiatiki Katastrophi*), Athens 1962.

MALLOSIS, I. *Political History of Dimitrios P. Gounaris* (*I Politiki Istoria tou Dimitriou P. Gounari*), Athens 1926.

* MANTOUX, PAUL. *Les Déliberations du Conseil des Quatre*, 2 vols, Paris 1955.

* MARKEZINIS, SP. V. *Political History of Modern Greece (Politikι Istoria tis Neoteras Ellados)*, 4 vols., to date, Athens 1966–68.

MAZARAKIS-AINIAN, GEN. ALEXANDROS. *Memoirs (Apomnimonevmata)*, Athens 1948.

* METAXAS, I. *Diary (To Prosopiko tou Imerologio)*, vols. ii and iii, Athens 1952, 1964.

* MINISTRY OF FOREIGN AFFAIRS. *Greece in Asia Minor (I Ellas eis tin Mikran Asian)*, 2 parts, Athens 1921, 1922.

MOSTRAS, V. D. *The Asia Minor Venture (I Mikrasiatiki Epicheirisis)* 2 vols., Athens 1966. An annotated text of Gounaris's speech of defence at the Trial of the Six.

NICOLSON, HAROLD. *Curzon: the Last Phase*, London 1934.

NICOLSON, HAROLD. *Peacemaking 1919*, London 1933.

OECONOMOS, L. *The Tragedy of the Christian Near East*, Anglo-Hellenic League pamphlet no. 50, London 1923.

PALLIS, A. A. *Greece's Anatolian Venture – and After*, London 1937.

PALLIS, A. A. *Greeks Abroad (Xenitemenoi Ellines)*, Athens 1954.

PALLIS, A. A. 'Racial migrations in the Balkans during the years 1912–1924', *Geographical Journal*, lxvi, no. 4, October 1925.

* PAPANASTASIOU, A. *Studies, Speeches, Articles (Meletes, Logoi, Arthra)*, Athens 1957.

PAPANDREOU, G. *Political Topics (Politika Themata)*, vol. i, Athens 1941.

PARASKEVOPOULOS, L. I. *Memoirs (Anamniseis)*, Athens 1933.

* PASSAS, I. D. *The Agony of a Nation (I Agonia enos Ethnous)*, Athens 1925. (The apologia of Papoulas.)

PENTZOPOULOS, DIMITRI. *The Balkan Exchange of Minorities and its Impact upon Greece*, Paris 1962.

PHESSOPOULOS, G. TH. *The Disputes of our Officers and the Dissolution of our Army in Asia Minor (Ai Dichoniai ton Axiomatikon mas kai i Dialysis tou Stratou mas en M. Asia)*, Athens 1934.

POINCARÉ, RAYMOND. *Histoire politique: chroniques de quinzaine*, 4 vols., Paris 1920–22. (Poincaré's articles in *Revue des Deux Mondes* from 15 March 1920 to 15 January 1922.)

POLYBIUS. *Greece before the Conference*, London undated.

* *Proceedings of the Trial of the Six (I Diki ton Ex – ta Estenographimena Praktika)*, Proia edition, Athens 1931.

PSIROUKIS, N. *The Asia Minor Disaster (I Mikrasiatiki Katastrophi)*, Athens 1964. (A Marxist account.)

PSOMIADES, H. J. *The Eastern Question: the Last Phase*, Salonika 1968.

RAWLINSON, A. *Adventures in the Near East 1918–1922*, London 1923.

RENTIS, K. TH. *Greek Foreign Policy after 1 November (I Exoteriki Politiki tis Ellados meta tin 1 Noemvriou)*, Athens 1922.

RIDDELL, LORD. *Intimate Diary of the Peace Conference and After, 1918–1923*, London 1933.

* RODAS, MICHAEL. *Greece in Asia Minor (I Ellada sti Mikran Asia)*, Athens 1950.

ROSKILL, STEPHEN. *Hankey, Man of Secrets*, vol. ii, London 1972.

SAKELLAROPOULOS, K. M. *The Shadow of the West (I Skia tis Dyseos)*, 2nd edition, Athens 1960.

SARAPHIS, STEPHANOS G. *Memoirs (Istorikes Anamniseis)*, vol. i, Athens 1952.

SETON-WATSON, CHRISTOPHER. *Italy from Liberalism to Fascism, 1870–1925*, London 1967.

SEYMOUR, CHARLES. *Letters from the Paris Peace Conference*, Yale 1965.

SKLIROS, G. *The Contemporary Problems of Hellenism (Ta Synchrona Provlimata tou Ellinismou)*, Alexandria 1919.

SPYRIDONOS, G. *War and Freedom (Polemos kai Eleftheriai)*, Athens 1957.

STAVRIDIS, E. A. *Behind the Scenes of the K.K.E. (Ta Paraskinia tou K.K.E.)*, Athens 1953.

STEVENSON, FRANCIS. *Lloyd George, a Diary*, ed. A. J. P. Taylor, London 1971.

* STRATIGOS, X. *Greece in Asia Minor (I Ellas en Mikra Asia)*, Athens 1925.

* STREIT, GEORGIOS. *Diary—Archive (Imerologion—Archeion)*, 3 vols, Athens 1964-6 (volumes published to date cover only 1914–15).

TEMPERLEY, H. W. V. *A History of the Peace Conference of Paris*, vol. vi, London 1924.

* TOYNBEE, A. J. *The Western Question in Greece and Turkey*, London 1922.

TRIAL OF THE SIX. See *Proceedings of the Trial*.

TRIANTAPHYLLOU, K. N. *Asia Minor Disaster (Mikrasiatiki Katastrophi)*, Patras 1962.

TRIKOUPIS, N. *The Command of Large Units in War 1918–1922 (Diikisis Megalon Monadon en Polemo 1918–1922)*, Athens 1935.

VAKAS, D. *Venizelos as War Leader (O Venizelos Polemikos Igetis)*, Athens 1949.

VELLAY, CHARLES. *L'Irrédentisme hellénique*, Paris 1913.

* VENIZELOS, E. K. *Greece Before the Peace Congress*, no place or date of publication.

* VENIZELOS, E. K. Diary, published in *Tachydromos*, issues nos. 788–91 of 16 May to 6 June 1969. A short diary covering the period (May 1919) of the Greek landing in Smyrna. *Tachydromos*

also published some interesting letters from Venizelos to Repoulis (1918–20) from the archive of D. Lambrakis (ed. G. Roussos), in issues nos. 792–7 of 13 June–18 July.

VENTIRIS, G. *Greece 1910–1920 (I Ellas tou 1910–1920)*, 2 vols., Athens 1931.

VLACHOS, G. *Political Articles (Politika Arthra)*, Athens (Galaxia edn.).

VOZIKIS, GH. *The Defence of the Victims in the Trial of the Six (Ai Apologiai ton Thymaton tis Dikis ton Ex)*, Athens.

WALDER, DAVID. *The Chanak Affair*, London 1969.

ZAKYTHINOS, D. A. *Political History of Modern Greece (I Politiki Istoria tis Neoteras Ellados)*, 2nd edition, Athens 1965.

ZALOKOSTAS, CHR. *Alexander (Alexandros)*, 2nd edition, Athens 1952.

ZAVITSIANOS, K. G. *Recollections of the Historic Dispute of King Constantine and Eleftherios Venizelos (Ai Anamniseis tou ek tis Istorikis Diaphonias . . .)*, 2 vols., Athens 1946, 1947.

Index

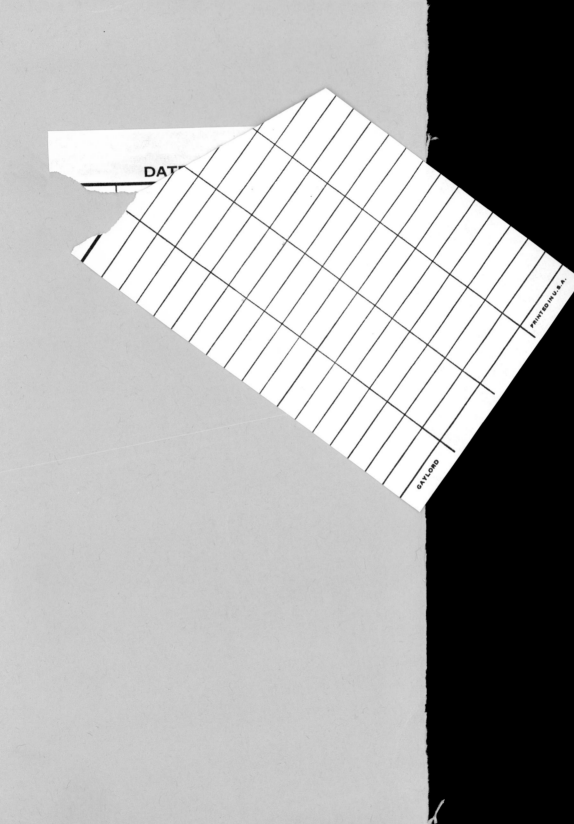

DATE

GAYLORD

PRINTED IN U.S.A.